The Legal Handbook for Trainers, Speakers, and Consultants

The Legal Handbook for Trainers, Speakers, and Consultants

The Essential Guide to Keeping Your
Company and Clients Out of Court

Patricia S. Eyres
Attorney-at-Law

McGraw-Hill

New York   San Francisco   Washington, D.C.   Auckland   Bogotá
Caracas   Lisbon   London   Madrid   Mexico City   Milan
Montreal   New Delhi   San Juan   Singapore
Sydney   Tokyo   Toronto

Library of Congress Cataloging-in-Publication Data

Eyres, Patricia S. (Patricia Stearns).
    The legal handbook of trainers, speakers, and consultants : the
essential guide to keeping your company and clients out of court /
Patricia Eyres.
        p.   cm.
    Includes index.
    ISBN 0-07-063512-9 (cloth) : alk. paper)
    1. Employees—Training of—Law and legislation—United States.
    2. Employee training personnel—Legal status, laws, etc.—United States.
    3. Business consultants—Legal status, laws, etc.—United States.   I. Title.
    KF3559.Z9E97   1998
    346.7303—dc21   97-48502
                                                                           CIP

McGraw-Hill

A Division of The McGraw·Hill Companies

    2 3 4 5 6 7 8 9 0   FGR/FGR   9 0 3 2 1 0 9 8

ISBN 0-07-063512-9

*The sponsoring editor for this book was Richard Narramore, the editing
supervisor was Jane Palmieri, and the production supervisor was
Tina Cameron. It was set in Palatino by Renee Lipton of McGraw-Hill's
Professional Book Group composition unit.*

Printed and bound by Quebecor/Fairfield.

McGraw-Hill books are available at special quantity discounts to use as
premiums and sales promotions, or for use in corporate training programs.
For more information, please write to the Director of Special Sales,
McGraw-Hill, 11 West 19th Street, New York, NY 10011. Or contact your
local bookstore.

This book is printed on recycled, acid-free paper containing a
minimum of 50% recycled, de-inked fiber.

*In memory of Dr. Herbert M. Stearns,
whose steadfast encouragement
continues to inspire me*

Contents

3. How to Avoid the Injury Lawsuit   67

4. Designing Training Programs: How to Avoid Potential Legal Problems   93

5. Legal Issues in Diversity Training   110

9. Legal Challenges to New-Age Programs and How to Avoid Them   205

10. Certifying Trainers and Training Programs: Legal Dos and Don'ts   220

11. Terror, Violence, Sickness, and Stress in the Workplace: The Role and Responsibilities of Training   235

12. Training to the Rescue: How to Use Training to Improve Performance and Prevent Liabilities   249

Part 2. Legal Dos and Taboos for Speakers (and Stand-Up Trainers)

13. The 10 Most Common Legal Problems for Presenters and How to Avoid Them   271

14. How to Meet Your Legal Responsibilities to Participants With Special Needs   298

Part 4. Copyright Issues: What Every Trainer, Speaker, and Consultant Must Know

Appendixes

Acknowledgments

I am very grateful to the following people for their assistance with the preparation of this book:

Barbara S. Boarnet, Esq., for help with the extensive legal research; especially the state-by-state legislation.

Terri Shea for a superb job throughout the preparation of the manuscript, particularly her exceptional attention to details.

Richard Narramore, Editor at McGraw-Hill, for providing focus and constructive suggestions and for his gentle reminders to limit the "legalese."

Brian Eyres for his steadfast support and patience, and for serving as a sounding board for my ideas.

My colleagues at ASTD and ISPI for their help in identifying specific issues of concern to trainers and performance technologists.

My associates in the National Speakers Association, particularly members of SpeakerNet, who responded promptly and generously when I solicited input on legal issues of concern.

Introduction

Why You Need This Book and How to Use It

From communication about workplace hazards to complex skills training to unconventional programs designed to unleash human potential, there are legal land mines out there that you don't want to step on if you are a trainer, speaker, or consultant. Some basic knowledge about legal issues that affect your work could save you a lot of grief and expense in the future. For example, are you aware of the legal restrictions on the scope and content of your presentations so that you don't accidentally violate the rights of others to religious freedom, equal employment opportunities, and privacy? You must also be careful to honor the proprietary rights of others, and you will benefit from knowing how to legally protect your own work product.

Trainers can forge partnerships with management to ensure that their organizations comply with the myriad regulations governing public and private sector employers. As an information professional—trainer, consultant, or speaker—you cannot afford to be a source of legal liability to yourself, or to your employers and clients.

This book is a practical guide to how the legal system affects your work. Each chapter provides information in plain English on how to recognize potential legal pitfalls, avoid or overcome such challenges, design and deliver legally defensible programs, and defend yourself against unavoidable legal challenges. You will also find guidelines for proactive management of your work, useful checklists for key activities, and practical solutions to real-world challenges. Legal challenges to trainers, speakers, and consultants are neither inevitable nor insurmountable. It isn't necessary to be risk-averse, but the practical realities of the legal system do require that you be risk-aware.

You don't need to read this book from cover to cover. It is a reference work designed to make it easy for you to jump around to the topics that relate to the specific work you're doing, whether it's diversity training, contracting to conduct an offsite team-building intervention, designing curriculum and test instruments, or giving a motivational speech at a sales meeting.

This book is structured in five separate parts, with the first three devoted to legal issues of concern to trainers, speakers, and consultants, respectively. A number of legal risks are relevant to all three disciplines, and where appropriate, you will be directed to other chapters with specific page numbers for ease of reference. Part 4 addresses in detail what every trainer, speaker, and consultant must know about copyright issues. These chapters will help you avoid infringing protected materials and protect your own work product.

Despite your best efforts, you may still face legal challenges. You cannot absolutely prevent accidents, contract disputes, business losses, or the lawsuits that invariably follow. But you can protect yourself and have the best opportunity for a successful defense if you follow consistent procedures, don't panic, and know what to do when trouble strikes. Part 5 provides a chapter addressing what to do at the first sign of legal trouble, with comprehensive appendices of sample contracts, documentation, and laws relevant to your work.

This introductory chapter ends with an Executive Summary of the 10 most common legal problems facing trainers, speakers, and consultants. If any of them sound like they may be relevant to your situation, page references after each of the items will tell you where to find the details in this book. If you're not yet convinced that you need basic knowledge about the laws affecting your work, the next two sections are full of stories of legal nightmares that may cause you to rethink your position!

Don't Let This Happen to You! Legal Horror Stories From the World of Training, Speaking, and Consulting

Readers who believe legal challenges happen to someone else may not be convinced that this book is relevant. Here are stories about actual trainers, speakers, and consultants who found themselves facing legal challenges. Perhaps they too believed it couldn't happen to them.

The Unwary Trainer

It is important to provide realistic training, particularly in situations where the need to react under adverse conditions is critical to safe and successful job performance. However, during the training itself, individual trainers are responsible for ensuring that equipment used during the course is reasonably safe for its intended use and for effective supervision of the training facility. One clear-cut example of a personal injury occurring during a training exercise, followed by an expensive lawsuit, is *Tabone v. State of New York.*[1]

At the time of the accident, the injured party was employed as a firefighter and was enrolled in a class known as "Essentials of Firemanship." The class was planned, directed, supervised, and instructed by a certified state employee, and was made available to the county and its firefighters. The state furnished workbooks and lesson plans, while the county provided the facility, a smokehouse for training drills, and classroom-related equipment.

The lesson on the fateful night included a smoke drill that was intended to train the students to use air packs. The objective was to realistically simulate smoky conditions. This exercise was conducted in the smokehouse, and a device thought to be a smoke bomb was employed. In reality, it was a white phosphorus antipersonnel grenade commonly used by the military.

While assisting the instructor in carrying a mannequin to be "rescued" in the drill, Tabone was handed the sealed canister. The instructor told him to pull the pin, and when he did it exploded in his hand, showering him with white phosphorus and setting him on fire. A jury awarded him over $2 million, finding the state 75 percent at fault for its trainer's negligence. The trainer's employer, the county, was found 25 percent at fault for the negligence of its personnel, although it settled prior to trial for an amount greater than this share.

Significantly, the court also found the trainer negligent in representing to the class that the canister contained a smoke bomb despite his lack of direct knowledge. Additionally, because he did not ascertain the risk of harm, he failed to effectively supervise the drill by not insisting that appropriate protective gear be worn by all those foreseeably in harm's way, including the injured man.

The Unsuspecting Speaker

Discrimination laws, by definition, apply only to the actions of employers, don't they? Not necessarily. While employers are usually legally responsible only for the conduct of their managers, supervisors, and employees, a growing area of law imposes responsibility for all aspects of the work environment, including actions by nonemployees, such as speakers.

One speaker attempting to keep his audience alert sprinkled slides of bikini-clad women into a technical presentation on fingerprinting analysis. The result: a claim for harassment and sex discrimination by two female employees. The presenter was a guest lecturer. The employer that hired him—and sponsored the program—was liable for the damages.

Another case involving speakers, *Markham v. White*,[2] has received adverse media attention. The charge is sexual harassment stemming from a series of presentations to law enforcement officers. The defendants are *individual instructors* employed by the U.S. Drug Enforcement Administration (DEA) and retained as speakers for state, county, and municipal law enforcement officers. The presentations, offered repeatedly over several years, contained explicit sexual references, jokes, and derogatory and demeaning references to women in general and female audience members in particular. Officers from five states attended these seminars, where the speakers allegedly:

- Promised male participants at the beginning of each seminar that they would go home and have aggressive sexual encounters with their wives

- Inserted graphic slides with pictures of nude women between instructional slides

- Referred to women in derogatory terms, using words starting with *b*, and referred to African American women as "brown sugar"

- Grabbed their own genitals throughout the seminar

Certifying a nationwide class action, the judge concluded that the classes constituted a sexually harassing training environment. If you use humor with sexual, ethnic, racial, or disability-based overtones, you may embarrass yourself and your client and leave both parties open to a lawsuit. Consult Chapter 13, pp. 281–284, to recognize and avoid these legal risks.

Other significant areas of legal exposure for speakers—including damaging reputations, invading privacy, providing discriminatory content, and infringing copyrights—are addressed fully in Chapters 13, 14, 18, and 19.

The Unprepared Consultant

Independent consultants are not immune to liabilities. You face a host of responsibilities in designing and delivering effective service to your clients. Consultants are accountable to provide professional and competent services as well as to honor contractual commitments and refrain from infringing protected intellectual property rights of other consultants and trainers. These issues are fully covered in Chapters 15 through 19.

One issue of great concern to consultants is the potential for your own lack of preparation to reflect badly on your client, and even subject the client to legal detriment. One example is the need to take appropriate steps to maintain confidentiality for sensitive work product. Diversity consultants, for example, provide services ranging from training to conducting a "diversity audit" of the organization. However, in discrimination litigation, the results of the audit may be requested in the discovery process. The discovery process and production of documents in litigation are discussed in the Executive Summary that follows, as well as in Chapter 20, pp. 419–425.

One case highlights the challenges facing an employer as a result of court-ordered production of a diversity consultant's work product. In *Hardy v. New York News, Inc.,*[3] the employer was ordered to turn over to the plaintiffs an "EEO report" that had been prepared by external consultants at the company's request. The court ruled that the materials were not protected by any legal privilege because they were generated in the normal course of business rather than in anticipation of litigation. Since the consultant was not an attorney, the attorney-client privilege, which protects the intended confidentiality of communications between client and lawyer, did not come into play.

In support of his decision, the judge found several factors justifying disclosure of the consultant's report, which reflected lack of care by the consultant (and, in fairness, by the employer client) to maximize the potential for confidentiality. The following factors were included:

- The documents were not marked "confidential" or "privileged."
- The documents were addressed to the company itself rather than to the company's legal department.
- The documents did not refer to the development of an affirmative action plan in the context of pending minority-hiring litigation.
- The documents were not treated as confidential, and were widely disseminated and commingled with other personnel documents.

Although the client also assumed a share of the responsibility to maximize the potential for confidentiality, proactive steps by the consultant would have minimized the potential for this costly disclosure. Chapter 16, pp. 344–347, provides guidance for consultants on a range of confidentiality issues.

In addition to potential legal action by clients, consultants are frequently jointly responsible to third parties who are injured by their acts or omissions, such as their clients' employees. A consultant's negligence may result in additional liability for both the employer *and* the consultant. In this arena, external facilitators owe a duty of due care to avoid injuries to participants in their training. The story of one consultant's encounter with the legal system underscores the point.

The case involved an experienced consultant who taught a certified scuba diving class. In *Leno v. Young Men's Christian Association*,[4] the consultant taught the program for the YMCA, which provided the tanks, regulators, and harnesses used by the students. The volunteer trainer provided the weight belts, maintained all the equipment, and filled the air tanks. The students purchased their own fins and snorkels. The consultant had two decades of diving experience, and had volunteered for this organization for several years prior to the accident that led to the lawsuit.

One student died because of negligent supervision by the consultant and his team of instructors. The court concluded that the individual trainers—lead and assistants—were negligent and had personal accountability. As the sponsoring agency, the YMCA was legally culpable, as was the individual consultant.

The court found, consistent with the law in most states, that the use of an independent contractor or consultant to perform high-risk or inherently dangerous instruction may create liability for failure to take the necessary precautions to ensure safety and competent training.

The following Executive Summary provides an overview of the most significant issues you may face in your career, with specific page references to locate more detail.

The 10 Most Common Legal Problems for Trainers, Consultants, and Speakers and How to Solve Them

1. Your company is sued for failing to perform government-mandated training.

Safety Programs

One explosive area of training liability involves programs that are supposed to educate employees about workplace hazards. The legal risk arises when a law or regulation imposes a *requirement* to train employees in specific content areas, within prescribed time frames. Trainers, independent consultants, and their employees and clients can be found legally responsible for failure to comply with the required content, timing, or methods of effective training. Generally, however, the penalties are more severe following a fatality, a serious injury, or a flurry of illnesses.

The best way to solve these potential problems is to recognize when federal or state law requires training in your industry or work environment. Chapters 2 and 3 provide details you need to know on design and delivery of effective safety training. Appendix A provides a snapshot of federal statutes with a training component, and a state-by-state guide to regulatory requirements.

Workplace Security and Violence Prevention

The National Institute for Occupational Safety and Health (NIOSH) reports that over 7600 employees, an underestimated number, were killed on the job over the last 10 years. Twelve percent of that number were workplace homicides. When a violent incident occurs in the workplace, lack of state or federally required training can make an employer liable for significant penalties.

The Occupational Safety and Health Act (OSHA) requires employers to provide a workplace that is safe and to develop practices and procedures—including training—that are reasonably adequate to meet this obligation. OSHA defines a serious violation as one for which "there is substantial probability that death or serious physical injury could result." Implicit in this standard is the proposition that employers must provide a workplace free from the dangers of foreseeable incidents of violence.

The federal government, through OSHA, now recommends workplace security and violence prevention training, similar to that required in California, Michigan, Washington, and other states. These guidelines and suggestions on the content, timing, and delivery of training on coping with violence and its aftermath are discussed in Chapter 11, pp. 243–246. If your organization doesn't have a workplace security and violence prevention program that includes effective training, consider recommending one to senior management. If you are called upon to design or deliver these programs, Chapter 11 guides you through the process.

Discrimination Prevention

Employers and their authorized agents and employees are responsible for maintaining a discrimination-free work environment, a mandate that includes obligations to conduct training on harassment prevention. Some states require such training by statute. Even in the absence of a state law mandating training, federal courts have concluded that an employer's obligation to maintain a nondiscriminatory work setting includes a specific requirement to train supervisors and employees on the definitions and scope of inappropriate behaviors. One such case is *Robinson v. Jacksonville Shipyards, Inc.*[5]

The case gained national media attention because of protests by the unions that sexual harassment liabilities for off-color calendars and pinups violated the First Amendment. However, the court ruled that the absence of formal training on preventing sexual harassment led to the employer's liability. As part of the court's order, the shipyard was required to implement annual training for supervisors, managers, and investigators by "experienced sexual harassment educators."

One solution to these problems is to understand where training can rescue your employer's legal defense through comprehensive needs assessment, effective program design, and systematic documentation. Chapters 6, pp. 153–157, and 12, pp. 255–257, guide you through the process.

2. Someone sues your company for emotional trauma suffered during your new-age team-building session, or is physically injured during your outdoor retreat activities.

Adventure Training

Whether you call it adventure, wilderness, or outdoor training, there are several potential areas of liability for design and delivery of nontraditional programs:

- Personal injury lawsuits and workers' compensation claims for illness, injury, or other damage the participant suffers during the training

- In extreme situations, emotional distress lawsuits, or claims of stress-related disability due to "delayed reaction" or posttraumatic stress disorder brought on by the training

- Discrimination charges from a disabled employee who is completely excluded from the program, refused a reasonable accommodation to allow full participation, later excluded from advancement opportunities, or retaliated against for his or her inability to participate

The primary solution to reduce your legal risks and still facilitate valuable programs is to anticipate and prepare for inevitable accidents. You should also carefully plan to provide disabled people with equal opportunities to participate. Chapter 14, pp. 300–303, includes guidance on addressing these special needs. Chapter 8, pp. 192–195, takes a comprehensive look at how to design and facilitate safe adventure training programs, cope with participants' anxiety or fear, and limit your own and your employer's or client's liabilities for unavoidable accidents.

New-Age Training

New-age or nontraditional training programs have captured the attention of both the Equal Employment Opportunity Commission (EEOC) and the courts. Designed to unleash the human potential of participants, by taking them out of both traditional classroom settings and their own "comfort zones," these programs are frequently provided for managers.

New-age programs have been legally challenged on three primary grounds, which might be called the "Three I's":

- Infringement of religious beliefs
- Invasion of privacy
- Infliction of emotional distress

Several cases involve claims by employees that new-age training programs infringe on their protected rights of religion. Other nontraditional methodology may cross the line into invasion of trainees' psychic well-being. Some cases have resulted in adverse media attention, such as the ABC *Nightline* report that the U.S. Federal Aviation Administration initiated a stress management program taught by a consultant who was an initiate of the New-Age Ramtha School of Enlightenment. According to a 1995 Inspector General's report, highlighted on *60 Minutes* in March 1997, stress management training at the FAA included tying some employees together with strips of bed linen for 24-hour intervals, and subjecting others to verbal and psychological abuse.

One way to prevent lawsuits is to make these workshops voluntary, fully advise participants about the content and methods before the programs begin, and be sensitive to concerns raised during the training. Chapter 9, pp. 215–218, focuses on how internal trainers and external consultants can select, design, and deliver nontraditional training while minimizing the legal risks.

3. You are sued for infringing the intellectual property rights of another person.

Information professionals—trainers, speakers, and consultants—create and distribute written materials, artwork, or other intellectual property. The materials may be stand-alone products, or part of a presentation. In each of these instances, the creator should take certain legal steps to protect that work from infringement. The intellectual property of a business has intrinsic and commercial value which the law protects. Participant materials, workbooks, or other documentary material used in training programs are all subject to copyright protection.

In addition, instructors and speakers frequently use materials from other sources, as part of their audiovisuals, music, cartoons, or pictures, in conjunction with their presentations. The creator of that work may have protections against the unauthorized use of the materials, if copyright protection has been obtained. The subsequent unauthorized use of the material gives rise to a lawsuit for infringement. The remedies in this context may also be civil or criminal; they are stiff when the unauthorized use is willful or flagrant.

The World Wide Web is a valuable source of research, data, and ideas for valuable material in a training program or professional speaker's presentation. You may unlawfully infringe existing copyrights by downloading and making use of protected intellectual property via the Internet and other public bulletin boards.

The range of copyright issues of concern to trainers, speakers, and consultants—including copying handouts, designing training manuals, using audiovisual aids and training instruments, knowing when and how to obtain permission to incorporate copyrighted materials into a larger presentation, and understanding how to protect your own work product—are addressed in detail in Chapter 19, pp. 387–388 and 403–405. Chapter 13, pp. 271–279, highlights special issues for speakers using cartoons, graphics, and sound.

4. The content or delivery of your training or speech is discriminatory.

Diversity Training

In addition to the various employee relations problems that can result from the implementation of diversity programs, diversity training has had adverse legal implications for employers in defending against employment discrimination lawsuits. The primary dangers of diversity programs from a legal standpoint are racial, ethnic, or sex-based remarks, made in diversity training sessions, that may be used in later employment discrimination litigation as evidence of management bias. When your diversity training materials, flip charts, or group activity notes contain candid remarks by managers that could be construed as racial or sexual bias, or when a "diversity scan" reflects unfavorably (statistically or through anecdotal evidence) on your employer's record with minorities or women, admission of such information in a subsequent discrimination lawsuit can be damaging to the employer's case.

A primary example is *Stender v. Lucky Stores, Inc.*[6] In 1988, Lucky Stores sought to determine the cause of the glaring lack of promotions for women and minorities within the organization. As part of its attempt to remedy the situation, the company conducted an in-house diversity training session for all store managers. The managers took part in an exercise that is commonplace in many diversity training seminars—they were asked to list various stereotypes that they had heard about women and minorities. This list later wound up in court as evidence against Lucky Stores. Chapter 5 addresses the full range of legal issues surrounding diversity training.

Training Methodology

In addition, the training methodology in a diversity program must be appropriate to meet the learning objectives and must not itself create a separate basis for significant liability. To professional trainers this seems obvious, but a new sexual harassment case with a training twist provides a graphic reminder.

Throughout 1994, the Federal Aviation Administration (FAA) conducted, as part of its diversity training, a confrontational exercise drawn from the Navy's Tailhook episode. During the exercise, men were subjected to a one-minute trip through a gauntlet of women, who were told to tease, taunt, and fondle them. The stated purpose: to turn the tables on the men and give them a blunt lesson on what many women regularly experience in male-dominated environments.

This kind of activity has the potential for violating Title VII of the 1964 Civil Rights Act and the Civil Rights Act of 1991, based on targeted adverse behavior of a sexual nature. The 1991 act significantly expanded the remedies available to participants adversely affected, including the right to a jury trial by their peers. The genuine risk to the organization, *and* to individual trainers who harass participants, is liability for the very discrimination that the training is intended to prevent. If you design or deliver diversity or EEO compliance training, you will find relevant details on how to minimize your legal risks in Chapters 5, pp. 114–117, and 12, pp. 259–266.

Presentation Content

Even when the training does not focus on controversial or emotional topics, the presenter's content can result in troublesome legal problems, both individually and for the employer or client that sponsors the program. Jokes, graphics, and other "ice-breaking" material sprinkled throughout a program may be designed to engage the audience and generate interest. When used appropriately, these tools enhance a professional presentation. When the content strays into inappropriate areas—such as sex, race, religion, ethnicity, or disability—the consequences range from embarrassment (for both the presenter and the employer or client) to discrimination claims. The presenters from the DEA (see Introduction, p. 4) who used graphic content to generate interest in an otherwise "dry and technical" program now find themselves defendants in a class action lawsuit. Legal concerns about discriminatory content in presentations are addressed in Chapters 6, pp. 143–150, and 13, pp. 280–285.

5. Your company is sued for injuries caused by the human error of an employee who, it is claimed, was inadequately trained.

Even when your employer complies with the minimum training standards prescribed by a federal or state law, a court may find that your program design or delivery fails to comply with a legal duty to provide adequate training.

Injuries Due to Human Error on the Job

Employers and their trainers are most vulnerable to personal injury lawsuits when employees are killed or injured in workplace accidents. Training participants litigate when they are injured, and other employees sue when they are harmed as a result of a coworker's mistake caused by poor training. Even nonemployees are also beginning to seek redress when their injuries or property damages result from human error which is allegedly caused by inadequately trained personnel.

In the wake of a violent workplace incident, some courts have been quick to pin the blame on the employer's failure to provide effective training. For example, in *Gonzales v. Southwest Security & Protection Agency, Inc.,*[7] an employee of a security firm injured a bystander through negligent use of a nightstick. The New Mexico court of appeal found that when employees are given the tools to commit violent acts, their employer may be legally responsible for an injury if their training in the use of the tools was deficient. The court concluded that the employees had not been properly trained to use the weapons, or to appropriately detain suspects.

In the case of faulty training curriculum, the most frequent claims involve allegations that the methods used did not impart sufficient learning to ensure successful knowledge application or skill performance on the job. Negligent course design is the most common allegation.

Injuries During Training

Realistic training is an essential element of performance-based training, particularly in situations where the need to react under adverse conditions is critical to safe and successful job performance. However, during the training itself, individual trainers are responsible to ensure that equipment used during the course is reasonably safe for its intended use and for effective supervision of the training facility.

The solutions to most legal challenges involving injury lawsuits are to understand when the law—statute or judicial precedent—requires you to meet a legal duty of due care, anticipate when and how injuries may occur, and take proactive steps to provide performance-based training to enhance safe and productive workplaces. Chapter 3, pp. 82–88, has a complete discussion of how to avoid facing injury lawsuits from employees and third parties. Chapter 4, pp. 97–109, details the legal issues surrounding curriculum design and supervision of the training facility, and Chapter 12, pp. 255–257, provides a checklist for designing performance-based training.

6. You discriminate against employees in their access to training.

Although workplace safety is vital, employers *and their trainers* are required to balance the need for safety with the individual rights of employees to be free from improper discrimination in America's workplaces. Many training programs, and the selection criteria for participation in training opportunities, are under judicial and regulatory scrutiny. Time-honored methods of testing and evaluation are closely monitored by the EEOC and parallel state commissions.

Many of the training discrimination cases raise allegations of "disparate treatment" or "adverse impact" arising from the methods of selecting employees for training opportunities. Disparate treatment cases involve treatment of one individual (or group) differently from another because of race, color, religion, sex, national origin, age, or disability. Proof of discriminatory intent is critical in disparate treatment cases, but in some instances discriminatory intent may be *inferred* from differential treatment. Thus, actual ill-will or "malice" is not required.

Discrimination can also occur in the assignment to positions that provide on-the-job training necessary for future promotions. Federal law requires that individuals be given the opportunity to compete equally for jobs on the basis of objective, job-related criteria. Thus, in *Wilmore v. City of Wilmington*,[8] the court found discrimination when minority employees were not assigned the administrative jobs that provided on-the-job training for promotions in the fire department. Likewise, in a class action against a supermarket chain brought in April 1997, female employees complained that they were denied training routinely given to their male counterparts.

At the heart of most cases dealing with inequality of access to training is the exclusion of qualified trainees from programs that can give them the skills necessary for advancement. The situation falls into the category of "glass ceiling" litigation and is discussed in Chapter 6, pp. 129–141. When a judge rules that an organization has illegally discriminated, he or she may impose broad remedies to reduce or eliminate workplace bias. One favored approach to negotiated settlements is a mandatory order requiring broader outreach for training to enhance promotional opportunities. This is fully discussed, with case examples, in Chapter 12, Figure 12-2.

Perhaps the number-one area of discrimination *in access to training* is age. The claims involve selection of trainees for advanced or technical skills programs, and the content or delivery of those programs. Even worse, stereotypes about the aging process have led trainers to discriminate against employees by refusing to train them on advanced automation equipment (industrial robots, for example) because of a concern that they are "too set in their ways" or otherwise unreceptive to change. In addition, older workers have complained that they are treated differently in training and are singled out for "ageist" comments by instructors.

At other times, denial of access to training results in adverse employment actions. In an era of downsizing and restructuring, employees who are denied opportunities to learn new skills face more than a stalled career; they fear outright job loss. Likewise, workers who are not provided with education to stay abreast of the needs on their current jobs may have poor performance evaluations and demotions. In these contexts, the denial of equal access to training can result in tangible job detriment leading directly to litigation.

Many courts have concluded that a deprivation of training which leads to a demotion is sufficient job detriment to constitute discrimination. For example, in *Carrero v. New York Housing Authority*,[9] the complaining party prevailed on a claim that discrimination led to a denial of training and subsequent demotion, despite the employer's argument that "mere failure to train" was not a denial of a tangible job benefit.

The solutions to the challenge of providing true equality of opportunities are to recognize the variety of overt and subtle forms of discrimination, to establish objective job-related qualification criteria, and to apply consistent performance standards to all employees. Chapter 6 focuses on all aspects of unlawful discrimination in selection and delivery of training, providing specific guidance on how to develop objective standards and avoid common legal challenges.

7. Your posttraining testing and evaluation tools are challenged because they invade privacy or exclude qualified trainees.

Use of any kind of test has the necessary effect of weeding out certain employees. If the test tends to exclude women, minorities, or other identifiable protected groups, it may have an unlawful "adverse impact" under the employment discrimination statutes. Adverse impact involves an employment policy or practice (the test) that is neutral by its terms, but that has a discriminatory effect on an identifiable protected group. This usually occurs in two settings:

- An employer has no intent to unlawfully discriminate, but establishes qualification criteria that are not related to a business necessity and that have a disproportionately adverse impact on disabled individuals. For example, a "neutral" posttraining test may be given in a location that precludes or limits a physically disabled applicant, even though the disability does not hamper the applicant's ability to perform the essential functions of the job with a reasonable accommodation.

- Seemingly neutral qualifications have an adverse impact on disabled or ethnic groups. An example is the requirement for reading and writing ability to take a test, when reading and writing are not required to perform the job. In order to prevent adverse impact, an employer's performance requirements *must be directly job-related* and should replicate essential tasks to be accomplished on the job.

In essence, trainers may use a test only if they can establish that it is both job-related and a valid predictor of successful job performance. Legal challenges to employment tests have generally centered on arguments that the tests (1) had a disparate or differential effect on minorities and (2) were not demonstrably valid predictors of an employee's job performance. In 1971, the U.S. Supreme Court ruled that even if an employer did not intend to discriminate by the use of tests, any test that had an adverse effect on women or minority groups would have to be validated as being job-related in order to avoid a finding of illegal discrimination by the employer. To prevent unanticipated legal consequences, you can use validated tests and administer your tests fairly. Chapter 7, pp. 174–183, provides a step-by-step approach to defensible testing procedures.

Actionable discrimination also occurs when trainees are either excluded or bumped from training on the basis of discriminatory motives rather than objective job performance. Frequently, the indicia used to establish "motive" fall short of direct evidence of biased intent. It is rare indeed—although not unheard of—for a trainer to pronounce: "I'm failing you because you are a [racial minority]" or "I just don't think a [female] can cut it in this program." In the context of disabilities, legal trouble is invited when an incorrect determination about the availability of a reasonable accommodation is used to justify removal from training—as in, "We're sorry, but your physical limitations make it unsafe for you to participate." Chapter 7 focuses on all aspects of test selection, design, administration, and validation.

8. You are sued for failing to honor your contractual commitments.

As a consultant, speaker, or contract trainer, you are delighted when you receive new business. You move into the relationship with high expectations. When your client's high expectations are the results of representations you make about your qualifications, experience, and ability to complete assignments on time with expected measurable outcomes, you may have created contractual promises.

As in a marriage or personal relationship, the consulting relationship requires both trust and accountability. And, just as the parties to a personal relationship rarely anticipate or discuss roadblocks to their happiness, the parties to a consulting or speaking contract often focus on the strengths of their relationship, without addressing reciprocal accountability for possible bad times. Contractual commitments— promises—are made that, when not fulfilled, result in client dissatisfaction and possible litigation. The client may claim business damages from the delay, or seek to avoid or discount the contractual fee.

The best way to avoid these problems is to anticipate and discuss your mutual responsibilities and expectations. Decide in advance what your reciprocal obligations will be and spell them out in the agreement. Provide a realistic schedule for work completion, by anticipating the potential external delays that may impede your work. It isn't necessary or desirable to avoid making promises; rather, pledge only what you can realistically complete under all the circumstances.

Training and consulting professionals increasingly face legal actions from dissatisfied clients on theories akin to professional malpractice. These negligence actions, alleging that errors and omissions by the professional consultant damaged the client's business, often stem from misplaced expectations about the work to be performed.

One source of erroneous perceptions by the client is overstated qualifications. In extreme cases, bragging about experience you don't quite have can result in a fraud action when the work product is not as expected. More often, the client's expectations are unrealistic because all variables have not been fully disclosed. There is no substitute for frank discussion *before* the work commences on what all parties may realistically expect from the relationship.

All joint responsibilities should be built directly into the contractual agreement to reduce the potential for costly misunderstandings that lead to lawsuits for breaches of contract or professional responsibilities. Additionally, it helps to address the consequences if a client does not follow your advice, and a third party is injured.

The full range of contractual issues, with samples of effective contract language, are addressed in Chapters 15 and 16, Figures 16-1 through 16-8, and Appendix C. Joint responsibilities to third parties are addressed in Chapter 8, pp. 199–202.

9. You find that your documentation is ineffective or nonexistent.

In any legal dispute—an OSHA regulatory inspection, an EEOC discrimination investigation, an injury lawsuit—the decision maker must make several determinations: what happened, who was injured or damaged, how it occurred, who was responsible, and what penalties or damages should be assessed. As in most conflicts, memories fail, recollections differ, and stories definitely change. To reach a responsible conclusion on the issues, the agency representative or civil jurors must ultimately determine whose recollections are most credible. The existence of effective, accurate, and consistent documentation helps immeasurably. Conversely, the absence of documentation can destroy even the best technical defense.

Documentation is a written record of an event, discussion, or observation by one or more individuals. Most organizations rely on documentation to record their activities and those of their employees. Any written information, whether formally or informally generated, can be considered documentary evidence if it is pertinent to a legal action or a regulatory proceeding. Why is documentation so important? Simply because a written record of events is the best evidence of what actually occurred. Many times in litigation—particularly in civil lawsuits for damages arising out of a workplace accident—the events leading up to the accident took place months *or years* before the evidence is actually presented in court.

A common thread throughout the reported cases in all aspects of training liabilities reveals that the absence of documentation hinders an effective defense, *even when the facts would otherwise support your position.* There are few substitutes for complete records pinpointing the steps you and your organization took to provide safe, nondiscriminatory training—and to do so within the bounds of applicable laws and company policy. Conversely, the presence of clear, forceful, and *accurate* documentation can save the day, and bring the training department to the rescue of the organization. These issues are fully discussed in Chapters 12, pp. 251–257, and 20, pp. 429–433.

10. You are confronted with ethical lapses and unlawful behaviors before and during litigation.

You may take comfort in the fact that not everything is illegal! However, when the activities are not outright unlawful, but nevertheless pose ethical problems, trainers, speakers, and consultants will be expected to make appropriate judgments, and to balance their legal obligations with ethical considerations.

Common ethical issues involve maintaining client confidences, avoiding conflicts of interest, and refraining from using another professional's noncopyrightable ideas without crediting the source. Although not necessarily unlawful, each of these actions requires appropriate exercise of judgment. Principles of integrity are paramount, even when the behavior may not violate a specific law.

Much more difficult challenges arise when trainers and consultants are faced with choices about participating in improper—even unlawful— activities. Internal trainers may be in the difficult position of having to stand up against improper, unethical, or even unlawful actions by their employer. The same dilemma arises when a client behaves improperly and expects—or requests—that you adhere or, worse, actively participate.

In essence, you may have to "blow the whistle" on improper conduct by the organization that pays you. The notion of whistleblowing has been used to cover a variety of situations confronting professional trainers and consultants:

- Refusal to commit or participate in an unlawful act for an employer
- Refusal to carry out illegal or unethical instructions
- Reporting a perceived impropriety to a supervisor or through other internal channels
- Responding to lawful requests for information or documents by a government agency, even when instructed by an agent of the employer to withhold such information
- Actively reporting improper activities to a government agency, or enlisting an employee or consultant to falsify documentation

Many of these situations begin as ethical dilemmas, but can easily transcend to full-blown liabilities. The most common problem arises with the creation, maintenance, and disclosure of documentation. (Most chapters in this book address when and how to generate appropriate documentation in particular situations.) The ethical and legal conundrum develops when records are requested by an outside agency (such as OSHA) or documents are sought in civil litigation. At a minimum, it is a breach of ethics to alter, fabricate, hide, or destroy relevant documents. Professionals facing an instruction to do so should advise their employer or client about the consequences. Refusal to participate in improper activities is both good judgment and legally protected activity. It is discussed in Chapter 20, pp. 426–429.

It is critically important for employers to adopt and maintain effective document management procedures and for individual trainers to understand and comply with these policies. Guidelines on the creation, use, maintenance, and disclosure of documentation are presented in detail in Chapter 20, pp. 429–431.

Chapter 1 starts with a road map through the legal system to orient you to the information in the rest of the book.

References

1. *Tabone v. State of New York*, 456 N.Y.S.2d 950 (1982).
2. *Markham v. White*, Northern District of Illinois, No. 95 C2065 (January 29, 1997).

3. *Hardy v. New York News, Inc.*, 114 F.R.D. 633 (S.D.N.Y. 1987).

4. *Leno v. Young Men's Christian Association* 17 Cal.App.3d 651 (1971).

5. *Robinson v. Jacksonville Shipyards, Inc.*, 760 F.Supp. 1486 (1991).

6. *Stender v. Lucky Stores, Inc.*, 803 F.Supp. 259 (N.D.Cal. 1992).

7. *Gonzales v. Southwest Security & Protection Agency, Inc.*, 665 P.2d 810 (New Mexico 1983).

8. *Wilmore v. City of Wilmington*, 699 F.2d 66 (1982).

9. *Carrero v. New York Housing Authority*, 890 F.2d 569 (2d Cir. 1989).

1
What You Should Know About the Legal System

Which Laws Apply? A Practical Guide to Legislation Affecting Trainers, Consultants, and Speakers

In order to understand and manage your legal risks, you should have a basic knowledge of the legal system and how it operates. This chapter provides a road map through the legal system. There are three areas of legal standards affecting trainers, speakers, and consultants: statutory law, administrative regulations, and state common law. The following overview of these areas is intended to guide you through later chapters.

The Role of Statutes

Statutes are the results of legislation passed by elected lawmakers. Federal statutes are enacted by Congress, and are referred to interchangeably as *laws* or *acts*, such as the Americans With Disabilities Act. State legislatures and municipalities also adopt statutes, which are sometimes called *codes*, such as the Labor Code and the Penal Code.

Federal and state laws can either forbid illegal acts or impose affirmative responsibilities to act. Most criminal statutes are prohibitive, and violations result in stiff sanctions. Violations of criminal laws are generally referred to as *illegal* acts. Civil statutes may also forbid conduct, such as particular types of employment discrimination. The term *unlawful* is used to describe civil infractions.

Other civil law statutes, such as labor codes mandating payment of overtime, require specific compliance. In still other circumstances, a civil law may restrict some behaviors while mandating others. One example is the federal Family and Medical Leave Act (FMLA), which *requires* employers to provide unpaid leave of absence for eligible employees and *prohibits* retaliation against employees who exercise their rights under the act.

Most statutes governing training are compliance-driven. When prescribing required training, these laws generally specify the nature of the required conduct (such as the substantive training to be conducted), the required time to conduct the training, and the penalties for failure to comply. The statute may impose monetary fines or other specific affirmative orders and will usually specify whether it provides an exclusive government remedy, thereby precluding a private right of action for damages by an injured person.

Some statutes, such as the Occupational Safety and Health Act (OSHA), provide mixed remedies depending on the number and severity of the violations. That is, the statute provides for *both* criminal and civil remedies to the enforcing government agency. In these situations, the choice of proceedings is made by the prosecuting authorities.

The most frequent question from training professionals is: "Which statutes apply to their industry or workplace?" Throughout this book, you will find references to special laws that relate to training. Also, Appendix A provides a list of federal laws mandating training and a state-by-state resource guide for mandated safety training.

Criminal Statutes. In order to withstand constitutional scrutiny, every criminal statute must set forth the basic compliance requirements—specifically, a description of the conduct that violates the statute and the range of penalties for illegal acts. Criminal statutes also require "intent" to violate the law, such as *willful* safety violations under OSHA.

Criminal laws are prosecuted by "the people," through the Department of Justice (federal) or the district attorney (state or county). Punishment for illegal conduct may be incarceration (jail time) and/or monetary fines. In some cases, "restitution" may be ordered as a form of compensation to an injured person, and is enforced by the court.

In some circumstances, individuals who are injured by a criminal act may also pursue independent actions for damages in a civil court action. For example, *People v. O. J. Simpson* was pursued by Los Angeles County prosecutors, and the penalty, upon conviction, would have been incarceration. The families of the victims pursued a separate action for civil damages under state law. In the training context, an employer or trainer may be prosecuted criminally for failure to provide hazard communication training (see Chapter 2, pp. 46–47), and may also be subject to a civil lawsuit for damages by injured parties (see Chapters 3, pp. 69–82; 4, pp. 94–103; 8, pp. 186–191; and 11, pp. 238–240).

Civil Statutes.   In contrast to criminal statutes, civil statutes provide for fines and/or court orders restraining further unlawful activities. The distinction is significant, because criminal convictions may result in jail sentences for individual managers or executives, harsher penalties ("megafines"), and/or probation for repeat offenders. Probation may result in conditions placed upon ongoing operations.

Civil statutes frequently authorize a private right of action for damages by an injured party. For example, an employee who is denied an equal employment opportunity may seek redress in court. Under the federal antidiscrimination statutes, the employee must first file an administrative claim with the Equal Employment Opportunity Commission, which will investigate and decide whether to proceed with an enforcement action. The EEOC and the Federal Office of Contract Compliance may also bring their own civil enforcement actions, independent of the individual employee.

Still other statutes provide for civil remedies, but can be invoked *only* through a private lawsuit for damages. One example relevant to training is the federal civil rights act known as Section 1983,[1] which penalizes state and local governments whose employees violate a person's civil rights. This is distinct from Title VII of the federal Civil Rights Act of 1964, which governs discrimination by employers and their agents. The statute has been invoked by citizens seeking damages from cities and their law enforcement divisions for civil rights deprivations to citizens allegedly caused by inadequate police training.

State Workers' Compensation Codes.   Another set of familiar statutes are state workers' compensation codes. Workers' compensation systems provide benefits for employees with work-related injuries, including those sustained during training. In most states, the workers' compensation codes are an exclusive remedy, precluding an injured employee from filing a lawsuit for damages unless he or she can prove that the employer's conduct was willful or grossly negligent. However, these exclusivity provisions have been riddled with exceptions in some states. These issues, as they affect lawsuits involving injuries during training, are addressed in Chapters 3 and 8.

Specialized Orders Mandating Training Following Occupational Injuries. Some statutes permit a court to devise specialized orders to fit the circumstances. These orders are in the nature of civil penalties, but they usually require the violator either to cease conduct (abatement) or take positive steps (affirmative action) rather than pay damages to compensate for past injuries.

Health and safety violations may result in specialized orders from enforcement agencies mandating training programs and/or further safety measures.

The Role of Administrative Regulations

Federal and state statutes define the basic elements of a crime or a civil infraction. Regulations are then required to interpret the law. Regulations are established and enforced by administrative agencies, which derive their authority from the statutes themselves. For instance, OSHA enforces the Occupational Safety and Health Act, while the EEOC investigates discrimination claims and enforces the antidiscrimination statutes. Likewise, state industrial relations or labor departments administer claims under state codes.

Although most legislation may seem cumbersome and detailed, statutes cannot possibly define every nuance of appropriate or unacceptable conduct. Administrative agencies adopt regulations to interpret the laws and provide enforcement guidance. For example, the U.S. Department of Labor (DOL) adopted regulations to implement and enforce the Family and Medical Leave Act. Federal regulations are set forth in the Code of Federal Regulations. Readers can identify federal regulations when they are cited as C.F.R. in the end-of-chapter references throughout this book.

In addition to the Code of Regulations, enforcement agencies issue *guidances* from time to time to provide compliance direction. For example, a recent EEOC guidance provides interpretative information concerning hiring and reasonably accommodating qualified people with psychiatric disabilities.

Administrative agencies provide written enforcement directives or *compliance manuals* for their investigative personnel to ensure effective compliance with the governing statutes. You will find references to enforcement guidances and compliance directives issued to OSHA inspectors in Chapters 2, pp. 52–54 and 60–64, and 11, pp. 236–238.

Figure 1-1 identifies the agencies most likely to affect your work as a trainer, consultant, or speaker.

Figure 1-1 Description of Government Enforcement Agencies.

Equal Employment Opportunity Commission (EEOC)

If your organization has more than 15 employees, you are governed by most of the equal employment opportunity statutes. The EEOC has broad investigative powers under all statutes that it enforces. It may investigate and gather data, enter and inspect business locations and records, interview employees, and impose record-keeping and reporting requirements. In addition, the agency may advise employees of their rights and advise employment agencies and labor unions of their responsibilities.

In connection with administrative proceedings, the EEOC may require the appearance of witnesses and the production of documents and other evidence, supervise the payments of amounts owed, and institute actions in the courts to obtain relief on behalf of an aggrieved person.

Office of Federal Contract Compliance Programs (OFCCP)

If your organization is a government contractor or is otherwise subject to affirmative action requirements, you may come into contact with the OFCCP. This agency enforces Presidential Executive Order 11246 relating to affirmative action compliance. Enforcement powers include auditing of affirmative action plans for mandated employers, ongoing compliance reviews, and investigation of complaints of discriminatory employment practices.

Once it determines that there has been a violation of Executive Order 11246, OFCCP may begin either administrative or judicial proceedings, seeking a variety of sanctions against violating employers. Alternatively, the agency may refer the matter to the Department of Justice for investigation by the Attorney General.

Occupational Safety and Health Administration (OSHA)

OSHA enforces the Occupational Safety and Health Act. Its powers include the right to inspect facilities, issue citations, and bring enforcement action. OSHA ensures compliance with the act by inspecting employers' work sites, issuing citations, and proposing monetary penalties for conditions violating OSHA standards and regulations.

Civil penalties for each violation are proposed by OSHA and assessed by the Occupational Safety and Health Review Commission (OSHRC) after considering the employer's good faith, business size, previous violation history, and the gravity of the violation. The penalty

---

(Continued)

may be as high as $7000 for each serious or nonserious violation, and as much as $70,000 for each repeated or willful violation.

Occupational Safety and Health Review Commission (OSHRC)

OSHRC was created under the OSH Act as an independent agency to hear appeals of OSHA citations. The employer may contest the alleged violations, the time allowed for abatement, the amount of the penalties, or all of these factors.

After a contest is filed with OSHRC, it is assigned to an administrative law judge (ALJ), who has the authority to conduct a variety of prehearing investigations and proceedings. The ALJ has the authority to change the characterization of a violation from that charged by OSHA. The ALJ may affirm, increase, decrease, or vacate the proposed penalty. A formal hearing may also be conducted, and the ALJ will issue a written decision. The commissioners may review the judge's decision at the request of a party or on their own initiative. The employer does not have a right to review. Any party can appeal the final OSHRC decision to a federal court of appeal.

Department Of Labor (DOL)

Trainers and consultants are most familiar with the DOL's enforcement of overtime laws under the Fair Labor Standards Act (FLSA). The agency also enforces the Federal Family and Medical Leave Act (FMLA). The DOL is required to receive, investigate, and attempt to resolve complaints of violations of leave rights (FMLA) and minimum wage and overtime claims (FLSA). Enforcement powers include investigating complaints, mediating disputes, and filing enforcement actions on behalf of employees.

Department of Justice (DOJ)

The DOJ enforces the public accommodation requirements (Title I) of the ADA for all covered employers. It also enforces the Title II (employment) provisions of the ADA for state, county, city, and other municipalities.

National Labor Relations Board (NLRB)

The NLRB, which deals with union organizing rights, enforces the National Labor Relations Act. The remedies for discrimination under that act are exclusive and are not affected by the enforcement of Title VII by the EEOC. The NLRB can entertain claims of unfair representation by employees of a labor union or of retaliation for opposing unfair practices. The NLRB has the power to require a union to process an employee's grievance.

Case Law Established by Judicial Precedent

In addition to statutes enacted by legislative bodies and regulations adopted by administrative agencies, court cases may establish legal requirements which bind employers and their individual trainers, consultants, and speakers.

Judicial precedents are created in two ways: through interpretation of a statute and as state common law. For example, Title VII of the federal Civil Rights Act of 1964 prohibits employment discrimination based on gender, but the statute does not define every form of sexual discrimination. The EEOC has issued guidances further defining and providing examples of "hostile work environment sexual harassment." When individual employees pursue private civil cases against their employer on the basis of Title VII, the court has the authority to further interpret whether the conduct at issue falls within the parameters of a hostile environment claim. The resulting decision may further define the parameters of hostile environment harassment through a published judicial opinion.

The second way case law becomes binding precedent is through state common law principles, derived either from public policy or from the body of case precedents. These cases arise when there is no specific statutory remedy, but the alleged improper actions of the defendant violate public policy. The most common examples in the training context involve negligence lawsuits, which are addressed throughout Chapters 3, pp. 69–82; 4, pp. 93–100; 8, pp. 186–192 and 199–202; and 11, pp. 238–240.

Case law is created at both the federal and state levels through the following court structure:

Trial court	Federal district trial court
	State trial courts
Intermediate court of appeal	Federal circuit courts
	(1st through 13th circuits)
	State appellate courts
Highest court of appeal	U.S. Supreme Court
	State Supreme Court/High Court
	(courts of last resort)

Figure 1-2 depicts the geographic breakdown of the federal circuit courts of appeal.

When lawsuits are filed, they proceed through the judicial system in stages. The initial stage is the trial court, in which the parties present

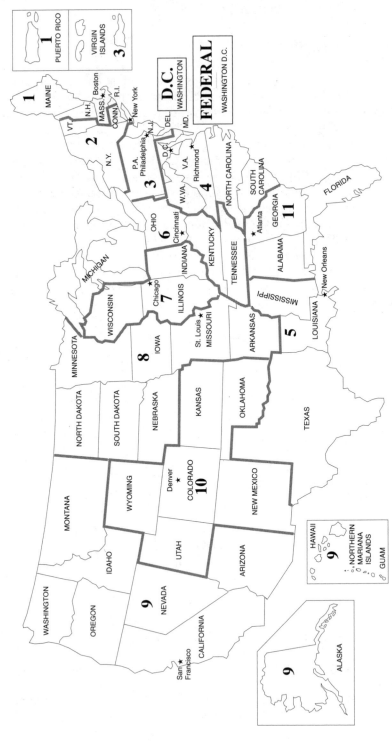

Figure 1-2 Geographic Breakdown of the U.S. Circuit Courts of Appeal. [*Source:* Public record from *Federal Reporter.* (See 28 U.S.C.A. §41.)]

witnesses and documents to prove the elements of their claim or to refute the factual allegations made against them. A decision is then reached by the trier of fact, which in many cases is a jury drawn from the local community. The losing party may then file an appeal, which is submitted to a panel of judges through written briefs and transcripts from the trial. In the federal system and in most states, the losing party has the right to a first-level appeal.

The losing party in the court of appeal may petition the state's highest court through a discretionary appeal. The highest courts of most states do not accept every case for determination. The same is true for the U.S. Supreme Court. Generally, the Supreme Court docket is so full that review is limited to questions involving interpretation of federal law, disputes between states, or issues in which there is a "split of authority" within the federal appellate courts.

It is not uncommon for rulings of federal circuit courts of appeal to conflict on similar issues of law, with some circuits imposing stricter requirements than others. For example, the federal courts are split on the issue of whether "same gender" sexual harassment claims are actionable under Title VII of the federal Civil Rights Act. This issue is ripe for decision by the Supreme Court, with a hearing held in December 1997 awaiting a decision in 1998.

Such splits may create confusion for trainers, consultants, and speakers about which case must be followed. The following guidelines generally apply:

- U.S. Supreme Court cases establish binding precedent throughout the country.

- Federal appellate decisions are binding only on parties within their jurisdictional area, but may be persuasive authority in other jurisdictions. For example, a 9th Circuit decision stemming from a California lawsuit is binding precedent in all states governed by the 9th Circuit (western United States), but is persuasive authority only in New York, which is the 2nd Circuit. A contrary ruling in the 2nd Circuit would control.

- State appellate court decisions are binding on their geographic area, but in the absence of contrary controlling cases, they may be persuasive in other areas of the state. The state's highest court always has the option to accept an appeal when conflicts arise within the rulings of its lower appellate courts.

A court's written decision, called an *opinion*, establishes the precedent. Federal trial court district court judges often issue written opinions, while state trial court judges almost never do. All appellate court decisions are rendered through a written opinion, but unless they are "certified for publication," they are neither binding precedent nor able to be cited as official authority in briefs submitted to another court. As noted above, published cases in the governing jurisdiction must be followed, unless they are overruled by a higher court. Trainers and their employers will be expected to adhere to state and federal case interpretations of statutes when those opinions are the controlling authority.

A Word About Case Citations

Relevant cases are referenced throughout this book. Citations to the written opinion or other identifying citations are provided in the end-of-chapter references.

Supreme Court opinions are referenced as U.S. or S.Ct. References to F.Supp. are federal trial court decisions. For example, 20 F.Supp. 25 (N.D.Cal. 1997) refers to Volume 20 of the Federal Supplement, page 25, decided by the Northern District of California in 1997. Federal Circuit Court decisions are cited consistently as F.2d or F.3d. For example, 210 F.2d. 118 (9th Cir. 1997) refers to Volume 210 of Federal Cases, page 118, decided in 1997 by the 9th Circuit Court of Appeals.

How Legislation and Court Decisions Affect Your Work

Federal Preemption of State Laws

Workplace activities are governed by a variety of laws, regulations, and common law judicial precedents. Some are overlapping. Others may even contain conflicting provisions. Employers with multistate facilities may have differing requirements for similar jobs. A frequent question raised by employers involves federal preemption of state law enforcement. In other words, which laws control?

The concept of federal preemption over enforcement of state laws applies when the federal government, acting through Congress, intends to regulate every aspect of a given activity. Congress is then required to enact sweeping legislation and to mandate accompanying regulations so that they cover every facet of the activity. In this way, Congress "occupies the field" to the exclusion of state or local laws.

For example, the OSHA Hazard Communication Standard[2] specifically preempts all state laws relating to evaluation and communication of hazardous chemical information. However, right-to-know laws with wider coverage or more stringent requirements than the federal standards were adopted in a number of states prior to the 1987 expansion of the federal standard. The result has been conflict in state court decisions concerning which laws apply.

Many states administer safety and health programs under the 1970 federal OSHA (FED-OSHA) provisions, which permit states to manage their own occupational safety and health programs, *provided that the state programs are at least as effective as the federal program.* Currently, 23 states and 2 U.S. territories are approved to operate their own OSHA programs. FED-OSHA specifies that when the state program meets this requirement, the state may assume exclusive jurisdiction over the health and safety of employees within its jurisdiction. OSHA then monitors the state's enforcement of its own standards. FED-OSHA continues to govern when new standards are adopted, until the state adopts standards at least as effective.

Some states, like California and Florida, have adopted OSHA statutes that provide *more stringent* penalties than FED-OSHA. Others have enacted industry-specific statutes mandating training and documentation requirements that surpass FED-OSHA requirements. If you have work sites in different states, you may have more than one standard to meet. Appendix A contains a state-by-state summary of occupational health and safety laws impacting training.

Many federal EEO statutes expressly state that it is the intent of Congress that the statute *not* preempt state or local law. For example, Title VII of the 1964 Civil Rights Act, Section 708, expressly preserves the applicability of state and local EEO laws, so long as they are not inconsistent with Title VII. The regulations state that nothing in Title VII shall be deemed to exempt or relieve any employer from any duty, liability, penalty, or punishment provided by any existing state or local law or any enacted in the future.

Similarly, the regulations promulgated under the Americans With Disabilities Act expressly provide that the ADA does not preempt any federal, state, or local law that provides greater or equal protection for the rights of individuals with disabilities. Additionally, someone with a disability may pursue claims under a state discrimination statute or common law tort principle simultaneously with the remedies provided under the ADA, when those laws provide greater or different relief. This means that an employer may be faced with multiple avenues for liability if it discriminates against a qualified disabled applicant or employee in training, testing, or evaluation.

Likewise, discrimination statutes vary from state to state, with some providing greater protection to workers than others. Appendix B contains a summary of the civil rights and equal employment opportunity laws of the 50 states.

The Civil Discovery Process

If you, your organization, or your client are ever a party to—or a witness in—litigation, you can expect to encounter one or more forms of *discovery*. The discovery process affects every lawsuit.

The parties to a lawsuit typically engage in a lengthy process to exchange information. There are—or should be—no surprises by the time the parties get to trial. All sides make extensive efforts to identify and gather their own relevant documentation and to seek disclosure of pertinent documents from their adversary.

In most states, the standard for disclosure is very broad, essentially requiring the production of all documents that are relevant to the subject matter of the case, or that may lead to discoverable information or witnesses. Accordingly, the existence or absence of documentation often has a significant impact on the case results.

Pretrial discovery takes several forms: interrogatories (exchange of written questions and answers), document productions, and deposition testimony under oath. The parties are also required to exchange lists of expert witnesses prior to trial, so that the witnesses too may be subject to deposition after they produce their reports and files.

In cases involving significant claims of damages, many witnesses may be called for deposition, including individual trainers, curriculum designers, and others involved in the events leading to the lawsuit. It is not uncommon for a witness to be questioned extensively about documents generated years earlier. Witnesses may also be interrogated about the absence of key documentation. The latter process may reveal haphazard record keeping, which is merely negligent treatment or destruction of documents, a criminal act.

Once testimony is given under oath, any inconsistencies are invariably the subject of unfriendly cross-examination, with resulting negative impact on the witness's credibility. The impact of the discovery process cannot be overemphasized. Cases are won on the strength of evidence produced before the trial. Likewise, inconsistencies or evasion often devastates a defense. The solution is to be aware of how the discovery process—particularly production of documents—may affect both your work and subsequent litigation.

Trainers, consultants, and speakers who understand how the discovery process operates, who recognize how documentation—or lack of it—can be used in court, and who stay prepared with effective documentation will be in the best position to add value to the defense of any litigation. Chapter 20 provides practical guidelines for generating effective documentation and coping with the discovery process.

Monday Morning Quarterbacks: How the Jury System Operates and Why It's Relevant

"We'll take our chances with the jury."

With such bravado, fictional attorneys in courtroom dramas often espouse confidence in their case, or the wisdom of jurors to mete out "true justice" for their clients. In the real world, litigants—and their counsel—must consider carefully the wisdom of asking a jury to determine their fate.

The jury system is intended to provide litigants with an opportunity for an impartial verdict by their peers: ordinary people drawn from the surrounding community, people just like you and me. Sometimes, this is a scary thought. In the legal climate of the 1990s, high-profile jury cases have captured the attention and the imagination of the media as never before. Newspaper headlines scream the results of large jury verdicts in all types of cases.

Following a controversial verdict, editorials and commentators sometimes decry the "vagaries" of the jury system. Yet the right to a jury trial is an ingrained part of our justice system. The constitutional guarantee of an impartial jury trial in criminal cases is unquestioned. Even in civil lawsuits, litigants often turn to the jury trial as a forum for a neutral determination. As recently as 1991, Congress extended the right to a jury trial for the first time in federal employment discrimination actions and a flood of such lawsuits followed.

For better or worse, jury trials are here to stay. What this means for you as an individual trainer, consultant, or speaker, as well as for your employer and clients, depends upon your preparation for the inevitable and your understanding of how the system operates. Jurors are the ultimate "triers of fact." They are never experts on the law. They are rarely well versed in the technical subject matter of a lawsuit. In fact, jurors with any background in a litigant's industry will likely be excluded from considering the case, because the juror's role is to assess disputed facts, not to rule on the law. Legal decisions are the province of the judge; factual disputes are within the broad discretion of the jury.

In judging the facts, the jurors assess the credibility of every witness. Most cases that reach trial involve disputes about what happened. Witnesses have different recollections, and documentary evidence may be inconsistent. Jurors are asked to consider all the testimony and evidence, and then determine the true facts. They will ask themselves: "What makes sense? What doesn't make sense? Who is telling the truth and who is mistaken? Who is believable and who is not?"

The issue of reasonableness is uniquely the role of the jury to decide. Was it reasonable for an employer to have taken certain action? Did the injured party's own conduct contribute to an injury? Did an individual trainer act reasonably under all the circumstances? Should the consultant have been better prepared for potential problems? Did the speaker's content cause harm to another person?

When complex factual issues are key to a decision, the jury will be aided by expert witnesses. These individuals, usually subject-matter experts or people experienced in the industry, will provide opinions on the technical issues. The jury must then determine which of the dueling experts is most credible. In injury lawsuits a jury's assessment of the relative credibility of experts can be critical to the outcome.

Once all the testimony is presented, and documents are introduced into evidence, the judge will *charge the jury* by instructing jurors on the law they should apply. The attorneys have substantial input into the language used to frame these instructions, which the judge then literally reads to the jurors. In a few jurisdictions jurors are permitted to take the written instructions into their deliberations. Most of the time, they rely only on their notes, although they can ask for the court reporter to reread the instructions to them.

Once deliberations begin, the fate of the parties rests largely with the jurors. In criminal prosecutions, constitutional standards require a unanimous decision. In the absence of total agreement, the case is *mistried.* In civil cases, the jurors may reach a verdict with as few as nine of twelve jurors.

In criminal cases, the verdict is straightforward: guilty or not guilty. The jurors must reach their conclusion *beyond a reasonable doubt.* In civil cases, on the other hand, the burden of proof is a *preponderance of evidence,* which is often described as a "scintilla" of evidence weighing in favor of the prevailing party.

In civil cases, the jury may be required to make multiple determinations. First, is liability established or not? If not, the defense wins and the case is over. If liability is established, the jurors usually must assess an amount of damages to compensate the victim for injuries and other losses. This is often a hotly contested issue. Basically, the jurors must determine "what it's worth." The resulting verdict of *compensatory damages* is literally to compensate the injured person for medical expenses, pain and suffering, lost income, and sometimes emotional trauma.

In civil cases involving allegations of intentional wrongdoing, the jurors may be asked to award *punitive damages.* Such monetary fines— sometimes called the equivalent of the "corporate death penalty"—are assessed to punish the wrongdoer and make an example for future employers. The goal is deterrence. Punitive damages capture headlines, but legal commentators hotly disagree on their deterrent value.

Personal Liabilities and What They Mean for You

With most of the legal challenges addressed in this book, the employer will be the primary or target defendant, because it may have both direct liability for its own actions and indirect liability for agents (including internal trainers and external consultants whom it hires and authorizes to act). In some instances, individual trainers, speakers, consultants, managers, or supervisors may also face claims for personal liabilities. Consider these examples.

- Someone who engages in sexual harassment has independent personal liability and may be sued individually by the victim. As a result, individual instructors from the DEA are now the sole defendants in a class action alleging sexual harassment during training. (See the Introduction, p. 4, and Chapters 5, pp. 114–117, and 13, pp. 281–284, for this and similar examples.)
- Some courts have ruled that supervisory employees may be personally liable for committing discriminatory acts under the Americans With Disabilities Act. An example is *EEOC v. AIC Security Investigations, Ltd.* (Illinois 1993).[3]
- The manager or supervisor of a hazardous work or training environment may be charged individually with criminal violations or negligence. An example is *People v. Cargill, Inc. and Leslie Salt Co.*[4]

In the context of civil or criminal proceedings, individual liability is very different from personal consequence. There are personal consequences simply to being accused of wrongful conduct: diminished morale, embarrassment, damage to reputation. And those found responsible for discrimination or other violations face potential adverse employment action. The effects can devastate careers.

These very real personal repercussions should not be minimized. However, personal liability is even more significant. Personal liability permits the injured party to sue an individual as a separate defendant. At a minimum, this results in expenses for defending against the claim. In some situations, such as negligence claims arising from a workplace injury, the employer may provide a joint defense, and thereby absorb the tangible costs involved. But when an individual's alleged intentional wrongdoing is in issue, the employer may decline to provide a defense and is prohibited by public policy in most states from paying any resulting punitive damages assessed against the individual.

In very extreme criminal cases, individuals can be sentenced to jail or levied hefty fines. In the civil context, a personal judgment can also be collected. The images of a moving van pulled up to O. J. Simpson's home, with deputy sheriffs removing personal property to satisfy a large civil judgment, were burned into the consciousness of a large television audience. There are a variety of methods to execute a judgment to satisfy an award of damages, and courts typically give broad authority for this process.

This chapter is not intended to encourage you to immediately homestead your house or put your property in someone else's name. (The latter action is unlawful after a personal liability has been established.) Rather, the purpose is to highlight potential legal pitfalls for professionals—trainers, consultants, and speakers—so that they will recognize when, and under what circumstances, personal liabilities may arise and then take proactive steps to prevent the problems in the first place.

References

1. 42 U.S.C. §1983.
2. 29 C.F.R. §1910.1200.
3. *EEOC v. AIC Security Investigations, Ltd.*, Federal District Court (Chicago 1993). (Source: EEOC news release following verdict on March 19, 1993, reported in CCH, *Accommodating Disabilities*, March 1993, pp. 1, 2; verdict reduced: Illinois 61 EPD ¶42, 289.)
4. *People v. Cargill, Inc. and Leslie Salt Co.*, California Superior Court (Solano County 1995).

PART 1

Legal Dos and Taboos for Trainers

2

What Every Trainer Should Know About Health and Safety Training

When You Are Required to Train Employees and What Can Happen When You Don't

A maze of federal and state laws governs the process of training employees, adding to the burden of regulating the workplace both profitably and legally. The Occupational Safety and Health Act establishes comprehensive federal standards for health and safety training, standards which are enforced by the Occupational Safety and Health Administration. Many states have equivalent requirements, administered by their own state OSH agencies (e.g., CAL-OSHA, NJ-OSHA). In the absence of a state standard, FED-OSHA will control. States are able to supersede FED-OSHA requirements only by enacting more stringent regulations. A comprehensive overview of every state standard for training is set forth in Appendix A. Enforcement agencies—and courts—will continue to demand that your workers:

- Be fully warned about hazards and understand the warnings

- Receive adequate training on how to work safely

- Have workable state-of-the-art protective devices, and know how to use them effectively

Although the FED-OSHA general-duty clause mandates training, the most comprehensive legislation is the Hazard Communication Standard, which requires employers to train all workers who may be exposed to hazardous chemicals under normal operating conditions or in foreseeable emergencies. In addition, workers who may become ill from exposure to dangerous substances in the facility—even though not in the direct performance of their job—must receive a level of hazard training that is sufficient to alleviate the risks.

This is the most explosive—and expensive—area of training liabilities. Failure to meet the strong mandates to educate employees about workplace hazards continues to lead the list of penalties. The FED-OSHA general-duty clause spells out required training on general hazards and workplace safety rules. Most approved state plans do the same. However, the Hazard Communication Standard—the right to know and understand—provides the framework for much broader legal risks.

The Employee's "Right to Know"

At their core, hazard communication and safety training are part of the broad requirement that employees be adequately informed about dangerous aspects of their jobs. In essence, they have the right to know what the hazard is, how they may be harmed, how to protect themselves, and what to do if injuries and exposure occur. Figure 2-1 provides a snapshot of the FED-OSHA training requirements.

The *Federal Register* of August 24, 1987, contains the text of the Hazard Communication Standard. The legislation requires that employees exposed to hazardous substances receive at least annual training. New employees must be trained before they are placed into environments where hazardous substances are being used. Additional training is required whenever exposure changes as a result of new processes or substances in the workplace. The training must include:

- The nature of the hazard
- Protective measures that must be taken
- How to read and use a material safety data sheet (MSDS) and chemical warning labels
- How to monitor exposure levels
- Precautions for handling the hazardous substances
- Required protective equipment
- Methods for preventing or minimizing spills, leaks, and explosions
- Emergency procedures to be followed in the event of a spill or accident

Figure 2-1 Health and Safety Training Requirements Under the Federal Occupational Safety and Health Act.

General-Duty Clause. If a recognized hazard exists at the workplace that is not covered by a particular standard, training is required in safe operating procedures in relation to the hazard. Instruction on general safe work practices means work practices that apply to most of the employees at the work site. Examples: lifting procedures, use of protective equipment, knowledge of exits, emergency evacuation procedures, fire protection procedures, handling of flammables, and medical and first-aid procedures.

Specific instruction is required for hazards unique to any job assignment. Example: proper use of machine guards and equipment and specific protective measures to use during normal operating conditions or in foreseeable emergencies.

General Industry Standards. The General Industry Standards issued by OSHA apply to all employers unless specific regulations state otherwise. These standards are divided into categories that include hazardous materials, occupational health and environmental controls, personal protective equipment, first aid, fire protection, and materials handling and storage.

Specific Industry Standards. In contrast to the general-duty clause, OSHA, the Department of Transportation and other federal agencies have promulgated specific standards for general industry, and other specific standards for specialized industries, such as health care, construction, and agriculture. When a specialized standard applies to an industry, or a workplace because of hazardous materials in use at that site, trainers must be aware of the specific training, evaluation, and documentation requirements.

Hazard Communication Standard. Although the FED-OSHA general-duty clause mandates training, the most comprehensive legislation is the expanded Hazard Communication Standard, which requires employers to train all workers who may be exposed to hazardous chemicals under normal operating conditions or in foreseeable emergencies. In addition, workers who may become ill from exposure to dangerous substances in the facility—even though not in the direct performance of their job—must receive a level of hazard training that is sufficient to alleviate the risks.

The *most frequent OSHA violation* in four of the last five compliance years is of the Hazard Communication Standard. The agency has not been reluctant to issue significant citations and then assess large fines for failure to meet hazard communication requirements. Figure 2-2 highlights a few significant examples.

Information About Hazardous Materials

Exposure to hazardous materials is broadly defined to include ingestion, inhalation, or absorption through skin contact. Even if the amount of the hazardous material is very small, its presence in the workplace during normal operations or under anticipated conditions triggers the need to warn and train all workers who may foreseeably be at risk of exposure or contact.

McCrory Corp. (1993). The proposed penalty came after a May 16, 1991 fire at McCrory's Huntington Station department store in New York. The $3.1 million penalty included $49,000 each for six locked doors. Additionally, OSHA fined McCrory's for a *failure to train* the 58 employees at the store in emergency evacuation procedures— $49,000 for each untrained employee, for a total of $2.8 million.

Triangle Pacific Corp. (1994) was charged with 46 willful, repeat, and serious violations at its wooden cabinet systems manufacturing plant in Nashua, New Hampshire. The charges included failure to develop a training program for employees required to perform machine setup and maintenance, and *lack of a blood-borne pathogens training program* for employees who perform first-aid functions.

Taraco Environmental Service & Excavation (1995). An underground storage tank installer and removal company was charged with willful violations after an investigation of an explosion that injured four employees. Among the charges: *inadequate employee training* in the hazards associated with entering and cleaning petroleum-based fuel tanks and failure to develop and implement a written hazard communication program.

Figure 2-2 Examples of OSHA Penalties Assessed for Failure to Train Employees Properly.

If your company has never trained employees on working with hazardous substances, then you need to plan three kinds of training:

- Catch-up training for all experienced employees who have not been trained on the subject

- Regular, ongoing orientation on hazardous substances for new workers before they are assigned to their work areas (required by the standard)

- Retraining when new substances are introduced to the work setting, when new information surfaces about the hazards of a substance currently in use, or when the nature of employee contact with the substance changes because of job redesign or the introduction of new technology

Some trainers use the material safety data sheet (MSDS), prepared by the vendor of hazardous materials, as the basis for the training content. You are better served by a complete instructional package—containing a description of objectives, content, delivery methods, evaluation methods, and so forth—to show OSHA inspectors. In addition, take extra care to document everything carefully—identify all employees who attended training, how well they learned the material, what subjects were covered, and how often the training and refreshers took place.

Employees must be trained at the time they are assigned to work with a hazardous chemical—that is, *before* they begin to work with the chemical. The intent of this provision is to prevent adverse health effects. OSHA inspectors generally believe that an employer can't meet this objective if training is delayed until a later date.

Additional training is to be done whenever a new *hazard* is introduced into the work areas, not a new *chemical*. For example, if a new solvent is brought into the workplace, and it has hazards similar to existing chemicals for which training has already been conducted, then no new training is required. Of course, the substance-specific data sheet must be available, and the product must be properly labeled. If the newly introduced solvent is a suspected carcinogen, and there has never before been a carcinogenic hazard in the workplace, then *new training* for the carcinogen hazard must be conducted in the work areas where employees will be exposed to it.

When a new employee joins the work group, complete retraining is not automatically required if the new employee has received training from a past employer. It is highly unlikely that no additional training will be needed, since employees will need to know the specifics of their new employers' programs—such as where the MSDS is located and details of the employer's in-plant labeling system, if appropriate.

If it is determined that an employee has not received training or is not adequately trained, the employer is responsible regardless of who provided the prior training. Trainers are responsible to evaluate an employee's level of knowledge with regard to the training and information requirements of the standard, and their own hazard communication program, including previous training that the employee may have received. The law's training requirements also apply if an employer becomes aware of exposure to hazards at multiple work sites for which employees have not been previously trained.

Training need not be conducted on each specific chemical found in the workplace, but may be conducted by categories of hazard (e.g., carcinogens, sensitizers, acutely toxic agents) that are or may be encountered by employees during the course of their duties. This approach is especially useful in training employees about the types of hazards they may encounter at another employer's worksite.

Emergency Procedures

A requirement that safety trainers frequently overlook is instruction on emergency procedures. If the chemical is very hazardous, more information would be expected to be provided on the MSDSs. Therefore, the training for emergency procedures, including information about the characteristics of the chemical and precautions to be taken, would need to be more extensive.

The scope and extent of training regarding emergency procedures will necessarily depend upon the desired responses of employees to foreseeable emergencies. If you intend merely to evacuate the work area, the training in emergency procedures would be quite limited, but should include information on the emergency alarm system in use at the worksite and evacuation routes and areas where applicable. However, if your employees are expected to take appropriate action to moderate or control the impact of the emergency, or to serve as emergency responders, then additional training will be required. At a minimum, training these responders on the "emergency procedures" required under the Hazard Communication Standard should include, as applicable, leak and spill cleanup procedures, use of appropriate protective devices, decontamination procedures, shutdown procedures, recognizing and reporting unusual circumstances (incidents), and where to go (evacuate to) in an emergency.

You cannot satisfy the standard simply by giving an employee a data sheet to read. OSHA views the Hazard Communication Standard as performance-based, requiring the trainer to provide a forum for explaining to employees not only the hazards of the chemicals in their work areas but also how to use the information generated in the hazard communication program. The training can be accomplished in many ways (e.g., audiovisuals, classroom instruction, interactive video), and should include an opportunity for employees to ask questions to ensure that they understand the information presented to them.

Furthermore, the training must be comprehensible. If employees must receive job instructions in a language other than English, then training and information will probably also need to be conducted in a foreign language.

Use of Personal Protective Equipment

One of the primary areas of mandated safety training is personal protective equipment (PPE). OSHA's published PPE standards apply to equipment intended to protect an employee's head, face, eyes, hands, and feet. Protective equipment is an important element of an overall safety program that includes administrative and engineering controls, workplace hazard analysis, *and training* as the final protection between a worker and harm. PPE is to be used in emergency situations, as a backup measure to protect a worker against existing or unexpected hazards, or when normal safety measures are temporarily impossible.

The most significant element of the standards mandate hazard assessment and employee training. Employers are required to assess the workplace to determine if hazards that require the use of PPE are present or are likely to be present in foreseeable situations. If so, employers must select appropriate protective equipment and ensure that employees exposed to the hazards use it properly.

Employees must be trained to know when PPE is necessary under normal operating conditions and in foreseeable emergencies, how to use and maintain the equipment, and what steps to take if the PPE malfunctions.

As you implement these mandated programs, it is your responsibility to emphasize the reasons for wearing each piece of personal protective equipment and how your employer will deal with noncompliance through disciplinary measures. Both federal and state workplace safety laws require enforcement of disciplinary policies for employees who disregard the training, particularly in the proper use of PPE. Although you are not necessarily responsible for adopting or enforcing those policies, you will be expected to address them in training. Policies that punish noncompliance must be plainly stated, well understood, and consistently enforced. Enforcement must be across the board for all visitors, managers, supervisors, vendors, and employees.

Significantly, you must certify in writing that the training has been carried out and that *trainees understand it*. Each written certification should contain the name of the employee trained, the date or dates the training occurred, and the specific subject matter. This standard—even more than the Hazard Communication Standard—requires effective posttraining testing or evaluation to confirm each trainee's level of knowledge and ability to apply the instruction on the job. (For a further discussion of effective testing and evaluation, see Chapter 7.)

Be a Manager, Go to Jail: How to Avoid Becoming a Defendant in a Criminal Case

Absence of safety training in your organization can also result in prosecution by state enforcement agencies. A New York grand jury handed down a 14-count indictment following a 1988 explosion fatality, charging an employer and two of its managers with manslaughter and criminally negligent homicide. The indictment stated, in part, that "neither [the deceased] nor his assistant had been trained in tank cleaning safety."

An example of expanded criminal remedies is California's Corporate Criminal Liability Act, which is part of the Penal Code. This statute is unique; it imposes criminal penalties on managers for their failure to warn or train employees about serious concealed hazards in the workplace, even if the failure is due to *simple negligence*. A danger is considered concealed if a reasonable person under similar circumstances would not appreciate the danger.

The Corporate Criminal Liability Act provides, in part, that liability is generally dependent on a manager's actual knowledge of a serious concealed danger. For purposes of the act, the term *actual knowledge* is defined to mean that a corporation or individual manager has information that would convince a reasonable person in the circumstances in which the manager is situated that the serious concealed danger exists. This is the same standard as simple negligence in a civil law context.

One of the early prosecutions under this act, *People v. Reclamation Services, Inc.*,[1] involved an alleged absence of training. In February 1992, Reclamation Services hired an 18-year-old day laborer and ordered him to move a desk with a forklift. Unfortunately, the employee had no training in forklift operations, and the forklift tipped over on top of him and killed him. CAL-OSHA assessed penalties for serious and willful violations. The district attorney then charged the company with violating the Criminal Liability Act. The company eventually agreed to pay an additional five-figure penalty.

Subsequently, in *People v. Cargill, Inc. and Leslie Salt Co.* (1995),[2] an employee who normally worked in Leslie Salt Company's shipping department was assigned to do cleanup work in the plant. While the employee was sweeping around an unguarded bag-flattening machine, it is believed that he reached through an opening and activated the machine. The machine grabbed the employee's gloved hand and crushed him to the waist. He died several days later. CAL-OSHA cited Leslie for serious violation of California regulations. The Alameda County district attorney also charged Leslie and its parent company, Cargill, Inc., with a criminal misdemeanor in violation of the California Corporate Criminal Liability Act. Leslie pleaded nolo contendere (no contest) in January 1992.

The zeal with which district attorneys intend to prosecute employers for violating laws on health and safety training is underscored by an official memorandum issued by the Los Angeles district attorney. Explaining the sanctions imposed by the Criminal Liability Act, then DA Ira Reiner stated:

> We strongly believe some managers will fail to report and warn [train]. *They will be vigorously prosecuted.* Others may attempt to shield themselves from liability by failing to implement a comprehensive program for hazard identification. Those who take this course subject themselves to criminal prosecution..."[3]

California lawmakers have called this the "Be a Manager, Go to Jail" Act. It's a catchy slogan, but not very funny if you are a manager—directly or indirectly responsible for training—who must, under the act, warn and train workers about "serious concealed hazards" in the workplace or face criminal prosecution. Trainers in other states should not heave a collective sigh of relief yet; several states are considering enactment of similar legislation.

Seven Critical Requirements for Effective Safety Training Under the Occupational Safety and Health Act

There are seven critical requirements for a lawful safety training program under the Occupational Safety and Health Act.

1. Identify and comply with all training requirements under the general-duty clause that are applicable to your industry or workplace.

In order to achieve full compliance, an employer must be aware of the requirements for training workers on safe work practices and hazardous conditions. The responsibility for determining what safety training is required, and when, frequently falls on the training and/or risk management department. If your organization does not have appropriate or fully effective safety training in place, you should seriously consider recommending it to senior management.

First, undertake a complete review of all applicable laws and regulations to determine which requirements apply to your operations. Each separate worksite or facility must identify the specific regulations applicable to its operations. The process requires internal or external regulatory compliance experts or technical specialists to monitor the steady flow of new regulatory requirements, condensing regulations into terms that facility personnel can easily understand and act upon. Appendix A provides a summary of federal statutes and a state-by-state guide to required safety training.

Once an employer identifies the regulatory standards applicable to each worksite or facility, the training department should identify individuals within the organization responsible for carrying out the compliance activities. Don't forget that all trainers, compliance specialists, and others responsible for designing and delivering the worker training should also be provided training on how to meet their obligations. Trainer training requires more than identifying regulatory standards for which an individual is responsible; it also requires that each trainer understand the precise conduct necessary to satisfy the legislative requirements.

Finally, managers and those responsible for delivery of training should demonstrate a personal commitment to the company's compliance program. Employees at every level of the organization should understand that safety and environmental health concerns are taken seriously, and trainers serve as visible role models. Management should also model this organizational commitment with their personal conduct and back the compliance program with sufficient resources to ensure consistent enforcement.

2. Identify hazards in your workplace and develop a written hazard identification and abatement program.

Hazard identification and control is the heart of an effective compliance program. Periodic inspections and procedures for identifying existing or potential hazards in the workplace should be an ongoing process. The required hazard assessment survey must be made by a qualified person. Technical experts and supervisors should be called upon to help with the specifics for their work environments. Inspections should be conducted by personnel who are trained to identify actual and potential hazards and understand safe work practices. It is often useful to pair a technical expert with a trainer, to record information in a manner that will be useful during curriculum design and development.

It is important to conduct unscheduled, surprise inspections and continuous workplace reviews. Individual supervisors should be asked to continuously observe the areas under their direction and control for indications of unsafe conditions or work practices. It is also helpful to obtain information from employees who have worked on the job site for a reasonable period of time and are familiar with the specific needs of the work setting. Employees should be encouraged to tell trainers or supervisors of possible hazardous conditions, knowing that their reports will be given prompt and serious attention without the threat of retaliation. The survey produces knowledge of hazards that exist in the workplace, as well as conditions, equipment, and procedures that could be potentially hazardous.

3. Conduct appropriate analysis and plan for training.

Once you know the scope of mandated general-awareness safety training or job-specific training, you can identify the needs of your specific workplace. The primary component is a job analysis to determine what an employee needs to know in order to perform the job safely. A job hazard analysis consists of carefully studying each step of a job, identifying potential hazards, and determining how to eliminate or control the potential hazards. The job analysis can be developed by examining material safety data sheets, equipment instructions, or other content of the specific OSHA standard. In addition, supervisors or technical job experts can assist in the process. This job analysis should serve as the framework for your needs assessment before you design your program.

A secondary approach is to use the hazard assessment together with a job hazard analysis. The approach is to study and record each step of the job, identifying existing or potential hazards and determining how best to perform the job to minimize or eliminate the risks.

Finally, a review of company records may reveal areas of concern. Records of accidents, injuries, illnesses, and near-misses provide useful data. Also, you can request that supervisors observe employees on the job, and review safety procedures for updating. Concurrently, you should identify experienced employees who can provide specific descriptions of the tasks, materials, and equipment they use on the job, and their understanding of safety issues surrounding their performance.

OSHA also suggests that you identify employees for training by prioritizing: those who must be trained by regulation, those whose positions directly involve the actions the training is to cover, those who may reasonably be expected to be assigned to the job, and technical experts or supervisors whose work may take them into potentially dangerous areas.

4. Conduct all required training, and refresher training, within the time frames required by federal or state law.

Training is unquestionably the most important element of the safety program. Effective training allows employees to learn their jobs properly, and to develop skills for working safely and effectively. An effective program includes training for both employees and supervisors.

Employees should be provided with all required substantive training at the following intervals:

- Training for all employees when the program is first established

- Training in general workplace safety and job-specific health and safety instruction whenever new employees are hired

- Job-specific instruction and any new general workplace safety information whenever employees are given new job assignments for which they have not previously been trained

- Specific training and instruction whenever new substances, processes, procedures, or equipment presenting a new or different hazard is introduced to the workplace

- Specific training and instruction whenever new protective equipment or different work practices are used on existing hazards

- Specific training and instruction whenever the employer becomes aware of a new or previously unrecognized hazard

- Training for all supervisors to ensure that they are familiar with the safety and health hazards to which employees under their immediate direction and control may be exposed

Supervisor training is critical. When you design these workshops, inform line supervisors about all policies, procedures, and safe work practices. In addition, your training objectives and content should underscore the fact that supervisors are key personnel responsible for enforcement of safety policies and procedures within their areas of authority. They should also be fully informed about hazards to which an employee is exposed, how to recognize them, the potential effects of these hazards, and the rules for safe work practices.

Supervisor instruction should also include skills training on how to investigate accidents and take appropriate remedial steps to prevent them in the future. Emphasize the importance of strong, consistently enforced disciplinary policies for violation of safe work practices or failure to use protective equipment as instructed.

5. Audit your programs and evaluate trainee performance to ensure effective transfer of knowledge and application of information to safe work practices.

Some form of evaluation is necessary to ensure that the knowledge has been transferred, and employees understand how to work safely. See Chapter 7 for a full discussion of testing procedures and legal issues surrounding testing.

In addition to establishing each trainee's qualifications to proceed to the work environment, the evaluation provides information for program improvements. If evaluation indicates that the training did *not* produce effective results, it may be necessary to revise the curriculum or provide periodic retraining. Important questions to determine program effectiveness include whether the content was confusing or distracting, whether anything was missing from the program, what trainees learned or failed to learn, and how the skills they learned were transferred to on-the-job performance. This is an area where trainers can become partners with line supervisors to obtain follow-up information and feedback about the applicability of program content to actual job-related performance.

6. Effectively document each employee's training, including your objectives, content, and steps to accommodate learning differences and special needs.

Careful record keeping is an essential element for satisfying regulatory inspections. Even more significantly, complete documentation of your compliance efforts and your accomplishments provides the best method for defending against charges and citations.

Most of the regulations specify the record keeping required to demonstrate compliance. At a minimum, documentation must include:

- The name (or other identifier) of the trained employee
- The inclusive dates of training
- The type of training provided, with a summary of content
- The identity and qualifications of the trainer
- An indication that the trainee was tested or evaluated following training to ensure that he or she understood and could act upon the safety instructions

The primary purpose of maintaining documentation of training and other aspects of compliance is to present the information to an inspector at the time of a regulatory visit to your place of employment. Complete, legible, concise, and easy-to-understand documentation provides the best opportunity to avoid costly enforcement proceedings.

Documentation is a written record of an event, discussion, or observation by one or more individuals. Most organizations rely on documentation to record their activities and those of their employees. Any written information, whether formally or informally generated, can be considered documentary evidence if it is pertinent to a legal action or a regulatory proceeding. This applies to OSHA inspections, OSHA investigations, OSHA enforcement proceedings, criminal prosecutions for violations of statutes, and/or civil lawsuits by injured parties for damages.

Documentation techniques are addressed in detail in Chapter 20, p. 425–431.

7. Cooperate with inspections and compliance investigations.

To survive in today's complex regulatory climate, you must maintain credibility with the regulators as well as with the public. OSHA and similar agencies are given broad authority to inspect work sites and to issue citations or assess penalties. Accordingly, it is a good practice to make all documentation readily accessible, and to identify knowledgeable people within your organization to participate in the inspection process.

OSHA Inspections: How to Prepare

Regulatory agency inspections can occur at any time, with or without notice. OSHA inspections are generally triggered by an employee complaint alleging imminent danger or past unsafe practices, a workplace fatality, or an accident causing the hospitalization of five or more employees. An inspection may also occur as a follow-up to prior enforcement activities.

The inspectors will request the following information as part of the inspection and audit process:

1. Designation of person(s) responsible for conducting training
2. Description of the training methodology (audiovisuals, classroom instruction, etc.)
3. Substantive elements of the training program—for comparison with the elements required by the Hazard Communication Standard
4. The procedures used to train new employees when they are assigned and to train current employees when a new hazard is introduced into the workplace
5. The procedures used to train employees about new hazards that they may be exposed to when working on or near another employer's work site (i.e., hazards introduced by other employers)

Individual trainers should be aware that during the walk-around inspection, the inspector may request an interview with responsible trainers or record keepers. Follow these guidelines:

- Be cautious, but courteous. Provide access to all workplace facilities, but insist that an authorized company representative escort the compliance officer at all times.

- Be accurate. Do not volunteer information not specifically requested.

- Determine the nature of the visit and identify the person(s) most likely to have custody of the documents requested for inspection.

- Take detailed notes of the questions you are asked.

- Remember that you have the right to remain silent. Silence does not mean guilt or responsibility. All company positions should be taken consistently by authorized representatives.

- Do not admit that any condition is a violation.

- Do not guess or speculate about when training was conducted, or who was present. Always defer to the documentation (e.g., if asked when a particular employee was trained, respond by checking the records).

- Never speculate about the cause of an accident or injury (e.g., "She must not have followed instructions" or "I guess he should have been more aware of how to use personal protective equipment"). The specific cause of an injury can be established only by safety or medical experts.

- Never answer the question "Did management know about this?" or "How long has it been this way?" Defer to a review of the documentation and to knowledgeable, *authorized* spokespeople for the organization.

- Appoint a representative to take detailed notes of all that is said and done. Make sure the notes are dated (with month, day, and year) and that the originals are stored immediately in a safe place. Make a minimum number of "working copies," for use by authorized company representatives during the investigation and follow-up process.

Back to Basics: The Fundamental Rights of Employees to Understand On-the-Job Hazards

Training Multinational Workforces

When you design or present safety training, you should be alert to situations where a trainee's English-language limitations impede the effectiveness of the communication. The law requires you to *effectively* warn about workplace hazards, and OSHA interprets such a warning as "readily understandable" instruction. Arguably if you train a multinational workforce, you must make sure that your training effectively communicates to employees with diverse backgrounds, experiences, literacy levels, and primary languages.

Federal standards recommend, but do not require, bilingual safety information and training. OSHA inspectors are generally told, however, that if employees must receive their job instructions in a language other than English, then safety training and information will probably also need to be conducted in that foreign language. At a minimum, you should anticipate this issue being raised in a compliance audit or penalty inspection.

Balancing the Right to Understand Workplace Hazards With Business Needs

In addition to the right to know about hazards, and the right to understand the danger, employees have a right to act upon that knowledge without fear of reprisals or other employment-related penalties for doing so. This is a strong component of both federal statutes and state laws.

Under right-to-act legislation, when employees have received hazard communication training informing them of hazardous conditions to avoid, they have the right to refuse to work in a situation where the hazard exists unabated. The federal OSH Act makes reprisals against such employees unlawful. Reprisal can result in additional citations and penalties. It can also result in a civil action for damages under state statutes and common law.

An example of such a case was an award of damages and attorneys' fees to a zookeeper who suffered harassment, demotion, and constructive discharge in retaliation for making safety complaints to OSHA and the Department of Agriculture. After a fellow worker lost an arm while feeding a polar bear, the zookeeper told OSHA that hand-feeding was a common practice among the keepers, and that they lacked training in bear handling. Following her complaints, the keeper was demoted to an entry-level job, allegedly for safety reasons, and was suspended when she refused to accept the transfer without explanation.

The employee then filed a lawsuit for retaliatory demotion under Ohio law, and the court ordered her reinstated to her original job. Following reinstatement, she was denied access to necessary records and prevented from listening to safety tapes. Her state law claim for retaliatory discharge in violation of public policy was not preempted by the OSH Act. See *Haynes v. Zoological Society of Cincinnati, Ohio*.[4]

Still another example is a jury verdict awarding both compensatory and punitive damages to an employee wrongfully terminated for expressing his unwillingness to work in a cyanide leach pit while he had an open surgical wound. The worker had learned of the need to protect unhealed wounds from cyanide absorption at one of the employer's required safety courses. The appellate court, in upholding the jury verdict, found that the employee was exercising appropriate safety precautions when he advised his supervisor that he should not and would not work around cyanide with his wound, *in accordance with the training he received*. The discharge violated Nevada public policy under the state OSH Act, which expressly prohibits requiring employees to work at a site which is not safe and healthful. The employee was not limited to the act's remedy for retaliatory discharge. Because the statute provides only for reinstatement and back pay, and does not allow for other forms of damages, he was able to pursue an action for "tortious discharge against public policy."[5]

Balancing Safety Training Mandates With Equal Employment Opportunity Requirements

Effective safety training is vital for two reasons. First, the law requires compliance, which encompasses trainee understanding of the material presented *and* ability to demonstrate that understanding through appropriate posttraining performance testing. Trainers who are responsible for delivery and posttraining evaluation are prohibited from allowing untrained employees, or those who cannot safely apply the information, to remain in the work environment. You add real value as a business partner with management when you recognize the need to provide effective safety training and recommend programs that protect the company from the legal and practical risks of noncompliance.

Second, compliance with right-to-know and right-to-understand laws reduces injuries. In order for training to be effective, and legally defensible, trainers must be satisfied that the training has been suitably completed. This is a significant challenge when portions of the worker population have learning disabilities or other special needs.

When employees have special needs, you are required to make reasonable accommodations in the training process. Specifically, you need to design and deliver training that provides the appropriate safety information in a manner that the employee can understand, apply, demonstrate knowledge of, and act upon.

In the context of health and safety training, participants with special needs fall into two primary categories: trainees with learning or cognitive disabilities and participants with English-language challenges.

English-Language Barriers. Workplace safety laws must be properly balanced with employment discrimination requirements. Employers have a legal duty under the OSH Act and other legislation to provide safe workplaces for employees, including providing intelligible safety instructions. The more extreme the safety or health risk, the higher the duty to overcome language barriers. Some employers have been tempted to refuse to hire, promote, or train employees whose primary language is not English, or to mandate that only English be spoken in the workplace. In the absence of a business necessity to do so, such selection criteria may violate federal (and many state) nondiscrimination provisions based on national origin, ancestry, or culture.

The primary federal statute prohibiting national origin discrimination is Title VII of the Civil Rights Act of 1964, which is enforced by the EEOC. The EEOC has promulgated Guidelines on Discrimination Because of National Origin, in which it defines national origin discrimination as the denial of equal opportunity "because of an individual's, or his or her ancestors', place of origin; or because an individual has the physical, cultural, or linguistic characteristics of a national origin group." Under current EEOC regulations and ample judicial precedent, at least the following are unlawful for employers with 15 or more employees:

- Denying employment opportunities because of an individual's foreign accent or inability to communicate well in English.[6]

- Training or education requirements that deny employment opportunities because of an individual's foreign training or education, or that require an individual to be foreign-trained or -educated. (For a further discussion of selection criteria that discriminate against employees by depriving them of an equal opportunity for training and advancement, see Chapter 6, pp. 129–141.)

- English-only rules that require employees to speak only English at all times in the workplace. The EEOC has taken the position that this is a burdensome term or condition of employment, because it includes work breaks and lunchtime, when employees may be most comfortable speaking in their native language.[7] English-only rules must be justified by business necessity.

In one case, the EEOC found that an oil refinery's English-only policy qualified as a business necessity. The policy required employees to speak English during emergencies and in specified areas where there was a potential for fires, explosions, and other casualties.[8] Safety may be included in the criteria applied to determine if work rules limiting the use of languages qualify for a business-necessity defense under Title VII.

Other than English-only rules, it is unlawful to exclude otherwise qualified employees from jobs, opportunities, training, assignments, or other advancement opportunities because of their national origin—or a characteristic of their national origin, such as English-language proficiency. (Chapter 6, pp. 135–141, has a full discussion of selection criteria for training, and Chapter 7, pp. 163–171 and 178–182, addresses testing and evaluation.) Also, national origin discrimination doesn't make good business sense, since many foreign-born employees are highly educated, knowledgeable, technically skilled, and valuable. These individuals are entitled to both equal employment opportunities *and* effective safety training.

Learning Disability Barriers.   Trainers cannot simply assume that all English-speaking employees are able to read, analyze, synthesize, and respond to safety training. Employees who are literate in English but nevertheless have profound reading difficulty for other reasons are even more reluctant to alert the trainer when they cannot read, write, or comprehend the instruction. They too have the fundamental right to know and understand the hazards they face. This situation surfaces most frequently with cognitive disorders and learning disabilities.

The EEOC has defined learning disabilities as follows: "Specific learning disability means a disorder in one or more of the psychological processes involved in understanding or using language, spoken or written, which may manifest itself in an imperfect ability to listen, think, speak, read, write, spell, or do mathematical calculations."[9] Trainees and workers with learning disabilities are protected from discrimination under the Americans With Disabilities Act and many comparable state antidiscrimination statutes. These equal opportunity laws require the employer to make reasonable accommodations to the known disabilities of employees, where possible and appropriate. Accommodation ensures balance between health and safety requirements and the equal employment opportunity laws.

Participants with learning disabilities in a health and safety program may have challenges in any of the following areas:

- *Visual/reading* (inability to understand concepts in written format)
- *Auditory* (inability to combine a variety of tones into meaningful words or to understand spoken language)
- *Attention* (limited attention span, manifested in hyperactivity, drowsiness, or inability to concentrate for sufficient comprehension)
- *Processing/analytical* (inability to process and store information in short-term memory; inability to draw conclusions from analogies or to interpret data)
- *Social* (inappropriate social conduct often caused by inability to interpret body language or to appreciate serious dangers)

The presence of employees with learning disabilities in a training class on safety or health-related issues poses a significant challenge for the instructor. Trainees with disabilities have dual rights: the right to know and understand hazards they may face on the job, and the right to equal job opportunities. People with disabilities cannot be automatically excluded from the opportunity to attend training, to successfully complete the posttraining evaluation, and to be placed on the job. Yet the federal occupational health and safety laws mandate that employees not be placed into jobs for which they are ill prepared to work safely.

In the context of safety training, it is critical to inform participants that their lack of understanding may result in two significant consequences. First, they may be injured or cause injury to a coworker and second, they may not be able to return to the work environment until they satisfactorily pass the posttraining evaluation or test. This information, when presented accurately, forcefully, and with compassion, should encourage participants with special needs to come forward. If necessary, the trainer's openness and understanding should be emphasized repeatedly.

Testing ensures that trainees understand and can apply material presented during training when they return to their jobs. Testing should measure knowledge, skills, and abilities. Giving people with disabilities an equal opportunity to take and satisfactorily pass a test may require accommodations in both the physical and substantive aspects of the test. (Chapter 7, pp. 167–171, has a complete discussion of reasonable accommodations in testing.)

Participants in health and safety training programs must be provided with an opportunity to fully engage in and complete the course. The trainer's job is to ensure that training materials, presentation, and posttraining evaluation are modified as necessary to accommodate participants with special needs. The objective is to provide effective training so that employees are adequately prepared to work safely. Effective training becomes especially important when OSHA inspectors visit, since they may identify and question employees about their knowledge of safe work practices.

People with disabilities may be excluded from a job when (1) they cannot perform the essential functions of the job, with or without a reasonable accommodation, or (2) they present a direct threat of harm to themselves and others. These restrictions provide a defense to a claim of discrimination, but *only* when the burden of establishing the direct threat to safety has been met. Because this is an affirmative defense, the employer bears the burden of proof; and, to protect against discrimination, Congress made the required level of proof significant. Indeed, the EEOC has specifically stated in its Technical Assistance Manual for ADA compliance:

> An employer may require that an individual not pose a direct threat of harm to his or her own safety or health, as well as to the health or safety of others. However...such determinations must be strictly based on valid medical analyses or other objective evidence related to this individual....A determination that a person might cause harm to himself or herself *cannot* be based on stereotypes, patronizing assumptions about a person with a disability, or generalized fears about risks that might occur if an individual with a disability is placed in a certain job. Any such determination must be based on evidence of specific risk to a particular individual.
>
> Where there is a significant risk of substantial harm to health or safety, an employer must still consider whether there is a reasonable accommodation that would eliminate this risk or reduce the risk so that it is below the level of direct threat.[10]

Evolving Legal Standards for Ergonomics, Process Safety Engineering, Blood-Borne Pathogens, and More

Cumulative Trauma Disorder and Repetitive Stress Injuries

The common tolls of the modern workplace have generated a host of new workplace injury claims. Cumulative trauma disorders (CTDs) and repetitive stress injuries are rising as more employees are exposed to computer keyboards, computer mouse-pointing devices, adding machines, automated checkout registers, laser scanners, a variety of hand-held tools, and even hand-held cellular phones.

Headlines have called attention to many of the perceived ergonomic hazards—video display terminal (VDT) diseases such as radiation emission levels, pregnancy disorders, carpal-tunnel syndrome, cataract development, and related physical stresses arising from office automation. Repetitive motion injuries result from working in awkward positions using improper work tools, or doing the same tasks over and over, especially when applying force. Chronic back pain, arm and leg nerve and muscle problems, tendinitis, and other disorders may arise from cumulative trauma over an extended time period. One of the most frequent disabling injuries is carpal-tunnel syndrome, resulting in pain and in extreme cases intermittent paralysis of wrists and hands.

A single repetitive stress injury (RSI) can easily range in cost from a few thousand to as much as $80,000. Such additional costs would include items such as increased medical premiums, reduced departmental productivity (work disruption), lost work days, increased pressure from other workers, added time and energy to accommodate new workloads, alternative work assignments, and the cost of training new temporary employees, as well as the deluge of paperwork and forms to be completed for workers' compensation claims.

The difference in cost is often directly related to early identification of the hazard(s). If your employer provides education on how to prevent such problems, most strains and injuries can be recognized early and nonsurgical rehabilitation can be implemented. Early identification saves both considerable expense and the employee's long-term productivity. Accordingly, training is an essential part of an effective ergonomics program. Everyone involved in the program—from managers, supervisors, and engineers to trainers, curriculum designers, employees, and maintenance staff—should be trained. The depth and detail of the training will depend on the role you expect each person to play in your repetitive stress control program.

The program coordinator should have the most intensive training. On-site medical personnel will need training in recognition and treatment of repetitive stress injuries and early detection principles. Supervisors will need training to help them identify and correct problems on the production lines they supervise. This type of training may involve several days of instruction. Some organizations set up ergonomics teams that try to spot and correct ergonomic problems. These groups will need special training.

Training enables managers, supervisors, and employees to understand ergonomic and other hazards associated with a job or production process, the prevention and control of such hazards, and their medical consequences. Figure 2-3 highlights the elements of an effective ergonomics program.

Occupational Exposure to Blood-Borne Pathogens

OSHA has published model exposure control plans for blood-borne pathogens to protect workers exposed to infectious diseases such as HIV and hepatitis B virus. A covered employer must have complied with the first phase of the regulations by establishing a written exposure control plan by May 5, 1992. The plan must include, in part, a classification of jobs in which employees risk occupational exposure to blood-borne diseases, a schedule and methods for implementing precautions,

---

Ergonomics training should include the following information:

- The varieties of cumulative trauma disorder and how they occur
- What risk factors cause or contribute to such disorders and how to prevent them
- How to prevent cumulative traumas or minimize risks through appropriate use of office equipment and adopting safe work practices
- How to recognize and report symptoms
- How to correct and report workstation problems
- The essential elements of the employer's ergonomics program and methods used by the employer to minimize repetitive motion injuries

---

Figure 2-3 Components of an Ergonomics Training Program.

and procedures for training employees and for keeping records of training.

Implementation of "engineering and work practice controls" must have been completed by July 6, 1992. These controls include protective equipment and clothing. Employers are also required to advise employees, through labeling and training, on occupational exposure to blood-borne pathogens. Figure 2-4 highlights the essentials of an effective program in any workplace where occupational exposure to blood-borne diseases exists.

Workplace Security and Violence Prevention

When your employer learns that a current or former employee has threatened violence against managers, supervisors, or other employees, you may have to take certain preventive steps under the guidelines provided by FED-OSHA and several states. Encompassed within the general-duty clause is an obligation to do everything that is reasonably necessary to protect the life, safety, and health of employees, including the furnishing of safety devices and safeguards and the adoption of

---

Blood-Borne Pathogens Training

- Identify the blood-borne hazards that exist in the particular workplace, including modes of transmission.
- Describe who is foreseeably at risk of injury or exposure through potential contacts with infectious materials.
- Describe how employees at risk can protect themselves from exposure through "universal precautions" or use of protective devices.
- Identify the symptoms of disease and/or warning signs of exposure.
- Describe—and demonstrate—how good work practices (including labeling, decontamination procedures, and safe disposal), engineering controls, and effective use of personal protective equipment can reduce the risks of infection.
- Inform trainees what to do if they are exposed or believe themselves to be at risk.

Figure 2-4 Components of a Blood-Borne Pathogens Training Program.

practices, means, methods, and operations reasonably adequate to create a safe and healthful workplace.

FED-OSHA has used the general-duty clause to encourage employers to take steps to prevent injury to employees. In 1996 the agency issued guidelines focusing on preventing workplace violence in several industries, including health care operations, retail, and related public service establishments. Although the guidelines do not carry enforcement authority and do not affect current compliance activities, FED-OSHA has noted that it will continue to issue citations for workplace violence under the general-duty clause whenever criminal activity endangers workers.

Some state safety and health agencies either have or are developing safety standards or guidelines with the same goal of motivating employers to address workplace violence. This is the case in California, where the California Occupational Safety and Health Act of 1973 (CAL-OSHA) imposes a general duty upon employers, similar to that imposed by the federal law, to provide "employment and a place of employment which are safe and healthful for the employees therein."[11]

Similarly, Washington State requires retailers to implement a formal accident prevention program.[12] The program must include training in crime prevention for retail employees as well as posting notices and taking certain precautions with respect to the placement of cash registers and lighting.

The role of training in addressing terror and violence in the workplace is discussed in greater detail in Chapter 11, p. 235–240.

Mandated Training on the Dangers of Drugs

Another federal law mandating training is the Omnibus Anti-Drug Abuse Act (known as the Drug-Free Workplace Act) of 1988. It covers employers who have or seek federal government contracts for goods or services of $25,000 or more. Also covered are recipients of federal grants, which are usually municipalities and nonprofit organizations. There is no minimum number of employees, so very small employers with the requisite government contracts or grants must also comply.

The act provides that no employer shall be eligible for a federal contract unless it certifies to the federal contracting agency that it will "provide a drug-free workplace" by meeting six separate policy and enforcement functions. Four of the functions relate to training, including publishing a policy statement to notify employees that "the unlawful manufacture, distribution, possession, or use of a controlled substance is prohibited in the [employer's] workplace" and establishing a "drug-free awareness program" to inform and train employees about the dangers of drug abuse in the workplace.

Where to Go for Help When You're Not Sure What Training Is Required and When: A Resource Guide

All these training requirements may seem overwhelming. The key is to focus the training on those laws or industry regulations that are applicable to your organization. There are many resources available for identifying applicable standards, and for keeping up with changes as they occur. Here are a few general guidelines.

- Consult trade or professional associations in your industry for information. Many have legislative specialists who keep up with emerging standards.

- Retain a consultant to assess your company's needs and to either design a focused training program or assemble the material for you to do it.

- Consult your local OSHA or EPA office for written information. Do not be fearful of drawing an audit or inspection by using this resource.

- Send your employees to outside programs or seminars about hazardous materials handling and disposal.

- Consult officials at your local university or community college, particularly in the extension programs. They may be willing to help you design a program to meet specific regulatory requirements.

- Take advantage of federal, state, or local government training programs. OSHA, EPA, and DOT offices all have materials which may be used, with appropriate customization, by similar organizations. Often it is not necessary to reinvent the wheel.

- Network with other trainers in your geographic area or industry. Share information and resources to the extent that you can do so without disclosing confidential information about your internal programs.

- Evaluate off-the-shelf programs carefully. Many are directly applicable; others are so generic that you may risk wasting resources on inapplicable subjects, missing an essential component, or even worse, providing instructions that are inaccurate when applied in your own work environments.

The complete text governing OSHA training requirements can be found in the *Federal Register* at 48 F.R. 53310-12 and 48 F.R. 53337-38. *Chemical Hazard Communication* (U.S. Department of Labor, OSHA 3084, revised 1988) describes the requirements in less imposing language. The latter publication also contains information about government and government-funded organizations that provide training and other technical services for employers with fewer than 300 employees.

Several publishing and training film firms also sell or rent excellent off-the-shelf packages. Some are appropriate for briefing managers on training requirements. Others are more appropriate for training employees.

Consultation Services

Considerable help, much of it at low or no cost, is available to employers that need assistance in establishing or improving a safety training program. The OSHA consultation program is administered through the states and can be reached by calling the OSHA regional office. Appendix A contains telephone numbers for OSHA offices in all 50 states.

In addition, workers' compensation carriers, medical insurers, and other health maintenance organizations are extremely interested in controlling workplace costs and reducing illness and accident rates. They frequently have libraries, publications, videos, and consultants available. Similarly, trade associations and professional training companies have training resources and databases of consultants or vendors who may be helpful.

OSHA Training Outreach

In addition to consultation services, OSHA maintains an Office of Training and Education, which includes the OSHA Training Institute, located in Des Planes, Illinois. The institute was established in 1982 and offers courses on safe work practices, hazardous waste site operations, ergonomics, process safety management, and various environmental hazards.

OSHA area offices also frequently supply useful information, such as availability of speakers, publications, audiovisual aids, and technical advice. These offices provide funds to nonprofit organizations to conduct workplace training and education in substantive areas where OSHA has determined that such training is lacking or deficient.

FED-OSHA and states such as California and Texas have specialized consulting services for delivering training in multiple languages. They can assist in identifying relevant videotaped products and other resources for providing general safety instructions in Spanish, Vietnamese, and other languages. OSHA also provides some hazard communication information in multiple languages.

References

1. *People v. Reclamation Services, Inc.,* California Superior Court (Alameda County 1995).

2. *People v. Cargill, Inc. and Leslie Salt Co.,* California Superior Court (Solano County 1995).

3. Ira Reiner and Jan Chatten-Brown, *California Law Imposes New Level Of Corporate Responsibility,* Memorandum, Office of the Los Angeles District Attorney, p. 4.

4. *Haynes v. Zoological Society of Cincinnati, Ohio,* 567 N.E.2d 1048 (December 22, 1993).

5. *D'Angelo v. Gemco; Western States Minerals Corp. v. Jones,* 819 P.2d 706 (October 24, 1991).

6. Title VII, §1601.6(b)(1).

7. EEOC Decision 71-446.

8. EEOC Decision 83-7.

9. EEOC Technical Assistance Manual on Compliance with the Americans With Disabilities Act (1992).

10. EEOC Technical Assistance Manual on Compliance with the Americans With Disabilities Act (1992), §4.05 (emphasis in original).

11. California Labor Code, §6400.

12. WAC 296-24-102, 296-24-10203.

3

How to Avoid the Injury Lawsuit

What Types of Personal Injury Lawsuits Involve Training?

Employers and individual trainers are most vulnerable to personal injury lawsuits when employees are killed or injured in workplace accidents. Employees and training participants litigate when they are injured during training, or when they make a mistake on the job that they assert wouldn't have happened if they had been properly trained. Even nonemployees turn to the courts when they are injured or sustain property damages because of an employee's human error allegedly caused by inadequate training.

Personal injury lawsuits are pursued by individuals rather than by government enforcement agencies. Typically they seek compensation, or compensatory damages, for lost wages, medical expenses, and general pain. In rare instances, a criminal statute will authorize *restitution*, which is a form of compensation to victims of a violation of the law. When a statute provides for restitution, the government or the injured party can seek a court order requiring payment of direct out-of-pocket costs on terms the court imposes.

Most injury lawsuits are brought in state civil courts, and are based on the law of negligence. The ordinary legal definition of negligence is a failure to exercise due care under circumstances in which a legal duty of care is owed to another person. Litigation of workplace negligence involves an examination of the existence of a legal duty. The more foreseeable the risk of harm to identifiable parties, the greater the need to exercise reasonable care to prevent that harm. When negligence is alleged, the courts are required to determine on a case-by-case basis whether state law imposes a duty of care in the particular circumstances. There is no clear body of precedent identifying a duty of care in particular circumstances. The evolution of negligence law has been a case-by-case process of injured parties arguing that courts should recognize the existence of a duty of care under particular circumstances, even when legislation has not imposed such an obligation.

Not surprisingly, the most significant area of potential legal risk for individual trainers and their organizations involves programs that educate employees about workplace hazards. In high-risk work environments, such as manufacturing plants using toxins, chemicals, or potentially dangerous equipment, human error can pose a real threat to trainees and other employees. When people are injured in an accident, they often search for culprits in the department least able to reconstruct or document the steps it took to prevent foreseeable risks of harm. Unfortunately, increasing attention in these lawsuits is placed on the training department.

You would not see a lawsuit entitled "John Doe v. XYZ Corporate Training Department." Rather, the injured party would name the employer as the defendant, and would typically raise more than one theory. For example, a person injured by an explosion at a work site might allege three different grounds for negligence: failure to effectively train employees whose error caused the explosion, inadequate supervision of the workplace, and failure to exercise appropriate care in the handling of hazardous materials. Liability may arise from one or more of these circumstances. Since human error is a factor in most accidents, the trend throughout the country is for lawsuits to focus on training—or lack of it—to establish liability. One recent high-profile example: In March 1997, a South Carolina jury found USAir at fault for the July 1994 crash that left 37 people dead and many injured. The primary factor cited by survivors and families of the deceased: USAir "did not properly train its pilots and improperly allowed them to fly into thunderstorms."

You should anticipate that questions will be raised about the training you provided to employees who cause or contribute to an injury-producing event. These questions will certainly focus on how well the employees were prepared to do their jobs. If you are unable to reconstruct or document the steps you took to design and deliver appropriate, timely, and effective training, you may quickly become "target zero" for a negligence allegation.

Claims for negligent training typically focus on an alleged failure to train, inadequate training design, failure to disclose potential exposure to toxic or hazardous materials, and negligent selection of instructors or vendor-sponsored programs. This chapter focuses on the most common types of lawsuits and how to avoid them. Chapter 4 addresses negligence in curriculum design and supervision. Chapter 8 focuses on personal injuries during adventure or outdoor training.

When Training to Government Standards Is Not Enough and What to Do About It

Chapter 2 focuses on compliance with government-mandated training. Many trainers are under the mistaken belief that if they meet federal requirements they will avoid all liabilities. Government requirements addressing the design, content, timing, and delivery of training provide a baseline standard; but they are *only a minimum*. In fact, you may be found negligent for failing to provide sufficient training, even when your programs meet the minimum standard prescribed by OSHA, *if* under all the circumstances the jury finds that the timing, content, or delivery of the training was insufficient to reduce the risk of foreseeable harm to your employees or visitors to your work sites.

In essence, when an employer (acting through its responsible agents, such as trainers) knows, or reasonably should know, that additional training and skill building are required for employees to appreciate dangers and/or to work safely, you will have a legal duty to act reasonably to provide the additional training. The failure to do so may be negligent. Training to a blind level of compliance (i.e., simply meeting the letter of the statute regarding subjects covered, timing, and record keeping) is frequently insufficient in a personal injury lawsuit. Likewise, simply providing material safety data sheets or other reading material is generally not enough to ensure that the trainee has learned, has absorbed, and can effectively apply the knowledge to safe work practices. To comply with the law, you need to make sure workers *really understand* the information and skills training they receive.

The biggest challenge for health, safety, and skills training is literacy. Because there are so many employees in varied positions with widely different levels of education, literacy, English proficiency, and basic communication skills, trainers should make sure that competency problems are not a concern when developing written safety and health programs. To combat such problems, trainers should link with line supervisors and management to provide comprehensive evaluation of competency levels and then design training using a variety of methodologies to meet the needs of diverse work environments.

Figure 3-1 provides a checklist for effective training and worker understanding of important information about hazardous conditions in the workplace.

Six Ways Your Legal Duties Are Established and Expanded by the Courts

A successful negligence lawsuit requires proof of several specific elements. These include the existence of the legal duty of care owed by the employer or individual trainers, a breach of the duty, causation (a nexus or direct connection between the breach of duty and the injury), injury or damage, and the amount of the damage.

In an injury lawsuit, legal duty is based on the applicable "standard of care" for trainers in a particular industry. Standard of care is often defined as the level of conduct expected of similarly trained professionals in a given field. For example, a physician has a duty to provide medical care for patients that is within the accepted standards adopted by members of the medical profession in the area where the physician practices. When the doctor is a specialist (a cardiologist, say), a higher standard of care is imposed.

The determination of whether a duty of care exists is generally a question of law for the courts to decide; whether the defendant breached this duty of care by acting unreasonably under the particular circumstances is a question for the trier of fact. In most civil cases, either party may request a jury trial. If a jury is waived by both parties, the trier of fact will typically be a single judge. The courts impose a legal duty in six ways.

1. A minimum standard of care may be established by a statute or other regulatory scheme that governs the particular subject or industry.

Although an OSHA violation does not create a private right of action by an injured party, it may establish a minimum or threshold legal duty to train to the mandated level. In these instances, the requirements of the legislation establish the standard of care and satisfy the element of "duty." In high-hazard industries, the standard of care (duty) may be more stringent than the statute itself. When this occurs or when there is

Figure 3-1 Checklist for Effective Training in Diverse Work Environments.

Encouraging Compliance

Does the corporation encourage compliance with the spirit and letter of right-to-know regulations by:

- Demonstrating management concern?
- Reminding supervisors of their training and warning responsibilities?
- Supporting the discipline or discharge of employees who consistently fail or refuse to comply?

Knowing When to Train or Warn

Do employees receive safety information and training about hazards:

- When first hired?
- When a new hazard is introduced in their work area?
- When transferred to a new work area?
- When a previously unrecognized hazard becomes known?
- At least once a year, as a "refresher" course?

Showing What's Important

Are employees taught how to "get to the heart of the matter" with written materials—for example, to ask themselves basic questions about the information on material safety data sheets, such as:

- What is this? (identify hazardous chemical or equipment)
- What harm can it do to me? (particularly health hazards)
- Are there other dangers? (possibility of fire or explosion)
- What should I do to protect myself? (prevention and self-protection)
- What do I do if I've been injured or exposed? (self-protection and emergency medical attention)

Coping With Reading or Language Difficulties

Is the employer or are individual trainers aware of workers who may have problems reading and understanding written information about workplace hazards because of:

- Illiteracy, poor reading skills, or learning disabilities?
- English as a secondary language?

If so, what steps have been taken or planned to help these workers understand important hazard information?

(Continued)

Expanding Training Methods

Along with written materials, are workers trained using other techniques such as:
- Videos or films?
- Small group discussions?
- Role playing and demonstrations?
- Question-and-answer sessions?
- Simulated exercises?
- Realistic workplace simulations?
- Realistic workplace conditions, such as stress, reduced oxygen, or other reasonably foreseeable physical challenges?

---

no government regulation, the standard of care may be imposed by judicial decisions, by the employer's own safety policies, or by a combination of these elements as described below.

A relevant statute establishes a threshold *minimum* standard of care. Evidence of a statutory violation might be introduced to establish negligence "as a matter of law," where the element of duty is met without further required proof. Here, the duty and its breach are automatically established. However, the injured party still must prove that the breach of duty was the legal (proximate) cause of the injury. The amount of damages is universally a question for the jury. See the discussion of the role of jurors in Chapter 1, pp. 33–35.

2. Regulations issued by a federal or state enforcement agency may provide a legal duty to provide specific training.

Congress and state legislatures pass legislation (statutes or laws) that govern training. They also extend broad authority to administrative agencies to issue regulations, which then have the force and effect of laws. Such regulations may supply a legal duty to train. One example is the Federal Aviation Administration, which prescribes the level, timing, and scope of training required for commercial airline pilots and airlines.

The FAA also has the power to issue civil penalties for failure to meet its standards. The agency doesn't hesitate to use it, as reflected in a March 1997 penalty of $52,000 proposed against Delta Airlines for allegedly failing to provide proper training, testing, and evaluation of security personnel.[1] Upon notification, Delta took full corrective action.

3. Legal duty may be based on the standard of care for organizations or individual trainers in the particular industry.

If other companies in the same industry provide training that exceeds the minimum, a court will expect you to meet that higher standard. In essence, standard of care is often defined as the level of conduct expected of similarly trained professionals working in the same field, or under the same circumstances. The elements of industry standards and expert witness opinions to establish standard of care were addressed by the Alabama Supreme Court in *Thompson v. Liberty Mutual Ins. Co.*[2] The court relied upon the affidavit of a professor of mechanical engineering who concluded that industry standards were not followed with respect to the instruction and training of an injured worker on a piece of equipment.

A brief case study illustrates why you should keep up with industry standards and advise management when your training programs need updating. In *Vons Companies, Inc. v. Seabest Foods, Inc.*,[3] customers of Jack-in-the-Box restaurants in several states suffered from exposure to *E. coli* bacteria traced to hamburgers sold at the restaurants. Many became ill and some died. The parent company, Foodmaker, blamed the *E. coli* contamination on its meat suppliers, including Vons. In turn, Vons sought indemnity (reimbursement) from several Jack-in-the-Box franchises, including Seabest Foods, Inc., alleging that they were negligent.

Prominent among the allegations of wrongdoing was the franchisees' failure to require adequate qualifications *and training* for their cooks. Vons alleged that the Foodmaker franchise agreement mandated standardized procedures and training that did not meet industry standards. According to Vons, the franchisees failed to cook the meat to the proper internal temperature because of deficiencies in the cooking and training procedures and equipment requirements provided by Foodmaker on a systemwide basis. The California Supreme Court agreed, finding the training procedures "systematically deficient when measured by industry standards."

This case exemplifies how training—or lack of training—can become one theory among many in a negligence lawsuit. The basis for focusing on the *legal duty to train* arose from industry standards for internal cooking temperature and related training. The California Supreme Court found that the franchise relationship, with its uniform standards for cooking food, training employees, and buying equipment was a primary source of injury to Vons, whose reputation was adversely affected by claims of tainted meat.

4. A legal duty of care may be established by your employer's own policies and practices, particularly when there is evidence that the employer regularly exceeded minimum statutory requirements.

Your legal duty to provide effective training may also be established by your own company policies. For example, when you undertake to provide training not directly required by a statute or industry practices, you must perform the training consistently and effectively. The failure to do so may be negligent. An Illinois case provides a relevant example. In *Decker v. Domino's Pizza, Inc.*,[4] a "manager in training" at the pizza chain brought a negligence action after he suffered severe injuries during an armed robbery.

On the day of the incident, this manager in training was working the evening shift. Shortly before the robbery, some employees noticed a suspicious person outside and he went to investigate. The robber began to hit him over the head with a pistol and kicked him in the lower back. Forcing the management trainee (plaintiff) back into the store, the robber shot another employee and then demanded that the plaintiff open the safe. The plaintiff told the robber that the safe was on a time delay, but the robber did not believe him. After attempting to shoot the plaintiff in the face, the robber fled from the store. The plaintiff suffered severe personality disorders and physical lacerations to his head and hands. He was hospitalized for three days. The jury concluded that Domino's was negligent, and returned a verdict of $400,000.

Prior to this incident, Domino's had formed a standards committee to review proposed security measures for its stores. It also hired an outside consultant to review security procedures and to be sure that managers in training were instructed in safety and security. The consultant was not directly responsible for the training, since this was the responsibility of the franchise owner. Significantly, Domino's Pizza, Inc. required certification of the local franchise's trainer/manager.

At the time of this incident, there were no federal or state occupational safety standards mandating training on workplace security or violence prevention, nor were there state laws requiring certification of trainer/managers or any specific curriculum. Domino's voluntarily established the standards requiring franchisees to train employees through certified trainer/managers.

At trial and again on appeal, the company strenuously argued that its legal duties should be construed narrowly, and should be limited to the mandatory use of a time-delay safe. The court disagreed, finding that Domino's had voluntarily assumed a duty to provide proper training on workplace security and violence prevention. The court found that the training was ineffective and haphazard, violating the company's own policy. Essentially, once the employer adopted the policy, its trainers were required to provide effective, timely, and consistent training. Essentially, the court imposed liability for the negligent performance of the duty voluntarily undertaken through this employer's specific policies.

5. Duty may be established by past practices of your employer, particularly if there is no reasonable explanation for why the training was cut back or abandoned.

When your employer adopts policies and then fails to enforce them, you and your company will invariably find yourselves in a worse position than if the policies had never been created. Courts regularly conclude that if you adopted a policy you must have determined that it was consistent with your business needs. To make matters worse, there may be memos from management justifying the creation of the policy in glowing terms, such as "This will make us work smarter and safer" or "This will enhance our employees' skills to handle all challenges they may face." Then, when the policy is haphazardly enforced, it is "Murphy's Law" that an injury will occur to an employee who did not receive the requisite training under the policy. The result? Failure to meet your self-imposed standard of care.

As a trainer, you should make sure that you enforce consistently all published policies within your areas of responsibility. When your company fails to follow its own policies, potential cross-examination of executives *and trainers* can occur and be quite uncomfortable. Consider the hypothetical cross-examination depicted in Figure 3-2.

6. A legal duty may be created or expanded by court cases in the particular state.

Even when your employer complies with the minimum standards prescribed by a statute, a court may find that you have breached the standard of care by providing training that is "inadequate" under all the circumstances. The standard of care may be expanded through court cases that explore appropriate training techniques and instructional design principles. In these cases, instructional design specialists with pertinent experience in the same industry or locale give expert testimony in court about standard practices in the training field.

The injured party may try to prove that although a company met the minimum requirements of a statute, the circumstances demanded additional training, or a different type of training. For example, OSHA

Q. You knew that such training was necessary for the safety of your workers?

A. Yes.

Q. You would not have created a policy that did not add to the safety of your workplace?

A. Of course not.

Q. And after you provided that level of training, your employees worked safely and effectively?

A. We assumed so.

Q. Isn't it a fact that your trained employees never caused or received an injury?

A. Yes, indeed.

Q. Then why didn't this employee [the injured one] receive the level of training you *knew* was necessary?

A. I don't know.

Q. Why didn't you follow your own policies?

A. I can't really say.

Q. Isn't it true that [the injured employee] wouldn't have been injured if he had been trained like all the others?

A. (Silence!!)

Figure 3-2 Sample Cross-Examination Highlighting Failure to Adhere to Training Policies.

does not require that training be conducted in more than one language, and most statutes do not require companies to pair employees with supervisors who speak the same language. However, since training often occurs on the job, particularly in high-risk work environments, the employer's failure to ensure on-the-job training that meets the worker's needs may result in substantial liability if an employee is injured.

In the absence of a statute, employer policy, or guiding case precedent, most states measure the standard of care (legal duty) by what the "reasonable person" would do under all the circumstances, balancing the risks and the objectives. In essence, the trier of fact—typically a jury—will decide whether you have met the standard of care required of reasonable trainers under the circumstances. Frequently, expert witnesses are called to provide opinions on what similarly situated trainers would do.

"Causation": The Legal Nexus Between the Breach of Duty and the Harm

The existence of a legal duty and evidence of its breach are only two elements of the typical negligence lawsuit. The injured party also bears the burden of proof to demonstrate that the breach of the duty actually caused his harm. The legal term for this is *proximate cause* or *causation*. In plain English, it means a direct link between the breach (inadequate training) and the harm (the accident or injury). If the harm would not have occurred "but for" the breach of duty, negligence liability is established.

Consider a case from Texas. *Mahavier v. Beverly Enterprises, Inc.*[5] provides a clear example of a successful defense to a negligence claim when the admittedly inadequate training did *not* directly cause the injury. The plaintiff sought damages for the pain and suffering of her husband, who died in a fire while a patient in the defendant's hospital. The deceased suffered from cancer, and by all accounts had a short time to live. While he was hospitalized, a fire broke out in his room. The fire burned for almost 10 minutes before it was detected, and when the nurses rushed in they were ineffective in extinguishing the flames. The deceased suffered third-degree burns over 20 to 40 percent of his body. He lived for several hours afterward. The death certificate noted that the immediate cause of death was carcinoma, but body burns and smoke inhalation were significant contributors.

The allegations against the hospital included failure to provide adequate equipment *and training* to its personnel to fight foreseeable fires. A jury concluded that the hospital did fail to properly train its personnel and that this was the cause of the decedent's pain and suffering. On appeal, the appellate court found the evidence concerning inadequate training to be extensive. The testimony indicated that there were fire extinguishers on the wing where the fire occurred. Three contained water for fighting wood and paper fires. The fourth, located at the nurses' station, was a carbon dioxide extinguisher designed primarily for putting out electrical fires. Neither of the nurses present at the fire knew which to use. They could not remember ever having had a fire drill.

The hospital's maintenance supervisor stated that fire drills were occasionally conducted and that a seminar on fire fighting had been held several years earlier, but he could not remember which personnel had participated in the training. There was no documentation to answer this question. He further testified that a "fire plan" had been prepared by the hospital administration and was posted at each nurses' station, but there was no enforcement to ensure that the document was read by employees.

On the basis of this evidence, the appellate court concluded:

> It is clear to us that the hospital personnel lacked adequate training and lacked proper equipment for use in case of fire. Having been alerted to the fire, each of the nurses should have picked up a correct fire extinguisher to help extinguish the fire....From all of the evidence, the jury could properly have inferred that had the nurses been adequately trained in fire fighting procedures and had access to the proper equipment, they could have extinguished the fire sooner.

The next question was whether the lack of training actually caused the injuries. The court ruled that it had not, explaining:

> In order to bridge the causal connection between the negligent acts of the hospital personnel over to the deceased's injuries, the jury would also have had to supply one additional inference, and that is, that, had the nurses been able to put out the fire sooner, the deceased would not have sustained the injuries of conscious pain and suffering. . . . The jury's finding could only be based on speculation in this case.

In essence, the court found a legal duty to train personnel to avoid foreseeable injuries to third parties, and further found a clear breach of the duty. The missing evidence was a direct connection between the failure to train the nurses to promptly respond effectively to the fire and the burns. Since the burns may have occurred in the first minute of the fire, the element of "causation" was not established.

Readers should be cautiously optimistic when considering this case. The hospital may have dodged the bullet only because the medical evidence of when the burns were sustained was impossible to prove. The absence of effective training for a foreseeable emergency, coupled with the paucity of documentation regarding training, could have been devastating.

Damages

Courts require proof of injury as part of a negligence claim. An injury is any invasion of some legally protected right or interest. Punitive damages can be awarded when the employer's or trainer's total disregard for safety training or reckless disregard for safe practices results in injuries. Punitive damages punish the defendant, either to prevent the act from occurring again or to set an example for others.

Long-Term Health Risks or
Delayed Illness From Exposure

Long-term health problems from occupational exposure is a significant issue on the horizon. High-risk jobs pose a unique hazard to the American workforce. One of the thorny issues of the 1990s involves employee allegations of ill-health as a result of long-term exposure to toxic substances though ingestion, inhalation, or skin absorption. Such exposure can be quite expensive for the employer, taking the form of lost work days, increased workers' compensation benefits, and lost productivity from other employees who begin to perceive themselves at risk. Sometimes, the adverse health effects are not detected until many years after the exposure. When the information becomes known to the employer, a duty may exist under state common law to notify former workers who are at risk, even though congressional attempts to impose a notification mandate have not mustered enough support.

One area of common law judicial decisions that presents significant financial exposure to employers, and to individual trainers, is the injury lawsuit technically called the *toxic tort*. This civil action usually seeks both compensatory and punitive damages, and is an outgrowth of the "delayed injury" claim. A toxic tort involves claims of injuries and/or illnesses caused by exposure to toxic materials. The damage typically stems from exposure to hazardous materials in or leaked from a work site. The exposure may occur from a single event, such as a chemical spill, or may result from long-term exposure to workplace hazards. The injuries may be sustained from inhalation, skin absorption, or ingestion of noxious, poisonous, or carcinogenic materials.

The types of injuries vary from deadly to chronic. In recent years, some large groups of people have even been able to recover damages for anticipated future illness (or injury aggravation) and even the emotional distress caused by fear of becoming ill. As an example, cases involving "fear of developing cancer" from an adjacent business have been successful in some states. Most toxic tort lawsuits involve multiple claimants, making the financial exposure significant.

The most common claimant in a toxic tort case is a former or current employee who asserts that the employer, *acting through individual trainers,* failed to provide accurate, timely, or complete warnings on the nature of the chemical hazard. A common corollary argument is that the training on when and how to use protective devices was deficient. The worker typically alleges that if a warning had been given properly or promptly, the exposure would have been avoided through safe work practices or protective equipment.

Health and safety trainers can use your compliance with the Hazard Communication Standard, and your training curriculum, to bolster your defense to a toxic tort action, because you are required to document periodic training. If your record keeping is complete, it should reflect at least that the MSDS was thoroughly explained, that the employee was effectively trained about the hazards, and that he or she demonstrated acceptable levels of knowledge and ability to apply the information to safe work practices.

Negligent Selection of Vendors and Trainers

You and your employer can't escape liability for damages by releasing control of safety training to an outside consultant or vendor. In most states, the law assumes that the vendor is acting on your behalf. Additionally, most statutes provide that the duty to train cannot be delegated.

The common law of negligence in most states requires an employer to conduct an appropriate investigation before hiring an instructor or consultant. Particularly with training that involves hazard communication, the employer is responsible for ascertaining the vendor's qualifications, experience, and skills before making a choice. It's also wise to have representatives from the training or human resources department monitor the scope, content, and delivery of the training to ensure that the necessary topics are covered effectively.

In most states, trial courts impose a "nondelegable" duty on an employer to provide appropriate training, particularly on safe work practices. In plain English, this means that the employer cannot absolve itself from its own liability by relinquishing control to a vendor or consultant.

Several cases illustrate the point. *Suich v. H.&B. Printing Machinery, Inc.*[6] involved an employee's injury on a piece of industrial equipment. The injured employee sued both his employer for negligence and the manufacturer of the equipment for a defective product. The jury returned a joint verdict for over $2 million, allocating 20 percent of the blame to the manufacturer and 80 percent to the employer. The negligence claims against the employer were based on failure to provide adequate training.

The evidence revealed that the only instruction the employee received on the equipment was during on-the-job training from journeymen pipe fitters. The employer didn't train its service personnel, including the injured man, in the proper use of the equipment. A central issue was whether the employer, or the manufacturer, was responsible to instruct on the proper use of this heavy equipment. Over the employer's objection, an expert called by the manufacturer testified that this employer was obligated to train its employees in using the equipment. The expert suggested that the machinery was designed for a "sophisticated industrial user," and that it was dangerous only in the hands of an untrained person. The comment rendered the testimony about the effectiveness of on-the-job training extremely relevant.

The appellate court determined that the employer was indeed negligent, because it failed to meet its legal duty to train its employees. This duty was independent of any duty or responsibility of the manufacturer to supply a safe product. The court reasoned:

> This independent duty owed Carrier's employees was to provide a safe place to work. Carrier cannot seriously contend that an employer can furnish a sophisticated tool or piece of equipment to an employee and rely solely on the manufacturer to provide all necessary instruction on its use. This obligation is different than and in addition to the manufacturer's duty to produce a product that is reasonably safe. . . . *Carrier failed to adequately train and supervise its employees in proper rigging techniques.* . . . These deficiencies were unrelated to the allegedly unsafe condition of [the equipment].[7]

Finally, on an evidentiary issue, the employer argued that it was an error to allow its employees to be questioned on the training they received. The court disagreed, noting that this testimony was relevant to demonstrate the injured employee's subjective knowledge and understanding of the risk. The lesson is to expect testimony from your trainees—years later—on the effectiveness of your program.

The result was the same in a California case in which an employee sustained very serious injuries while disconnecting a liquid hose from an ammonia storage tank. In *Levels v. Growers Ammonia Supply Company et al.,*[8] the employee sued both his employer, Fredlo Farms, and Growers Ammonia Supply Company, the supplier of the large ammonia-filled tanks and related equipment for use on the job site. Fredlo Farms was aware that the injured employee had no experience in using such equipment.

Growers provided a trainer to conduct on-site instruction. While the injured employee was told how to use the equipment, a Fredlo Farms manager stood out of earshot talking to others. In the process of giving instructions, the Growers representative hooked hoses to incorrect valves, causing the compressor to freeze and become inoperative. The manager who witnessed the incident "became concerned as to whether or not [the instructor] was competent to instruct in the operation and use of the equipment." However, the manager did not move closer so he could observe or hear the instructions.[9]

The instructor gave verbal information through only one complete cycle of filling the tanks and no written instructions or diagrams. A state regulatory safety order pertaining directly to the transfer of ammonia required that during transfer at least one attendant familiar with the installation remain in attendance. The order specified that an attendant could be considered familiar with the equipment only after he or she had been provided with a set of operating instructions and had been personally instructed through a minimum of three full cycles of operation. Neither Fredlo Farms nor Growers was unfamiliar with these requirements, and Fredlo Farms did not comply.

The accident occurred when the employee attempted to fill a different tank in the same way, but mistakenly removed a hose that was still under pressure. The explosion severely injured him. The problem for Fredlo Farms was its complete reliance on the contractor to provide safety use instruction. The fact that the trainer was an independent contractor did not absolve Fredlo Farms. Fredlo had a nondelegable duty to provide its employees with a safe place to work, to comply with all applicable safety regulations, and to be sure that all vendors and contractors met appropriate standards of competency and qualifications.

Is this a catch-22 for employers operating under high-hazard conditions? On the one hand, you have an obligation to provide a safe workplace and effective training; on the other hand, business realities—and legal prudence—require that you rely on technical expertise of manufacturers and equipment suppliers. If you rely on external contractors without adequate investigation of their qualifications, competence, and complete curriculum, you may be legally accountable for their mistakes. If you attempt to provide technical instructions using unqualified internal trainers, you may be just as legally culpable.

How to Protect Yourself From an Injury Lawsuit: A Checklist

Administration and Compliance With Legal Duties

1. Identify the person or people from the training department selected to assume responsibility for ensuring that training design and delivery standards will be followed by all trainers. This person should be thoroughly trained on how to administer risk management programs in the training context.

2. Be aware of your legal duties to employees and third parties. You need to know what standard of care applies to your organization,

and whether it varies from program to program. Keep in mind that you are always expected to exercise reasonable care under the circumstances to prevent or reduce the potential for foreseeable risks of harm.

3. If your organization elects to expand training beyond the applicable state or industry standards, understand the effect of that judgment. If you reduce your training requirements later, be prepared to explain why your action was both appropriate and justified by business necessity.

4. Comply with all federal and state laws and regulations regarding content of training. There are a wealth of publications, particularly with regard to the Hazard Communication Standard, other OSHA safety training, and of course industry standards to help keep you abreast of changes in the requirements.

Conduct Effective Safety Training

5. Be sure that your training program covers the five essential questions:

- What is it?
- How can it hurt me?
- How can I protect myself?
- How do I know if I've been injured or exposed?
- What do I do if injured?

6. Train workers on job-specific safety issues. Monitor the need for follow-up training and refreshers even if those are more frequent than required. If you elect to do more training than the minimum required by an applicable statute, understand how your standard of care (based on employer practices) may be affected.

7. Maintain and update all occupational health and safety training programs that instruct employees in general safe and healthy work practices, and provide specific instruction with regard to each employee's job assignment and general workplace safety.

8. Make sure employees are fully warned about the hazards, and understand the warnings and the consequences of ignoring them.

9. Establish a system for identifying and evaluating the types and scope of training required for the organization. Identify the level of training necessary to meet the standards of applicable statutes, regulations, industry practices, or employer policies.

10. Establish a system for communicating with employees on all matters relating to occupational health and safety, and required skill

levels, including provisions that will encourage employees to notify the employer of workplace hazards without fear of reprisal.

11. Establish and consistently enforce a system for ensuring that employees comply with safe and healthy work practices, including disciplinary action for employees who fail or refuse to comply with codes of safe conduct or fail to use protective devices as they are instructed.

12. Be sure that all warnings about hazardous substances and processes are clear and unambiguous and that, as a result of the warning, employees know of the danger and the recommended means to avoid it.

13. Signs, warnings, and training materials should use accepted "signal words" to convey the degree or nature of the danger associated with the hazard. OSHA regulations specify several major signal words, such as *danger, caution,* and *warning,* along with colors to alert workers to the relative degree of the hazard (red, yellow, and orange, respectively).

14. Signal words should be followed by text describing the specific danger and how to avoid it. Do not weaken the warning with conditional phrases intended to reduce anxiety about the hazard. Use other methods to reduce anxiety, such as assurances that the safety precautions will serve their intended purposes.

Set and Enforce Appropriate Learning Objectives

15. Establish measurable learning objectives and enforce them rigorously and consistently. Document each trainee's performance. Why? Because an employee who receives training in June 1991 may not commit an error until 1993. In many states, the judicial process is four to five years. Will you or your instructor remember in 1998 what occurred on June 4, 1991? Documentation should include the following:

- What specific training did the employee receive?
- What methodology was used?
- Who did the training, and what were the trainer's qualifications?
- How did the trainee perform?
- What were the performance criteria, and how was the employee's performance evaluated?
- Was the employee's English language or literacy barrier an issue?
- If so, what steps were taken to overcome it?

    If this seems akin to a cross-examination, it's *mild.* Whoever must represent or testify for the company needs to present a credible position—from actual memory, refreshed memory, or intimate knowledge of the company's record-keeping procedures. *Documentation is the key.*

16. Develop objective, job-related performance standards that include quantitative and qualitative criteria.

Select Contractors and Vendors Carefully

17. Determine the scope of any mandated training. Do federal or state laws require specific content, timing, or methodology? Is the vendor familiar with these requirements?

18. Ask for appropriate information from the vendor's safety training records. What steps will the vendor take to comply with applicable regulations? Are there sample compliance programs that the vendor will share?

19. Determine whether the vendor has ever been cited by a regulatory agency for safety infractions. You should treat this information with great care, ensuring confidentiality where appropriate. Remember that unproven allegations should be given limited weight. Allow the vendor to explain any challenges or discrepancies in its safety records.

20. Determine the level of qualifications and experience of each individual instructor. If technical expertise or relevant certification is important, ask for documentation. If it is not forthcoming, request the right to seek verification from educational, institutional, or licensing agencies. Don't be reluctant to ask for specific information on the extent of the trainer's hands-on experience.

21. If you are purchasing new equipment, and a manufacturer's representative will provide on-site instruction, determine the nature of this person's training experience. Is the representative a salesperson, a career trainer, or a technical expert? What type of instruction will be provided—classroom, on-the-job, or other methodology? Ask for references from similar programs.

22. Ask for a description of any personal protective devices to be utilized during the training, and determine who will supply these items. Determine who is responsible for making sure the equipment is in working order. What steps will be taken to be sure there is enough protective equipment for all participants, in the sizes they require? Identify who will be responsible for determining the effectiveness and quality of the equipment and spell out (preferably in writing) your respective responsibilities.

23. If the training will be conducted on site at your workplace, ask the vendor for a description of what you must provide. Will the vendor provide assistance in setting up the training facility? If ventilation or climate control will be a factor, ask for written specifications. Identify and spell out your respective responsibilities for monitoring climactic conditions throughout training and after the external trainers have left your premises.

24. Ask for several references from employers of differing sizes and industries, where appropriate. Have a set of specific criteria you will ask the references. Avoid general questions, such as "Were you satisfied with the training?" Instead, ask targeted questions about the length, substantive scope, and quality of the instruction.

25. Inquire about the vendor's evaluation mechanisms. How does the vendor determine the effectiveness of its instructions? Are written or on-site evaluations used? Ask the vendor to share its data on success rates with you (without disclosing confidential information about other employers' practices or employee records, of course).

26. Specify in writing the roles and responsibilities of the external trainers and your internal personnel. Documentation will provide the maximum opportunity to uncover any gaps in responsibilities or communication barriers. Remember, your purpose is not so much to bind the other party to contractual obligations as to ensure consistency and adequate training.

27. Spell out your respective responsibilities in the contractual documents. Although you cannot relieve yourself of your own negligence—and that of your employees—you can seek contractual indemnification for any losses you sustain from the vendor's negligence or affirmative misrepresentations to you. Remember, the contract will only define the relationship between your organization and the vendor; it will not relieve either of you from liabilities to an injured party.

28. Thoroughly document your investigation of the vendor's safety records and references. The reality of the U.S. civil justice system is that litigation can consume several years. Your investigation may be fresh in your mind at the time, but you may be required to reconstruct your efforts as much as four years later. (For a complete discussion of documentation, see Chapter 20.)

Establish and Enforce Appropriate Evaluation and Testing

29. Make sure that evaluation and testing techniques mirror the performance standards you have established.

30. Design appropriate evaluation and testing procedures to measure the employee's understanding, retention, and application of the material.

31. Establish performance and instructional objectives that include all tasks required to work safely and effectively.

32. Establish objective standards of performance for instructors and instructional designers. Enforce the standards consistently.

Policies and Procedures

33. Develop comprehensive policies and procedures for safety and hazard training.

34. Develop job-specific and measurable evaluation standards, and administer them across the board. To avoid claims of discrimination, make sure every trainee undergoes the same job-specific evaluation. In the case of foreign-born workers, a delicate balance must be maintained between avoiding discrimination and being sensitive to language barriers that call for differing training or evaluation needs.

Accommodate Special Needs

35. Accommodate trainees who have special needs and document the entire process. Your specific, job-related training objectives and precise evaluation techniques will be helpful here.

36. Develop departmental checklists for generating the appropriate documentation. Once again, consistency is the key ingredient.

37. Develop and enforce visible and consistent methods of communicating between line management and the training department about the content, scope, timing, and updating of mandated training.

Documentation, Documentation, Documentation

38. Document the *who, what, when, where,* and *why* of the training that each employee receives. Follow the requirements of OSHA orders on documentation formats. Many computer programs will assist in this effort, but simple manual records will suffice if they are accurate, up to date, legible, specific, consistent, complete, and truthful.

39. Preserve all appropriate documents and records concerning steps taken to implement and deliver the appropriate training.

40. Make sure that training records reflect all of the following:

- The names of all employees attending the training
- The inclusive dates of the training
- The substance of the training, including enough technical information to establish the adequacy of warnings
- The performance objectives of the training, tied directly to the tasks the employee will perform and/or the conditions of the work environment
- When the employee was provided with initial training, refresher training, or warnings about new, previously unrecognized hazards
- The employee's performance on posttraining testing and performance evaluations, with test scores, observation of performance, or equivalent objective verification
- Evidence of the employee's attendance for the entire time frame of the training

It is very helpful to have the original signature of the employee at both the beginning and end of the program. The signature can be used to "refresh" the employee's memory if a dispute regarding attendance arises.

The Role of Trainers as Expert Witnesses: Challenges and Opportunities

In injury cases involving claims of inadequate hazard communication training, the parties frequently turn to expert witnesses who can address the clarity of warnings and the effectiveness of the instruction. Experts may serve critical roles in both the pretrial and trial phases of an injury lawsuit. In the pretrial phase, experts are particularly helpful in assessing the required duty of the employer and the training department.

The threshold question for the jury in most cases is: "What would the reasonable trainer do under the circumstances?" The expert can determine and testify about what standard of care applies, and how it was created. An expert with direct, hands-on experience in the particular industry is uniquely positioned to provide credible testimony regarding the role of the training organization, the standards applicable to its work, and of course whether the organization met its standard of care (i.e., performed its duty to the trainee).

Who is better suited to provide expert testimony than a professional trainer with the same or equivalent experience? An independent expert with appropriate experience can review the documentary records, assess the quality and timing of the training, and reach a conclusion concerning the efficacy of the training. The best experts are full-time practitioners in the relevant field. As witnesses, practitioners are especially convincing when they testify about their own observations, experience, and skills. For example, an expert who designed and delivered training for emergency response technicians was uniquely suited to testify in a negligence lawsuit involving a chemical spill. The allegations were that the emergency responders had been trained on the substance and theory, but had been deprived of skills training to simulate both the emergency and the foreseeable stressful conditions under which they would operate. In essence, there are few substitutes for "been there...done that!"

During the trial phase, experts move beyond their roles as advisers and educators. They become responsible for interpreting and clarifying technical information and for providing opinions on central issues of liability. The weight that a jury or judge gives to the expert's testimony will often hinge on the expert's credentials.

Many injury lawsuits, particularly those involving toxic torts, become a battle of the experts. Thus, in addition to objective qualifications such as degrees, licenses, relevant publications, and eminent professional accomplishments, the expert's direct experience in a comparable work environment will often affect credibility. An independent expert is valuable precisely because he or she serves as a neutral evaluator of how trainers or their organizations performed. Most trainers who serve as experts are professionals from the same or similar industries, but they neither are employed by a party to the lawsuit nor have a direct stake in its outcome.

The good news: Testifying as an expert witness can be a valuable service and a substantively challenging exercise. Additional benefits include enhanced professional recognition and, of course, financial compensation.

The bad news: Expert witnesses who have served as trainers sometimes must render an opinion that the trainer or organization defending the lawsuit failed to meet the standard of care required of similarly situated professionals. So, how do you minimize the possibility of adverse expert testimony about your work?

How to Avoid Being Caught in the Crossfire of Dueling Experts

Expert testimony is, by definition, opinion testimony. The expert may rely on direct evidence, inferences drawn from the facts of the case, and even hearsay. Hearsay, which is an out-of-court statement offered to prove the truth of an assertion, may include statements by various workers or other witnesses which are not independently admissible. If a witness is not available for cross-examination in court, his or her hearsay statement would be inadmissible, but it can be relied upon by an expert to support an independent opinion. Hypothetically, in a case involving a participant injured in a training exercise because of alleged negligent management of the training facility, an expert could rely on hearsay statements of coworkers to support an opinion that the equipment was not operating safely during the week the accident occurred.

Opposing experts often have divergent opinions. When the subject of your expert testimony is the efficacy of the training that the injured plaintiff received, your professional work will take center stage. Dueling experts will focus squarely on the design, delivery, preparation, integrity, and performance of the training staff. When this occurs, your role in the design or delivery of the training will be thoroughly examined. Your preparation and planning will be dissected. Your documentation will be scrutinized. You may be asked to help prepare answers to a series of written questions, which are usually provided by the party under oath. You may be called to give sworn testimony at a pretrial deposition, testimony that carries the same effect as if given in court. You will certainly be called upon to explain or verify the accuracy of any documentation you personally created.

The reality in most states is that complex litigation consumes several years in the pretrial and trial processes. Therefore, all your responses to written questions and your testimony under oath can be reviewed, analyzed, and used by expert witnesses to form an opinion about the quality of work you may have done years earlier. Expert opinions will be based on what the standard of care was at the time the training was designed or completed, *not* at the time of trial.

The following are a few techniques for minimizing the possibility of being caught in the crossfire of dueling experts:

1. Prepare your documentation as if you will be questioned about it years later. Avoid all but the most common abbreviations. Make sure your handwritten notes are complete and legible.

2. Always date your documentation with the month, day, and year. Although you may know when you make the entry that it is January 1998, you may not be sure if you are questioned at trial in the year 2002.

3. As a curriculum designer, document the steps you took to plan the content and design of the program. How was your lesson plan connected to the job-related skills needed by the trainees?

4. As a presenter, document the content and delivery of training. For employees with special needs, be sure to memorialize the steps you took to accommodate learning.

5. Keep your documentation simple and objective. When you must use subjective criteria (other than test scores) to evaluate trainee performance, avoid relative terms such as *frequent, excessive, too many,* and *too few.* Specify the objective performance standard, and then use a concrete example to rate an individual trainee:

   Instead of: "He was too slow in putting on protective gloves."

   Use: "He took four minutes to put on protective gloves, and must be able to do so in two minutes."

6. When you design your training curriculum, be sure you thoroughly understand the standard expected. Are you complying with:

   - A statute, such as an OSHA regulation?
   - An industry standard or practice?
   - A specific policy of your employer?

   Document the steps you took to make your content, timing, methodology, or delivery compliant with the applicable standard of care.

7. When called upon to explain your documentation, don't guess or speculate. If you cannot remember, and you cannot reconstruct events from other documentation, don't be afraid to respond truthfully with "I don't remember" or "I don't know." This is far better than being confronted with inconsistencies.

8. When giving testimony, stick to your personal knowledge. Do not guess, speculate on, or "interpret" what may have occurred. If you cannot remember, and cannot refresh your memory from documentation you created or are personally familiar with, just say so. This is far better than having to recant a guess that later turns out to be wrong.

References

1. Reuters News Service, March 7, 1997.
2. *Thompson v. Liberty Mutual Ins. Co.,* 532 So.2d 129 (Alabama 1989).
3. *Vons Companies, Inc. v. Seabest Foods, Inc.,* 14 Cal.4th 434 (December 12, 1996).
4. *Decker v. Domino's Pizza, Inc.,* 268 Ill.App.3d 521; 644 N.E.2d 515 (December 30, 1994).
5. *Mahavier v. Beverly Enterprises, Inc.,* 540 S.W.2d 813 (Texas 1976).

6. *Suich v. H.&B. Printing Machinery, Inc.*, 185 Ill.App.3d 863 (June 27, 1989).

7. *Suich v. H.&B. Printing Machinery, Inc.*, 185 Ill.App.3d 863 (June 27, 1989) (emphasis added).

8. *Levels v. Growers Ammonia Supply Company, et al.*, 48 Cal.App.3d 443 (1975).

9. *Levels v. Growers Ammonia Supply Company, et al.*, 48 Cal.App.3d 443, 446 (1975).

4

Designing Training Programs

How to Avoid Potential Legal Problems

Who Wins More Negligence Suits for Faulty Curriculum and Why

Sometimes total absence of training is not the issue. When you have conducted training and someone is still injured, the focus may turn to your methodology or the way you personally supervised the training. Most statutes mandate the content and timing of training, but *not* the instructional methods or techniques. Mercifully, legislators have left that decision to training professionals. However, this doesn't mean your work can't be challenged. Your decisions on curriculum design and instructional methods must be based on the needs and rigors of the particular job for which you are conducting the training. The threshold question is: "What would the reasonable curriculum designer do?" Even when you comply with the minimum standards prescribed by a statute, a court may find that you have breached your legal duty by failing to meet the standard of care for similarly situated professionals. Chapter 3, pp. 70–76, provides a complete explanation of the six ways your legal duties may be established by the courts in negligence lawsuits.

High-risk or technical skills training programs are particularly susceptible to legal challenge on the basis of the training *methods* used. For instance, in a case involving a chemical spill, the injured third parties claimed that the workers were inadequately trained for effective emergency response. The trainees received classroom instruction, which included explanations of emergency response and technical procedures, but not on-the-job instruction or simulated exercises. When an actual emergency occurred, they did not perform as quickly and efficiently as desired. Uncertainty and panic adversely affected their performance. The trial focused on whether the injuries might have been prevented if the emergency responders had been trained in a more realistic setting. The trainers were allegedly negligent because even though they complied with all statutory content and timing requirements, their methods were still *ineffective* in addressing foreseeable emergency conditions.

You can try to protect yourself by designing specific and measurable training objectives that mirror the tasks that trainees will be expected to perform under normal operating conditions and when faced with foreseeable emergencies. Each trainee's performance on those job-related skills should be individually evaluated. And each stage of the training process—design, delivery, and evaluation—should be well documented.

Negligence claims for faulty curriculum design and training supervision fall into two primary categories. The first encompasses personal injuries occurring during training. The second encompasses injuries, property damage, and/or business losses stemming from an employee's poor or marginal performance. The gist of the second claim is that the employee would have performed more competently with training, thereby avoiding the harm to the third party.

Injuries During Training

When an employee is injured in the course and scope of employment, benefits may be available through the state workers' compensation system. When the injuries are the result of willful misconduct by the employer or individual trainers, the civil courtroom may provide alternative relief. Consider several instructive case examples.

Ehlinger v. Board of Education of New Hartford[1] involved an allegation of negligence in course design which led to a personal injury. Although the case involved a public school student, the court followed the same negligence principles applicable to public and private sector employers. The injured girl dislocated her right elbow when she struck the gymnasium wall while running the speed test portion of the New York State physical fitness exam. The legal claims focused on the trainer's negligence in designing the course and in failing to adequately supervise the test.

The manual for the test advised that "to assure maximum safety and performance...leave at least 14 feet of unobstructed space beyond the start and finish lines." In this case, the finish line was placed 8 feet from the wall. Several participants testified that the trainer's only instructions were to run around the cones three times, while a partner recorded the student's time.

The court focused on whether the school *and the individual trainer* had a legal duty to exercise reasonable care in providing instructions and supervision. The evidence demonstrated that the state guidelines were specifically adopted to prevent foreseeable injuries like the one that actually occurred. The court found negligence, explaining that "the recommendations in the manual were sufficient to put the instructor on notice of a possible safety hazard created by the proximity of the finish line to the wall, and she was under a duty to warn students of that danger and instruct them to take necessary precautions."[2]

When training occurs during employment, an injured trainee's primary claim is against the employer. Your actions as a trainer or curriculum designer, operating within the scope of your employment, are your employer's legal responsibility, and in most states you will *not* have personal liability for negligence. However, contract trainers or independent instructors, who are not employees of the sponsoring organization, may find themselves to be individual defendants in a lawsuit arising from injuries during training. And the sponsoring organization still has independent primary legal accountability.

A California case against the YMCA, involving a scuba-diving class, provides an instructive example. In *Leno v. Young Men's Christian Association,* which was highlighted in the Introduction, p. 6, the instructor volunteered his time to teach the course, in an ongoing relationship with the local YMCA. In this setting, he operated in the capacity of an independent contract trainer.

One significant issue was instructor certification. The contract trainer was not certified by either the national YMCA or the National Association of Underwater Instructors. On one occasion, the physical education director at the YMCA (who, in the court's view, served as the trainer's "supervisor") asked if he wanted to take a national YMCA certification test, and offered to pay for it. The trainer later testified that he agreed to do so, but then decided not to take the test even though he knew that the YMCA preferred certified instructors and that someone in the national organization was pushing for it. He called the supervisor, who indicated that it was up to him whether or not to take the test.

At one point the YMCA asked one of the leading scuba experts in the area to evaluate this trainer's course design and teaching methods. The report rated the course as "fair," but stated that it was unsafe because there was no emergency life-saving instruction. The report was submitted to the supervisor, who never questioned the reviewer or discussed it with the trainer.

For the YMCA, the sponsor of the program, these facts were devastating. First, the YMCA knew prior to the fatal accident that this trainer was uncertified—possibly in violation of its own policies requiring certification. The policy of using only certified instructors created a standard of care which the local YMCA did not meet. (See the full discussion of standard of care in Chapter 3, pp. 70–78.) Second, and more troublesome, was the YMCA's knowledge from its own consultant's report that the course curriculum was deficient because of the total absence of an important safety component.

Trainees who successfully completed the 12-session course received a YMCA certificate of proficiency. A student could not earn a certificate without passing the ocean checkouts, and the YMCA mandated qualified instructors on ocean checkouts.

The student in question had some problems with his regulator and mouthpiece, which he brought to the attention of an assistant instructor, and then followed her instructions to surface and use the snorkel. She later instructed him to swim to shore underneath the kelp, and lost sight of him. She then followed a trail of bubbles until she found him lying on the bottom. She released his weight belt, but could not administer CPR because *she had not been so trained.*

The court concluded that the individual trainers—lead and assistants—were negligent *and personally accountable.* The primary issue on appeal was the YMCA's responsibility for the contract trainer's negligence in his course design, and his failure to train assistants in emergency life saving. The court determined that the instructor was indeed the agent of the YMCA and that it was independently responsible for his negligence. The YMCA owed a duty of care to people who paid a fee for diver training advertised under its auspices, supervised by its physical education director, held on its premises, and conducted with equipment it supplied.

The court found, consistent with the law in most states, that an independent contractor who performs high-risk instruction may be held liable for failure to take the necessary precautions to ensure safety and competent training. In most states, the YMCA would have a right to sue the contract trainer to recover amounts it was forced to pay the injured party. The basis for the trainer's liability to the client would be either state law negligence principles or contractual indemnity. The latter is explained in Chapter 16, pp. 331–333. The sample contracts in Appendix C have indemnity clauses.

Injuries to Third Parties From Errors of Poorly Trained Personnel

Frequently, errors by untrained or ill-prepared employees result in foreseeable harm to third parties, and courts have no problem recognizing negligence claims under these circumstances. The most common claims focus on teaching methods and allege that the trainees received inadequate skills training to meet their job responsibilities. In California, for example, a medical university owed a duty of care to patients who were under the care of its residents to make sure the residents were properly trained and supervised. In *County of Riverside v. Loma Linda Univ.*,[4] the court found the university negligent in discharging its duties to educate and train the residents and to supervise their training—negligence that resulted in damage to patients' well-being.

In a similar case in Michigan, *McCullough v. Hutzel Hospital*,[5] a medical malpractice case included allegations of inadequate training. A resident-trainee was permitted to perform a surgical procedure, which he did negligently. In addition to traditional malpractice claims, the injured patient raised a unique theory by claiming that the hospital and its supervising physicians were responsible for inadequately training and supervising the resident. The court held that specialists who undertake to supervise residents taking advanced training have a legal duty to see that surgery is performed properly. The basis for the ruling was that the specialists have the necessary qualifications and training to judge the competency of the resident's performance and to design effective training methods to develop the needed skills.

If your company does not use effective methods for training and developing employees whose errors may injure the public, you should seriously consider addressing the issue with senior management. When your employer's business involves certain known risks to a particular clientele, the employer is at risk of being found negligent if you fail to take any steps to avoid those risks. Thus, in *Estate of Arrington v. Fields*,[6] a security guard company was sued after a scuffle in which one of its employees shot a patron at a convenience store, believing the man to be a thief. The guard had been issued a handgun, but was not effectively trained in its use. This alone, the court concluded, constituted negligence. As a trainer or curriculum designer, you can assist your employer in avoiding legal risks by focusing on the importance of effective curriculum design.

How to Prepare the Training Facility and What Can Happen When You Don't: A Case Study and Checklist

The individual trainer is on the front line in the training room. Literally. This means that you have both authority and responsibility for everything that happens throughout the training. At times, you may share the risk with the owner of the facilities and others in your organization, but during the program itself you are directly accountable.

High-Hazard Training Activities

It is certainly important to provide realistic training, particularly in situations where the need to react under adverse conditions is critical to safe and successful job performance. In such cases, you must ensure that your equipment is reasonably safe for its intended use and that you can effectively supervise the training facility. One clear-cut example of a personal injury occurring during training is *Tabone v. State of New York*,[7] also highlighted in the Introduction, p. 3. The class was planned, directed, supervised, and instructed by a certified state employee, and was made available to the county and its firefighters.

Since the objective was to realistically simulate smoky conditions, a device thought to be a smoke bomb was used. In reality, it was a white-phosphorus antipersonnel grenade commonly used by the military. The device was obtained by a county employee, who admitted that he had some experience with smoke and metal bursting grenades, but none with the white phosphorus. The state instructor had no experience with such devices, as evidenced by an inquiry he made at the beginning of class when he picked up the sealed canister and asked if any of the students knew what "WP Smoke" meant. He received no reply, and he didn't open the canister. Had he done so, he would have seen the clear markings "BURSTING TYPE." In essence, the trainer was completely unaware of the contents of a device he intended to use during a class exercise. Nevertheless, he represented to the class that it contained a smoke bomb to be used in the drill.

The injured firefighter arrived late and wore no protective equipment. While assisting the instructor in carrying a mannequin to be "rescued" in the drill, he was handed the sealed canister. The instructor told him to pull the pin, and when he did it exploded in his hand. Although the firefighter ultimately survived, he suffered second- and third-degree burns over 35 percent of his body, including his face, neck, chest, arms, hands, and upper thighs.

A jury awarded him over $2 million, finding the state 75 percent at fault for its trainer's negligence. Although the trainer was not personally sued, he was the source of significant liability for his employer.

The state appealed, contending that its trainer relied upon the representations of the county supervisor who provided the device. The appellate court was asked to analyze the state's liability. The court underscored the individual instructor's duty to exercise reasonable care to avoid injuries during the training exercise, a duty that required both knowing that the equipment was safe for its intended use and adequately supervising the training exercise. The court concluded that the grenade was "highly inappropriate for use as a smoke-making device," and that the trainer breached his legal duty to open the sealed canister himself to make certain that it contained a smoke bomb rather than relying solely on the representation of the county fire coordinator.[8]

The court also assessed liability for the trainer's representation to the class that the canister contained a smoke bomb, because he lacked direct knowledge. Additionally, he failed to supervise the drill effectively by not insisting that appropriate protective gear be worn by all participants who were foreseeably in harm's way, including the injured man.

To prevent mishaps and disasters from ruining your training—and adversely affecting your employer's bottom line—there are steps you can take to prepare the training room or facility for safe, comfortable, and effective training. If you are using personal protective equipment, make sure that you have a sufficient quantity and that all is in working order. If life vests or masks are required, take the time to make sure that the fit is correct on *every participant.* Accept responsibility for checking all equipment and tools yourself. Don't rely exclusively on the representations of others about the equipment you are using. If you feel it is beyond your area of expertise, seek out the assistance of an expert before the program begins. If you have any reasonable doubt about the safety of a tool or piece of equipment, don't use it. For a complete discussion on precautions to take during wilderness or other high-risk training activities, see Chapter 8, pp. 189–191 and 202–204.

Low-Hazard Training Programs

Programs with little apparent physical risk can also be a source of legal exposure if participants are injured. To avoid common injuries, you should make sure all exits are clearly marked and are operative throughout the program. If you are in a secured building, instruct the participants before you start on where they can find exits and what to do in the event of a fire or other need to evacuate.

If the need to evacuate the facility is a reasonable possibility, select a participant to serve as your monitor to make sure that everyone, including physically challenged participants, can be removed from the building in a timely and safe manner. For a complete discussion of your responsibilities to trainees with special needs, consult Chapter 14.

Consider the ventilation systems carefully. If your program takes place in a very hot or humid location, make sure there is enough air circulation to ensure comfort throughout the entire program. Your primary concern may be just keeping everyone awake. Still, nothing disrupts a program more than a participant passing out from heat exposure.

Avoid furniture or equipment obstructions in the aisles and walkways. Sometimes participants must leave during the training, and in their haste not to interrupt they fail to watch where they are going. Bruises and serious eye and head injuries can result. If you are using projection equipment, make sure the cords or wires are taped down and out of the way of people (yourself included) who must walk by. A single fall can cause a serious back injury.

Take seriously your responsibility to keep participants from injuring others. The problems range from horseplay to serious forms of fighting. Make sure you are truly in charge, and exercise your responsibility to remove unruly participants, where appropriate and necessary.

Finally, encourage participants to report any unsafe conditions or nonfunctional equipment to you immediately. When they do so, you should be prepared to take appropriate action to remedy or minimize the condition. If you are on notice of an unsafe condition and ignore it, you will risk further injuries and may jeopardize the applicability of insurance coverage.

Actions versus Words: When Interactive Methods Are a Legal Necessity

Sometimes there is absolutely no substitute for realistic training. When the consequences of human error are high, and the training curriculum must reflect authentic workplace conditions, enforcement agencies and the courts will scrutinize your curriculum to determine whether you effectively achieved the training objectives. Figure 4-1 highlights examples of legally faulty training design.

Likewise, when flawless performance under adverse conditions is critical, juries will scrutinize your training methods after the fact, just like Monday morning quarterbacks. (See the discussion of how the jury

- Following several critical incidents, the Federal Aviation Administration mandated increased flight attendant training, including the mandate that they be trained to respond to emergencies by using real protective smoke hoods and fighting real fires.

- After an accident investigation involving a USAir jetliner in New York, the National Transportation Safety Board report cited the airline for inadequate training, stating that the pilot training was "degraded by an absence of realism" and "lacking in challenge."

- In the aftermath of a chemical spill at a manufacturing plant, the site operator was sued for injuries, some of which were aggravated by delays by the emergency response team in evacuation and triage. The team had received significant classroom instruction and participated in announced drills. Yet team members failed to perform effectively when it counted in a real emergency. The culprit, according to the expert witnesses, failed to provide realistic (unannounced) simulations that mirrored the personal anxieties and fears of the people on the team.

- In the civil rights litigation arising out of the videotaped traffic stop of motorist Rodney King in Los Angeles, a primary allegation involved the absence of realistic training at the Los Angeles Police Department academy; specifically, the failure to inject genuine stress levels into the training, in order for the officers to learn to channel stress into positive, and lawful, behaviors.

Figure 4-1 Examples of Cases Alleging Inadequate Training Methodology.

system operates in Chapter 1, pp. 33–35.) In these situations, interactive methods may be the only legally defensible training. In essence, realistic simulations and role plays may be essential to establish the effectiveness of your training programs.

Simulations duplicate events for which specialized skills are required. Effective exercises enable the trainees to perform skills by creating real-life situations in which they must function. Simulations are representations of actual situations, designed so the trainees focus on specific skills. The simulation of an emergency, for example, duplicates the elements of the actual event and highlights the skills and responses that will be required.

In the chemical spill litigation profiled in Figure 4-1, the expert witnesses concluded that "practice drills" were ineffective because the participants had advance notice. In effect, they always knew it was a "drill," so their foreseeable fear for families and friends was absent. When the real event occurred, the miscues, delays, fright, and fatigue of some responders interfered with their performance, because they had not been provided with genuine scenarios under which they could practice, debrief, and learn from their mistakes.

In any situation with potential panic, realistic training is indispensable. While creating emergency action plans for fire or natural disaster evacuations, trainers should consult with safety engineers and local fire officials to prepare and observe realistic drills. Former New York City fire chief Samuel Cahan told the American Society of Safety Engineers in 1996 that "for people exposed to discipline, control, and training, the likelihood of panic is minimized. Trained people react with training."[9]

Performance-based training and certification of training programs are extremely useful because they focus *specifically* on job-related skills. This focus serves the dual function of (1) increasing the likelihood that the trainee will learn to handle hazardous situations properly on the job and (2) facilitating consistency in training.

Simulators should replicate foreseeable conditions, including foreseeable equipment failures and similar emergency scenarios. These techniques provide participants with practice that closely replicates the actual environment, but with the opportunity for immediate feedback. The simulations should be repeated regularly, with changes that maintain appropriate levels of challenge. In order to achieve training objectives, the simulations must be carefully designed and administered to ensure that trainees gain an appropriate appreciation of how to respond in real situations.

Role plays are another interactive method that, in some situations, may be essential to your successful legal defense. In role playing, participants act out a particular problem or situation, and then discuss their reactions. In contrast to specific skills addressed in simulations, role plays focus on providing relevant situations for the development of "soft skills," such as feelings, attitudes, and behaviors. Relevancy translates into authenticity. And adults learn these skills best by practice, feedback, and interaction. This is especially important in training supervisors on the skills they will need to manage effectively within the law. Thus, role plays and other interactive methods may be the best method to ensure that participants learn skills for preventing and investigating sexual harassment, or effecting legally enforceable discipline and termination decisions.

Although absence of interactivity may not itself be the source of liability in every case, proactive use of these methods may serve as a defense to a claim that you were negligent. The issue in a lawsuit alleging negligent workplace conditions is whether the trainer or curriculum designer took reasonable steps to prevent the risk of foreseeable harm to identifiable people. (This issue is discussed in detail in Chapter 3, pp. 70–78.) When you can demonstrate that interactive methods were used as the best approach to skills development under realistic (foreseeable) conditions, your defense may carry the day. In this situation, the design of the training program actually bolsters the employer's defense. For details, see Chapter 12, pp. 249–255.

Are Your Trainees Stressed Yet? How to Determine When You Must Properly Simulate Working Conditions

Some participants may become stressed—even ill—from the realistic anxieties you inject into a simulation. Stress is unfortunate and should be minimized by appropriate instructional design, but there are times when it simply can't be avoided. Fortunately, workers' compensation will typically provide benefits to trainees who suffer the effects of stress-induced illness. Several states—notably, California, Colorado, Michigan, Florida, and Texas—permit workers' compensation disability claims for stress-related illness, sometimes in the absence of any physical manifestations. These are variously called "psych" claims or "stress disabilities."

When stress is an integral part of the job, employee training must be realistic. Could we reasonably expect to train air traffic controllers, pilots, and others without determining whether they can meet the rigors of the tasks they are assigned, *including* working under stress? In a *Los Angeles Times* article entitled "Lack of Skills Leads to Violence" (January 30, 1990), a professor of justice at the American University in Washington and a former police officer asks a rhetorical question: "How can we expect to end unnecessary citizen-police shootings if officers are inadequately trained?" He recounts that unnecessary violence occurs when well-meaning officers lack the skills to resolve confrontations without resorting to violence. In the worst cases, they shoot their way out, or end up in civil rights litigation like *Rodney King v. LAPD*.[10]

Once again, there is no substitute for complete job task analysis and performance-based training. If the job performance requires working under extremely stressful circumstances, simulated situations should be a regular part of the training. Your documentation to support the determination that performance-based training required injection of realistic anxiety levels will help defend you against personnel-related lawsuits by trainees who claim stress on the job or from your workshop. See the detailed discussion of documentation in Chapter 20.

Do Your Curriculum Design Standards Meet Applicable Legal Requirements? A Checklist

Curriculum design requires significant attention to substantive detail and appropriate methodology. Your methods must be appropriate to achieve the objectives of safe and skillful job performance. Always work from the framework of concrete learning objectives.

What do you want the learners to be able to remember, apply, and act upon? What skills will they be expected to perform, and under what level of supervision? Will their work be reviewed by others or will their performance (acts or omissions) unilaterally bind the organization? Will they work individually or as part of a team? How will their individual roles contribute to the entire performance of the company? How will the trainees be accountable for their performance, judgments, and actions when they return to the workplace?

These and other questions are critically important in designing an effective—legally supportable—curriculum. The overriding objective is to ensure that the trainees are effectively prepared to perform their jobs safely and competently. The following checklist provides a basis for appropriate curriculum development and methodology.

Preliminary Planning

1. Why is the training being conducted?
   - Is it to comply with laws, industry regulations, or employer policies?
   - Is it prompted by a significant incident or event in the workplace?
   - Is it to correct recurring performance problems?
   - Is it to impart new skills and procedures required in the workplace?
   - Is new equipment being introduced into the workplace?
   - Is it prompted by other legal concerns?

2. What are the consequences of poor performance?
   - What are the foreseeable risks of harm from untimely or inadequate job performance when the trainees return to the job site?
   - Who is at risk of harm? What behaviors or responses by the trainees will eliminate or reduce the risk?

3. Are the trainees new to the organization? Will orientation to basic employer procedures be required before the substance of the planned program is addressed?

4. Are existing employees being retrained for other jobs? Will this require orientation to new systems, procedures, or facilities?

5. Who are the trainees, and what is their level of education or experience?

   - Do any participants have special needs? (See the extensive discussions in Chapters 2, pp. 56–59; 7, pp. 167–171; and 14, pp. 300–305.)
   - Are participants likely to be receptive or reluctant to receive this training? How can their reluctance be overcome through interactive methods?
   - What is their relevant past experience with training of this type?
   - Will you have sufficient time to learn about the participants prior to the program? What are the basics you need in order to prepare customized materials and instructional aids?

6. How soon must the training take place? Will you have sufficient lead time to develop the materials?

7. Will technical subject matter expertise be required? If so, how quickly can it be obtained?

   - Must technical experts be available as consultants only, or will you need them to review course materials and/or participate in presentations?

Develop Substantive Content

8. Develop a task analysis that identifies routine, important, and high-liability substantive issues to be included in the program.

9. Determine whether a content expert or technical specialist is required to ensure substantive accuracy of program content and materials.

10. Use a consistent instructional systems development model to design content.

11. Prioritize the areas of subject matter content, from the most important to the least important.

    - Identify and prioritize the risks of poor job performance, from physical injuries to business consequences.
    - Design your course presentation to be consistent with these priorities.

12. Conduct a comprehensive analysis of the knowledge level of your expected group of trainees. Design a presentation appropriate to this knowledge. Nothing is worse than beginning at a level beyond the comprehension of the group.

13. Get input early from line supervisors on the skills they will require on the job.

   - What skills are excellent?
   - What works at an acceptable level?
   - Where is improvement required?
   - Most important, what leads to error and misjudgments?

14. Work backward from supervisors' experience to build an effective substantive program. Make sure that your written materials and audiovisual aids are appropriate to the language and education level of the group. Document the steps you take to ensure an acceptable level of understanding. See the comprehensive discussion of safety training that meets special needs in Chapter 2, pp. 55–59.

Use Appropriate Methodology

15. Identify those areas where classroom instruction is appropriate. Determine what percentage of the overall program this will entail, and build it into the appropriate sequence in the program.

16. Evaluate the level of interactivity required. Are the skills you intend to impart best conveyed by "doing" rather than by being told what to do? If so, you must build into the program sufficient interactivity to achieve the required result: participants who can perform the skill.

17. Will the trainee be expected to perform under stress? What are the anticipated environmental issues in the workplace? Will physical exertion be required? How about mental or emotional energy? Design your content and methodology to simulate these "real world" conditions.

18. Determine whether video can reasonably substitute for the actual workplace. If not, how can you bring the vagaries of the workplace into the training facility?

19. Use realistic simulated exercises.

   - Identify and prioritize the risks inherent in lack of realism, and design the content accordingly.
   - Obtain input from technical experts, managers, line supervisors, and job incumbents, as appropriate, to accurately reflect real— not ideal—working conditions.

- Always use the same tools, equipment, machinery, and protective devices that the trainees will use on the job. Coordinate with line management to ensure realism.
- In high-risk work environments, build in realistic "failure" scenarios on the basis of foreseeable emergencies. For example, if protective gear may fail under realistic conditions, build it into the exercise, and then debrief the participants' reactions. For example, certification training for scuba divers invariably includes scenarios for dealing with equipment malfunctions.
- In emergency response training, include authentic life-saving techniques, such as CPR and proper personal protection skills.

20. Make role plays vivid and relevant to the trainees' actual workplace.

- Provide nonthreatening opportunities for feedback on performance.
- Design a discussion component of critical issues that relate to the training objectives, and integrate them into the program.
- Rather than attempting to change "attitudes," focus on specific behaviors that the participants will be expected to model on the job.
- Provide conflicting ideas on how to resolve a problem.
- When confrontation or hostility is expected in "real life," build it into the program. Confrontation is especially important in management training to conduct performance appraisals, convey termination decisions, and defuse conflict in the workplace. Lack of effective supervisory skills in these areas can be a significant liability, as discussed in Chapter 11, pp. 241–244.
- Avoid creating more conflicts than you can resolve in the allotted time. Leaving managers with more questions than answers can be unnerving. In addition to heightened stress for the managers, it may result in inappropriate responses to actual situations with employees.

21. If the training is designed to address performance management or interpersonal communication, determine whether realistic case studies will be useful to develop the skills.

22. Your methodology should match your learning objectives. Don't "sugarcoat" simulations for complex or high-intensity tasks. Trainees should be able to perform under realistic conditions. Unrealistic training has been a recurring theme in litigation and regulatory investigations of plane crashes. In one case, the National Transportation Safety Board cited an airline for pilot simulation that "lacked realism and was degraded by an absence of challenge."

Prepare to Handle Stress During Simulations and Role Plays

23. Explain the potential for stress before starting the role play.

24. Be prepared to handle emotional problems or difficulties that may arise as a result of realistic role plays.

25. Provide a comfortable and nonjudgmental environment for discussion.

26. Build discussion around the anxieties and fears raised during the role play.

27. For very high-anxiety simulations, be prepared to deal with illness during the program.

    ▪ Understand how people react to stress, and assist those with inappropriate reactions in safely completing the role play.
    ▪ Obtain medical attention if required.
    ▪ If the simulation is a group exercise, prepare to handle the anticipated reactions of other participants to a colleague's illness or anxiety attacks.

Prepare Effective Instructional Materials

28. Materials should be an adjunct to your program. They serve as very effective documentation if later litigation develops, because they establish what the participants received.

29. Assure yourself that the written materials are error-free on substantive issues. Keep track of those courses whose content may be affected by new processes, techniques, or laws. Use of an outdated program can spell trouble.

30. Design your materials to address the reading and comprehension level of the group. For participants with special needs, consider adjunct materials. See Chapter 14, pp. 300–305, for specific techniques to accommodate these participants.

Exercise Care in Selecting External Consultants

31. Select consultants carefully. When simulations are involved, request information and references on past usage. Take care to ensure that the simulations realistically represent your work environment.

32. Work with consultants to develop customized approaches to your specific work environment. Role plays and simulations that are not relevant pose a twofold problem: They don't convey the skills and

behaviors you need, and they can be counterproductive by turning participants off.

33. Document the steps you take to investigate a vendor's safety record and on-site emergency services.

These techniques will help you design effective and legally defensible training. When you are unsure about what standards apply to your industry, seek assistance. Chapter 2, pp. 64–66, and Appendixes A and B direct you to available resources.

References

1. *Ehlinger v. Board of Education of New Hartford,* 465 N.Y.S.2d 378 (July 11, 1983).

2. *Ehlinger v. Board of Education of New Hartford,* 465 N.Y.S.2d 378, 379 (July 11, 1983).

3. *Leno v. Young Men's Christian Association,* 17 Cal.App.3d 651 (1971).

4. *County of Riverside v. Loma Linda Univ.,* 118 Cal.App.3d 300, 317 (1981).

5. *McCullough v. Hutzel Hospital,* 88 Mich.App. 235 (1979).

6. *Estate of Arrington v. Fields,* 578 S.W.2d 173 (Tex.Civ.App. 1979).

7. *Tabone v. State of New York,* 456 N.Y.S.2d 950 (1982).

8. *Tabone v. State of New York,* 456 N.Y.S.2d 950, 985 (1982).

9. *BNAC Communicator,* Fall 1996, p.6.

10. *Rodney King v. LAPD,* Los Angeles Superior Court and Federal District Court (1994).

5
Legal Issues in Diversity Training

Diversity training programs are popular staples in many organizations. When properly presented, they are essential. When improperly designed—or worse, when delivery is itself discriminatory—diversity programs can be legally indefensible.

Diversity programs teach managers to appreciate diversity as a potentially valuable business tool. Culturally diverse employees can provide new and different perspectives on solving problems and can help market the company's services to cultural groups that the company has not previously pursued, thus creating new business opportunities. Further, consideration of all types of diversity, including age, background, education, and traditional issues of gender and race, helps companies communicate more effectively with the international business community in an increasingly global economy.

When Design of a Diversity Workshop Can Land You in Court and How to Protect Yourself and Your Company

Critics of diversity training maintain that some programs do more harm than good from an employee relations standpoint. Stressing cultural diversity within a business, they argue, may have the effect of polarizing the workplace, emphasizing differences between employees rather than unity, perpetuating stereotypes, and exacerbating any problems that already exist in culturally diverse settings.[1] Despite the rapid growth and value of good corporate diversity programs, internal trainers *and* diversity consultants should be alert to the negative legal effects of implementing them.

The methods used to train employees to understand and value diversity vary greatly. The primary goal of diversity training is to eliminate conscious or unconscious prejudices by making employees aware of their own subtle biases, sensitizing employees to differences, and teaching employees to value a variety of differences. One technique in diversity training is to force employees to confront their own prejudices through various exercises such as role playing, volunteering common stereotypes and racial or ethnic slurs, or even drawing pictures. Diversity trainers also facilitate vignettes containing examples of office racism and sexism.

Another aspect of diversity training is valuing differences. This approach may consist of explaining the various personal, psychological, and social traits held by different cultural groups. Managers are made aware of these cultural factors and how these factors translate into an employee's behavior in the workplace, in order to foster an understanding of cultural differences among individuals.

Although diversity training is designed to foster harmony and understanding among employees, programs have been challenged as polarizing the workplace, emphasizing differences rather than unity, and exacerbating problems that already exist between employees. As one commentator has noted, many 'diversity approved' stereotypes are uncomfortably close, if not identical, to common sexism and bigotry."[2] According to diversity critics, even "positive" stereotypes can be damaging in that they "raise barriers against looking at workers as individuals."[3]

Some methods of diversity training have been challenged as provoking hostility and antagonism among employees by bringing prejudices to the surface, encouraging employees to vent negative feelings, or attempting to "blame and shame" certain groups. An article entitled "The Unfortunate Side Effects of Diversity Training," *The New York Times*, highlighted several examples of diversity training gone wrong:

> At one federal agency in Washington, participants in a seminar were asked to provide stereotypes about minority-group members. Later a list of them, including comments like "All blacks like watermelon," was printed on the agency letterhead and distributed by the diversity trainer to employees who had missed the seminar. Many employees complained, . . . [and another] consultant [was] called in for damage control.

In another instance, . . . a diversity trainer asked white male managers to volunteer stereotypes, which elicited responses like "Women cry under pressure." Women and minority groups were encouraged to vent their anger about being excluded in the workplace. By the next day, the managers were taunting the women about what they'd said, and the women were upset about what the managers had said.[4]

In one case that involved methodology in a workshop, *Fitzgerald v. US West Communications, Inc.,*[5] the appellate court addressed the issue of diversity training in a slightly different context. US West Communications was found liable as a result of racially charged comments made by Ms. Sapp, an in-house training instructor, when she was selecting outside facilitators to conduct the company's diversity workshops. The court concluded:

This developing area of diversity training has, at its motivating core, highly emotional areas of interpersonal relationships with real and potentially volatile strong conflicts, and its purpose is to cause those involved to recognize and deal appropriately with such as they find within themselves and others.

. . . Unfortunately, the very workshop format which was designed and intended to expose strong, unacceptable emotions and responses so that they could be examined and controlled, in Sapp's case engendered an emotional response that while not uncommon, was one that Sapp herself was unable to deal with."[6]

Watch Out for Those Flip Charts! When Workshop Materials Can Haunt You in Court

One of the most serious legal challenges to diversity training stems from use of the participants' comments as later evidence of management bias. Indeed, racial, ethnic, or sex-based remarks made in diversity training sessions have come back to haunt trainers and their employers in later employment discrimination litigation.

The leading example is *Stender v. Lucky Stores, Inc.*[7] In 1988, Lucky Stores tried to determine the cause of the glaring lack of promotions for women and minorities within the organization. In an attempt to remedy the situation, the company conducted an in-house diversity training session for all store managers. As part of the training, the managers took part in an exercise that is commonplace in many diversity training seminars: They were asked to list various stereotypes that they had heard about women and minorities.

Later, a number of female employees filed a class action alleging sexual discrimination on the basis of lack of female promotions. During pretrial discovery and over the objection of Lucky Stores, the court ordered the company to produce the flip charts and notes from the in-house diversity training session containing the managers' flagrantly stereotyped comments.

The court rejected Lucky's claim that the materials were privileged, electing to narrowly construe a privilege that allows a business to protect itself from disclosing information it gathers for its own critical self-evaluation for affirmative action compliance. Second, the court held that the attorney-client privilege, which usually shields confidential communications between lawyer and client, did not apply because the managers' meetings were held, not for the purpose of "facilitating the provision of professional legal services to a client," but rather for training managers.

The court relied on the notes as evidence that Lucky's managers harbored discriminatory attitudes toward women. The judge found that the comments were not just portrayals of social stereotypes, but reflections of what many Lucky managers firmly believed. Thus, the court concluded that the notes constituted "evidence of discriminatory attitudes and stereotyping of women" by Lucky's managers.

Lucky contended—unsuccessfully—that the notes were taken out of context and were examples of stereotypes and not actual opinions of the managers. The trainer used those responses to show that people have biased preconceptions of a good worker. Plaintiffs alleged that the training was conducted only to ward off an EEOC investigation.

After a lengthy trial with no jury, the judge found for the plaintiffs and awarded over $90 million in damages (remember, there were many claimants). Thus, although the company initiated the diversity training in order to remedy the lack of promotions for women and minorities, the feedback that came out of the training sessions turned out to be a significant factor in the employer's losing the lawsuit. The *Stender* case was ultimately settled, and in addition to a significant monetary payment, the store agreed to spend at least $20 million implementing new personnel policies, procedures, training, and affirmative action goals.

The solution is *not* to drop valuable diversity programs. Rather, it is to be proactive in your approach to collecting workshop materials and practical in your use of those materials. If you conduct diversity training, you should be aware of the *Stender* case, and develop appropriate policies on the use and retention of flip charts, notes, and other documentation of participants' comments. Don't stifle interaction or honesty, but create a climate of mutual respect and dignity for all participants. Make sure that participants understand the purpose of their interaction during the workshop. Consult your human resources or legal department for guidance on record retention.

Beware of Confrontation! When Workshop Exercises Can Haunt You in Court

Another frequent source of discrimination complaints involves sexually harassing *content or presentation* of diversity training. These cases stem from sexually offensive written materials, verbal content (jokes and banter), and related conduct in the presentation of the instruction.

Your curriculum design and training methodology must be appropriate to meet the learning objectives and must not itself create a separate basis for significant liability. To professional trainers this seems obvious, but a sexual harassment case with a training twist provides a relevant example.

In 1994, the Federal Aviation Administration sponsored a confrontational exercise as part of a much larger program on diversity. The activity was drawn from the Navy's Tailhook episode, but was later ridiculed by the participants and the press as "Malehook." During the exercise, men were subjected to a one-minute trip through a gauntlet of women who teased, taunted, and fondled them. The stated purpose: to turn the tables on the men and give them a blunt lesson on what many women regularly experience.

The men subsequently complained that they were forced to walk through the gauntlet of women, who were instructed to shout crude sexual remarks and reach out to touch their chests, legs, and buttocks. Some men complained of very intrusive physical touching. One former controller who participated in a settlement between the Air Traffic Controllers Union and the FAA claimed that his trip through the gauntlet had a grave effect on his marriage and forced his wife into therapy. As he described it:

> I was escorted through a door and into a room crowded with women who "started saying 'my, he wears tight jeans' and 'there's a nice bulge in his pants' and one woman started rubbing my chest, and another put her hands in my back pockets and said 'what a nice rear end' or something like that.... Another started playing with my belt and reaching into my pants pockets.[8]

On September 2, 1994, 11 air traffic controllers filed a sexual harassment lawsuit against the U.S. Department of Transportation arising out of this mandatory workshop. The male plaintiffs alleged that the program created a hostile and offensive working environment. Douglas Hartman, an 11-year veteran of the FAA, became the lead accuser. He claimed that when he objected to the exercise, he was ridiculed with lewd and demeaning comments by a manager. Then, following the workshop, he suffered further harassment, anguish, and lost promotional opportunities because of his objections during the exercise. Although he filed an internal complaint in September 1992, it was not acted upon and he allegedly experienced further retaliation.

Further, elements of graphic sexual harassment were used as course materials. According to a judge's written opinion refusing the government's request to throw out the suit, the trainers conducted a discussion, following the gauntlet, in which the men were numerically rated "with their names on a chart subscribed to drawings of male genitalia." The pictures were graphic, and the men were allegedly humiliated by being compared to these large-scale graphic posters. The judge also found this graphic material, and the accompanying verbal discussion, grounds to allow the controllers to seek a jury's opinion on the "reasonableness" of their feeling that the training environment was hostile and offensive. The government chose instead to settle for an undisclosed sum. See Chapter 1, pp. 33–35, for an explanation of the role of jurors as "Monday morning quarterbacks."

Douglas Hartman complained to no avail to his immediate supervisor that the gauntlet exercise was so stressful that he preferred to sit out the rest of the training. Part of the problem was the supervisor's alleged failure to take the complaint seriously and his cavalier reaction to Hartman's genuine distress. An even larger problem for the FAA was the fact that the same program was repeated several times over the following months, despite other complaints.

According to Joseph Bellino of the National Air Traffic Controllers Association, the FAA's problems with its diversity training extended beyond gender and sexual harassment issues. Bellino described one exercise in which "black employees were encouraged to go off by themselves and discuss their problems in a 'white, male-dominated society,' and then return to the main room and verbally assail some individual white male employees."[9]

Until 1993, the Department of Transportation programs also included addressing participants as "jerks and jerkettes," and racial groups were allegedly encouraged to exchange epithets. These types of confrontational exercises, with the objective of raising awareness, have resulted in dissatisfaction and even backlashes by employees, particularly white men who have perceived the programs as "bashing."[10]

Such methodology does little to encourage full participation and comfort, so it may in fact defeat the very purpose of the program. Of more concern in legal circles is the real potential for targeted adverse behavior of a racial or ethnic nature to violate Title VII of the 1964 Civil Rights Act and the Civil Rights Act of 1991. The 1991 act significantly expanded the remedies available to participants adversely affected, including the right to a jury trial by their peers. The genuine risk to the organization is the very discrimination the training is intended to prevent.

The FAA is not the only employer to face charges that its diversity training methodology crossed the line of propriety—and legality. *The Wall Street Journal* reported on February 13, 1997, that R. R. Donnelley suspended its diversity awareness training after employees criticized the program and threatened legal action.

Finally, there is always the danger that the content of an *appropriate* diversity program will be used by participants, out of context, and will come back to bite you. Consider the widely criticized Texaco executives caught on tape making remarks about "black jelly beans...falling to the bottom of the bag." This specific phrase was at least partially drawn, apparently out of context, from a diversity awareness program they had attended. Does this mean that you must discontinue any sensitive training because your participants may misuse or mischaracterize your content? Of course not. But awareness of the legal pitfalls can reduce the potential for unintended consequences.

Because of the sensitive nature of diversity training, it is critical that you choose the right methodology. There is no formal certification of licensing for diversity trainers. Thus, the level of training, experience, and skill will vary considerably. For this reason, it is critical to use diversity trainers—internal or external—who are well versed in your unique needs. Effective diversity trainers understand and adapt to the culture of an organization and should be able to tailor a program that will enhance rather than detract from your diversity efforts.

Successful, and legally defensible, diversity training encompasses at least the following considerations:

1. Making sure the program and the individual trainers reflect the demographics of the company's employees. Trainers should balance their experiences with well-researched information on the organization and its individuals.

2. Creating a welcome atmosphere for everyone, including straight white males who may be put off by accusations that they are racist or homophobic.

3. Including all aspects of diversity in the program—specifically, age, geography, work experience (e.g., military vs. civilian, government

vs. private sector, corporate vs. small office), educational background, and lifestyle preferences.

4. Focusing on your knowledge of how people are influenced by cultural values, and model respect for those differences during the program. Be sure to include all participants, especially those who are from the majority culture in the particular workplace.

5. Providing substantial opportunities for interaction and dialogue by all participants. Nobody should leave the training program feeling unheard or disrespected.

How to Audit Your Diversity Training for Legal Pitfalls

Why You Should Conduct a Self-Audit

There are many reasons to conduct a self-audit, but here are two big ones. First, local, state, and federal employment laws are so complex that it is easy to do something unlawful without even realizing it. Most organizations want to comply with the law. An audit furthers that goal by highlighting trouble spots before they get out of control.

Second, if a violation is uncovered through a government investigation or the filing of a lawsuit, serious financial exposure can result. When you and your organization are proactive, you can minimize the cost, disruption, and legal risks of an outside investigation or audit.

Who Should Conduct the Audit

In order for your audit and legal compliance program to be successful, it is important that senior management and training directors fully support the program. Sometimes operating management recognizes the need for such a process. In other situations, you may need to sell the idea. One way to do so is to identify the very real and personal risks of noncompliance with applicable laws. This is made easier by the specter of "Texaco-like" public relations disasters, large judgments, and personal liabilities for employment law violations.

Appoint an Audit Team

Once management decides to conduct an audit, a team should be appointed to oversee the process. This team will collect and analyze data about current training policies and legal compliance, recommend areas and methods for improvement, and monitor the company's success or failure at legal compliance.

For important legal reasons, including the ability to shield audit results from pretrial disclosure to adverse parties, the team should have at least one lawyer member. For the important reasons given below, the training department must be represented on the audit team.

Train the Audit Team

Here is where your skills and experience are most valuable. Before a self-audit is undertaken to determine compliance with employment laws, team members need to have some important information, including:

- A general overview of the various employment laws applicable to the employer
- The importance of maintaining the confidentiality and legal protection of information obtained during the audit
- The proper procedures for handling such information
- Operating procedures to be used by the team

Several questions naturally arise before a self-audit begins. Since the audit is designed to determine the company's compliance with employment laws, the first issue is establishing which employment laws apply to the organization. This is no small task, since there are many sources of employment-related laws, and their requirements are often complex. Appendixes A and B and Chapter 6 provide relevant information for your initial analysis.

Identifying Diversity Training Procedures

Once the applicable law has been identified, the audit team must consider the company's internal training policies and procedures and past practices, all of which have an impact on potential legal risks of diversity programs. The process is usually straightforward, but it may help to break down the company's system into various components, such as:

- Selection procedures for diversity training opportunities
- Procedures for evaluating course content

- Procedures for curriculum design, including methodology
- Procedures for selecting consultants and contract trainers
- Record retention systems and documentation procedures

Conducting Audit Interviews

One effective means of compiling information during an audit of selection practices is to interview a wide range of existing employees who are involved in those procedures. The following categories of personnel should be interviewed:

- Members of senior management, especially department heads who send employees to training
- Employees at various organizational levels who have applied for training opportunities
- Members of the training staff who have significant involvement in employee selection for training

Protecting Confidentiality

One legitimate reason that trainers may be wary of conducting self-audits is the likelihood that negative information uncovered in the process will come back to haunt them in court. For example, suppose an internal audit discloses a serious problem with sexual harassment in a training program. Even if the employer acts to resolve the problem when it is uncovered, an employee who took the class may later sue the employer for sexual harassment. The employee's attorney may then make every effort to gain access to the employer's audit findings and attempt to use that information in the lawsuit.

A number of legal doctrines may protect the employer from disclosing self-audit results and other confidential internal material, but each requires that the employer act with great care in generating and maintaining such data. Two of these doctrines are explained below.

Attorney-Client Privilege

Both federal and state law protect certain communications from disclosure during litigation because of the importance of the attorney-client relationship. Generally, this privilege serves to prevent disclosure of communications between attorney and client when (1) legal advice is sought (2) from a professional legal adviser acting in that capacity (3) involving a communication relating to that purpose (4) made in confidence (5) by the client. The privilege protects against disclosure of confidential information by either the client or the lawyer, but it may be waived by the client.

Before conducting self-audit interviews—indeed, before even beginning a self-audit—the corporation should have the company's chief executive officer or board of directors specifically authorize the self-audit for the purpose of securing advice from the corporation's attorneys regarding legal compliance. This authorization should be in writing.

Self-Evaluation Privilege

A few courts have recognized a privilege based upon a discovery in litigation of some information produced as a result of an organization's internal evaluation of its operations. In doing so, the courts have relied on the important public policy to be advanced by having organizations improve their legal compliance through candid, thorough, and self-critical reports. When applied, however, this privilege has been limited to the evaluative portion of the reports. Purely factual information, such as how many minority members applied and were hired for particular jobs, is discoverable. Unfortunately, few state decisions recognize the self-evaluation privilege.

References

1. See, for example, Heather MacDonald, "The Diversity Industry," *The New Republic*, July 5, 1993, 22 at 24–25; Kathleen Murray, "The Unfortunate Side Effects of Diversity Training," *The New York Times*, August 1, 1993, at F5; Mobley and Payne, "Backlash! A Challenge to Diversity Training," *Training & Development*, December 1992.

2. Heather MacDonald, "The Diversity Industry," *The New Republic*, July 5, 1993, 22 at 25.

3. K. Murray, "The Unfortunate Side Effects of Diversity Training," *The New York Times*, August 1, 1993, at F5.

4. K. Murray, "The Unfortunate Side Effects of Diversity Training," *The New York Times*, August 1, 1993, at F5.

5. *Fitzgerald v. US West Communications, Inc.,* Federal District Court, No. 93-1142 (1995).

6. *Fitzgerald v. US West Communications, Inc.,* Federal District Court, No. 93-1142 (1995).

7. *Stender v. Lucky Stores, Inc.,* 803 F.Supp. 259 (N.D.Cal. 1992).

8. *Hartman v. Pena,* No. 94C 5416 (N.D.Ill. Dec. 27, 1995).

9. *Fortune,* October 17, 1994.

10. *Newsweek,* November 25, 1996.

6

How Trainers Discriminate Illegally, Without Realizing It

After reading about regulatory penalties for failing to meet legal mandates (Chapter 2, pp. 39–47), and lawsuits for negligent training design (Chapter 3, pp. 67–78) and supervision (Chapter 4, pp. 93–104), you may be tempted to encourage your employer to restrict the individuals selected for advancement to high-risk jobs. Resist the urge to do so.

Although workplace safety is vital, employers are required to balance the need for safety with the individual rights of employees to be free from improper discrimination in America's workplaces. Many training programs, and the selection criteria for participation in training opportunities, are under judicial and regulatory scrutiny. Discrimination compliance lawsuits are being filed at record levels. A significant number involve alleged denial of access to training because of gender, ethnicity, or disability.

Which Equal Employment Opportunity Laws Affect Your Training?

The premise of all federal equal employment opportunity legislation, and many parallel state statutes, is that an employer and its agents must not permit managers, supervisors, trainers, or employees to make employment decisions on the basis of gender, race, color, religion, national origin, age, or disability. Some states include separate protections for sexual orientation. Individuals who fall within these protected groups are also entitled to be free from harassment by managers, coworkers, and even vendors.

EEO laws require both public and private employers to hire, promote, train, and retain employees on the basis of qualifications and merit. To comply, you must make consistent, job-related decisions when considering employees for all job opportunities, including training and advancement. Employment decisions most commonly affected by employment discrimination laws are placement, assignment, training, performance appraisal, discipline, and discharge. Decision makers cannot take into account personal characteristics that are not job-related or consistent with business necessity.

The question of qualifications, skills, and experience to perform a job must be objectively applied to all candidates for the opportunity. Even when a unique skill is required, such as fluency in a particular foreign language, the courts have determined that the job qualifications must focus on the ability to perform, not on the personal characteristics of the performer. For example, when you advertise for a training opportunity that requires fluency in Spanish, look for an individual with that skill, *not* necessarily an individual of Latino descent.

Likewise, under the Americans With Disabilities Act, employers and their trainers must select individuals for training and advancement opportunities on the basis of their ability to perform, not on the disabilities or disorders they may have. Such a selection criterion requires careful consideration of the essential physical, cognitive, and emotional functions necessary for the specific training opportunity, so that the candidate can be considered relative to those requirements. Individual trainers are also responsible for considering reasonable accommodations to the known disabilities of their trainees, both during workshops and in posttraining evaluations.

Because your employer can act only through managers, supervisors, and trainers authorized to make these employment decisions, your organization relies heavily on you to avoid discriminating in your own employment decisions *and* to ensure that all training activities are bias-free. Appropriate intervention may be required during the training to make sure that other participants don't create a discriminatory environment. Figure 6-1 summarizes each discrimination statute, highlighting its impact on training.

There are four primary areas of concern in maintaining an equal opportunity workplace. Stated another way, trainers must *avoid* discriminating on any of the following bases:

Figure 6-1 Legal Framework of Federal Equal Employment Opportunity Statutes Affecting Training.

Title VII of the Civil Rights Act of 1964

Title VII is the most widely enforced antidiscrimination statute. The statute prohibits employers from discriminating in employment on the grounds of gender, race, color, religion, or national origin. In addition, the Pregnancy Discrimination Act of 1978 established that Title VII treats adverse employment decisions based on pregnancy, childbirth, or pregnancy-related medical conditions as unlawful gender-based discrimination (commonly called sex discrimination).

Title VII protects job applicants and employees in any of the above-mentioned groups from discrimination in hiring, compensation, training, terms and privileges of employment, and termination of employment. Claimants who allege that they have been discriminated against must first file an administrative claim with the EEOC. Following an investigation, the EEOC may elect to proceed with a case or to close the file. If the EEOC closes the file, it issues a "right to sue" letter, and the applicant or employee may then proceed with a lawsuit in a civil court.

Type of Discrimination	Training Context	Defense
Sex Discrimination: Title VII prohibits discrimination in employment against any individual, male or female. When the gender of an individual is one of the factors upon which an employment decision is based, the resulting decision is unlawful.	1. Refusal to hire, promote or train an individual for a certain job on the basis of his or her gender.	1. *Bona fide occupational qualification (BFOQ).* In very rare instances, gender may be either an appropriate qualifying or disqualifying factor. Gender must be reasonably necessary to carry out a particular job function, or participate in a particular training program, in the normal business operation.
	2. Disparate treatment in employment, including training, based on pregnancy or childbearing capability.	
	3. Sexual harassment, including jokes, innuendos, and other verbal, physical, and/or graphic content of training.	2. Business necessity. This is primarily used when necessary for safety on the job or in the work site.

Religious and Ancestral Discrimination:
Title VII defines religion as including all aspects of religious observance, practice, and belief. This includes atheists and agnostics. Religious or ancestral discrimination occurs when an individual is required by an employment rule or policy to choose between abandoning a fundamental precept of religion or culture or losing an employment opportunity.

1. When an employee is precluded from observing a Sabbath because of training or testing schedules.

2. When an employee notifies the employer that a training program or technique conflicts with his or her religious beliefs, and the employer fails or refuses to provide a reasonable accommodation.

3. National origin harassment, such as jokes, insults, or epithets; a manager or supervisor promoting a particular religion or religious belief during training, or mocking a detectable accent.

BFOQ. Undue employer hardship in providing reasonable accommodation.

(*Continued*)

Figure 6-1 (*Continued*) *Legal Framework of Federal Equal Employment Opportunity Statutes Affecting Training.*

Age Discrimination in Employment Act of 1967 (ADEA)

ADEA is a federal statute that applies to all employers with 20 or more employees. It prohibits discrimination against individuals age 40 and over. When originally enacted, the federal law applied to people age 40 to 70, but the maximum age 70 was eliminated in 1987 with very narrow exceptions. Any adverse employment decision in hiring, terms, and privileges of employment, training, discipline, or firing that is based on age is prohibited by ADEA. It also prohibits mandatory retirement policies.

Type of Discrimination	Training Context	Defenses
Age Discrimination: Job applicants and employees 40 years of age and older are protected from employment discrimination in all aspects of employment, including hiring, compensation, benefits, pensions, discipline, appraisal, training, and termination. Under ADEA, individuals who make a successful claim of age discrimination have a wider array of remedies, including certain forms of compensatory damages.	1. Refusal to promote or train an individual for a certain job on the basis of his or her age. The EEOC has found such discrimination especially prevalent when managers and supervisors make subjective training and promotion decisions on characteristics such as "energy," "ability to be trained," and "flexibility," using preconceptions concerning older workers. 2. Age harassment, such as "ageist" comments, innuendos, conduct, jokes, and insults in training materials or presentations.	*BFOQ.* Business necessity.

Disability Discrimination

The Americans With Disabilities Act took effect on July 26, 1992, for employers with more than 15 employees. It applies to all such employers, including federal agency contractors. The ADA prohibits employers from discriminating against qualified individuals with a broader range of physical or mental disabilities than the Rehabilitation Act of 1973.

Type of Discrimination	Training Context	Defenses
Employers must maintain a discrimination-free work environment with respect to individuals who have a substantial impairment of a major life activity as defined by the Americans With Disabilities Act of 1990.	1. Refusal to promote, train, or make reasonable accommodations in training for an individual because of his or her disability.	*BFOQ.* Reasonable business necessity.
Reasonable accommodations for disabled workers may include modifications to the job, retraining, or installing equipment or machinery that accommodates the disability.	2. Refusal to make a reasonable accommodation so that a disabled employee may perform the essential functions of the job, or participate in training, provided that the reasonable accommodation does not place an undue hardship on the employer, such as extensive costs or danger to other employees at the work site.	Undue hardship in making reasonable accommodations.
	3. Harassment, such as insults, disparaging remarks, jokes, or innuendos in training materials or training presentations.	

1. *Intentional discrimination.* The employee or trainee is treated differently from similarly situated coworkers. This is often referred to as "disparate treatment." Intent does not necessarily mean malice or ill-will; intent to make the employment decision is sufficient when a discriminatory result occurs. Disparate treatment includes:

- *Overt:* blanket exclusion of all members of a specific group. An example is excluding disabled workers or people over 40 from eligibility for a physically demanding training program. This overt exclusion targets protected groups without reference to individual qualifications, skills, abilities, and attitudes.
- *Special rules:* enforcement of a special employment rule against trainees who are members of a particular protected group. An example is preventing trainees with high blood pressure from participating in physically demanding programs, while allowing trainees with other disabilities to participate.
- *Subtle stereotypes:* special rules or disparate treatment based on stereotypes or assumptions. In one EEOC decision, it was ruled discriminatory to train white workers on the job while sending all employees with Hispanic surnames to the training facility. Such a practice falls under the "intentional" category even though the trainer may be well intentioned and not malicious or "bigoted."

2. *Adverse impact.* An employment practice or policy that is neutral by its terms has a discriminatory effect on a protected group. For example, a "neutral" posttraining test may limit physically disabled applicants from completing the test, even though their disability does not prevent them from performing the essential functions of the job with a reasonable accommodation.

3. *Perpetuating the effects of past discriminatory policies and practices.* An example is a policy of selecting applicants who are referred by employees before placing other applicants in a training program. The EEOC has found that if the existing program is entirely Caucasian or male because of past discrimination, use of employee referrals tends to perpetuate the all-white, male-dominated nature of the program.

4. *Harassment or hostile work/training environments.* A hostile training atmosphere permits insults, pranks, innuendos, slurs, derogatory comments, and embarrassing or humiliating activities that offend people on the basis of gender, age, race, religion, ancestry, or disability.

Trainers need only scan a morning newspaper to recognize that access to training is a key element of a truly equal employment opportunity. The trend toward large-scale employee class actions has been especially newsworthy. Consider these examples:

- Fifteen current and former employees of the Washington, D.C., Metro Transit Authority filed a lawsuit seeking a collective $200 million in damages, citing discriminatory exclusion from training and other advancement opportunities on the basis of race, national origin, and gender discrimination. The claimants contended that "there is no question this is perpetuated in such a consistent manner that it can only be [agency] policy." The lawsuit also named several Metro managers and supervisors as individual defendants.[1] See the discussion of personal liabilities in Chapter 1, pp. 35–36.

- A federal trial judge allowed a class action lawsuit to proceed against Dominick's Supermarkets, Inc. Among the allegations was the failure to provide women with equal access to training given routinely to their male counterparts.[2]

- The Immigration and Naturalization Service faced a class action brought by up to 4700 Latino agents, seeking back pay and compensatory damages. The complaint alleged discrimination in performance evaluations, assignments, and access to training for preferred-duty positions.[3]

Many of the discrimination charges of failure to provide equal opportunities for training involve large numbers of employees and span significant time periods. For example, in 1996, 48 current and former employees at Bell Atlantic Corp. filed a class action alleging that the regional telephone company discriminated against black employees by denying them training and promotional opportunities, dating back to 1983. Others claimed that the company trained white coworkers, who were then given preferred positions for advanced management training.[4]

In an era of corporate restructuring, excluding employees from the skills training they need to keep pace with technological or industry changes can devastate their careers. Equality of access requires that selection procedures for advanced training programs be provided on an objective basis. Exclusion from training opportunities is a key area for discrimination claims against employers and their training professionals.

Exclusion From Training for Advancement

An employer may also discriminate by excluding trainees from on-the-job training for future promotions. The law requires that individuals be given the opportunity to compete equally for available positions on the basis of job-related criteria. Thus, in a case involving a fire department, the court found discrimination when minority employees were never assigned the administrative jobs that provided on-the-job training for promotions.[5] Most cases dealing with inequality of access to training focus on the inability to acquire skills necessary for advancement. This category could be broadly labeled "glass ceiling" litigation, in which the complainants allege that advancement to more responsible management jobs has been stalled.

Exclusion From Training Leading to Adverse Action

Sometimes the exclusion from training results in adverse employment actions. During downsizing, employees who are denied opportunities to learn new skills face more than a stalled career; they fear outright job loss. Likewise, workers who are not provided with education to stay abreast of the needs on their current jobs may face poor performance evaluations and demotions. In these contexts, the denial of equal access to training can result in tangible job detriment, and become illegal discrimination.

Many courts have concluded that a deprivation of training which leads to a demotion is sufficient job detriment to constitute discrimination. For example, in *Carrero v. New York Housing Authority,*[6] the complaining party prevailed on a claim that discrimination kept him from training and caused a subsequent demotion. The court flatly rejected the employer's argument that "mere failure to train was not a denial of a tangible job benefit."

There are no uniformly acceptable or unacceptable selection criteria for advanced skills training or on-the-job instructional opportunities. Whether the criteria are found to be nondiscriminatory may depend on several factors. Statistical evidence of discrimination, the structure of the selection system, the particular training program or job in question, the relationship between the criteria and the job, and the consistent application of the criteria to all employees frequently are more important than the substance of the actual criteria.

Among the selection criteria that have been upheld by the courts are experience (if the requirement is job related), skills, productivity, absenteeism/tardiness, and disciplinary records. In establishing selection procedures for your training programs, consider the following policies to ensure that the system is as objective as possible and capable of consistent enforcement:

- Publicize all training opportunities uniformly to all potentially interested employees.

- Provide those responsible for the selection of trainees with written guidelines specifying the weight to be given to each selection criterion.

- Establish job-related criteria for training opportunities. It is usually impossible to immediately accommodate every employee who wants—or needs—training; set up an objective schedule based on the highest need. Consult with line supervisors and management to determine an appropriate schedule, and then follow it consistently. Make exceptions only under extreme conditions, and be prepared to support them with evidence of business needs.

- Make sure all employees are aware of the requirements they must meet for admission to the training program.

- Establish objective qualification standards for skills training programs, including prerequisites as appropriate. Prerequisites can include prior training, on-the-job experience, or an objective skills test.

- When employees request and are denied a training opportunity, provide appropriate feedback on the qualification or timing factors. Make sure that all explanations given to the employee's supervisor or other managers are consistent. In the eyes of a jury, inconsistent explanations are far worse than no explanation at all, because they permit the jury to infer that the reasons given were a pretext for discrimination. See Chapter 1, pp. 33–35, for a discussion of the role of juries, and remember that under the Civil Rights Act of 1991 all employees are entitled to a jury trial in a discrimination dispute.

Ageism and Access to Training

Ageism is an emerging concept in the workplace. As in the case of sexism and racism, discrimination against an applicant or an employee because of his or her age (40 or over) is unlawful under the Age Discrimination in Employment Act (ADEA). There has been a significant increase in the number of age discrimination claims before the EEOC. Thus, this is an area where managers, supervisors, and trainers should continue to update their awareness of circumstances that may result in discrimination complaints.

The ADEA applies to all terms and conditions of employment, including advertising, placement, training, performance appraisal, and promotional opportunities. Under the ADEA, it is unlawful for an employer, a supervisor, and/or an individual trainer to fail to select a trainee for a program; to indicate any "preference, limitation, specification, or discrimination" based on age in training advertisements; or to retaliate against any employee who asserts rights under the ADEA.

When age is used as a factor in making an employment decision and it isn't job-related, the decision is unlawful. This is true even when other job candidates are over 40 and the exclusion is based on relative age. The rule has been confirmed by the U.S. Supreme Court in *O'Connor v. Consolidated Coin Caterers Corp.*,[7] in which relative age was used as a factor in terminating a 57-year-old and replacing him with a 44-year-old. Although the latter was also protected by the ADEA, the employer used age as a factor in making the employment decision when it was *not* job-related or consistent with business necessity. Thus, if you use age to "break the tie" between two equally qualified candidates for your training opportunity, you cannot defend your selection on the ground that other "older" (over-40) people participated.

Age discrimination claims encompass both the selection of employees for advanced or technical skills programs and the content or delivery of those programs. Most trainers would acknowledge that refusal to select a female for advanced training because she "might" decide to take an extended pregnancy leave is unlawful under Title VII. Yet many employers have been charged with similar discrimination based on age when they pass over individuals for advanced training on the premise that their potential retirement will prevent the company from recouping its training investment.

Even worse, stereotypes about the aging process have led trainers to discriminate against employees by treating them differently during training on advanced automation equipment (e.g., industrial robots) in the belief that older employees are "too set in their ways" or otherwise unreceptive to change. In addition, older workers have complained that they are singled out for "ageist" comments by instructors. You should regularly remind instructors and facilitators that offensive comments or activities based on age are unlawful (just as they are with sex, race, ancestry, and disability).

Although you may legitimately use lack of training as a ground for layoffs, when the reason an employee received no training is related to age, you violate the ADEA. In *Coates v. National Cash Register Co.*,[8] two long-term field engineers were denied training on newer equipment because they had the most experience on the old equipment which was being phased out. They were laid off when they couldn't operate the newer equipment, a move that the court concluded was age discrimination.

The U.S. Environmental Protection Agency settled a similar discrimination suit filed by a senior agency attorney who claimed that she was not promoted because of her age and gender and was then retaliated against for filing a bias complaint. The plaintiff alleged that after she filed the EEO complaint, her supervisors responded by denying her training and travel opportunities and downgrading her performance evaluations.[9]

Trainers should avoid stereotypes that tend to deprive older workers of equal access to training and advancement opportunities.

1. *Older workers are physically unskilled, even infirm.* This stereotype persists despite rapidly emerging medical advances. Indeed, entrepreneurial magazines routinely discuss the opportunities for expansion of businesses that cater to the needs of older people for physical activities and entertainment. Although some seniors may require accommodation if they must stand or sit for lengthy periods, older workers are *not* necessarily infirm. Likewise, capable aging employees who are exposed to increased activity and intellectual stimulation help to dispel the notion that confusion accompanies the aging process.

2. *Older workers resist change.* A common negative stereotype is that older employees are not "trainable" on new technology and procedures because they are resistant to change. In 1983 at the NATO Symposium on Aging and Technological Advances, Gwyneth G. Donchin reported on a study of 4000 workers in a high-technology company. The results challenged traditional notions. Over half the employees believed that management was not interested in training them in new technology. Donchin concluded that older workers "will accept change according to their degree of involvement in planning for it and their perception of management's intent." Accordingly, an employer that resists retraining existing employees on new automated systems may be engaging in veiled age discrimination.

3. *Older workers cost too much to train.* Generally, older workers are more stable and loyal to the employer. Consequently, they are more willing—not less inclined—to remain in their positions long enough for the company to recoup its training investment. The fact that seniors have not engaged regularly in classroom instructional settings does not mean their learning skills are materially different from those of younger workers. In fact, seasoned workers tend to emphasize accuracy over speed. Thus, they are good candidates for training in technically advanced or detail-oriented jobs.

4. *Older workers' salaries are disproportionate to their contributions.* Although it is true that longevity of employment puts the seasoned employee in a much higher compensation bracket (with respect to both salaries and fringe benefits), it is legally risky to assume that "new blood" will bring a fresher or more productive approach to the work site.

A demotion or discharge that stems, in any way, from management's decision to cut overhead by replacing more highly compensated individuals with entry-level workers is blatantly in violation of the ADEA. Such an action would probably draw a discrimination claim. However, a more subtle form of unlawful age discrimination is adoption or enforcement of a policy that is age-neutral, but nevertheless has a negative impact on older workers. Thus, it is unlawful to make any change in health insurance, disability leave, or other existing fringe benefits that will affect older workers disproportionately. A prime example is a physical examination requirement which singles out employees over 40 but does not apply to *job-related* health standards.[10]

5. *As workers age, they become "soft" and cannot cope with stressful work situations.* This stereotype is frequently used to exclude seasoned employees from programs that appropriately inject stress into the curriculum. (See Chapter 4, pp. 100–101 and 103–104.) It is impermissible to pass over an otherwise qualified person for training simply because of management concern that advancing age will render the employee incapable of dealing with the rigors of the job. Few actions will draw a bias complaint faster than putting an active employee "out to pasture." Even in the absence of loss of wages or benefits, the emotional damages that accompany such decisions often warrant sizable monetary awards.

6. *Older workers are just going through the motions until they retire.* This assumption is used to exclude older workers from training—particularly on advanced technologies—on the basis that the employer will not "recoup its training investment." Certainly employees who have spent 30 years or more in the workforce think about what they will do when they retire. However, the implicit assumption that these employees are mentally in another world is as inappropriate as the notion that a working mother will not concentrate on her responsibilities while at work because her attention has been divided by family matters. Managers, supervisors, and trainers who assume that workers approaching retirement are either inattentive or uninterested in their job performance invite a legal challenge if they make employment decisions on this basis.

Long-standing notions about the productivity and contributions that older employees make to a workforce must be closely examined. Managers, supervisors, and trainers may not assume that older workers are unable—or unwilling—to do the required job. Sensitivity to these and similar myths about maturing employees should be included as a regular part of management workshops to minimize liability for inappropriate management conduct (see the discussion in Chapter 12, pp. 258–267). Sensitivity training efforts can help ensure a claim-free environment, and will enhance the morale and productivity of all segments of the workforce.

Questions You Should *Never* Ask a Candidate for Your Training Programs

Recruitment and Advertising

When you are advertising vacancies for a job or training program, it is unlawful to state a preference based on race, color, religion, sex, or national origin. It is also unlawful to indicate an exclusionary intent— by making references, say, to "young trainees" or "healthy individuals." Examples include:

- "Single *man* for extensive travel"
- "Will train *young graduates* on advanced systems design"
- "Candidates must be *healthy, robust,* and *physically fit*"
- "A *mentally challenging* training opportunity"

Courts have repeatedly considered evidence of advertisements referring to a specific characteristic, such as gender or age, in finding a pattern and practice of discrimination. Indeed, in one sexual discrimination case a federal appellate court stated: "[T]he advertising evidence is useful and probative insofar is it goes to establish motivation and hiring policies....Even if the advertisements were placed out of a sincere belief that females would not be interested in the job [or the training], such a belief is precisely the kind of stereotyped assumption that Title VII is aimed at eliminating."[11] Review the language of your workshop advertisements, flyers, postings, and registration forms to be sure you don't discriminate without realizing the effect of the language you choose.

Personal Interviews

When you ask a question that improperly solicits information about sex, age, race, religion, national origin, and/or disability status for purposes of *pretraining selection,* you risk violating the discrimination laws. Especially in the personal interview, you should be aware of areas of questioning that are impermissible. In most instances involving sex or age, it is not the question itself that is unlawful; it is how you use the answer. However, under the Americans With Disabilities Act, asking any question about disabilities, disorders, limiting conditions, or illnesses is flatly unlawful and gives rise to an immediate bias claim. About 25 percent of all complaints to the EEOC involve improper questions asked of applicants for employment opportunities.[12]

Employers should rely on probing questions to elicit factual information that can be used to support a negative decision on a marginal candidate. Questioners should be careful to make sure that their notes, which may become evidence in a later bias claim, reflect only permissible selection criteria.

Figure 6-2 provides an overview of the primary areas of lawful and unlawful pretraining interview questions. Although the list is *not* exhaustive, it highlights issues of discriminatory exclusion of candidates for training opportunities. The following are specific questions you should never ask a candidate for your training.

On the Basis of Disability

- Have you ever had or been treated for any of the following conditions or diseases?

- Have you ever been hospitalized? If so, for what condition?

- Have you ever been treated by a psychiatrist or psychologist? If so, for what condition?

- Is there any health-related reason you may not be able to complete the training?

- Have you had any major illness in the last five years?

- How many days were you absent from work because of illness last year?

- Do you have any mental or physical defects that preclude you from performing certain kinds of work? If so, can you describe such defects and specific work limitations?

- Are you taking any prescribed drugs?

- Have you ever been treated for drug addiction?

- Have you ever filed for workers' compensation benefits?

- Do you have the physical stamina to complete a rigorous 12-week training program?

- Are you physically capable of traveling out of the country on a regular basis after you finish the training program?

Figure 6-2 Examples of Lawful and Unlawful Preplacement Interview Questions.

Preemployment Inquiries		
Area of inquiry	Lawful	Unlawful
Name	For access purposes, to inquire into whether the applicant's work records are under another name.	To ask if a woman is a Miss, Mrs., or Ms. To request applicant to give maiden name or any other previous name she has used.
Address/ housing	To request place and length of current and previous addresses. To ask for applicant's phone number or how he or she can be reached if a number is not available.	To ask applicants if they own their own home, rent, or live in an apartment or house. Specific inquiry into foreign addresses.
Age	To require proof of age by birth certificate _only_ _after hiring._	To ask age or age group of applicant. To request birth certificate or baptismal record before hiring. To ask _date_ of high school graduation.
Birthplace/ national origin		To ask birthplace of applicant or that of his or her parents, grand-parents, or spouse. Any other inquiry into national origin.
Race/color	If ability to speak a specific foreign language is a BFOQ, to ask if applicant is fluent in _that_ language. To indicate that the institution is an equal opportunity employer. To ask race for affirmative action plan statistics, _only after hiring._	To ask about "native tongue" or foreign language. Any inquiry that would indicate race or color. To require photograph.

(_Continued_)

Area of inquiry	Lawful	Unlawful
Sex	Indicate that the organization is an equal opportunity employer.	To ask applicant anything that would indicate sex (unless job related), childbearing issues, family responsibilities, or maiden name.
Marital/ parental status	To ask status (married or single) _only after hiring_ for insurance purposes. Number and ages of dependents and/or spouse _only after hiring_ for insurance purposes.	To ask marital status _before_ hiring. To ask the number and age of children, who cares for them, and if applicant plans to have more children.
Religion/creed		To ask an applicant's religion or religious customs and holidays. Request recommendations from church officials. Any inquiry about willingness to work on Sabbath or any particular religious holiday.
Citizenship	To ask whether a U.S. citizen. If not, whether the applicant intends to become one. If U.S. residence is legal. If spouse is a citizen. Require proof of citizenship _only after hiring_.	To ask if native-born or naturalized. Proof of citizenship before hiring. Whether spouse or parents are native-born or naturalized. Date of citizenship.
Relatives	To ask name, relationship, and address of person to be notified in case of emergency, _only after hiring_.	To ask for names of relatives working for the employer. Identity of nearest relative.

Area of inquiry	Lawful	Unlawful
Military service	To inquire into service in the U.S. armed forces. Rank attained. Branch of service. Any job-related experience. Require military discharge certificate _only_ after _hiring._	To ask type of discharge. To request military service records. To ask about military service in armed service of any country but the United States.
Education	To ask what academic, professional, or vocational schools attended. To ask about language skills, such as reading and writing foreign languages.	Specifically to ask the nationality, racial, or religious affiliation of schools attended. To ask how foreign language ability was acquired.
Criminal record	To request listing of convictions and other misdemeanors.	To inquire about arrests.
References	To request general and work references not relating to race, color, religion, sex, national origin, or ancestry.	To request references specifically from clergy or any other people who might reflect race, color, religion, sex, national origin, or ancestry.
Organizations	To ask organizational membership (professional, social, etc.) so long as affiliation is not used to discriminate on the basis of race, sex, national origin, or ancestry. Offices held, if any.	To request listing of _all_ clubs applicant belongs to or has belonged to.
Photographs	May be required _after hiring_ for identification purposes.	To request photographs before hiring. To take pictures of the applicant during the interview.

(Continued)

Area of inquiry	Lawful	Unlawful
Work schedule	To ask willingness to work a required work schedule. To ask if applicant has military reservist obligations.	To ask willingness to work on any particular religious holiday.
Disability	To inquire for the purpose of determining applicant's capability to perform the job. (Burden of proof for nondiscrimination lies with the employer.)	To exclude disabled applicants as a class on the basis of their type of disability. To inquire whether applicant has or can qualify for a driver's license, where driving is not a BFOQ.

On the Basis of Gender

- Do you have appropriate child care arrangements?
- What does your spouse do for a living? Is your spouse likely to be transferred out of state?
- Are you planning a family? What are your family obligations?
- Will your family commitments keep you from traveling on business?

On the Basis of National Origin

- What is your native language?
- What are your parents' names?
- Where were you born? Where were your parents born?
- Have you lived in a foreign country?

On the Basis of Religion

- What church or synagogue do you attend?
- Are you religious? When do you attend Sabbath services?
- Do you think your religion will conflict with your work schedule? Will you object on religious grounds to working or training on Sunday?

On the Basis of Age

- How old are you? Are you over 40?
- When (or in what year) did you graduate from high school?
- Do you have retirement plans? When will you retire?
- How are your reflexes?
- Do you think you have a sufficient energy level to travel extensively?

How to Avoid Discriminating Against Disabled Participants

Training directors, curriculum designers, and presenters must be especially mindful of the Americans With Disabilities Act. The ADA protects a broad group of trainees who are qualified by education, skills, and experience because they "can perform the essential functions of the job, with or without reasonable accommodation."

To comply with the ADA, you may not refuse to train, promote, evaluate, or otherwise provide employment benefits to a job applicant or employee who has a "covered disability." Covered disabilities may be physical challenges, cognitive impairments, emotional disorders, or a combination of these conditions.

The ADA defines disability broadly to include chronic illnesses, disfigurements (e.g., severe burns), certain emotional conditions (e.g., history of depression), and past drug or alcohol dependencies as well as sight, hearing, and physical impairments. AIDS-infected and HIV-positive individuals are also included.

The ADA defines disability in three separate ways:

1. A person who has a physical or mental impairment that substantially limits one or more of the person's major life activities; or

2. A person who has a record of such impairment; or

3. A person who is regarded as having such an impairment.

To be protected under the laws, a person must be both disabled and "otherwise qualified" to do the job. The candidate is "otherwise qualified" if he or she is able to meet all the essential requirements of the job with or without reasonable accommodation.

What Is a Covered Disability?

The applicable statutes treat disability broadly to include a physical or mental impairment that substantially limits one or more of the individual's major life activities. Physical impairments may involve the ability to sit, stand, walk, talk, see, hear, move, manipulate with hands or feet, and/or work. The condition must be permanent and not transitory (broken limbs or temporary back injuries are not covered as disabilities under the ADA, but if they are work-related, workers' compensation still applies). Mental or cognitive impairments may involve the ability to learn, reason, or analyze. They include learning disabilities such as dyslexia and attention deficit disorder, mild retardation, Alzheimer's disease, and related syndromes.

The ADA also covers psychiatric disabilities, including clinically diagnosed depression, bipolar disorder, phobias, and dementia. The EEOC issued its newest guidance on discrimination and reasonable accommodations for psychiatric and mental disorders in April 1997.

The second part of the definition includes a record of such impairment, such as posttreatment for cancer, kidney disease, HIV- or AIDS-related syndromes, and other chronic illnesses. It also includes treatment (through a certified rehabilitation program) for drug and/or alcohol dependencies.

The third part of the definition, being regarded as having the impairment, includes conditions that are not *in fact* disabling (because they do not actually impair a major life function) but that the employer or supervisor may *erroneously perceive* to be disabling. Included are medically controlled hypertension, heart disease, diabetes, or epilepsy as well as burns or other disfigurements that affect physical appearance. "Front office appearance" requirements will be carefully scrutinized.

Who Is a Qualified Individual?

The key question in a discrimination case is whether the individual is qualified by education, skills, or experience to perform the job, engage in the training, or participate in the advancement/skill-building opportunity. A *qualified individual* is someone who, with or without reasonable accommodation, can perform the essential functions of the job that he or she either currently holds or desires. This definition requires an assessment of whether a person, though disabled, nevertheless can be accommodated under the ADA.

Essential functions refer to the fundamental duties of the employment position that a person holds or desires. Marginal functions of the position are not included. A job function may be considered essential if the job cannot exist without it, if a limited number of employees are available for distribution of the tasks, or if the function is highly specialized and the incumbent in the position was hired specifically for his or her expertise.

In addition, to be considered a qualified person with a disability, a candidate must not pose a direct threat to his or her own health or safety or to the health or safety of others when performing the essential functions of the job. "Direct threat" means a significant risk of substantial and imminent harm that cannot be eliminated or reduced to an acceptable level by reasonable accommodation. A threat that is remote or theoretical is not sufficient to conclude that a candidate is not a qualified person with a disability. The assessment of whether a person poses a direct threat must be made on a case-by-case basis, considering the duration of the risk, the nature and severity of the potential harm, the likelihood that the potential harm will occur, and the imminence of the potential harm.

How Can You Discriminate Without Realizing It?

As a trainer, you may not limit, segregate, or classify a candidate for your training in a way that adversely affects the individual's opportunity to participate. For example, if a disabled person wants to register for your training and meets all the selection criteria except one, which the candidate is unable to meet because of the disability, that criterion must concern an essential aspect to participation in the training in order to be considered nondiscriminatory.

For more detailed discussions of the ADA and steps you must take to reasonably accommodate disabled trainees, see Chapter 7, pp. 167–171 (testing), Chapter 8, pp. 192–195 (physically challenging training, such as adventure programs), and Chapter 14, pp. 298–305 (accommodations by speakers for participants with special needs).

Handling Harassment in the Training Room

High-profile cases have focused national attention on the subject of sexual harassment in the workplace. Sexual harassment is prohibited both by Title VII of the Civil Rights Act of 1964 and by many state statutes. Unfortunately, the training facility is not immune to claims of sexual harassment.

The most easily recognized form of sexual harassment is a quid pro quo ("this for that") situation in which a power holder threatens job detriment unless the victim submits to demands for sexual favors. Most instances of this "conditional harassment" have their roots in the use and abuse of power. Managers, supervisors, and even trainers have power over those who receive opportunities for training and advancement, hiring, promotion, performance appraisal, and post-training testing.

In many industries, the 1980s and 1990s brought unprecedented opportunities for advancement for women. It also brought the power relationship to female supervisors, who control the livelihood and job benefits of both men and women. Just as some men abuse their power over females in demeaning and sexually explicit ways, some women do the very same thing over men. When this occurs, quid pro quo sexual harassment claims follow. Male employees or trainees confronted with unwanted sexual attention don't like it any more than do female employees. The conduct is equally sanctionable under Title VII.

In the training context, quid pro quo involves the threat to deny training opportunities that are conditioned on exchange of sexual favors. It is the proverbial "Sleep with me or I won't offer you training, provide safe training, or pass you successfully through training." Quid pro quo training cases are relatively rare. Typically, individual trainers have neither the regular contact with trainees nor the power to make the credible threats usually found in conditional harassment cases. Unfortunately, such cases do occur.

The work environments most ripe for quid pro quo training cases are law enforcement and the military. The lengthy training process, the constant and close proximity of instructors to trainees, and the extensive authority (power) provided to trainers in these settings create the potential for unwelcome sexual advances that threaten a job opportunity.

In *Henson v. City of Dundee*,[13] a female police dispatcher alleged quid pro quo harassment, basing her claim on the denial of an opportunity to attend the police academy because she rejected her supervisor's demands for sexual favors. After the rejection, she was subjected to a series of incidents that interfered with her ability to do her job and succeed in the training. The court ruled that the claim was actionable, because the dispatcher's training opportunities were conditioned on demands for sexual favors.

Trading test scores or training evaluations for sexual intimacies is also uncommon, but not unheard of. Most of these claims are against faculty members who demand sex for grades. Although Title IX of the Civil Rights Act prohibits such behavior, it has rarely been applied in the workplace. Exceptions occur when the workplace and the training academy are virtually synonymous, as in military training facilities. In this context, failure to pass training that is based on conditional harassment, if it results in removal from the workplace, is unlawful under Title VII.

The highest-profile quid pro quo training cases in recent years have involved trainers at the U.S. Army's Aberdeen Proving Grounds. By last count, when this book went to press, the Army was investigating over 1074 allegations of sexual harassment, including rape, forced and unwelcome sexual encounters with drill instructors, threatening conduct, and an extremely hostile training environment. Much of the media attention has focused on the fact that these trainers had absolute authority over their subordinates. The instructors were in a position to abuse their power, and breach the trust placed in them by trainees.

Hostile Work or Training Environment

Claims of unwelcome behaviors of a sexual nature during training are much more common than claims of conditional harassment. Unfortunately, they seem to be increasing. Sexual harassment in the content or delivery of training typically falls into the same patterns as general workplace harassment: verbal, physical, and visual behaviors of a sexual nature that create a hostile, offensive, or intimidating training environment.

Actionable hostile environment sexual harassment occurs when an employee is forced to work or be trained in a setting that is offensive, intimidating, or hostile because of sexually explicit or demeaning behavior: not necessarily outright sexual advances; not necessarily by a supervisor or someone in a "power" position over the victim; not necessarily threatening any job-related benefit; not always socially unacceptable verbal behavior (in contrast to racial, ethnic, or religious jokes).

To establish a hostile environment sexual harassment claim, a trainee must provide evidence of *conduct or behavior* (physical, verbal, visual, or a combination), that is *of a sexual nature* and is *unwelcome* by anyone who does not want to see, hear, or feel the conduct. The conduct must create *for that person* (the victim) an *offensive, intimidating, or hostile work or training environment*.

Examples of hostile training environments are programs that contain sexually explicit graphics, words, or gestures, including innuendo; use of off-color or sexually demeaning, explicit, or graphic words, jokes, or other verbal/nonverbal communications, including body language of the instructor or other trainees; physical touching of a sexual nature by an instructor; and distribution or display of sexually explicit cartoons, pictures, or graphics in handouts or other program materials.

Physical Harassment During Training

Physical harassment involves unwanted touching, pinching, patting, rubbing, and other sexually suggestive behavior. In some cases, there is no actual physical contact; rather, the harasser uses intimidating or offensive gestures or other sexually suggestive body language. The latter cases are often called "leering." Many arise in the context of training programs, particularly those involving coaching, close contact, and demonstrations of physical activities.

The training facility is an integral part of the work environment. Even when the training is not mandatory, employees who are part of a team are not truly free to exclude themselves from a training situation when they find the environment hostile, offensive, or intimidating.

Each trainee has an individual threshold of tolerance or comfort with physical or verbal behaviors that may be sexual in nature. In a later discrimination action, the trainee's reaction will be evaluated according to whether the behavior was objectively sexual and whether a reasonable person with similar life experiences would find the behavior offensive, intimidating, hostile, or abusive. All trainees should be encouraged to advise you or other facilitators if they have a concern about any aspect of the program. Assure them that their concerns will be addressed as confidentially as possible.

One case involving aspects of physical sexual harassment received significant media attention. In *Hartman v. Pena*,[14] the Federal Aviation Administration retained an external organization to design and deliver a series of diversity/sexual harassment workshops. Each set of trainees attended three complete days of training. A controversial exercise required male participants to walk down a "gauntlet" of female colleagues, during which the men were pinched, patted, and groped.

In a later complaint by 11 male controllers, the Chicago court found that "the cultural diversity workshop (CDW) was not a singular occurrence. It was a mandatory three-day program which employees not only had to attend, but also in which they had to actively take part at a place distant from the home office. The conduct complained of was more than an offensive utterance, or an isolated occurrence."[15]

This result is consistent with other cases throughout the country holding that a single incident of unwelcome and offensive touching will generally be sufficient to establish a claim for a hostile work environment. The training methods in *Hartman* are discussed in detail in Chapter 5, pp. 114–115.

Verbal Harassment During Program Delivery

Verbal harassment cases are common, even during training. They are based on words alone, often without any direct physical contact or suggestive body language. Most cases involve direct targeted words— "You have great [fill in the blank]," or "You would look terrific in a [fill in the blank]"—or graphic discussion about the harasser's own sexual prowess, fantasies, or activities. Just one overtly sexual statement when targeted to a particular individual is usually enough to satisfy the requirement of a hostile environment—if it is unwanted (the victim does not want to hear it), "of a sexual nature," and offensive, intimidating, or hostile *for that individual.*

Another type of verbal harassment involves off-color language and jokes that may or may not be targeted to a particular individual. If someone finds the content unwanted, sexually oriented, and offensive, a hostile working environment can occur if that person must hear the words while working at a desk, eating in the lunchroom, using the supply or xerox room, or taking breaks in a common area reserved for all employees. Once again, the employer must maintain a harassment-free work environment for all the terms and conditions of employment.

Don't assume verbal harassment claims can't happen to you. Examples from training are plentiful. One case, *Trent v. Valley Electric Association, Inc.,*[16] involved both sexual harassment and retaliation claims. The employee, a meter reader for a rural public utility company, was required to attend a safety program conducted by a contract trainer. She was the only female present at the lecture. She protested that the presenter used "foul language" and made a series of sexually offensive references, including a description of the sexual experiences of linemen at a Nevada brothel. While complaining to management, she told the general manager that she was not "one of the boys"—to which he retorted that "for some purposes" she was. Although the general manager did complain in writing to the contract trainer's organization, he also fired the complaining employee. The court of appeal allowed her to proceed with a retaliation and discrimination claim.

What about the "harmless" joke or icebreaker? If the trainer doesn't intend to offend or harass, how can a claim of discrimination be made? Actionable hostile-environment harassment occurs when an employee is forced to work or participate in an environment that is offensive, intimidating, or hostile because of sexually explicit or demeaning behavior. (This issue is also significant for speakers and presenters, and is addressed in that context in Chapter 13, pp. 280–285.)

Significantly, hostile environment sexual harassment is not necessarily *intended to discriminate or harm*. In fact, many people accused of harassment actually believe their behavior is "funny," "cute," or "attractive." What they think, believe, or intend is irrelevant. What matters is the reasonable perception of the victim who finds the conduct offensive, intimidating, or hostile and "of a sexual nature." Not surprisingly, many of the cases focus on the reasonable perception issue.

All of us have a different threshold of tolerance for behavior of a sexual nature, because we have unique life experiences. The court or the agency will adopt a very broad standard to determine whether it was reasonable for the victim with an individual set of life experiences to have found the conduct sexual and offensive, intimidating, hostile, or abusive.

Visual Harassment in the Training Room

Visual or graphic harassment is also a source of employee complaints and employer liabilities. The most common offenders are pinups, posters, placards, posted cartoons, and coffee mugs with sexually suggestive slogans or pictures. Displays of written or taped materials are actionable, particularly when the employer refuses to take immediate and appropriate corrective steps after a formal or informal complaint has been filed.

In *Stacks v. Southwestern Bell Yellow Pages,*[17] for example, the court found sexual discrimination and a hostile training environment. The finding was based on a supervisor's comment that "women in sales are the worst thing that has happened to this company," and on evidence that he permitted the showing of sexual videotapes and strippers at sales meetings and training sessions. The defendant argued that the incidents at these mandatory training sessions were "isolated," but the court disagreed and sent the case to a jury to consider appropriate relief for the employee.

Technology has created even more creative forms of sexual harassment: faxes, e-mail messages, and multimedia displays. The standards are the same: If the content is "of a sexual nature," is unwanted or unwelcome, and creates a hostile, offensive, or intimidating work environment, the material must be removed. This is true even if the visual material is serious art rather than sexual cartoons, although cases involving complaints about art are very rare.

Your Legal Responsibilities to Prevent Sexual Harassment

Your training facility is a work environment and you are in charge. In this capacity your own inappropriate conduct, or failure to stop offensive behavior by others, can spell legal trouble for you and your employer. When the program is mandatory, a trainee is not free to leave the room to avoid offensive, intimidating, or hostile conduct by instructors or by other class members. Even when a program is not absolutely mandatory, if skills or knowledge received in the training are necessary for job performance or advancement opportunities, the trainee is not required to remove himself or herself from the training to avoid unwelcome behaviors of a sexual nature. Thus, anything that occurs during training (or during a multipart program) is sufficient to constitute workplace harassment if the trainee establishes all the elements of a claim.

It is prudent not to take this issue lightly or to assume it is "political correctness run amok." Your actions as the facilitator (both in conducting yourself and in condoning the behavior of others) can get your employer into an expensive lawsuit quickly. If that isn't enough incentive, consider the fact that if your *personal conduct* is harassing, you are subject to individual liability.

Individual instructors who engage in acts of sexual harassment—whether verbal, physical, or visual—are individually responsible for their own conduct. You do *not* have to be a supervisor or manager for your actions to create a hostile, offensive, or intimidating training environment. As the instructor, you are at least an "authority figure" in the eyes of the trainees, a position that gives you the power to intimidate. Implied threats by body language, words, or gestures—even seemingly "in jest"—can, and do, result in hostile environment claims. Remember that when you are in charge of a classroom or training exercise, you are "the boss." Behave accordingly, and you will avoid potential miscues of a sexual nature.

To handle harassment in the training facility effectively, you should take two steps in order to deal with two main sources of concern:

1. Take every complaint—formal or informal—seriously and have the employer conduct a proper investigation.

The primary objective should be simply to *stop the offending behavior.* The courts and administrative agencies should be reserved for situations where the employer cannot—or will not—abide by federal and state law to stop gender discrimination in the workplace.

2. Avoid any form of retaliation against the complaining employee or witnesses. Retaliation may be direct—such as demotions, differential assignments, or other adverse actions that are not objectively job-related—or indirect, such as ostracism, ridicule, or even threats against employees who continue to complain.

Retaliation is an independent form of discrimination under federal and many state laws and is typically handled harshly by the courts and the administrative agencies. The reason is obvious: If any employee or trainee fears retribution, penalties, or intimidation for coming forward to get the harassment stopped, he or she will never do so and your best efforts to enforce a sound policy will be doomed. The remedy is hollow if only lip service is paid to equal enforcement of the laws against every person (including senior management, if applicable) who creates a sexually hostile environment for other employees.

How to Be an Affirmative Action Trainer

Affirmative action as a remedial policy to assist employers in providing equal employment opportunities has emerged as a primary issue in American politics. The definition of affirmative action, particularly in connection with hiring, promotion, and training/mentor programs, has become a moving target. Endless confusion has arisen about what distinguishes affirmative action from equal employment opportunities (EEO), as the two concepts were initially conceived in the Civil Rights Act of 1964 and later applied in public and private sector workplaces.

Adding to the confusion, the increasingly diverse workforce has spurred employers to adopt diversity initiatives, which seek alternately to appreciate the gender, racial, and other differences among employees and to manage those differences for maximum productivity. Diversity initiatives are proactive, while affirmative action is remedial. Diversity initiatives are never mandated by law; most affirmative action programs are established for compliance purposes. Despite these differences, diversity programs have often been labeled "affirmative action in disguise." This blurring of distinct concepts has added to both misunderstanding and mistrust.

In essence, both affirmative action and equal employment opportunities require that every *qualified* individual be given an opportunity to be "in the competition," and equal employment opportunities further require that the playing field be truly level at all stages of employment. In fact, it is well established in federal law that the playing field is uneven when "neutral" qualification standards exclude large segments of minority or female applicants—*not* because they cannot do the job, but because the qualification standards are inherently discriminatory. This violates EEO laws.

As the debate rages, it is critically important that trainers be informed about the issues in a clear, concise, and practical framework. It is even more essential that managers—particularly those charged with the responsibility of making legally defensible employment decisions—understand the present legal standards and be able to apply them consistently to all applicants seeking jobs and employees working for promotion.

Title VII contains a specific provision prohibiting employers from discriminating in their apprenticeship and training programs. Training programs can be a powerful tool in the affirmative action process. As a result, some employers have provided more openings in training programs to members of protected groups. Because federal government contractors have specific obligations to meet affirmative action goals under the Rehabilitation Act of 1973, remedial training programs aimed at upgrading female and disabled workers may be defensible. In fact, both the courts and employers have frequently fashioned remedial training programs for affirmative action purposes.

Affirmative action requirements are imposed only on government employers and contractors that perform services or sell products to the government in excess of $50,000. These requirements are designed to remedy the effects of past discrimination in many workplaces. Other employers are required to adopt affirmative action programs only if they are ordered to do so by a court, upon a finding of particularized discrimination in their workplace in the past.

The scope of affirmative action regulations, and the role of the Office of Federal Contract Compliance Programs (OFCCP) in auditing compliance with affirmative action goals and timetables is under review at the federal level. Similarly, many states are assessing their requirements for affirmative action and related programs for employers that do business with government agencies. Including effective training, mentoring, and coaching opportunities for underrepresented employees—in applicant and promotional pools—will remain a requirement of affirmative action compliance; however, the extent of liabilities for failure to establish goals or meet timetables will continue to be refined by the legislative and judicial actions in the next decade.

Affirmative action involves more than simply ceasing discriminatory practices. An affirmative action trainer *reaches out* and takes ongoing steps to widen the pool of qualified candidates for available training opportunities. These outreach efforts include expanded recruitment activities at colleges, trade schools, and other resource organizations to cast a wide net for qualified trainees.

Effectively applying affirmative action goals rests on understanding the concept of merit. Public officials and commentators at every point along the political spectrum urge that employment decisions be based on qualifications, without reference to skin color, ethnicity, or gender. The concept of opportunity based purely on merit enjoys wide intellectual and emotional support. If applied uniformly, the concept should prevent discrimination against every individual, whether he or she falls within the "majority" or the "minority" in a particular setting.

The federal courts have largely agreed. The key to complying with EEO laws is to make nondiscriminatory decisions by hiring or promoting only individuals who are qualified for the job. Affirmative action requires only affirmative steps to reach out, locate, and attract those *qualified* individuals who are members of previously underrepresented groups. Yet the courts are still filled with discrimination cases— over 110,000 in fiscal year 1996—many focusing on claims of discrimination arising from this central premise: *What does it mean to be "qualified" for a particular opportunity?* The excluded applicant claims to meet the required qualifications; the employer asserts that the applicant does not. The reality is seldom clear-cut, because "qualified" is rarely precisely measurable.

Your most concrete solutions rest with establishing objective, job-related qualification criteria that can be uniformly applied. Objective qualifications include education, experience (both on the job and in the workplace in general), job-specific training (skill- or safety-based), "hard" skills necessary for mechanical or intellectual tasks, and job-related knowledge.

However, the problem of determining whether unqualified people are being "favored" by affirmative action is compounded in most workplaces, where qualifications for the vast majority of jobs cannot be precisely measured by a numerically scored test. Even when civil service examinations rank candidates by test score, the handful of top performers are put through a personal interview process that results in some unavoidable subjective evaluation.

In the selection process, a myriad of "soft" skills determine whether an individual is "qualified" for a particular training opportunity. These include judgment, integrity, initiative, leadership, interpersonal attributes, and communication skills. These traits are much more difficult to "test" for, and frequently require subjective evaluation by the decision maker.

Even "communication skills" fall prey to subjective variables. Will the trainee need the ability to understand and be understood in the English language? Will the candidate need verbal or written skills, or both? Alternatively, does communication ability mean the expertise to communicate across cultural lines, such as American managers doing business in a global environment? Will the ability to "communicate" with management and coworkers in a corporate structure be important to the ultimate success of the candidate for a training program? In this context, who is "qualified" and who is not is a fuzzy proposition at best.

The U.S. Supreme Court ruled on this issue in 1996 in *Aderand v. Pena*. Now, all government affirmative action programs are subject to "strict scrutiny" to ensure that they do not, in fact, discriminate in their application.[18] This means that the plan must be motivated by a compelling government interest, such as remedying past discrimination by that government entity, and it must be very narrowly tailored to serve its intended purpose. Achieving a "balanced" workforce is not sufficient, under the constitutional mandates applicable to governments as employers. This typically means that government entities must always consider every race- or gender-neutral solution prior to taking conscious steps that include race or gender as a factor in the decision. Failure to do so may subject the plan to challenge and the employer to costly litigation.

In the private sector, employers that do not sell to the government may adopt voluntary affirmative action goals, but their affirmative action programs are subject to significant legal scrutiny to ensure that they do not, in fact, result in discrimination. Although private industry employers may set affirmative action goals to correct imbalances, their affirmative action programs cannot lawfully operate to exclude deserving employees from opportunities for which they are qualified.

How to Bias-Proof Your Training: A Step-by-Step Guide

Use Objective Qualification Standards for Trainee Selection

All training programs should have objective standards for measuring applicants' qualifications. The standards should reflect those skills, experience, aptitudes, abilities, and attitudes that are reasonable predictors of success on the job or in the training program. The more objectively measurable the standards are, the more difficult it will be for inappropriate factors—gender, age, disability, ethnicity—to invade the decision process.

Avoid Inappropriate Remarks
During Training and Evaluation

Actionable discrimination occurs when trainees are either excluded or bumped from training on the basis of discriminatory motives rather than objective job performance. Frequently, the indicia used to establish "motive" fall short of direct evidence of biased intent. Instead, circumstantial evidence is used, showing other remarks or conduct that implies a discriminatory motive. The jury is then asked to "infer" a biased intent from the facts presented.

In essence, a trainer can discriminate illegally without realizing it by using racial, sexual, religious, or other inappropriate expressions, even in a joking manner. Unquestionably, inappropriate verbal remarks come back to haunt a later decision. For example, when a participant fails to pass the training and the trainer is not able to establish objective, consistently applied performance standards used to evaluate and then drop the nonperformer, extraneous verbal remarks loom large before the trier of fact, which is usually a jury.

Sexual and racial remarks made about trainees may become evidence in a subsequent bias suit, if the trainee is excluded from participation or dropped from the program. Unfortunately, even when the remarks are not directly tied to the adverse decision, they are admissible to establish that the stated reasons for the firing were in fact a pretext for discrimination. A significant case involving a police recruit underscores this type of challenge. The trainee joined the Aurora (Illinois) Police Department and began a 10-week training program at the police academy. Once academy training is completed, recruits serve as probationary patrol officers until they successfully complete an officer training program. Recruits generally earn a first release from officer training after three months and a final release after the fourth month, although it is not unusual to spend longer in the program. If a recruit fails to earn a first and final release, his or her employment is terminated.

The female recruit at Aurora failed to earn her first release within four months. Her field training officers wrote daily performance reports, claiming that she was lacking in three specific areas. After six months without earning her first release she was terminated. The recruit then sued for racial and sexual discrimination, arguing that she was subjected to disparate treatment.

The court found discrimination because the woman was the only recruit who did not pass, and also was the only female, black recruit. The court noted that "because Brown performed well enough to earn her first and second releases, but did not, while other recruits did, she was singled out."[19]

The crux of the case was evidence of derogatory sexual and racial remarks by the field training officers (FTOs), directed at the trainee, and openly repeated throughout the training course. The recruit used these statements to claim that the city lied when it claimed she was terminated for poor performance—that in fact the reason was racial animus or sexual bias.

Among the most egregious remarks were FTOs referring to her as "missy-missy," ridiculing her for "feminine" shoelaces, commenting on her ponytail, remarking on her petite size, and telling her she "should be at home taking care of her daughter." One FTO commented that she would probably make sergeant before he did, because she was black and female.

A trainer's inappropriate remarks may be actionable even when they do not relate directly to the trainee's performance or status in the training program. According to the opinion of the appellate judge of the U.S. district court, this particular FTO strayed over the line of legal propriety by making a reference to a newspaper headline about integration in a particular neighborhood, and then telling the trainee that he was "glad that he no longer lived there and felt sorry for his friends who still lived there." The recruit alleged that another training officer told her that "all black kids come from broken homes," while another persistently made reference to "you people." These remarks—individually and collectively—supplied sufficient evidence for the appellate judge to conclude that the bias claim had enough potential to be sent to a jury for factual findings.

Each case will be analyzed on its own facts, focusing on the type and frequency of the remark, its context, the period of time between the remark and the adverse employment action, and whether the remark was made by the trainers, as decision makers. In this case, the *trainers* (FTOs) were the ultimate decision makers; each had significant input into whether the recruit would pass. Because one of the trainers used derogatory language almost daily and the remarks were "essentially made contemporaneously with the FTO's evaluation," the court found they could be appropriately viewed as evidence of animus toward working women or black women.

It is significant that the trainee did *not* allege workplace harassment in the form of a hostile, offensive, or intimidating work environment. Had she done so, she would have been required to prove only that verbal remarks of a sexual or racial nature created a hostile, offensive, or intimidating work environment. In that case, the issue would have been whether the words themselves were actionable discrimination.

In a similar case, a training supervisor's remarks to two women before they were fired convinced a federal appeals court to allow their case against State Farm Insurance Company to go to a trial by jury. Both women were fired nine months into a two-year training program for new agents, while a male trainee was retained. The reasons given for the terminations were "poor production," although the evidence reflected that the male's performance was not significantly better.

A major factor in the decision was the troublesome commentary of the training supervisor, who told one woman that she lacked motivation to be a successful agent because her husband made too much money and the company should not spend resources to train her merely to earn "pocket change." The same supervisor told the second woman that she might have marital problems when she started earning more than her spouse. The Utah justices concluded that it was up to the jury to determine whether these "stereotyped views" entered into the termination decision.[20]

Although most troublesome verbal comments in discrimination lawsuits involve race, religion, gender, and sexual orientation, such evidence has also been used successfully in age discrimination cases. Offhand remarks, sometimes made years before an adverse decision, may become part of the mix of evidence weighed by the jury in deciding whether a discriminatory motive exists. Frequently, the evidence is actually memorialized in writing.

The message from all these cases should be crystal clear:

- Avoid inappropriate commentary, "jokes," verbal expressions, or written opinions about race, gender, sexual orientation, age, disability, ethnicity, or religion. Such remarks, even when extraneous to any specific employment decision, can be used to establish biased motives in subsequent lawsuits. Assume that your words, like your deeds, may come back to bite you.

- Always have objective performance standards for successful completion of the training, and strive to apply those standards consistently to all trainees. (See the extensive discussion in Chapter 7.)

- Never evaluate performance on the basis of issues, opinions, attitudes, or beliefs not related to work.

- Always document a trainee's performance against the objective standards, and be prepared to justify an adverse decision as directly job-related.

Avoid Inappropriate Content

Written materials, methods, and presentation should also be free from sexually explicit, racially offensive, or otherwise discriminatory content.

Inappropriate content includes overtly sexual graphics or language (see Chapter 13, pp. 280–285), methods that infringe on religious freedoms (see Chapter 9, pp. 206–212), or other harassing methods (see Chapter 5, pp. 114–116).

References

1. Associated Press, April 10, 1997; and *BNA Discrimination Reporter,* May 1997.

2. Associated Press, April 9, 1997.

3. *BNA Discrimination Reporter,* May 1997.

4. *Richard v. Bell Atlantic Corp.,* 946 F.Supp. 54 (September 19, 1996).

5. *Wilmore v. City of Wilmington,* 699 F.2d 66 (1982).

6. *Carrero v. New York Housing Authority,* 890 F.2d 569 (2d Cir. 1989).

7. *O'Connor v. Consolidated Coin Caterers Corp.,* No. 95-354 (U.S.Sup.Ct. 1996).

8. *Coates v. National Cash Register Co.,* 433 F.Supp. 655 (1977).

9. *Kirk v. Browner,* Federal District Court, D.C., No. C93-584a (July 26, 1994).

10. FEHC Regulations, §7295.6(a), promulgated pursuant to California Government Code, §§12920, 12941-42.

11. *Capaci v. Katz & Besthoff, Inc.,* 711 F.2d 647, 660 (1983).

12. EEOC statistics.

13. *Henson v. City of Dundee,* 682 F.2d 911 (1982).

14. *Hartman v. Pena,* 914 F.Supp. 225 (1995).

15. *Hartman v. Pena,* 914 F.Supp. 225 (1995).

16. *Trent v. Valley Electric Association, Inc.,* 41 F.3d 524 (9th Cir. 1994).

17. *Stacks v. Southwestern Bell Yellow Pages* 27 F.3d 1316 (8th Cir. 1994).

18. *Aderand v. Pena,* U.S. Supreme Court (1996).

19. *Brown v. Aurora Police Department,* Federal District Court, N.Ill., No. 95 C2373 (September 30, 1996).

20. *Tomsic v. State Farm Mutual Ins. Co.,* U.S. Court of Appeals, 10th Cir., No. 95-4002, 85 F.3d 1472 (February 1997).

7

After the Training

Staying Legal With Performance Evaluation and Testing

How to Stay Out of Trouble When Evaluating Trainee Performance

Trainers are frequently required to evaluate trainees at the end of a class to determine whether they learned the content, can apply that information to job tasks, or can perform the necessary skills to succeed on the job. Some evaluation methods are objective, such as scored tests. Other appraisal tools are inherently subjective, requiring the trainer to assess trainees' capabilities through observations and other subjective criteria.

Evaluation and testing serve the necessary function of weeding out those who don't demonstrate an ability to perform on the job. Thus, a participant who is improperly excluded from a job assignment or advancement opportunity, on the basis of your evaluation of her performance, may lose tangible employment opportunities. Unfortunately, subjectivity breeds complaints for discrimination.

It is both practical and legally defensible to appraise trainee performance with reference to a set of standards that mirror the training objectives. You should develop specific, measurable learning outcomes or performance expectations for all participants in your training courses. Indeed, comprehensive performance criteria are an essential factor in avoiding discriminatory performance reviews. When you evaluate performance, you should understand and be able to articulate the essential learning outcomes, and the standards by which you will evaluate performance. This process accomplishes several important functions:

- It creates an objective set of measurable standards that can be quantified.

- It forces you to focus precisely on the knowledge, education, skills, or experience required to perform satisfactorily following training.

- It requires you to accurately assess the specific physical and/or mental functions of the job—in objective rather than subjective terms.

- It promotes consistency in standards for all participants.

- It promotes consistency in comparing a trainee's performance with acceptable performance criteria, because every trainee is judged against the same objective criteria.

- It increases the likelihood of placing or keeping an individual who can competently perform the requirements of the job following training.

- It facilitates good documentation of the essential learning objectives and the skills and/or knowledge required.

Setting Objective Performance Standards

Standards-based appraisals are an especially effective way to support and document your decision to hold an employee back, refuse to permit an employee to work without direct supervision, or promote one employee over another. First, every training program should have measurable performance standards. These standards should mirror what you expect of a trainee who completes your workshop.

Standards should apply to specific, significant tasks. If the trainee's expected skill or knowledge is expressed in vague, general language, it will be difficult—perhaps impossible—to write clear, meaningful standards for evaluation. Whenever possible, tasks should be expressed in concrete terms that describe definite actions that the trainee takes, and should reflect a fully acceptable or a satisfactory level of performance. Standards should be attainable and should reflect what is expected of a fully trained and competent employee. Standards must be high enough for the work unit to accomplish its objectives and should be reasonably achievable.

To be most effective, your standards should be expressed precisely. The more precise you are, the easier it will be to evaluate performance and give trainees guidance on your expectations. Vague or general words or phrases, such as *reasonable, seldom,* and *rapidly,* should be replaced with more precise terms whenever possible.

Specific Training Performance Appraisal Considerations

The performance appraisal process should be structured to ensure consistent application and to avoid unfounded charges of discrimination. As a trainer or evaluator, you can take several concrete steps to ensure consistency, objectivity, accuracy, and fairness throughout the training appraisal process.

1. *Perform candid appraisals.* It is always difficult to deliver bad news or to criticize likable people whose performance is unacceptable. To avoid discomfort, managers, supervisors, and even trainers turn to euphemisms, such as "The chemistry just isn't right," or "You're just not suited for this type of work," or "You really would be happier doing something different." When the precise bases for establishing inadequate performance are not documented, the unhappy employee asserts that the reason given for discharge, demotion, or discipline was a "pretext" for discrimination. Often the jury agrees.

- Do not avoid poor performance ratings out of fear of discrimination charges. Instead, address performance issues consistently for all employees on a timely basis.
- Be accurate and objective in your performance ratings. Rate good performance as well as poor performance. Rate performance for *all* participants, including those who excel. Doing so establishes your comprehensive documentation procedures.
- Address performance problems immediately—even during training, when necessary. Failure to identify poor performance early on allows the problem to continue. An employee who is not made aware of a performance deficiency cannot correct it.
- Keep complete and accurate records of your evaluations, and the specific bases for them—measured against concrete tasks and objectives. Failure to document poor performance can create a liability for the employer in legal claims of discrimination or wrongful discharge.

2. *Maintain objectivity at all times.* Focus performance evaluations on objective job-related criteria. Examples of objective criteria that have been upheld by the courts include quantity of work, quality of work, and completion of job-specific performance objectives.

3. *Communicate expectations early and often.* Regularly communicate standards or expectations to employees, and clearly identify each aspect of required performance. Specify the relative importance of each performance aspect. Employees should be told in advance what is expected of them, including relevant examples of performance on the different job criteria. Employees must understand the criteria upon which they are to be assessed, both to remain productive and to have truly equal opportunities.

4. *Stick to job-based criteria.* Relate the appraisal to the particular job. Avoid rating employees on items that are irrelevant to job performance. When items are irrelevant or of marginal relevance, indicate "not applicable." Consider the full rating period. Compare the employee's performance against a norm or performance standard rather than the performance of other employees.

5. *Record and memorialize.* All evaluations should be in writing, and any verbal feedback given during the evaluation period should be recorded. The language used on written appraisals should be as simple and easy to understand as possible.

6. *Be as specific as possible.* Review appraisals to ensure that high and low ratings are documented with anecdotal information showing what the employee did or did not do to earn the rating. Avoid vague or descriptive personal criteria, which may be misinterpreted or subjective. Examples include adaptability, demeanor, and social behavior (except to the extent that interpersonal skills are an appropriate element of job-related performance and are expressly addressed in the training).

7. *Confront performance problems positively and constructively during training.* Discuss and/or deal with performance problems at the time they occur. If the employee's performance is unsatisfactory, you should immediately counsel the employee on deficiencies and suggest concrete ways to improve performance.

8. *Consider reasonable accommodations when necessary.* When performance during or following training is unsatisfactory because of inattentiveness, failure to follow directions, or inability to concentrate, or when performance declines suddenly, your trainee may have a medical or disability-related problem. Follow your employer's policies with respect to medical examinations, referrals to an Employee Assistance Program sponsored by your employer, or evaluation of necessary reasonable accommodations. (See the discussion later in this chapter, pp. 167–171.)

9. *Specify consequences of nonperformance.* Clearly specify a final warning on the performance appraisal if performance is so poor that a discharge or exclusion from a posttraining position may occur.

10. *Strive for consistency.* Be consistent with appraisals. If poor performance is evident, document it as a basis to delay or deny completion of the training program. Inconsistency will reflect poorly in any subsequent legal proceeding.

11. *Plan your documentation.* Avoid making any notes on appraisal forms that may be deemed discriminatory or reflect a "mixed motive." Avoid contrived or pretextual statements. Avoid unreasonably harsh treatment of the employee that might lead to resignation, since your actions may be deemed a constructive discharge. Imagine having the appraisal enlarged and being viewed by a jury that doesn't know you or the employee. Can it be misinterpreted?

12. *Never back-date appraisals. Never* attempt to document something that did not occur. Always attempt to document events as they happen. Chapter 20, pp. 425–431, provides further specific direction on documentation techniques.

Causes of Distorted Training Performance Appraisals

The most significant discrimination cases involving performance appraisals reveal that there are many reasons for inaccurate or distorted performance reviews. Several may have legal consequences.

1. *Inadequate preparation.* Frequently trainers feel that they have too much to do and insufficient time. Unfortunately, curriculum content design, methodology, and presentation get more attention and time than development of objective evaluation systems. The result is lack of attention to details of language, and possibly incomplete descriptions of the employee's performance during training. Plan ahead, and make the time necessary to perform and document your appraisals.

2. *Lack of clear standards.* Clear, measurable performance standards during and after training are essential for accurate and legally defensible appraisals of trainee performance. Objective standards, communicated clearly and consistently to trainees, are an important component. Every participant should understand clearly what is expected.

3. *Inconsistency in ratings among trainers.* When they are passed over for placement or advancement, employees frequently allege employment discrimination on the grounds that other, similarly performing trainees were held to different standards. Sometimes inconsistency in ratings occurs with the same trainer, but more often it is the result of different perceptions among diverse trainers about what constitutes acceptable performance. If you assign multiple trainers for similar

skills-based programs, clarify performance standards for comparable jobs to achieve a better consensus among those trainers. Define and use performance-rating definitions applicable to all similar programs.

4. *Rating personality rather than performance.* Trainers are human too. You may respond quickly or strongly to personality traits, such as aggressiveness or active participation in a training program (through questions and interaction), that prevent you from objectively evaluating performance. The appraisal should focus only on actions, accomplishments, and specific instances of unacceptable performance during training.

5. *The contrast effect.* The exceptionally good (or bad) performance of one or more trainees may greatly distort the subjective evaluations that others receive. Contrasting the relative contributions of a group of trainees contributes constructively to the appraisal performance process. The rating of one employee should not shift the ratings for others except in extraordinary circumstances (such as a limited bonus pool).

6. *Subjective language in written appraisals.* Even carefully constructed written appraisals, by the most conscientious and well-intentioned trainer, may include language that can be misconstrued when viewed in the context of a later discrimination complaint. Sometimes assumptions about people, based on their personal characteristics, invade the appraisal process. Even when the comment is "positive," if you make reference to characteristics related to gender, age, ethnicity, or disability, you may be begging for a lawsuit.

In the absence of an objective road map to compare performance expectations against the particular participant's performance, you can't legally allow subjective, non-job-related factors to invade the evaluation process. When this occurs, the legal danger is twofold. First, subjective assumptions—even those made in "good faith"—might deprive the trainee of an equal employment opportunity. Second, the trainee's evaluation may reflect a "mixed motive," in which both proper and inappropriate factors are considered. In the latter situation, even a legitimate decision based on the performance appraisal may be successfully challenged, because the inappropriate factor was considered.

Balancing the Need to Test for Performance With Employment Discrimination Laws

Tests are used frequently to select trainees for advanced training, to verify an employee's skill and knowledge to meet legislative requirements, or to satisfy record-keeping requirements. Additionally, trainers use posttraining tests to identify trainees for corrective training.

Tests also identify skill deficiencies or knowledge gaps that translate into weak performance. The results of the tests are used to target specific training needs. Still other tests are used to help employees qualify for promotion, by identifying skills or management capabilities.

Use of any kind of test has the necessary effect of weeding out certain employees. If the test tends to exclude more women, minorities, or other identifiable groups protected under the employment discrimination statutes (see Figure 6-1), you may be discriminating by creating an "adverse impact."

In order to meet long-standing and emerging legal requirements, you must develop, administer, and validate tests to ensure that they serve a business purpose and do not discriminate. The greatest legal risks are posed by:

- Knowledge-based and skill-based tests that appear neutral and objective, but that unfairly exclude minority and disabled workers because the tests fail to measure job-related skills or are not accurate predictors of success on the job

- Tests that have a differential effect on groups with special needs (e.g., disabled and multilingual trainees)—such as requirements for reading and writing during the test—when these skills are not required or can be reasonably accommodated on the job

- Honesty, integrity, and personality tests that create privacy and discrimination considerations

- Test administration in a location that is inaccessible to people with disabilities

Legal Challenges to Testing and How to Solve Them

Legal challenges to employment tests have generally centered on arguments that the tests had an adverse or differential effect on minorities and were not demonstrably valid predictors of the employee's or trainee's job performance. In 1971, the U.S. Supreme Court ruled that even if an employer did not intend to discriminate by the use of tests, any test that had an adverse effect on women or minority groups would have to be validated as job-related in order to avoid a finding of illegal discrimination by the employer.

In 1978, after an effort of more than six years, the EEOC, the Civil Rights Commission, and the U.S. Departments of Labor and Justice jointly adopted the Uniform Guidelines on Employee Selection Procedures (Uniform Guidelines). The Uniform Guidelines apply to all employers subject to the federal discrimination laws and to all selection procedures, including "the full range of assessment techniques from traditional paper and pencil tests, *performance tests, training programs,* or probationary periods and physical, educational, and work experience requirements through informal or casual interviews and unscored application forms."

The Uniform Guidelines and the seminal U.S. Supreme Court cases of *Griggs v. Duke Power Co.*[1] and *Albemarle Paper Co. v. Moody*[2] form the foundation for lawsuits involving tests used as selection or performance assessment tools. Essentially, these cases involve a three-step inquiry to determine whether a test creates a discriminatory "adverse impact" on an identifiable protected group (such as women, the disabled, or racial minorities):

1. The complaining party bears the initial burden of showing that the test excludes protected individuals at a significantly higher rate than their counterparts. Although differential exclusion is difficult to prove, it is usually accomplished through statistical evidence.

2. If the person challenging the test does not meet this burden of proof, the court never reaches the question of the test's validity. When the evidence shows a statistical disparity that disproportionately excludes identifiable groups on the basis of gender, disability, or race, the burden then shifts to the employer or trainer/test designer to validate the test—that is, to show that the test is job-related. If you are challenged and fail to establish that your test is job-related, the court may order you to discontinue using it, and award damages to the complaining party. In order to establish "job-relatedness," you must show that the test is "demonstrably a reasonable measure of job performance" (*Griggs v. Duke Power Co.*[3]) or "bears a demonstrable relationship to successful performance on the job for which it is used" (*Walls v. Mississippi State Dept. of Public Welfare*[4]). It is this issue on which the EEOC's Uniform Guidelines attempt to shed some light.

3. If you establish job-relatedness, the challenging party may then attempt to rebut your proof by showing that the particular test is not required by business necessity because an alternative selection or evaluation device meets your objectives with less adverse impact on protected groups.

The validation techniques discussed in the Uniform Guidelines involve complex requirements, all of which have more to do with scientific testing procedures than with legal analyses. The guidelines adopted the three standards of validity utilized by the American Psychological Association in its 1974 Standards for Education and Psychological Tests. These three standards are criterion, content, and construct validity, as summarized in Figure 7-1.

Title VII of the Civil Rights Act of 1964 provides that it is not "an unlawful employment practice for an employer to give and to act upon the results of any professionally developed ability test provided that such test, its administration, or action upon the results is not designed, intended, or used to discriminate because of race, color, religion, sex, or national origin." Workplace tests, therefore, should be race- and gender-neutral predictors of job performance. Furthermore, tests should be prepared by experts and be validated according to the standards set forth in the Uniform Guidelines on Employee Selection Procedures.

If you bypass professionally developed tests in favor of those prepared in-house, you may find yourself facing charges of discrimination, because "homemade" tests are more difficult to validate than professionally researched tests. If a test is challenged by a trainee, you may be required to stop using it until it has been properly validated. In addition, a court may order you to place or promote trainees who were adversely affected by nonvalidated tests.

Psychological tests also have the potential for adversely affecting members of protected groups. Any general intelligence or aptitude test *must be validated.* If it is challenged, you must be prepared to produce evidence of validation *and* to demonstrate that the test is valid for the applicable jobs. Failure to do so can result in liability for discrimination.

Adoption of a sound, workable set of training policies and posttraining test procedures is your best defense against discrimination claims. Don't

---

■ Evidence of the validity of a test or other selection procedure by *a criterion-related validity* study should consist of empirical data demonstrating that the selection procedure is predictive of or significantly correlated with important elements of job performance.

■ Evidence of the validity of a test or other selection procedure by *a content validity* study should consist of data showing that the content of the selection procedure is representative of important aspects of performance on the job for which the candidates are to be evaluated.

■ Evidence of the validity of a test or other selection procedure by *a construct validity* study should consist of data showing that the procedure measures the degree to which candidates have identifiable characteristics that have been determined to be important in successful performance in the job for which the candidates are to be evaluated.

Figure 7-1 The Three Bases for Validating Tests Permitted Under the EEOC Uniform Guidelines on Employee Selection.

avoid written policies. Enhance your ability to defend against discrimination charges by putting employees on clear notice of their rights and responsibilities and by providing identifiable benchmarks of your organization's expectations. Clear, consistently enforced policies tend to limit the suspicion and distrust that lead to discrimination claims.

Accommodating Test Takers With Special Needs

Your posttraining tests should address your trainees' abilities to perform the tasks of the job, not their disabilities or disorders. The Americans With Disabilities Act (ADA) requires you to conduct tests in a place and manner accessible to people with disabilities. Trainees with impaired sensory, motor, or speaking skills should be offered modified tests or appropriate auxiliary aids to accommodate their disabilities, such as taped examinations, interpreters, and braille or large-print exams. In order to meet these legal requirements, you are justified in asking for advance notice of the reasonable accommodations and may also request proof of the participant's special needs.

When your company hires a qualified disabled employee and provides a reasonable accommodation to perform an essential job function, you must *also* provide appropriate reasonable accommodations for on-the-job and classroom training, and for testing and evaluation following the training. For example, a dyslexic trainee who will be reasonably accommodated on the job cannot be forced to take a pen-and-paper "test" following training without a similar reasonable accommodation. To so require would create a disparate impact on learning-disabled employees, thereby denying an equal employment opportunity. This is true even if the testing policy is facially neutral and applied to all trainees. The ADA's requirement for a reasonable accommodation would apply.

In designing reasonable accommodations, you should first determine the reason for the test itself. Once you know the objective for measuring "successful performance" on the test, you can evaluate alternatives for measuring the knowledge, skill, or abilities of the disabled test taker. You may have several objectives for testing during training.

First, you may use quizzes or other evaluation vehicles as teaching tools to assess the level of knowledge of participants at the outset of the training. In order to ensure that the training meets the needs of all participants, including the disabled, you should design the test to measure objective skills that are reasonably related to success in the training. Disabled participants are entitled to reasonable accommodations to allow them to achieve the benefits of tests as teaching tools.

Second, you may use evaluation tools to determine whether participants have retained content presented during the program and can apply that information to their job tasks. The results are typically used to determine future job placement. If the test is measuring job knowledge—rather than replicating a skill that the employee must perform on the job—a reasonable accommodation may be required to ensure equality for disabled test takers. If qualified people with disabilities are unable to complete the test, but *could* perform effectively on the job, the test violates the ADA unless you make a reasonable accommodation to take the test. This is particularly so in the safety area, where employers and trainers are *required* by occupational safety laws to prevent employees from working in an environment where they cannot perform safely. Disabled employees who cannot pass or complete the test itself—but could perform safely—must be provided with an alternative testing method to ascertain their retention and understanding of the safety training and their ability to work safely. (See Chapter 2, pp. 51–52.)

Third, tests are administered to narrow the field of qualified candidates for limited opportunities, which is a competitive process. Candidates are excluded on the basis of competitive rankings. If an applicant can prove that the testing was not administered equitably for all applicants, you may violate the ADA.

The obligation to reasonably accommodate a disabled test taker's needs includes making existing facilities accessible for the test, acquiring or modifying equipment or devices for the test, making appropriate adjustment or modification of test materials, and providing qualified readers and interpreters (for sight- or hearing-impaired test takers).

Several types of disabilities covered under the ADA are affected by tests. *Learning disabilities,* such as dyslexia and attention deficit disorder, affect the ability to perform effectively in a timed testing situation. *Sensory impairments,* primarily sight and hearing, affect the ability to read test questions and hear the instructions. Additionally, *motor coordination and dexterity challenges* impinge on the ability to sit, use a writing implement, or respond on a computer-based test; and *medical conditions,* such as diabetes, epilepsy, asthma, and environmentally triggered conditions, may require breaks during lengthy test situations.

The following guidelines are a starting point for analyzing when and how to consider reasonable accommodations in the testing process to ensure an equal employment opportunity.

General Issues for All Disabilities

Prepare in advance for special testing procedures. If possible, inform participants at the time of enrollment that there will be a test, and fully describe what is required to pass and how performance will be measured. If this is not feasible, make the announcement at the earliest possible time after training commences. Ask participants to advise you of any special requirements they may have to take the test, so that you have time to arrange for access, facilities, and related physical layout issues.

All tests should measure objective, job-related knowledge, tasks, and skills. This will ensure that all participants, disabled and otherwise, are being measured on the appropriate standards that will predict their success on the job. Tests should use a variety of formats, including true/false, multiple choice, and narrative. With computer-based tests, strive for a variety of interactive methods to test multiple skills. Provide separate instructions for each type of question.

Learning Disabilities

Remember that if the employee is not going to be required to read, analyze, synthesize information, recall information, and respond on the job within the same time parameters as the test vehicle, you are *not replicating on-the-job performance.* In these situations, you must consider a reasonable accommodation to take the test or to demonstrate knowledge and skill. Consider verbal tests, where appropriate, to ensure that reading difficulties do not adversely affect the trainee.

If you know in advance that additional time will be needed for a learning-disabled participant, establish the ground rules in advance. Although it is not necessary—and may be inappropriate—to advise other employees of why the disabled employee is being given additional time, let them know that a reasonable accommodation has been requested and granted. Make every effort to remove distractions and pressure from the test room. If you don't know the need in advance, and the participant requests additional time, or if it becomes obvious during the test that more time is needed, discreetly address the issue with the trainee.

Remember it is not necessary to reduce the performance standards, or to adjust the passing score in order to make a reasonable accommodation. Learning-disabled employees are not illiterate or dumb, and a reasonable accommodation is designed only to allow them to demonstrate their job-related knowledge and skills. Set your standards as high as possible, and then design procedures to meet the needs of the trainee—always maintaining the objective of measuring proficiency or anticipated success on particular jobs.

If the employee cannot read, but can write well, provide the test questions in a prerecorded format on a cassette tape, or supply a monitor to read the questions during the test. If a monitor is used, place the test taker in a separate room so that distractions to other participants are minimal. Conversely, if the learning disability precludes writing clearly, allow the participant to respond to the questions verbally or to record answers onto a cassette for later transcription.

In some situations, a take-home test may be an accommodation. If you are not required to monitor the test, this can be an option. You can take steps to provide a different test from that given to the other participants, but you should rely on the integrity of the accommodated employee.

Visual Impairments

Discuss with the trainees how to best test their job knowledge or skill. If the visually impaired employee or applicant is accustomed to a reasonable accommodation on the job, such as a magnifying instrument, braille materials, or a reader, permit the same accommodation in the testing situation.

Consider verbal tests, or prerecorded questions and answers, in areas that effectively measure job knowledge. If other participants are permitted access to materials during the test (e.g., the standard open-book or open-note format), strive to replicate that benefit for the visually challenged participant.

Hearing Impairments

Provide all instructions in writing, preferably transcribed exactly as those presented orally. If this is impossible, or if the test is interactive, consider an interpreter who can translate into American Sign Language. If you use an interpreter, take steps to minimize distractions to other participants. Consider providing additional time for the test taker to demonstrate proficiency with job tasks.

Mobility Impairments

If the participant has trouble writing, consider an oral test or tape-recorded questions. If physical agility is required, make sure the test reflects a job-related function *that is an essential function of the job.* If the trainee is limited in performing a function marginal to the job, exclusion on this basis will violate the ADA.

If the trainee will be using an adaptive device on the job to perform physical tasks, allow the same accommodation in the test setting, perhaps by testing in the job environment rather than in the test room.

Consult with the trainee in advance, or at the earliest time, to determine what type of accommodation will be helpful.

Medical Issues

Always consult with the participant regarding test-taking situations. For example, a diabetic may need to have food or beverage available during the test period, or take a break to test blood sugar levels. If so, provide an opportunity to extend the test by the amount of time needed for breaks.

If climactic conditions are an issue—for example, for employees with extreme allergies or other conditions affected by the test environment— make the determination of an alternative test site in advance. If the need for an accommodation does not become apparent until the test is under way, be flexible and prepared to make adjustments as needed. The test taker may need to be excused for illness during the test, and an alternative time and location will have to be set to repeat the exam. Again, although you cannot completely eliminate the potential for abuse, you should rely on the integrity of the employee and monitor *appropriately,* with direct observation and medical certifications where necessary.

These guidelines specifically address testing issues. For a discussion on accommodating the special needs of disabled participants *during the training class,* see Chapter 14, pp. 299–305.

Privacy Rights and Wrongs: What the Law Says About Test Content and Usage

Privacy rights of private sector employees represent one of the most rapidly developing areas of the law. The courts and several state legislatures are focusing increasing attention on employees' reasonable expectations of privacy during the employment relationship, even during training.

Federal law doesn't provide much protection for private sector employees. The Federal Privacy Act relates only to records maintained by federal agencies or government contractors. The U.S. Constitution, particularly the Fourth Amendment, protects the "right of the people to be secure in their persons, houses, papers, and effects against unreasonable searches and seizures." In 1965, the Supreme Court also ruled that the Bill of Rights created a "zone of privacy" that could not be violated by governmental action.

Many state constitutions provide similar protection to that offered by the Fourth Amendment. In some states, these protections are limited to government employers; in others, they have been extended to the private workplace.

State common law theories have been developed through case-by-case determinations. The basic definition adopted by many state courts for an invasion of the right to privacy is an intentional intrusion, physical or otherwise, into another person's private affairs or concerns in a manner that would be highly offensive to a reasonable person. These issues have made their way into the workplace, primarily in the context of medical examinations, drug and alcohol testing, physical searches, and electronic monitoring.

You should carefully consider privacy issues with respect to the results of any posttraining test, by asking the following questions:

- What do you or your employer *need to know* about the trainee's performance?

- For which trainees is the information needed?

- Within your organization who needs to know, and can the information be limited to trainers, supervisors, or managers with a genuine need to know?

- How long do you or your employer need to keep the information and how will it be filed or maintained?

In most states, invasion of privacy is subject to an individual lawsuit. The type of privacy interest that is often at issue in the workplace is an employee's reasonable expectation of privacy with respect to information of a highly personal nature. Your latitude in gathering information by testing depends upon your need for the particular information, which in turn depends upon the nature of the job at issue, or the objectives for the evaluation and testing being performed.

In most states, employers and their agents—such as trainers—have a qualified privilege to disclose information about an employee's fitness for a particular job. The privilege will be lost if the trainee demonstrates that the communication was made recklessly or intentionally, or to people beyond the limited "need to know." Leaving test results, scores, or other information in public view or at the photocopy machine is an abuse of the privilege, as is mentioning the information in a casual conversation with people (even other trainers) who have no specific need to know.

Polygraph Testing

Your employer's right to use polygraph tests to screen applicants and test current employees is governed by federal law. Some states also regulate the use of polygraphs. Any employer engaged in or affecting interstate commerce is subject to the Federal Employee Polygraph Protection Act of 1988. This act prohibits most private employers from using polygraph tests to screen applicants or test employees. However, the act recognizes three limited exceptions which involve misconduct investigations. Employers must provide written notice in compliance with the act.

The act contains detailed procedures for test administration and the use of test results. Employers who violate the act may be fined up to $10,000 by the Secretary of Labor. In addition, applicants and current employees have a private right of action, and may sue their employers in federal court.

Integrity and Honesty Testing

Written honesty tests are lawful in almost all states. One exception is Massachusetts, which prohibits such written tests. Likewise, Rhode Island requires that employers not use written tests to render a diagnostic opinion of the honesty of an individual as "the primary basis for an employment decision."

Prior to using a preemployment or preplacement integrity test, you should document the business necessity for the test by showing that job-related integrity is a necessary requirement for successful job performance. In addition, select a test that has been developed by professional and accredited personnel or organizations. It is prudent to confirm that the test publisher's claims of test performance are supported by appropriate validation studies.

Finally, you should provide training on proper test administration to all individuals who administer integrity tests. The content of their training should, at a minimum, include the importance of consistency in the testing process, the critical component of confidentiality of test results, what the test is designed to measure, how to score the test, and the limitations on use in employment decisions.

In addition, your training should focus on how to establish a proper testing climate, and how to provide feedback to test takers and detect language or cognitive barriers that may require a reasonable accommodation in the testing process.

Finally, appropriate record-keeping, test retention, and security practices within the organization are essential ingredients of effective honesty or integrity testing. Your documentation should bolster your position that you used the tests appropriately and only after careful consideration of your lawful business objectives.

Personality Testing

Restrictions on the use of polygraph tests have led some employers to try personality testing as an alternative in their selection procedures. Although employers have increased the use of written personality tests as a device to assess a variety of attitudes and personality traits prior to placement into training or job opportunities, these tests are now heavily affected by privacy laws.

Personality tests have been attacked as a violation of the right to privacy. A California court of appeal found that an employer did not demonstrate a compelling interest or job-relatedness in requiring security officer applicants to take the Minnesota Multiphasic Personality Inventory, which asked them to respond to true-or-false statements such as "I feel sure that there is only one true religion" and "I am very strongly attracted to members of my own sex."[5] The court determined that the test unjustifiably violated the applicants' constitutional right to privacy. The court also found the content of the test discriminatory because it invaded religious beliefs.

Six Critical Requirements for Lawful Administration of Tests

There are several critical requirements for lawful administration of tests.

1. Carefully prepare all test materials.

Advance preparation of test materials is critical to the success of any testing program. Plan and purchase all materials in advance, including test booklets, answer sheets, writing implements, and related tools. Consider all aspects of reasonable accommodation for mobility-impaired and physically challenged test takers.

It is equally important to ensure that all test materials are accurate and unambiguous. Yet errors do occur. If an error in a test question is brought to light, the test administrator should have the authority to handle the situation immediately.

2. Select qualified test administrators.

Sometimes the trainer who presents the program will be the administrator. This person should be as qualified to monitor and administer the physical examination as he or she is to present the substantive program.

This is especially important when the presenter is a subject-matter expert or manager with no experience in testing administration. In these circumstances, assign a separate qualified administrator to help with the testing itself. Alternatively, provide sufficient instruction to the presenter to ensure that the test will be administered fairly, consistently, and efficiently.

In order to make sure that disabled test takers are reasonably accommodated, the test administrator must be thoroughly familiar with the requirements of the ADA and any applicable state laws governing disability discrimination. The administrator should also have sufficient authority to address accommodation questions that come up during the test.

The training and qualifications required of test administrators will vary with the specific tests. All administrators should be thoroughly familiar with the directions and methods for recording answers. A qualified administrator should understand the importance of consistently applying test rules and providing unambiguous and consistent directions to all test takers.

Some tests require special techniques and professional knowledge to administer, score, and interpret. In such cases, qualifications should be carefully determined, and references checked. For example, the American Psychological Association's Standard 6.6 states:

> Responsibility for test use should be assumed by or delegated only to those individuals who have the training and experience necessary to handle this responsibility in a professional and technically adequate manner. Any special qualifications for test administration or interpretation noted in the manual should be met.[6]

Some publishers will not release a test without specifying the degree of training required to administer it. If you have purchased or licensed a validated test from a publisher but do not have a qualified test administrator on site, you should consider an outside consultant.

3. Ensure consistency in the administration of the test.

The most important element of test administration is standardization. Every time the test is given, it must be administered, scored, and directed in the same way under the same essential environment. This is especially important when test takers will be ranked or are competing with others. Any inconsistencies may provide the seeds for a discrimination claim.

Test administrators should also be prepared to minimize distractions or other factors that may affect performance. For example, although it is appropriate to provide a sign interpreter or reader for a sensory-impaired test taker, the room should be set up and monitored so as to avoid such reasonable accommodations from becoming a distraction to others.

Specified procedures should be carefully crafted prior to the commencement of the test. There is no substitute for thorough preparation and training on how to answer test takers' questions consistently, how to provide objective and clear instructions, and how to monitor the test in an authoritative manner. It is especially important not to project expectations about the participant's performance on the test—for instance, by giving less thorough answers to questions from particular groups of students, or appearing to favor one gender group over another.

It is, of course, axiomatic that no favoritism should be extended to any test taker. Careful monitoring of time in the use of references (open-book tests) or tools (such as calculators) should ensure consistent enforcement of the rules. When a protected trainee requires additional time, provide it efficiently, and if necessary quietly explain to others that a reasonable accommodation is in order. Always make an effort to avoid distractions to all concerned in these situations.

Administrators should be qualified to provide complete, clear, and concise instructions for all tests, including information on the purpose of the test, the time allowed for completion, how to record answers, what to do if the test taker has a question or a problem develops during the test, what to do when the test is finished, and the basics of how test takers must perform to achieve their employment goals.

Many successful employment discrimination claims result from employees not being given objective information on what is necessary to achieve success. At a minimum, each trainee who will be tested for a legitimate job-related purpose must be informed of the following: (1) the objective performance standards; (2) how well (or poorly) the trainee is meeting those standards; (3) what is expected of the trainee to stay employed, to advance, or to have other employment opportunities; and (4) the potential range of consequences for not meeting the objective performance standards. The responsibility for communicating this information rests with the test administrator or trainer/facilitator. If you don't have the information, make every effort to get it before the test. If you are not given the information, or if your employer's standards are unclear or expectations are undefined, you should raise the issue with the appropriate managers. This will help keep you and your employer out of legal trouble.

4. Be sure that all reasonable accommodations are met with respect to test takers with special needs.

Reasonable accommodation is thoroughly discussed earlier in this chapter, pp. 167–171. In addition, the subject is addressed relative to health and safety training in Chapter 2, pp. 56–59, and with respect to speakers and presenters in Chapter 14, pp. 299–305.

5. Be sure that all scoring is accomplished consistently by qualified administrators.

This is the most important aspect of test administration. A test that is not scored correctly will not be useful for its intended purpose, since it will not accurately measure knowledge, achievement, or aptitude. Inconsistent or unreasonably subjective scoring breeds complaints of discrimination, particularly by test takers with special needs.

Objective tests, such as true or false, multiple choice, and other numeric responses, have precise standards for scoring. They can often be scored by nonexperts, including nonhuman computer scanners. Subjective tests, such as essays, narratives, and other analytical responses, are more difficult to score. Psychological tests, such as personality and intelligence tests, may be largely subjective. Likewise, role plays, simulations, or responses to case studies are inherently subjective. All of these require qualified, trained, and experienced administrators to ensure both consistency and accuracy.

Many posttraining tests are administered in small groups or one to one. Once again, the content expert who presents the training may be ill-equipped to administer and grade the evaluation component. One successful approach is to use a team, with one presenter and one evaluator. If such a pairing is not suited to the subject matter or not within your reasonable budget, make an effort to train the presenter on lawful and objective evaluation techniques. This is critical to both the overall success of the program and to the legal defensibility of the evaluations.

If a candidate for an employment opportunity is disqualified because of an unacceptable score, the Uniform Guidelines require employers to provide "a reasonable opportunity for retesting and reconsideration." The EEOC's emphasis has been in preemployment selection; but the principle is equally applicable to an employee who is disqualified from further advancement—or barred from the work site because he or she can't pass regulatory compliance tests. In these situations, it is helpful to the defense against a discrimination claim to provide reasonable opportunities for retesting, particularly when the training or testing might be culturally biased or a reasonable accommodation is appropriate.

6. Maintain appropriate documentation and record keeping to satisfy compliance requirements, to establish your substantive and procedural work, and to ensure the confidentiality of trainee performance records.

Information about test takers' performance can be very sensitive and needs to be carefully controlled. This is especially important for personality, honesty, intelligence, and aptitude tests. Also, employees who have been retested should be assured that they will not be embarrassed or retaliated against in the process. Documentation techniques are discussed further in Chapter 20, pp. 429–431.

Test Validation Criteria: A Step-by-Step Guide

The threshold question in validating a test is whether the test in fact measures what it is intended to measure. If an adverse impact exists, you must present concrete evidence to demonstrate that the test accurately predicts how a person will perform on the job.

The Uniform Guidelines make it clear that a selection process that adversely affects employment opportunities for any protected group should be validated. If adverse impact has been established, then the employer should consider test validation for job requirements and performance. Under the Uniform Guidelines, validation can be achieved through three methods: content, criterion, and construct validity, as depicted in Figure 7-1. In addition to conducting a validation study, trainers should consider the use of evaluation methods other than testing to achieve a legitimate business purpose with less adverse impact.

Validity refers to the degree to which evidence supports inferences that are made from test scores. Thus, it is the inferences about the specific uses of a test that are validated, not the test itself. Your employer has the responsibility to ensure that a test it is relying on has been validated, because the employer is the one who draws the interpretations and inferences from test scores, and makes decisions on the basis of them.

1. Obtain professional guidance.

To ensure both the effectiveness and legality of posttraining tests, consider retaining competent professionals, whether they are outside consultants or a part of your organization, to design and administer tests. Expertise needed includes:

- *Test development expertise.* Development and supervision of development should be done by professionally competent staff or consultants in the field of testing psychology. Usually both a degree and related experience are required.

- *Content expertise.* The degree and kind of expertise needed will vary with the complexity and level of the contemplated tests. Sometimes, the expert knowledge comes from conferences or interviews with those directly associated with the job, such as trainees, current employees, and supervisors. At other times, experts from specific professional fields should be used.

- *Legal expertise.* Since the Uniform Guidelines were drawn up in consultation with professional psychological associations and were highly influenced by APA standards, it is quite likely that a competent testing psychologist will be familiar with the requirements of the guidelines. It is helpful, however, to have legal guidance if you are using a test for the first time or you have a significant percentage of multinational, multilingual, or multiabled test takers. A legal expert should be highly knowledgeable about litigation in the field of testing.

The Uniform Guidelines encourage, but do not require, professional supervision of an employment testing program. They note, however, that such professional supervision will not be considered as a substitute for documented evidence of validity.[7]

2. Determine what type of test to use.

A number of different tests are used in *posttraining* evaluation. Consider what job skills or learning you are attempting to measure, and use tests that will meet those objectives without having an adverse impact on test takers.

Power versus Speeded Tests.   Whether a test is timed or not will affect relative test scores. Power tests have no time limits. Trainees are allowed as much time as they wish. Speed or speeded tests have strict time limits. Time limits make tests convenient to administer and are effective for selecting employees who will need to work under extreme time pressure. Remember, your training curriculum should build in components that inject appropriate job-related stressors, and then test accordingly. (See the discussion on building stress into the curriculum in Chapter 4, pp. 100–104.)

If it isn't important to measure an employee's ability to perform under strict time limitations (because time pressures will not be present on the job), power tests are a better way of assessing a candidate's ability to do accurate, high-quality work. Also, unrealistically restrictive time limits may prevent disabled candidates from succeeding—not because they cannot do the job, but because they cannot pass the hurdle of the test. Such restrictions are unlawful under the ADA. (See the discussion on pp. 169–171 of this chapter.)

Paper-and-Pencil Tests versus Oral Tests versus Performance Tests. Paper-and-pencil tests are convenient to administer, but can be poor predictors of how well candidates will perform on the job. Performance tests, which involve simulations or "hands on" exercises, give candidates the chance to demonstrate actual work-related skills they learned in your program. Although such tests are usually legally supportable, they are less convenient to administer and may require the trainee to purchase or borrow expensive equipment.

Oral tests have the same question-and-answer structure as written tests, but they require the administrator to listen to each test taker's answers and consistently record all responses. However, oral tests generally make it easier for candidates to demonstrate their abilities and may be a reasonable accommodation for certain disabled trainees.

One advantage of nonverbal tests (i.e., performance tests) over verbal tests (i.e., written and oral tests) is that although directions must be given in words, nonverbal tests are otherwise language-free, and they are usually, but not always, less culturally biased. Another advantage is that many people with weak verbal abilities are unable to do well on verbal tests even though they have the skills that the tests purport to measure. Nonverbal tests are most likely to reveal the abilities of these types of candidates.

Objective versus Projective Tests. Tests may also be categorized according to how the test and scoring are structured. Objective tests probe for specific responses. Responses are scored according to whether they are correct or incorrect, or sometimes according to the degree of correctness or completeness. Projective tests are more open-ended. They allow trainees to provide answers that reflect their individuality. No two trainees will offer quite the same essay. The difficulty with projective tests is that different trainers will interpret and score the same responses differently. The resulting subjectivity may, even inadvertently, be culturally biased. Performance on projective tests can be assessed reliably only by trained examiners or administrators who will need to spend time reviewing the results. The additional costs may be justified in management training programs if a job placement decision can have significant long-term impact on both the individual and the employer.

Situational or Critical-Incident Tests versus Fact-Oriented Tests. A meaningful distinction can also be drawn between two important categories of job-knowledge tests. The first, situational or critical-incident tests, require candidates to demonstrate how they would respond in a given situation. Such tests focus on significant, judgment-related aspects of job performance that are not addressed in fact-oriented tests. Fact-oriented tests concern knowledge of facts, and may be heavily affected by the candidate's ability to memorize; judgment-related tests concern how knowledge is applied.

Although fact-oriented tests are comparatively objective and easy to assess, they do not measure a candidate's ability or apply facts learned in the training. Situational tests, by contrast, offer important information about how candidates are likely to perform on jobs that require the exercise of independent judgment, but do little to assess the candidate's factual knowledge or ability to memorize information.

3. Select a legally acceptable validation strategy for your particular test.

The three validation approaches depicted in Figure 7-1 are still accepted for demonstrating the validity of using a test to make an employment decision, including posttraining placement decisions. Although treated as separate approaches in the Uniform Guidelines, all three are closely linked. Construct validity is the most fundamental and embracing approach to validity, whereas content and criterion validity are aspects of an ongoing process of validation, rather than a one- or two-step procedure with final results.

Although the three approaches to validity are considered substantively valid, the Uniform Guidelines require only that one of the three approaches be used when showing the job-relatedness of a test that would otherwise violate Title VII. To meet EEOC requirements, an employer using a test can select any validation method that is (1) appropriate for the type of test, the job, and the employment situation and (2) technically or administratively feasible.

Content validation is appropriate primarily when it is technically and administratively feasible to develop work samples or other tests that mirror job behaviors. If test content reflects the training curriculum and is representative of job behaviors, you can establish validity without having to provide statistical evidence of how well the test works.

By contrast, a test based on inferences about mental processes cannot be supported solely or primarily on the basis of content validity, because it is testing analytical abilities or other cognitive skills. Thus, a content strategy is not appropriate for demonstrating the validity of tests that are intended to measure traits such as intelligence, aptitude, personality, common sense, judgment, leadership, and spatial ability.

4. Understand and employ standards for content-valid tests.

The Uniform Guidelines impose specific standards on content-valid testing. However, tests that do not meet these standards may nonetheless be shown to be valid using criterion-related or construct validation techniques. The standards are summarized in Figure 7-2.

Job Analysis

- A content validity study must include an analysis of the important work behaviors required for successful job performance.
- The analysis must include an assessment of the relative importance of work behaviors and/or job skills.
- Relevant work product must be considered and built into the test.
- If work behaviors or job skills are not observable, the job analysis should include those aspects of the behaviors that can be observed, as well as the observed work product.

Tests Measuring Knowledge, Skill, or Ability

- The test should measure and be a representative sample of the knowledge, skill, or ability.
- The knowledge, skill, or ability should be used in and be a necessary prerequisite to performance of critical or important work behavior.
- Either the test should closely approximate an observable work behavior or its product should closely approximate an observable work product.
- There must be a defined, well-recognized body of information applicable to the job.
- Knowledge of the information must be a prerequisite to the performance of the required work behaviors.
- The test should fairly sample the information that is actually used by the employee on the job, so that the level of difficulty of the test items corresponds to the level of difficulty of the knowledge as used in the work behavior.

Paper-and-Pencil Tests

- Paper-and-pencil tests that are intended to replicate a work behavior or a required job skill are most likely to be appropriate when significant portions of the job are performed in writing.

Figure 7-2 Specific Standards for Content Validation of Tests Under the EEOC Uniform Guidelines on Employee Selection.

Is Your Evaluation Program Legally Defensible? A Checklist

Although you can't guarantee a litigation-free workplace, the following checklist should help reduce the number of legitimate charges of unfair employment practices based on posttraining evaluation and testing.

1. All tests should be validated and administered in full compliance with the Uniform Guidelines on Employee Selection Procedures.

2. The objective task, skill, or knowledge requirements of all tests must be job-related.

3. Except under specific circumstances in which you can demonstrate that an available position is a steppingstone to other positions in the same job family, tests must be conducted and results evaluated only as they pertain to the presently available opportunity.

4. Employees and trainees should be fully advised of the purpose of any test, how it will be conducted, the conditions under which it will be administered, the role it will play in job placement or advancement, and who will have access to test results.

5. Have job experts take the test and weigh their opinions carefully.

6. Establish test validity. Validity measures how appropriate an employment test (or other employee selection procedure) is for making inferences about a candidate's ability to do well on the job. If a test is not a useful predictor of job performance, it is useless, inappropriate, and unlawful.

7. Consider test reliability. Reliability refers to the consistency, dependability, or repeatability of test results. A test that does not measure abilities consistently has little or no value. The various statistics on reliability, provided by test publishers, should be evaluated to determine if the test is acceptable from this point of view.

8. Consider fairness. The ideal test should not only be fair to all groups and individuals, but should also appear fair, so that test takers will accept the test and not feel uncomfortable taking it. A test is considered fair if, among other things, it has clear rules for administration and scoring so that scores may fairly be compared with each other; it is free of cultural, racial, or gender stereotypes and does not emphasize one culture over another; and it does not eliminate people with a disability, such as weak language skills or blindness, from a wide spectrum of jobs that they are capable of performing well.

9. Evaluate the test publisher. Test development is expensive and time-consuming, and there may be temptations for the publisher to take short cuts. Investigate the publisher's reputation. A reputable test publisher will not release a test without ensuring that the test has been properly researched with respect to reliability, validity for various applications, and fairness, and that it otherwise meets or exceeds the American Psychological Association's standards and other applicable guidelines. The publisher is also responsible for controlling who (among test administrators and test takers) has access to the test and for taking steps to ensure test security.

10. Administer the test using only experienced trainers, facilitators, or monitors.

References

1. *Griggs v. Duke Power Co.*, 401 U.S. 421 (1971).

2. *Albemarle Paper Co. v. Moody*, 422 U.S. 405 (1975).

3. *Griggs v. Duke Power Co.*, 401 U.S. 421, 424 (1971).

4. *Walls v. Mississippi State Dept. of Public Welfare*, 730 F.2d 306, 316 (5th Cir. 1985).

5. *Soroka v. Dayton Hudson Corp.*, 18 Cal.App.4th 1200 (1991).

6. American Educational Research Association, American Psychological Association, and National Council on Measurement in Education, *Standards for Educational and Psychological Testing* (1985).

7. Code of Federal Regulations, §1607.9.

8

Adventure/Outdoor Training and the Law

In today's competitive climate, creative management development programs are a must. It is neither productive nor necessary to be risk-averse. It is essential to be risk-aware.

The excitement of outdoor adventures, such as rock or tree climbing, and the bonding experience of intense group activities are largely responsible for renewed interest in adventure-based management development programs. These intense learning experiences are highly successful methods for bringing teams together, awakening self-awareness, and increasing motivation. The positive impact can increase profitability. Alternatively, one serious injury can destroy the bottom line and wipe out profits for years to come.

Do the risks outweigh the benefits? Not for careful and well-prepared organizations and their training professionals. Should external consultants who may shoulder a hefty portion of the liability get out of the business or shift to "safer" offerings? Not necessarily.

Outdoor programs are frequently used to improve managers' effectiveness in soft skills such as problem solving, interpersonal communications, and teamwork. Programs that are entirely outdoors include sailing, mountain climbing, and white water rafting. Structured activities may include ropes, harnesses, ladders, and other props. Many activities take place high above the ground, such as a tree-climbing exercise in which participants scale a 40-foot tree and then walk across a cable to a parallel tree. Another common exercise, called the "Spider

Web," requires a team to lift its members one at a time and pass them through the web of a rope to the other side. The exercise is repeated until the entire team has been transferred from one side to the other without touching the rope.

So-called adventure and wilderness training programs are typically provided by external consultants. They are nontraditional because they take place outside the work environment and involve elements of physical or emotional risk. The objective often involves team building, developing leadership skills, or encouraging risk taking.

Wilderness or adventure training is designed to require full engagement by all participants. You can't fully meet your objectives when one or more participants are frightened, fatigued, distressed, or embarrassed. The very purpose of bringing people closer together in an intense setting designed to evoke teamwork, risk taking, trust, or emotion can backfire when aspects of the exercises create panic, fear, anxiety, or embarrassment.

There are several potential areas of liability for design and delivery of these nontraditional programs. They include personal injury lawsuits and workers' compensation claims for illness, injury, or other damage suffered by participants during the training. In extreme situations there may be claims of emotional distress, stress-related disability due to "delayed reaction," or posttraumatic stress disorder brought on by the training.

Additionally, an adventure retreat gone awry may fuel discrimination charges from disabled employees who are completely excluded from the program, refused a reasonable accommodation to allow full participation, later excluded from advancement opportunities, or retaliated against for their inability to participate.

How the Courts Establish and Enforce Your Legal Duties to Participants

Trainers, consultants, and their respective organizations can minimize potential injuries to participants and reduce the risk of lawsuits by identifying relevant legal issues, carefully selecting program providers, and properly focusing on the safety aspects of program activities.

Any situation that results in death or serious injury to a trainee may lead to litigation. The most successful programs focus on anticipating and preventing participant injuries, both physical and psychological. Since program safety may be an issue in future litigation, program providers must depend upon the quality of the trainer's preparation and documentation to shield themselves from legal exposure. Take steps to anticipate and prevent injuries and clearly document that you have done so. Your efforts to maximize safety must be substantiated and should include investigations of vendor and equipment safety records.

Most negligence lawsuits involve some aspect of personal injury. In physical injury cases, damages may include pain and suffering, medical bills, and lost work time. Claims alleging emotional or psychological injuries seek recovery for emotional distress and related illnesses, as well as lost work. The latter are most frequently associated with "stress-related disabilities," which may be compensable under your state's workers' compensation codes.

In order to win—whether the case is based on personal injuries or property damages—the injured party must show that the facilitator (an internal trainer or external consultant) had a *legal duty* to provide safe and effective training, failed to do so, and through that failure directly caused the injuries. One successful defense is to demonstrate that the accident was unavoidable and that the harm would have occurred even with additional safeguards. In practical terms, this is the type of 20-20 hindsight that often fails to convince a jury when the injuries are extremely significant, such as permanent mobility impairments, brain damage, or burns. (See Chapter 1, pp. 33–35, for a discussion on how the jury system operates.)

As fully explained in Chapter 3, a successful negligence lawsuit requires proof of a legal duty of care owed by the event-sponsoring employer or individual trainers/facilitators, a breach of the duty, a legal nexus or direct connection between the breach of duty and the injury, and specific injuries or damages. In an injury lawsuit, legal duty is based on the applicable "standard of care" for trainers in a particular industry. Standard of care is often defined as the level of conduct expected of similarly trained professionals in a given field. For example, a physician has a duty to provide medical care for patients that is within the accepted standards practiced by members of the medical profession in the area where the physician practices. When the doctor is a specialist (a cardiologist, say), a higher standard of care is imposed.

Most of these cases are brought in state courts, where the common law of the state will apply. Decisions frequently involve sports coaches and physical education instructors, but the reasoning of the courts illustrates the risk factors that must be addressed by those responsible for supervising all types of physical activity programs.

Legal duty is the most important element in this type of lawsuit. The six separate ways that trainers' legal duties are expanded are explained in detail in Chapter 3, pp. 70–76. The duties of trainers who supervise the training activities are addressed in Chapter 4, pp. 94–100. There are very few statutes (legislation) or government regulations applicable to adventure training. Although the OSH Act's general-duty clause will certainly apply to the adventure training work site (see Chapter 2, pp. 40–46), these programs are not typically governed by specialized safety training requirements or industry standards.

Most states measure the standard of care by what the "reasonable person" would do under all the circumstances, balancing the risks and the objectives. In essence, the jury decides whether the trainer met the standard of care required in the particular work setting. Frequently, expert witnesses are called to provide opinions on the relevant standards and practices used by similarly situated adventure program trainers or sponsors. The jury then weighs the credibility of conflicting experts by evaluating their education, experience, credentials, and knowledge of similar workplaces or industries.

As a rule, facilitators of such programs owe concrete legal duties to participants to give adequate instruction in the activity, to supply proper protective equipment and instruction on how to use it safely, to provide effective supervision of each physical activity, and to use proper procedures to protect against aggravation if an injury should occur. These duties are not mutually exclusive. A reasonably safe program may require the responsible facilitator to provide safety instructions regarding necessary protective equipment and the risks associated with a particular activity. In addition, the facilitator should supervise the entire activity to ensure that safety rules and instructions are actually followed.

Expert witnesses and juries often conclude, however, that adventure program trainers must exercise *extraordinary care* because they supervise activities with little room for human error. Courts require reasonable and prudent *professional* supervision of higher-risk activities.

In the case of *Leahy v. School Board of Hernando County*,[1] a freshman football player was injured in what was described as a "nonaggressive" agility drill. Because of the lack of available equipment, the player was not issued a helmet. Players who had no helmets or mouth guards were given no special precautionary instructions beyond those given to players who had the equipment. Although the activity was called a "noncontact" drill, it was by nature a physical exercise. The injured player was the first without a helmet to attempt the drill. Under the circumstances, the court found the injury to Leahy was a foreseeable consequence of the failure to provide him with a helmet, the failure to give precautionary instructions, and the failure to limit the progressive intensity of the drill under the circumstances.

You can meet your legal duty to participants by following specific procedures.

1. Don't require participants to try any activity without first receiving proper instruction and preparation.

Instruction includes an explanation of basic safety procedures, suggestions for proper performance, and identification of foreseeable risks. Considerations in determining whether instructions are proper and sufficient include the difficulty and inherent danger of the activity, the experience of the participants, and the degree of advanced preparation for the activity.

2. Provide reasonable on-site supervision to prevent the injury.

Courts determine reasonableness of supervision by the same factors as reasonableness of instruction. The foreseeability of the risk is the major factor in determining whether a duty exists to supervise closely. The duty can be created by other court cases in the state where the training takes place, by your employer's policies, or by industry standards. Industry standards are rarely present in adventure training. Thus, you should look to your state case law precedents as well as your own policies. For example, if your employer has, as a matter of policy, always provided an on-site company representative trained in CPR at its adventure training programs, but fails to do so and a subsequent injury could have been prevented or minimized by prompt administration of CPR, the company may be found negligent for failing to comply with its own policies.

Always have a company representative present and available at the training site, especially when the risk of accident or injury is inherent in the program. Provide the on-site representative with the appropriate level of authority to make immediate decisions if participants need to be excused or require medical attention.

Similarly, if you have a detailed procedure for investigating vendors and their safety records, but neglect to do so with a new vendor, you may be questioned about why you did not conform to your own policies. In a subsequent negligence case, the injured party would claim that your detailed and (previously) consistent enforcement of the policy established the duty, and that you breached the duty by failing to investigate the vendor's records *this time*, without a reasonable explanation of why the policy was not triggered. If an injury occurred, and the cause of the injury was the vendor's shoddy safety procedures, the legal nexus of "causation" may be established—that is, "but for your lapse, the injury would not have occurred." Full details of the injury and requests for monetary damages would follow.

Likewise, assume that the facilitator you hire has a consistent policy calling for detailed inspection of safety equipment. Assume that a gear subsequently malfunctions, causing or contributing to an injury. The duty to inspect the equipment may derive both from the state common law and from the facilitator's own policies. Once your employee establishes that an injury would not have occurred but for the failure to detect an equipment defect through pretraining inspection, the necessary cause-and-effect relationship is preserved.

This is a double-edged sword: Your company should build into the retainer agreement an obligation for the vendor to meet all policy and appropriate safety standards. If the vendor fails to do so, your employer may have a claim to be indemnified (reimbursed) for any damages it must pay to the injured party. (The contracts in Appendix C provide examples of indemnity language.) However, as an internal trainer, you may also be culpable if you fail to ascertain that the vendor isn't meeting its own standards. One benefit here is the fact that consultants in this specialized area typically hold themselves out as "experts," thus raising their own standard of care.

3. Select an appropriate location for the activity.

Any area or site in which a program activity is conducted should be potentially safe and appropriate for the nature of the activity. It should provide the resources to meet the needs of the activity and not pose hazards that create unnecessary risks for participants.

4. Prepare all facilitators well so they can handle emergencies on any activity.

Formal orientation of *trainers* is a critical part of the safety of an adventure or wilderness program. The training should include "practice runs" so the staff can assess the trainees' readiness and ensure adequate instruction. Participants should be told of potential hazards and be taught proper techniques for dealing with them.

Nearly every aspect of an adventure training program depends on some type of specialized equipment. Instruction should ensure that participants know what the equipment is, what it is used for, how to properly use, maintain, and inspect it, and what to do at the first sign of malfunction.

Accidents sometimes occur regardless of the care or precautions taken. A review of the emergency procedures of a safe adventure training program should reveal that the provider is equipped and well prepared to cope with emergencies in a prompt and professional manner. Arrangements for emergencies should include coordination with groups capable of providing emergency medical services: sheriffs' offices, rescue teams, and hospitals.

You should anticipate participant errors, so it is essential to plan and train for rescue operations. Carefully monitor participants and their progress in the activity, and enforce established rules for participant behavior. Finally, train *all staff* to make reasonable efforts to get people out of danger, regardless of its source.

Participants put complete trust in their leaders, who should make every effort to help participants safely complete the activity. As an instructor, you should anticipate and sense dangerous situations and prepare to deal with potential problems. You should also anticipate participants' reactions to stressful situations, and be prepared to deal with them constructively and with sensitivity.

Even when you have breached your legal duty through unsafe activities, the injured party must establish that the breach of that duty was the cause of the harm. If unforeseen severe weather conditions or some other "act of God" (such as an earthquake or unanticipated fire) intervenes, your liability for negligence may be limited. However, you must still be prepared to handle reasonably foreseeable emergencies, and to implement rescue plans. If you proceed in the face of danger, even when the conditions giving rise to the new danger were unforeseen, you increase your legal risks and may assume new legal duties to handle the situation safely under the changed circumstances. Be prepared to stop the program in progress when unexpected situations arise.

How to Handle Stress, Fatigue, and Fear

The value of many adventure programs lies in the intensity of the experience. Participants frequently report life-changing results. Trainees have the opportunity to confront and overcome their own fears and in turn their internal barriers to success. Stress, even extreme fear, is intentionally injected into the program.

When stress is an integral part of their job, participants should be provided with realistic workplace scenarios. (See the detailed discussion in Chapter 4, pp. 101–104.) Once realistic anxieties have been injected into a simulation exercise, participants may experience illness arising from the training itself. Although this is unfortunate and should be minimized by appropriate instructional design, there are times when it simply can't be avoided.

Even for highly stressful management jobs, however, executives are not faced with climbing trees, hugging ropes, or performing other physically and mentally challenging tasks on a daily basis. Adventure training is typically *not* the type of program in which to realistically simulate the actual workplace. Nevertheless, your company and your professional vendor may conclude that introducing appropriate levels of tension into the experiential activities will yield positive results when participants return to the "real world" of their workplaces.

Once you have decided to weave physical and emotional pressures into the program, you should take precautions to limit the potential for injuries by informing all participants at the outset that some anxiety is anticipated and normal. Provide participants with an opportunity to discuss their fears in advance. Thoroughly debrief them after each activity to ensure that all participants have an opportunity to discuss how they felt and to proceed comfortably with the remainder of the agenda.

Honor the requests of any participants who are so stressed that they opt out of a particular activity. Make a special effort to include those individuals as integral parts of other exercises. Be alert to potential acts of intimidation or ridicule by coworkers or other participants, and put a stop to such behavior immediately.

Be alert also to the potential for extreme fatigue. Some trainees will not be physically ready for strenuous activities. Tell participants they may stop or ask for a rest break if they feel ill or fatigued. Emphasize that team participation never requires pushing oneself beyond reasonable endurance levels, and be sure facilitators and other participants don't embarrass or push a trainee too far by peer pressure, even when well intended.

Obtain immediate medical attention for any employee who has trouble breathing or becomes dizzy or disoriented by altitude or exertion. If first aid or medical attention is required, keep a complete record of what occurred. Take your notes from the field and incorporate them into a memorandum when you return to the workplace, so you can refresh your memory in case you are ever questioned by a workers' compensation carrier or in a courtroom.

How to Effectively (and Lawfully) Include Disabled Participants

The federal Americans With Disabilities Act (ADA) prohibits an employer from refusing to train, promote, evaluate, or otherwise provide employment benefits to a qualified disabled employee. A disabled individual is defined as a person who (1) has a physical or mental impairment that substantially limits one or more of the person's major life activities, (2) has a record of such impairment, or (3) is regarded as having such an impairment.

Covered disabilities that may affect an employee's ability to participate fully in an adventure training program may range from motor and sensory impairments (affecting sight, hearing, and mobility) to chronic disorders (such as epilepsy, emphysema, severe hypertension, diabetes, and asthma). The ADA is fully discussed in Chapters 6, pp. 141–143; 7, pp. 167–171; and 14, pp. 298–305. This chapter addresses the issue of disability discrimination relative to adventure training programs.

To be protected under the laws, a participant must be both disabled and "otherwise qualified." A participant is otherwise qualified if he or she is able to meet all the essential requirements of the job with or without reasonable accommodation. If one essential function of the job is participating in job-related training programs, then someone who cannot perform the training because of a disability can be appropriately excluded.

You should be mindful, however, that the primary objective of adventure training is to develop teamwork, problem solving, communication, and other soft skills that will make the participants better managers. The actual physical challenges of the program—trees, poles, logs, or ropes—will not be present when participants return to the workplace. The ability to climb a rope or navigate a raft through white water is not an essential function of any job; it is merely the tool used to develop new patterns of thinking or responding in team situations. In essence, the outdoor exercises don't replicate a task the employee will be expected to perform on the job.

Chapter 7, pp. 167–171, addresses disability discrimination in the context of posttraining testing. When a test measures job-related knowledge but does not replicate a specific job function, the test taker is entitled to a reasonable accommodation to demonstrate competency to perform the job. Just as a disabled employee who cannot overcome inherent barriers in the test procedure is entitled to a reasonable accommodation, so too is the disabled team member who cannot fully participate in the wilderness training activities.

You may not deny privileges of employment—including training and benefits—or otherwise adversely treat an employee because of a non-job-related disability. Thus, in the context of adventure training, you should always consider reasonable accommodations for disabled trainees with special needs. Discuss the need for an accommodation at the earliest possible time with the affected employee and with all facilitators or program designers.

Trainers should also address the issue directly with the disabled participant. For example, an insulin-dependent diabetic may be the best source of information on how you can provide refrigeration for the insulin, or incorporate regularly spaced meal periods for the individual. Likewise, a participant with hypertension or a severe heart condition may be able to consult a physician in advance to obtain input on which activities are appropriate and which are ill-advised. The program can then be altered, where feasible and appropriate, to maximize participation by the person with the disability.

Another potential reasonable accommodation in adventure training is the use of adaptive equipment. If a power source is necessary, make efforts to plan for full use of the equipment. Consider also accessibility and travel. In addition to the training site, evaluate in advance the accessibility of recreational areas, food services, sleeping areas, and emergency medical services. For example, some mountain retreats have only bunk beds, or place the food service at the top of a hill. Discuss any accessibility issues with the vendor and the management of the facility.

Don't make these programs mandatory if there is any question that they might be physically demanding or psychologically challenging. If the program is mandatory or strongly recommended, and a disabled employee is unable to participate, carefully consider an alternative method for the employee to acquire the same knowledge or workplace skill. Remember that the physical challenges in such a program are simply a method to achieve an understanding, a perspective, or a teamwork skill needed on the job; managers are not going to return to your work site to climb trees or perform other physical tasks. Thus, the disabled employee should be provided with an alternative method to achieve the same objective.

If you are taking an intact work group on a team-building workshop that involves physical components, and you have a disabled team member, make every effort not to exclude that member from the entire program. Find ways to accommodate participation to every extent possible. Consultants who develop adventure programs should already have addressed these issues, and can be helpful in designing exercises that will maximize participation by every member of the team. Remember that it is your legal obligation to inform an external consultant or facilitator about the need to consider reasonable accommodations for qualified disabled participants.

Alternatives to participation should be both nonthreatening and nonpunishing. This holds for both direct job-related actions and "subtle" forms of retaliation. It is a hollow remedy to allow an employee to "opt out" of a program because of a disability or medical condition only to be faced with ostracism or even ridicule from supervisors or coworkers. Make sure, through adjunct training, that supervisors don't punish those who do not participate when their performance appraisals are due. (See Chapter 12, pp. 259–268, for a full discussion of management training to prevent violations of the law.)

In each of these situations, planning is a critical component. In addition to fostering goodwill for all participants, and meeting your legal obligations to consider all reasonable accommodations, you and an external facilitator may be able to build into the program elements which the team members can carry back to their workplace as abled and disabled work together.

When an employee with a physical illness or disorder requires a medical clearance to participate, it is not discriminatory to request one in writing. This is a part of the reasonable accommodation, since it facilitates the individual's participation in a work-related event. However, to ensure complete effectiveness, the physician should be given all relevant information regarding the anticipated physical activities and any required medication. There should be no deviation from the physician's recommendations.

To protect the confidentiality of such personal information, and to comply with the significant restrictions imposed by the ADA on the receipt of medical information regarding a disability, you should request only as much medical information as is necessary to determine the nature and scope of the reasonable accommodation. This includes any physical restrictions, timing, or requirements for medication, and emergency treatment information in the event of a problem during training. Share the medical information only with the facilitator and those company representatives with an immediate need to know. All written records pertaining to the medical information should be filed separately from the employee's regular personnel file.

Investigating and Documenting Vendor Safety Records: A Checklist

Select vendors and consultants of adventure programs very carefully. First, decide whether the vendor's role will be to design and facilitate the entire program or to train your in-house trainers. The decision will determine the level of supervision you should exercise over the activities. Also, determine in advance the lines of authority between the vendor/facilitator and your authorized company representative. Give your representative the authority to excuse any participant who becomes agitated or ill.

Be prepared to examine the plans, the daily decisions, and the actions taken by providers to ensure minimum risk to trainees. Program design, safety procedures, organizational structure, emergency planning, medical services, and qualifications of *all* staff are essential features to examine when evaluating a provider's approach to safety. A good safety record doesn't just happen; it is the result of deliberate planning.

Any experienced provider of adventure training should be receptive to your request for safety records. For example, Outward Bound USA has an established accident reporting system and prepares an annual safety report to assist its managers in reviewing the safety of the year's program and in charting progress in reducing accidents, injuries, and illnesses. In addition, Outward Bound has instituted a review process whereby its safety program is independently audited every two years.

If the consultant you select is reluctant or appears offended when you request information, consider another provider. Indeed, consultants should be forthcoming for your mutual protection, since the principles of comparative fault will apply to all programs jointly sponsored or produced. (See the discussion in this chapter, pp. 199–202.)

Prior to the program, be sure that you know precisely what physical and emotional tasks will be required. Have an authorized representative of your organization attend one of the vendor's programs. If it is not possible to attend an actual program, obtain at least three references from similar organizations. Ask to speak to participants at several levels, such as the training director, the on-site trainer, and a representative sampling of actual participants. If the vendor is unwilling for you to make detailed reference contacts, consider using another vendor. However, the vendor may reasonably request that you hold proprietary information confidential, and otherwise engage in ethical and appropriate contacts at all times.

Carefully consider the facilitator's experience in providing such training for similar organizations. Assure yourself that the vendor is knowledgeable about your work environment, so the program is designed to maximize relevancy for your participants. Assure yourself too that the facilitator is experienced in basic emergency response and is well versed in the legal and practical requirements of providing training to a diverse group of participants. These requirements include being responsive to multicultural issues, communication styles, and the special needs of disabled trainees.

Determine how the vendor will handle situations if participants find the program physically demanding while it is in progress. Convey in writing to the vendor how you expect fear and fatigue to be handled during the program.

Provide your representative with the authority to intervene or stop an activity under specified circumstances. Try to anticipate the range of circumstances under which intervention may occur, and address the issues up front with the vendor. This will minimize open conflict in front of participants and reduce the potential for a later contractual dispute with the vendor.

1. Ask for appropriate information from the vendor's safety records. What is the vendor's accident rate? What on-site medical care is available? Is the vendor prepared for foreseeable emergencies?

2. Select vendors carefully. Demand to inspect safety records and determine in advance the first-aid and other safety measures that will be employed.

3. Determine how the vendor will handle individuals who decide in the middle of the program that the activity is too physically or emotionally challenging. Efforts must be made to avoid embarrassing them.

4. Ask for a description of any personal protective equipment (PPE) that will be utilized during the program, and determine who will supply these items. Who is responsible for making sure they are in working order? What steps will be taken to be sure there is enough PPE for all participants, in the sizes required?

5. Thoroughly document your investigation of the vendor's safety records and references.

6. Inform all participants in advance about the content of the program. Assure them that the program will be monitored closely for safety.

7. Consider sending a company representative from the training department to make sure the vendor complies with safety and emergency precautions. Inform participants that even though you are confident of the vendor's experience and professionalism, your company representative will also monitor the entire program.

8. Document the steps you have taken to protect employees' rights. This documentation should include a summary of your investigation into the content and methodology of the program, as well as the concrete steps you took to make it both voluntary and non-penalizing.

9. Document the steps you take to investigate the vendor's safety record and on-site emergency services.

How Unsupervised Consultants and Vendors Can Cause Legal Problems for Their Clients

The vendor you retain becomes your employer's agent in delivering the services you request. Under normal agency principles, everything the vendor does within the course and scope of the agreement is on your behalf. Your employer is responsible for the acts of its agent, and has "vicarious" liability for errors or omissions that produce injuries. Some courts use the term *respondeat superior* to describe this indirect liability. In plain English, the agent (the consultant) stands in the shoes of the principal (the employer). As an internal trainer, your role in selecting, recommending, or supervising the consultant is also a responsibility you fulfill for your employer. Your negligence may be imposed directly on your employer in the form of a damage judgment.

Under normal agency principles, an organization is not legally responsible for the acts of an independent contractor when the latter exceeds the scope of its authority. For example, if you hire a courier to deliver a package, and you authorize him to drive safely and within the rules of the road, he will be your agent if he negligently injures a pedestrian while following normal driving practices. However, if the courier drives intoxicated, and you have neither authorized him to do so nor learned of his impropriety, your legal responsibility may be limited. At least, as between you and the agent, he will be required to compensate you for any damages you incur through his excess of authority.

The employment relationship broadens your responsibilities and limits your ability to pass legal liabilities entirely to the vendor. Some employer duties can't be delegated, such as safety and discrimination prevention. This means that your employer cannot shield itself from its own liability by relinquishing control to a vendor or contractor. See Chapter 3, pp. 80–82, for a full discussion.

Because of the employer's independent duties to provide a safe, healthful, and nondiscriminatory work environment, the consultant's actions are deemed to be within the course and scope of his or her authority. This makes it extremely important to define the scope of responsibilities, and to set express limits, where appropriate, on the consultant's authority.

Address every aspect of the program, from when to excuse participation by a trainee who falls ill, to providing emergency services, to accommodating special needs of disabled participants. There is no substitute for preplanning to incorporate all foreseeable circumstances into the retention agreement.

In essence, if you fail to specify appropriate limitations on that authority, or don't effectively supervise the activities to ensure compliance with the scope of the agreement, you will be deemed to have extended the authority of the consultant as your agent. The employer, as the consultant's client, will be liable for negligent acts or omissions by the consultant.

In addition to this vicarious liability, your employer has an independent legal duty to effectively supervise all consultants you retain and provide with power over your employees. If you fail to ascertain qualifications, inspect safety records, or otherwise supervise, you risk independent liability for negligent retention. Under these circumstances, *both your employer and the consultant will have legal duties to program participants.* Their respective breaches of legal duty can give rise to a lawsuit in which they find themselves joint defendants. Some of their liabilities may overlap, such as when they have jointly directed the activities. In other instances the liabilities will be separate and independent, such as when the employer does not exercise appropriate control over the planning and performance of the training, and the consultant negligently causes an injury.

Sharing the Risk: Determining Accountability for Joint Activities

Comparative fault principles apply in all but two states and the District of Columbia. Comparative fault broadens the potential liability of "deep pocket" defendants. Under this doctrine, the jury must determine the relative degree of fault of all parties. Each party will then have a specific percentage finding of fault.

For example, suppose an employee is injured in a workplace accident and alleges that her employer is negligent in failing to train her. She also alleges that a vendor hired by the employer to design the program bears some responsibility, also for negligence. The employee is also partially at fault, because she ignored instructions on how to make sure the safety goggles fit properly. The ultimate eye injury would have been less severe, but not precluded, by correctly fitting glasses.

The jury must make findings of the degree of fault of each party, such as 5 percent for the injured employee, 45 percent for the employer, and 50 percent for the vendor. In a comparative fault state, the employee's recovery would be reduced by 5 percent, but the employee would not be completely out of court, as would be the case in a contributory negligence jurisdiction. In this example, the relative payments by the employer and the vendor are comparable.

An adjunct to the comparative fault concept is the doctrine of *joint and several liability,* which applies in most states. In plain English, this means that each party is responsible for its own percentage of fault ("several" or individual/separate liability), but also for the whole award ("joint"). By analogy, this is the equivalent of a joint bank account, in which both parties own the whole amount, even if they contribute different percentages of the total.

In the above example, if the award was $100,000, the injured party's 5 percent fault would reduce it to $95,000. Then, the employer would be responsible for 45 percent of the net, and the vendor the remainder. Equitable? Yes, but only because the relative degree of fault is essentially equal *if* both parties are financially capable of paying their individual ("several") share. But suppose the vendor is not able to pay most of its $50,000 share. The employer, which has "joint" (shared) liability for the whole judgment, must pay the entire amount. The result becomes even more inequitable if the fault is 80 percent for the vendor and 20 percent for the employer.

This doctrine was initially designed to avoid the harsh results of an injured party's being unpaid because of a financially irresponsible defendant. The result in many comparative fault jurisdictions has been to name as many potentially culpable defendants as possible, because even a very low level of fault by a wealthy defendant may result in the injured party's being made whole.

Thus, joint and several liability is often called the "deep pockets" doctrine. This partially explains why injured parties are not reluctant to bring their employer—and all potentially responsible departments and parties—into a personal injury lawsuit. Although the press and many business and industry groups have labeled comparative fault laws a "plaintiff's bonanza," the reality is that in a state with a comparative fault doctrine it is both legal and ethical to name all reasonably responsible parties and then to seek a specific apportionment of fault.

Comparative fault laws are governed by state statutes, so the state legislature may make changes at any time. In the absence of a legislative will to do so, initiatives can be placed on state ballots, as was done in California. Through a ballot initiative, voters modified the comparative fault doctrine by limiting the "joint" liability to economic damages— lost wages, reimbursement for medical expenses, and other "tangible" losses—with the portion of any award attributable to general pain and suffering to be borne only in relationship to fault. Thus, a training organization found to be only 10 percent at fault would pay a maximum of 10 percent of the economic damages, even if the party 90 percent culpable is broke. Any award for punitive damages (which are *not* available in a negligence action, since malice, oppression, or fraud is necessary) is a noneconomic component, and will be held to the strict apportionment standard.

Astute readers may be wondering how a financially sound organization with a high degree of fault can avoid the potential for a "joint" judgment with others with less culpability. After all, most lawsuits are settled out of court. Can a largely responsible party settle for a small amount and avoid the risk of going to trial?

It doesn't work that way. First, most injured parties obtain access to financial data early in the lawsuit and won't settle for a pittance if there is a concern about later recovery against other jointly responsible parties. In addition, most state laws have a good-faith settlement component that allows a settling party to obtain a judicial finding that its settlement is not grossly disproportionate to its ultimate potential exposure.

Contracting Issues

The providers selected for adventure programs should have the best safety records and most qualified staff. Get specific details about each provider, such as its injury record, type of program, emergency procedures, and orientation activities for participants. Before finally selecting a provider, get enough information to be able to respond to employees' questions regarding program safety.

As companies negotiate agreements for adventure training, liability issues arise. The main issue is discerning how much liability falls on the program sponsor and how much falls on the program providers. When contracting with a provider of adventure management training programs, you should obtain a *hold-harmless* agreement from the provider. This kind of agreement seeks to waive the company's liability for injury, illness, fatality, and public liability. You should also request supporting documentation that the provider carriers adequate liability insurance. Allocation of responsibilities for indemnification and hold-harmless agreements are generally handled by contract, as demonstrated in the samples in Appendix C.

Generally a written agreement details the relationship between program sponsor and program provider, including insurance and liability provisions. Despite agreements assigning liability to program providers, sponsors should carefully investigate program safety precautions, scrutinize site selections, and make certain that providers have adequate insurance coverage. Sponsors should also examine the safety record and financial viability of program providers. Courts look for deep pockets when grievous injuries occur and inadequate insurance coverage exists. For example, a large successful vendor will have deeper pockets than a nonprofit organization. Courts will have the deep-pockets company pick up a larger tab.

Waiver forms also are referred to as release forms, statements of understanding, or covenants not to sue. The legal value of these forms varies by jurisdiction. Have an attorney review and evaluate any waiver form. If waivers are used, even with limited contractual value, each participant should be allowed sufficient time to read and review the contents before signing; otherwise, the courts may decide that the participant was not fully aware of all the risks involved. Avoid possible claims by employees that they were coerced into signing the waiver as a condition of keeping their jobs.

How to Prevent Injuries During High-Risk Training and What to Do When They Occur

Business sponsorship of adventure programs has increased in recent years. These programs have more visible danger than traditional training. Suggestions for improving the safety of such programs include the following.

General Planning Considerations

1. Consider in advance the concrete objectives you have for the program.

   - Is it reasonably designed to impart a skill, knowledge, or analytical perspective that cannot be achieved with traditional methodology?
   - Will employees acquire a skill that can be tied directly to a business function?
   - How well are the objectives tied to a concrete determination of anticipated learning outcomes?
   - How will the success of the program be measured? How will participant performance be evaluated?

2. Obtain adequate health histories and, when appropriate, physical examinations of participants.

3. Provide current, step-by-step instruction. Make sure participants feel comfortable using equipment.

4. Do not pressure reluctant participants to continue the activity.

5. Foresee and avoid hazardous site conditions.

6. Explain risks and hazards before starting the activity.

7. Understand how people react to stress, and assist those with inappropriate reactions in safely completing the activity.

Emergency Procedures

1. Have first-aid materials present during the training. If possible, one member of the training team should be certified in CPR or other emergency procedures (a "plus factor" in selecting a vendor).

2. Make sure that all emergency telephone numbers are present at the site. Determine in advance the nearest medical care and/or hospital. This is also something the vendor should be prepared to accomplish. Of course you hope never to use such services, but it is wise to be prepared for all foreseeable contingencies.

What to Do in the Event of an Accident

1. Get professional help immediately, including medical or emergency response specialists or other qualified practitioners.

2. Remove other employees or participants from the immediate area, without creating panic or undue emotional distress.

3. Preserve evidence without exposing others to danger.
   - Take pictures of any existing conditions.
   - If there is no camera, draw a diagram and keep it with your notes.
   - Maintain the originals of the notes in a safe place, and date them with the day, month, and year.
   - Record the names, addresses, and telephone numbers of all those who witnessed the accident.
   - Notify your workers' compensation carrier and/or company risk management personnel as soon as possible.

4. Do not volunteer any opinions about the cause of the accident *to anyone*, including the vendor or facilitator's representatives. It is an unfortunate aspect of litigation that your friends, business partners, and colleagues may later be called upon to testify truthfully and in good faith about all communications surrounding an incident, and your genuine postaccident concern may be mischaracterized as an admission of liability.

5. Prior to the training, establish teams of individuals to contact in the event of an emergency. Teams may include safety personnel, management representatives, human resources specialists, and legal counsel.

Availability of Workers'
Compensation Benefits

Workers' compensation systems provide compensation to employees injured on the job regardless of fault. Moreover, these statutes provide some protection for employers against excessive liability. Work-related activities may include attendance at and travel to or from employer-sponsored activities. The courts will use the following issues to determine if an activity is work related:

- Did the employer pressure the employee to attend the function?
- Does sponsorship of the activity benefit the employer?
- To what extent did the employer sponsor control or participate in the activity?
- If the activity constitutes a benefit or consideration paid to the employee, such as activities awarded as sales prizes, workers' compensation does not apply.

Recent court decisions disclose a trend of extending benefits to employees injured while attending or traveling to or from employer-sponsored training programs. Sponsors should be informed about the legal risks to these programs and should choose or design their programs with safety in mind. A safety focus by all facilitators reduces the legal risk.

Reference

1. *Leahy v. School Board of Hernando County*, 450 So.2d 883 (Florida 1984).

9

Legal Challenges to New-Age Programs and How to Avoid Them

New-age or nontraditional training programs have captured the attention of both the Equal Employment Opportunity Commission (EEOC) and the courts. Designed to unleash the participants' potential by taking them out of both traditional classroom settings and their own "comfort zones," these programs are frequently provided for managers and supervisors.

There are as many definitions of new-age training as there are suppliers of such programs. Their techniques include self-hypnosis, guided visualization, therapeutic touch, biofeedback, and inducing altered states of consciousness to allow participants to achieve self-actualization, with the goal of improving motivation and productivity on the job. Defenders of new-age training respond that it is designed to enhance communication, open thought processes, and stimulate personal awareness that leads to productivity.

The Princeton Religious Center has defined new age as "an eclectic term for a wide range of beliefs held by some who may call themselves 'new agers' or 'aquarians.'"[1] Training programs that have been categorized as new age come in a variety of forms, including the teachings of mystics whose stated objective is to improve communication among employees, faith healers who read the "auras" of employees to improve their health, and consultants who aim to improve the "personal growth" of employees.

Critics of new-age training programs object to employers forcing employees to attend programs that attempt to "bend an individual's mind."[2] Other critics see such training as an attempt to introduce cultism and mysticism into corporate America. For example, Carl Rasche, an expert in religion and society, sees new-age training as a method used to "robotize employees by making them more compliant."[3]

The debate over the value of new-age training programs will continue as long as creative approaches to learning and professional growth are staples in the business world. However, a number of legal issues must be carefully considered to avoid potential costly lawsuits over invasions of employees' fundamental rights of privacy and religious freedom.

In 1988, the EEOC issued an addendum to its Compliance Manual relating to nontraditional training programs. The EEOC relied largely on two articles—one from *The New York Times* and one from *Time* magazine—in concluding that those programs may well violate employees' religious rights under Title VII.[4] *The New York Times* article described various instances of apparent conflicts between new-age training programs and employees' religious beliefs. One such instance involved a large California public utility that had been requiring employees to attend seminars based primarily on the teachings of a mystic, George Gurdjieff, who is associated with Eastern mysticism and the concept of "the power of positive thinking."

Employees complained that the seminars were a subtle form of mind control that sought to alter the employees' beliefs, self-concepts, and religious views. In one case, an employee was discharged by Firestone Tire and Rubber Company after he refused to participate in a new-age training program because the course focused on the individual and emphasized that the individual has the power and ability to deal with all problems. The approach conflicted with his religious beliefs that human fate is dependent on the will of God.

When Nontraditional
Methods Cross the Legal
Line and Why

New-age programs have been legally challenged on three primary grounds: infringement of religious beliefs, invasion of privacy, and infliction of emotional distress. Legal principles involve both discrimination under Title VII of the federal Civil Rights Act of 1964 and state laws involving personal injury claims.

Religious Infringement

Title VII of the Civil Rights Act prohibits discrimination on the basis of religion. Many states and local governments have similar laws. Under Title VII, an employer is required to accommodate the religious beliefs and practices of employees unless it can show that such an accommodation would constitute an undue hardship on the conduct of the employer's business.

Title VII prohibits religious discrimination against employees with respect to their pay, *training,* access to opportunities, and conditions or privileges of employment. The law defines religion as all aspects of religious observance and practice, including consistently held belief systems. Mere philosophical beliefs with no religious basis, no matter how strongly held, are not protected.

Title VII's prohibition of religious discrimination is not limited to situations in which the employee wishes to observe a Sabbath or holiday. Once an employee has stated a sincerely held religious belief that conflicts with one of your employer's requirements, including the content of training programs, you have a duty to address some type of accommodation. The employee has an obligation to cooperate in seeking a resolution of a conflict, and may not insist upon an accommodation of his or her own choosing. You need not make an accommodation if it will result in undue hardship to your employer.

Some aid in interpreting the definition of undue hardship comes from *Welsh v. United States,*[5] in which the Supreme Court interpreted the Military Selective Service Act, which exempts from "combatant training and service" any person "who, by reason of religious training and belief, is conscientiously opposed to participate in war." The Court relied upon its decision in *United States v. Seeger* that '[the] task is to decide whether the beliefs professed by a registrant are sincerely held and whether they are, *in his own scheme of things,* religious.'"[6]

The test is primarily economic. If an accommodation will cost your employer more than a modest amount or be unduly disruptive, then it may constitute an undue hardship. However, the less able you are to establish a sound business reason or necessity for the content, methodology, or timing of the training, the more difficult it will be to defend a lawsuit on grounds of undue hardship.

Several high-profile cases involve claims by employees that new-age training programs infringe on their protected rights of religion. The most notable case is *Kim v. DeKalb Farmers Market, Inc.,*[7] in which a mandatory training module for managers and employees allegedly required participants to disclose some very private information about their personal lives, which they felt infringed on their privacy. In addition, the vendor hired by the employer refused to excuse people and allegedly bullied them into participating. Also, employees contended that the trainers sought to impose values, doctrines, and thought processes that conflicted with the employees' religious beliefs.

Eight employees brought suit, alleging a violation of Title VII. Kim, who was a supervisor, claimed that he was urged by his boss to attend the training session, which was designed to create a breakthrough experience but which Kim claimed required emotional confessions by the participants and amounted to psychological conditioning and programming. The owner of the business told Kim to recruit his subordinates, and when he refused, conditions at work became so difficult that Kim was forced to quit. The case was settled out of court for an undisclosed sum.

The allegations dovetailed with a previous EEOC directive that referred specifically to new-age programs. The EEOC warned employers to be vigilant about protecting the rights of employees to practice their religion by allowing them to opt out of programs that conflict with their religious beliefs. In addition, a previously decided California case involving alleged "indoctrination" training at Pacific Bell was instrumental in the rapid settlement of *DeKalb Market.*

In another highly publicized case, a public utility sponsored a mandatory "leadership development" program that was designed to teach people to "think about thinking."[8] The consultant hired by the company used techniques derived from Eastern mystic teachings. As a result of employee complaints, the California Public Utilities Commission investigated the program, and concluded that the training created fear, decreased productivity, wasted time, and resulted in a split in the corporate culture and an intimidating work environment.[9]

In still another case, referred to as EEOC Decision No. 91-1 (January 1991), the subject training program was developed and marketed by a religious organization. The course materials instructed the course supervisor to make a convert out of every student by fully applying the religious teaching that the philosophy was "all-powerful and that the founder of the religious organization was a universal force believing in reincarnation."

The company president stressed that only by practicing the principles of the training program could employees attain professional and personal success. A communication consultant, marketing representative, and marketing supervisor brought the suit, alleging that their employer pressured them into participating in the training against their religious beliefs. Their refusal subjected them to extreme intimidation and coercion, creating an intolerable working environment. The president threatened to withdraw his support of any employee who resisted the training. He further harassed and degraded a supervisor in front of other employees when the supervisor refused to participate in the training. When the protestors were forced to quit, they filed a complaint with the EEOC, alleging discrimination on the basis of religious infringement, religious intimidation, and constructive discharge.

The EEOC ruled that the three employees had established a case of discrimination and that the employer failed to accommodate their religious beliefs, thereby violating Title VII. The company responded by alleging that the employees never requested an accommodation and that to provide one would have created undue hardship. Rejecting this defense, the EEOC stated: "To make out a...case of failure to accommodate, however, it is only necessary that an employee inform the employer of the conflict between his/her religious beliefs and the employment requirement." It was irrelevant that the charging parties did not actually use the term *accommodation* in making their requests.

The EEOC also rejected the assertion that attendance at the program was voluntary. The commission perceived the assertions as a mere pretext in light of the employees' credible allegations concerning intimidation and harassment.

Religious Intimidation

The courts and the EEOC have adopted a three-prong test for determining if an individual's beliefs or practices are religious. A belief or practice is religious if (1) it is sincerely held by the individual, (2) it functions as a religion in the individual's life, and (3) the belief is moral or ethical concerning right and wrong. If the employee is alleging religious intimidation, however, he or she must prove that the employer's new-age training program is religious and that it creates a religious atmosphere in the workplace. Under Title VII, an employer is required to maintain a working environment free of coercion or intimidation based on religion.

The *Kim v. DeKalb Market* case also had elements of religious intimidation. Employees were told to shed their own religious beliefs in exchange for a new system being taught by the instructor. The roots of the training had definite religious content, and the religious framework was concealed from some employees until advanced training sessions. Additionally, the facilitators promoted their programs as "life-changing," and the principles being taught were presented as essential to the personal and professional success of the employee. This met the EEOC's three-prong test to determine if the content is religious.

The EEOC specifically addressed a new-age program involving allegations of intimidation in a case known as EEOC Decision 71-1114 (February 18, 1972). The case involved an employer that permitted a supervisor to preach religion while on the job to two senior control tower operators. The operators complained about the activity to the director of training. The evidence established that the supervisor did discuss his religious convictions with other employees while on the job. The EEOC ruled that the employer violated Title VII by discharging one of the operators and constructively discharging the second by creating an intolerable work environment.

In response to employee complaints, the EEOC issued a policy statement on new-age training programs. The EEOC's Policy Statement on Training Programs Conflicting With Employees' Religious Beliefs, issued February 22, 1988, clarifies the nature of the conflict and the employer's duty to accommodate.

Reasonable Accommodations

The EEOC reaffirmed that an employer may not impose any religious requirements on the terms and conditions of employment without discriminating on the basis of religion. According to the policy statement, religion-based conflicts raised by new-age training programs "can be resolved under the traditional Title VII theory of religious accommodation." In its Compliance Manual, the EEOC states that "an employee need only demonstrate that participation in the program in some manner conflicts with his/her personal religious beliefs," and upon that demonstration the employer must:

1. Substitute an alternative technique or method not offensive to the employee's belief;
2. Excuse the employee from the particular offensive portion of the program; or
3. If the employee contends that the program itself rests upon concepts contrary to his or her beliefs, excuse the employee from the entire program.[10]

Thus, when you design and/or deliver new-age programs on behalf of your employer, you have a duty to make reasonable accommodations for the religious needs of your employees. The requirement for accommodation is to militate against employer policies, neutral on their face, that affect the ability of employees with sincere convictions to comply with the policies. In applying this provision, the U.S. Supreme Court has ruled that an employer need only "reasonably" accommodate the employee's needs—and only so far as such accommodation does not cause undue hardship on the conduct of the employer's business.

Some basic considerations of the courts in determining whether an employer has made reasonable efforts to accommodate employees' religious practices include the following.

- *The nature of the job or opportunity.* If the job or opportunity is specialized or unique, the employer may discharge or refuse to employ a person whose religious practices conflict with its needs. The right of refusal is limited to essential functions of a unique job, such as significant weekend travel which conflicts with Sabbath observances or safety constraints on the wearing of religious clothing.

- *The size of your employer's establishment.* If your employer is a large company, it may well be required to explain why it could not transfer the employee to a different operation, or provide an alternative training opportunity to allow the employee to acquire the information or learn the skill from a nontraditional training program.

- *The effect of transferring the employee to a different job, or providing an alternative training opportunity.* If a transfer means a substantial reduction in pay, or loss of other terms or conditions of employment, the employer may be required to show that no other method of accommodation is possible.

- *The employee's efforts in reaching accommodation.* If an employee fails to inform the employer of his or her needs or refuses to cooperate in trying to reach an accommodation, the employee may be considered as having forgone the right to reasonable accommodation.

The question of how far you must go to accommodate an employee raises the issue of undue hardship. In general, your employer must accommodate an employee until doing so results in undue hardship. The concept of undue hardship relative to reasonable accommodation of employees' religious needs under Title VII is a different and lesser standard than undue hardship under federal disability bias laws, according to the EEOC.[11]

The EEOC makes clear in its Compliance Manual that such training programs should not be made mandatory, as illustrated in the following hypothetical case.

> R requires its employees, as part of a training program, to participate in a form of meditation that involves emptying one's mind of all thoughts by repeating a meaningless word. The employees are taught that this meditation will bring them into contact with the "ultimate reality of the universe" which empowers them to reach the "supreme authentication" of their "True Self" and to become one with "All That That Is." R must accommodate the religious beliefs of its employees by excusing from this exercise, not only those employees who object because this conflicts with their religious beliefs, but also employees who object because they have chosen not to have

religious beliefs. In addition, *R's policy of requiring employees to attend a religiously oriented program discriminates on its face against all employees and potential employees on the basis of religion.*[12]

The burden to reasonably accommodate the religious needs of employees was also considered in the case of *EEOC v. Townley Engineering Co.*[13] The company's owners alleged that they made a "covenant with God" that their business "would be a Christian, faith-operated" business and required the attendance of its employees at a weekly devotional service held in the plant. The court found that the practice violated Title VII, because it conflicted with a bona fide religious belief of an employee and the employee was penalized in some way because of the conflict.

Once the employee establishes these elements, the burden shifts to the employer to prove that it made a good-faith effort to accommodate the employee's religious beliefs or practices. Finding that Townley made no good-faith effort, the court noted that

> the burden of attempting an accommodation rests with the employer rather than the employee. . . . [W]hen an employer does not propose an accommodation, or when its proposed accommodation does not eliminate the employee's religious conflict, the employer must accept the employee's proposal or demonstrate that the proposal would cause the employer undue hardship.[14]

The court concluded that a claim of undue hardship must be supported by proof of actual imposition on coworkers, disruption of the work routine, or impact on the business and bottom line.

Invasion of Privacy

As noted in the Introduction on p. 9, other types of new-age training programs involve methodology that invades employees' psychic well-being. Some programs have resulted in adverse media attention, including the U.S. Federal Aviation Administration's stress management program.

In addition, programs that pressure employees to disclose private thoughts or information have been challenged successfully. In one high-profile situation involving the Federal Aviation Administration, the agency agreed to pay $75,000 to an air traffic controller who suffered a mental breakdown after her past personal agonies resurfaced when intense group discussions turned to talk of intimate sexual experiences. The case was raised in the context of an unfair labor practices complaint against the FAA by the National Air Traffic Controllers Association.

According to press reports of the training, the controller broke down during an intense workshop in which the participants were required to disclose sexual experiences. The discussion brought out memories so disturbing that she couldn't concentrate, took leave without pay, and spent documented time in a psychiatric hospital. The agreement committed the FAA to assign her to a staff position.

An internal analysis of the training warned the agency that "too much confrontation can result in pushing trainees beyond their emotional limits, resulting in adverse psychological effects, or entrenchment in the attitudes and behavior the training was meant to change."[15] In subsequent personal injury lawsuits, if it becomes apparent that the agency continued to conduct this training despite learning of stress-induced illness among trainees, the agency will have increased legal liabilities to employees subjected to the program after the warnings.

This same program, with the objective of diversity training, was the source of a number of claims by male air traffic controllers of sexual harassment and mental distress arising from a reverse "gauntlet" exercise, in which the men were groped, fondled, and forced to listen to sexual banter directed at them by women. This portion of the program is discussed in Chapter 5, pp. 114–116.

The FAA reached a settlement of the complaint by the controllers' union by inviting any potentially harmed trainees to file claims of sick leave and medical expenses attributable to the controversial program. At taxpayer expense, this was a tough lesson on the consequences of nontraditional methodology gone awry.

Nontraditional FAA training was again in the news in mid-1997, when former Inspector General Mary Schiavo disclosed to a nationwide audience on *60 Minutes* her concern about FAA training, conducted at taxpayer expense, in which employees were asked to sit around in their underwear while the trainer requested that some employees relinquish their clothing for "sniffing" to determine their "essence." Whatever the stated objective for the training may have been, the uncommon methodology created, at a minimum, poor productivity and low morale and at worst, liability for invasion of privacy.

Infliction of Emotional Distress

Still other programs involve exercises designed to intimidate or indoctrinate employees into patterned thinking. The psychological effects of these programs may produce illness and lead to workers' compensation claims. When the content of the program is particularly invasive, the aggrieved employee may bypass the state workers' compensation system and proceed with a personal injury lawsuit through a common law claim of "intentional infliction of emotional distress." These actions generally seek compensation for medical bills, lost work time, and related "expenses" as well as general pain and suffering from emotional distress. In addition, the employee may seek punitive damages to "punish" the employer for its wrongful conduct.

In establishing a claim for intentional infliction of emotional distress, the offended trainee must establish that the employer's action— through the content or delivery of the training—was so extreme and outrageous that no reasonable person could be expected to endure attending. Who decides what is reasonable under the circumstances? A jury of ordinary people drawn from the community. Such a jury may spell trouble for the employer that initiates a psychologically intrusive or demeaning training program that is not tied to a concrete job-related skill needed by the employee. If the jury, as trier of fact, fails to see the relevance of such disturbing training methodology, it may not be receptive to arguments about "reengineering the company by getting employees to adopt alternative thought processes."

This does not mean that you should never inject stress into a training program. Quite the contrary. Employees who are being trained to perform jobs in which stress—and reactions to stressful situations— may spell the difference between success and disaster must receive realistic training to provide them with the tools to perform these difficult jobs under the most adverse conditions. To do otherwise may ill prepare them to perform safely in the workplace.

Accordingly, programs designed to teach law enforcement officers to respond to threatening situations (physical and verbal), simulated disaster drills for emergency responders, military tactical exercises, and realistic accident simulators for airline pilots have all been upheld against claims of stress-induced injury during the training.

The critical distinction: Does the training simulate actual working conditions? When the training directly bears upon a task or skill that the trainee must master, it is both lawful and necessary to effective curriculum design. Indeed, the trainees' performance under realistic conditions may determine whether they can perform effectively on the job. For a complete discussion of the value and necessity of injecting stress into your methodology, see Chapter 4, pp. 100–104.

In contrast, new-age programs rarely can demonstrate a direct nexus between the intrusive content of the workshop and a job-related skill. In the absence of a clear business justification, when faced with the potential for intrusive content, trainers should very carefully weigh the benefits of the program with the potential risks to the health and well-being of the participants and the legal exposure of the trainers.

In these types of lawsuits, the injured employees may sue both the employer and the consultant or facilitator. The actions are brought in the state courts, and may include claims for personal liabilities for the trainers or external consultants as well as liability for the sponsoring organizations. Because the claims involve an alleged "intentional wrong," any damage award may not be covered by insurance.

When and How to Use Nontraditional Training Methods Without Fear of Lawsuits by Participants

Employers should not necessarily scrap all creative or nontraditional training methods. However, several precautions will limit legal liabilities.

1. Do *not* make programs mandatory if there is any question that they might be described as new age or as religious indoctrination of any sort. The same approach should be considered with respect to intense, stressful methodology unless injecting stress into the program is directly job-related, as in law enforcement training. (See the discussion in Chapter 4, pp. 103–104.)

2. If employees elect not to participate on religious or privacy grounds, be sure that appropriate alternative training is available. For example, a program to develop creative thinking skills using techniques that some employees find objectionable should be supplemented by a different program on creative thinking skills. Consider alternative developmental approaches that result in the same performance outcome.

3. Alternatives should be nonpunishing. This holds for both direct job-related actions and "subtle" forms of retaliation. It is a hollow remedy to allow an employee to "opt out" of a nontraditional program on religious grounds only to be faced with ostracism or ridicule from supervisors or coworkers.

4. Do not punish those who don't participate when their performance appraisals are due.

5. The program should truly be voluntary. That is, employees electing not to participate on religious grounds must not be treated differently in conditions of employment or promotional opportunities, or otherwise deprived of opportunities to acquire skills that will lead to career advancement.

6. With psychologically demanding or stress-inducing programs, ask yourself what concrete objectives you have for the program.

- Is it necessary to inject realism or stress into the design? (See Chapter 4, pp. 100–104.)
- Will employees acquire a skill that can be tied directly to a business imperative?
- How well are the objectives tied to a concrete determination of anticipated learning outcomes?
- How will the success of the program be measured? How will participants' performances be evaluated?

7. Select vendors very carefully.

- Determine the content of the program and tell prospective participants about it in advance.
- Determine how the vendor will handle situations if participants find the program intrusive while it is in progress.
- Convey in writing to the vendor or consultant how you expect conflict to be handled during the program.
- Discuss in advance how the vendor will handle employees who become agitated or distraught during the program. Insist that the facilitator not embarrass or criticize the trainee publicly during the program, and monitor the consultant's actions closely. Such conduct would be considered retaliation. Because the consultant is your authorized agent, you will be directly responsible for such behavior. The problem is compounded if your on-site representative does nothing to stop it.
- Determine in advance the lines of authority between the vendor or facilitator and your authorized company representative. Give your representative the authority to excuse any participant who is having trouble or who reasonably complains about the content or methodology.
- Consider giving your representative the power to stop the program under specified circumstances. Try to anticipate the range of circumstances under which a break may occur, and address the issues up front with the vendor. This will minimize open conflict in front of participants and reduce the potential for a later contractual dispute with the vendor.

8. If you have determined an appropriate business basis for training that may be personally intrusive, offer employees an option to begin the program in small groups before bringing everyone together. It may be less intimidating.

9. If emotional conflict is anticipated, make sure the trainer or consultant is well prepared to deal with it immediately. If a participant becomes agitated or ill, be prepared to take appropriate

steps to obtain immediate medical attention. At the same time, closely monitor the effect of a participant's anxiety on other participants.

10. Make sure that supervisors and managers are trained to avoid intimidation, coercion, or "heavy-handed" discussions of their own religious beliefs or support for new-age thought processes.

11. Develop and enforce consistent policies that prohibit any form of religious coercion, intimidation, or harassment by employees and supervisors, and impose consistent disciplinary measures when appropriate.

12. Document the steps you have taken to protect employees' privacy rights and emotional well-being. Documentation should include a summary of your investigation into the content and methodology of the program, as well as the concrete steps you took to make it both voluntary and nonpenalizing.

How to Anticipate and Deal With Participants' Complaints

It isn't necessary to scrap or avoid intense training programs, as long as you anticipate the potential areas of conflict. Some very creative approaches to learning require participants to stretch—both physically and psychologically. The entire object of the program may be to take employees out of their traditional comfort zone, so they can unleash their potential or take acceptable job-related risks when they return to the office.

Always have a company representative present and available at the training site. This is especially important when the program's content may invoke strong reactions or may be uncomfortable. Be sure to provide the on-site representative with the appropriate level of authority to make immediate decisions if trainees refuse to participate or become agitated.

If you have carefully considered the program and your organization is satisfied that it is appropriate and reasonably designed to provide job-relevant skills, you are ready to proceed. Before the program begins, confirm again with all participants the anticipated nature of the content. Stress that attendance is voluntary, and identify the on-site representative responsible for dealing with problems that may arise during training.

The following additional steps will help minimize the risk of injury during the training or legal liabilities after it is over.

1. Consider in advance whether any content will infringe on religious practices, invade privacy, or inflict emotional distress. If so, warn participants to the extent possible and get feedback on their comfort levels and concerns.

2. Be open to feedback and constructive comments from participants. Try to avoid a defensive reaction to complaints.

3. Assure participants that an authorized company representative will be present during the entire program.

4. Assure participants that the company will not permit retaliation (subtle or directly job related) if they elect not to attend or decide not to finish the program. This is especially important when an employee's decision is based on religious convictions, since Title VII makes retaliation for the exercise of these rights a separate ground for discrimination. *Be sure that your employer has such a policy, and is prepared to enforce it consistently.*

5. Be alert *during the program* to overt signs of distress by participants who may not speak up because of shyness, fear of reprisals, fear of not being perceived as a team player, or cultural perceptions that to complain would cause a "loss of face" for both trainee and facilitator.

6. Be aggressive and creative in offering religious accommodations. Search for an accommodation that will benefit both the company and the employee. Do not take it upon yourself to determine what constitutes a religious belief. Even though some beliefs may be unfamiliar or uncommon, respectfully seek information from the complaining employee about his or her bona fide religious beliefs.

7. Do not make a determination until a review of all options has been made. Encourage a two-way dialogue with the complaining employee to determine how best to accommodate his or her beliefs while still meeting the objectives of the training.

References

1. Gustave Spohn, "Many Christians Hold New Age Beliefs," *Sacramento Union,* January 18, 1992, p. C-5.

2. Jeremy Main, "Trying to Bend Managers' Minds," *Fortune,* November 1987, pp. 95–106.

3. Jeremy Main, "Trying to Bend Managers' Minds," *Fortune,* November 1987, pp. 95–106.

4. Robert Lindsey, "Gurus Hired to Motivate Workers Are Raising Fears of 'Mind Control,'" *New York Times,* April 17, 1987, at A10, col. 1; Otto Friedrich, "New Age Harmonies," *Time,* December 7, 1987, p. 62.

5. *Welsh v. United States,* 435 U.S. 997, 98 S.Ct. 1650 (1978).

6. *United States v. Seeger,* 398 U.S. at 339, quoting 380 U.S. at 185 (emphasis added).

7. *Kim v. DeKalb Farmers Market, Inc.,* Atlanta, Georgia, trial court (1991).

8. R. Rubinstein, "To Be Kroned Is to Be Confused," *San Francisco Chronicle,* May 27, 1987.

9. California Public Utilities Commission, *Report on Pacific Bell's Leadership Development Program,* June 10, 1987, pp. 5–7.

10. EEOC, Policy Statement on Training Programs Conflicting With Employees' Religious Beliefs, issued February 22, 1988, at 4215-7.

11. Americans With Disabilities Act Employment Regulations, 403 FEP Manual 1561.

12. EEOC Compliance Manual, ¶5021 at 4215-8 (emphasis added).

13. *EEOC v. Townley Engineering Co.,* 946 F.2d 898 (1991).

14. *EEOC v. Townley Engineering Co.,* 946 F.2d 898 (1991).

15. Knight Ridder/Tribune News Service, September 22, 1994.

10

Certifying Trainers and Training Programs

Legal Dos and Don'ts

Certification signifies mastery of tasks or job requirements as measured by specific performance standards. Successful participants are awarded a credential, license, or certification that attests to their expertise. The credential signifies an anticipated level of content or skill mastery to perform competently on the job.

Programs that involve both training and certification generally include a precise process. The process consists of phases, beginning with initial screening of qualified candidates. Specific education, prerequisites, or experience may be required for entry into the program. Initial training is followed by advanced training and testing/assessment of the participant's mastery of the necessary skills. Certification may be followed by continued refreshers and supplemental training. In high-risk settings, recertification within a prescribed time frame is often required.

How to Determine When Certification Is Desirable and Keep Your Program Lawful

You may have several important reasons to design a training curriculum specifically to confer a certification.

1. A government regulation may mandate that people holding particular jobs be certified.

Government-mandated certification programs are most common in the area of safety and health standards, although not all safety training requires certification. The OSHA general-duty clause, and many specific safety training standards, require only that the training be designed and conducted with appropriate content and methodology. (See the detailed discussion of training requirements throughout Chapter 2.) Government standards require verification that trainees have completed the course and are competent to perform high-risk or technically complex jobs, and sometimes also require certification of specialized jobs like hazardous waste haulers and emergency responders.

2. Trainees may be subject-matter experts in a particular field or activity.

Certification of employees with unique expertise allows an organization to market its services as specialized. For example, manufacturers of industrial equipment or computer systems certify their field service engineers, and then warrant to their customers a high degree of proficiency. In addition to charging fees commensurate with the engineers' level of expertise, the manufacturers assure themselves that their customers are receiving appropriate service on their particular equipment. Some manufacturers honor their warranty on equipment only when it is serviced by certified technicians.

3. Trainees are being prepared to perform jobs requiring unique or specialized skills.

Certification programs are not necessary to impart basic skills or general knowledge. For specialized or unique occupations, such as emergency response personnel, computer technicians, field service engineers, and similar technical specialists, certification signifies subject-matter mastery.

One of the hallmarks of a certification program is that trainees must demonstrate superior competency in skills required in their work area to earn their certification. You must keep training records documenting whether each participant demonstrated competency for each required skill. Then, when the certified trainees are placed in specialized jobs, the employer can rely on the certification as evidence that they received a uniform and comprehensive curriculum.

4. Uniformity of content and delivery for every participant in the training program is highly desirable.

Specific standards for performance are typically required to earn certification. This requirement assures subsequent employers and customers that individuals placed into a job have completed rigorous, comprehensive instruction and have demonstrated their ability to meet those standards consistently. Certification programs frequently provide a core curriculum with consistent content, which provides a dependable basis to assure future employers that the individual has received specific job-related information in a systematic manner.

5. Uniform certification standards for specialized occupations provide a basis for customer or client reliance.

In specialized industries, uniform certification standards provide a basis for reliance by customers or the public which, if reasonable, may relieve the industry of certain liabilities. In essence, people dealing with your certified employees can reasonably expect competencies in particular skills. A case that highlights this issue is *Falkowski v. City of Baton Rouge,*[1] which focused on allegations of negligence by the city's emergency medical technicians, each of whom was certified. There were three classifications of EMT: *basic* (trained and certified in basic skills, such as first aid and splinting); *intermediate* (certified to perform additional skills, such as intravenous infusions); and *paramedic* (certified to perform monitoring and to administer drugs).

The injured party suffered an episode of hypoglycemia and became comatose. The responding EMTs, an intermediate and a paramedic, recognized the life-threatening situation and, following instructions of physicians via radio, initiated the intravenous hypoglycemia protocol. Although they saved the man's life, the way they administered the IV caused the patient to lose the use of his hand. He experienced extreme pain in the arm used to introduce the drugs.

In a malpractice lawsuit against the physicians, there was significant testimony about their reliance on the expected levels of skill and knowledge of the certified EMTs. One doctor testified that he did not instruct the EMTs on how to establish the IV, where to start the IV, or how to administer the drugs. The appellate court specifically addressed the reasonableness of this reliance, noting:

> As the testimony shows, when a physician authorizes a protocol, he does so relying on the fact that the EMTs are certified to perform the procedures listed. . . . These certifications mean that both were trained

and certified to initiate IVs and that the EMT paramedic was authorized to administer Dextrose-50.[2]

The court concluded that the EMTs were following the established protocol. Thus, the uniformity of standards and the structure of the certification program aided in the defense of both the EMTs and the physicians, because they followed established protocol and were not grossly negligent (a finding required by Louisiana law).

In contrast, some cases find that a certification *raises* the expected performance levels and in turn the standard of care for certified personnel. (How the courts establish the legal duty and standard of care in a negligence case is addressed thoroughly in Chapter 3, pp. 70–77.) For example, in *Simpson v. Sisters of Charity of Providence in Oregon*,[3] the certification involved an X-ray technician, certified by a national board after training and study in anatomy, radiographic positioning, and X-ray physics. A certain grade-point average and an extensive exam were required for certification. During the X-ray procedure the technician failed to correctly position a patient with a severe back injury, and the emergency room physicians didn't receive effective data. As a result, the doctors believed they couldn't get usable X-rays and ordered the procedure discontinued. The patient was then improperly allowed to sit up and dangle his legs, thereby suffering permanent paralysis.

The appellate judges ultimately concluded that the jury could reasonably find that because of his certification, the X-ray technician was not under the supervision and control of the treating physicians when performing his duties, and that his negligence led directly to the physicians' decision to stop taking X-rays. The court ultimately found that the certified technician failed to meet his legal duty to perform within the levels of his specialized training and expertise, a failure that resulted in substantial damage to the patient.

6. Certification is necessary in industries where the absence of both national standards and consistent training breeds incompetence and litigation.

Many times, a certification program is spurred by a perceived need to identify requisite skills in a specialized industry, and then train to those specific standards. For example, the Milwaukee County medical examiner is developing a training program for medical examiners and coroners, after a nationwide recognition that death investigators were neither uniformly trained nor held accountable to specific standards for performance. This situation creates a primary candidate for development of a certification program.

According to the *Journal of the American Medical Association*, the Death Investigator Training Program was developed because of the widespread lack of mandatory training programs, which exist in only seven states.[4] The program is based on 52 essential skills required of death investigators, as identified by a panel of experts. The program is approved by the National Association of Medical Examiners, but if a certification examination is included, it will require the creation of a certifying agency.

The movement toward mandatory national certification for coroners arose because of a recurring concern about the lack of adequate training in death investigation. Rather than a national standard for identifying—and training on—core skills for this specialized job, states and even counties had their own rules and perceptions of the level of training required. Experts determined that coroners, physicians, nurses, and others performing death investigations have been difficult to train because their responsibilities are not consistently defined.

The need for better training and certification was underscored by widespread recognition that inadequate training led to serious flaws in the service provided by hospitals and county agencies. The most serious cases involved incomplete data and inaccurate cause-of-death determinations. For example, at the 1995 annual meeting of the American Academy of Forensic Sciences, a report focused on South Carolina as one of many states with potential problems. Dr. Kim Collins, then a forensic fellow at the Medical University of South Carolina (Charleston), revealed that in about 40 percent of the suspicious deaths that coroners investigate, the cause of death is listed as "heart." However that percentage dropped substantially in one county after a physician was elected coroner. Her bottom line: "Coroner errors and lack of training [could] be inflating our coronary disease statistics."[5]

Individuals within and outside your organization will rely upon your representation that your certified trainees have the specialized knowledge and/or skills represented by the program. At a minimum, such a representation raises expectations. Thus, in making the decision to establish a certification program internally, trainers should determine whether it is necessary and/or appropriate to create higher expectations than may reasonably be required.

When you approach the decision to develop a certification program, you should consider several factors. First, are you required to do so by a regulatory or industry organization? Do you have specific jobs for which a license or certification is required? If so, you may build the certification into the job description and limit your search to certified candidates.

Second, consider what methods you have for locating certified employees to fill these positions. Are there external certifying agencies, or must you build a program in-house? If you can rely on an outside agency or government organization, you will reduce your own legal risk, and your employer's potential liability, because an in-house program must be consistent in content and delivery. Remember that internal programs you design and deliver will be scrutinized for content and methodology in a negligence lawsuit alleging inadequate performance by an employee you have certified. Thus, you may raise your standard of care by your own policies. See Chapter 3, pp. 74–75.

Third, do you sell or service unique equipment for which certified technicians will provide a competitive advantage? If your company is the manufacturer of unique or complex equipment, you may benefit from building your program internally to ensure consistent methodology, access to your own equipment, and confidentiality over your internal processes. The cost of developing equipment and training facilities may be built directly into your customers' purchase price. Alternatively, you may offer a service contract that provides incentives to customers who use your specially trained technicians.

Fourth, do you represent to your customers that your personnel have mastered specialized skills beyond the basic skill sets required to perform competently? If so, customers will have high expectations for performance and may bring a claim for damages on the basis of negligence, breach of contract, or even outright misrepresentation if your certified employees perform deficiently. If your employer is unaware of the legal effect of marketing materials and other sales representations—and you are responsible for any aspect of technical training—you should consider raising the issue with the appropriate level of management.

Fifth, are you prepared to rigorously enforce consistent standards for delivery and documentation of your certification standards? From a legal perspective, the more you hold your organization and its employees out to the world as having specialized expertise, the greater the chance that you and your organization will be held to a higher standard of care. By voluntarily creating a certification program that goes beyond what is required by law, you are creating a legal duty of due care. Subsequent failure to enforce your own high standards consistently may give rise to a negligence claim that would not have been viable under general common law standards. See the full discussion of standard of care in Chapter 3, pp. 70–76.

Finally, have you placed appropriate time limitations on the certification? Remember that by conferring a certification or other designation of expertise, your company and your individual trainers are representing that the trainee is competent in all aspects of the activities covered by the certification program. Since certification programs are typically limited to high-risk industries and/or technical jobs, there is often a time limit under which you can ensure continued high performance by your trainees.

If new knowledge or skills are required, your failure to provide refreshers or other updated instruction may render your certification both meaningless and legally risky. Likewise, if the passage of time may reduce the effectiveness of your trainees' skills in physically demanding or emotionally challenging environments, it may be essential to recertify them periodically for their own safety as well as the efficacy of your program.

How to Establish Objective Qualification Standards for Certified Curriculum Designers and Instructors

In addition to certifying training programs, you may be asked to certify your trainers. In order to meet your legal duty to registrants in your certification program, your trainers must be qualified in content design and delivery. Qualification is particularly important when the program will be used to certify participants as having specialized expertise.

Instructors certify that trainees are competent in the performance of specialized skills or techniques or substantive knowledge. If competence in a particular skill is required for the job, then the failure of an unqualified instructor to train to competence may give rise to a negligence claim. Examples of failure to train to competence include skipping required content areas, failing to utilize effective methodologies, passing someone through the program without requiring a specific demonstration of skill-based competence, or failing to develop a uniform assessment vehicle to measure competence. Accordingly, the qualifications and performance of the trainers—both curriculum designers and presenters—is often critical to the success of a certification program. Not surprisingly, it is also a key ingredient to delivering a legally defensible certification program.

At a minimum, competencies for certified trainers should include both knowledge and skill in curriculum design and content, supervision of the training facility, training delivery (including effective methodologies), expertise with specific measurement instruments used during the training, and mastery of assessment tools to ensure that certification standards are met.

In order to establish legally enforceable measures for certifying trainers, you should consider *objective* standards:

1. Is there a defined subject-matter discipline that merits certification? Why is it beyond the common expertise of seasoned trainers? What specific educational degrees are required to supply the necessary content expertise? (M.S., Ph.D., M.D., or other advanced degree?) Are there any other prerequisites to participation in a trainer certification program? Will it be desirable to pair a content expert with a seasoned instructor?

2. What content expertise will be required to complete the program? Is it beyond the expertise of an otherwise experienced trainer? For example, does the program cover specialized knowledge, techniques, or disciplines such as engineering controls, process engineering, or blood-borne pathogens? Should content experts also have training or presentation experience?

3. Are skill standards clearly defined? These standards should include identification—with specific examples—of knowledge, skills, and understanding needed to achieve competent performance during training and assessment. Each critical function should be supported by key activities and relevant levels of skill to perform each activity. Address skills necessary for coaching and feedback to participants and to other instructors. Consider also standards for effective facilitation of a variety of classroom activities, including high-risk activities.

4. What specific real-world experience is necessary to impart the knowledge or skill? Define it in terms of on-the-job experience.

5. Do the certified trainers have the requisite skills to evaluate trainee performance and provide qualitative, constructive, and nondiscriminatory feedback? Is certification in the use of a specific assessment instrument required? Is specific experience with particular assessment vehicles desirable? Can such training be delivered in-house, or must the instructor-in-training complete a separate program?

6. Are skills in distance learning and using on-line interactive tools and related technologies required? If so, establish evaluation processes that effectively determine whether the certified trainer can use these technologies in addition to other classroom presentations. Assure yourself that the certified trainer uses these technologies effectively.

Take a systematic approach to evaluating the certified trainer's expertise. This includes the skill to analyze the needs of trainees in content or on-the-job behaviors, to create concrete performance objectives and build the training around them, and to evaluate the training to be sure it is working.

Determine how the trainer will be evaluated as part of the certification process. Will it be a knowledge- or skill-based test? Is on-the-job observation required and if so, how will it be administered cost-effectively? Determine with as much specificity as possible the scope and nature of further required on-the-job apprenticeship or performance to master the skills necessary for certification.

Develop an objective set of minimum qualifications for entry into a train-the-trainer program to certify instructors. Candidates should demonstrate proficiency in skills to be imparted during training, specific experience in teaching or making technical presentations, and exceptional communication skills.

In connection with highly specialized training that encompasses proprietary information about the company, trainers should demonstrate appropriate knowledge and judgment concerning the necessary steps to protect the company's trade secrets and copyrights. See the extended discussion in Chapter 19, pp. 403–413.

Document the entire process you use to establish and enforce certification requirements that are objective, consistent, and job related. Keep complete records of qualifications, experience, and specialized training for your certified trainers and instructional designers.

How to Design Legally Defensible Certification Programs

In addition to the higher standard of care required of certified *trainers*, if you intend to certify participants who complete your training, it is your legal duty to provide the instruction, content, methodology, supervision, and evaluation needed to ensure that trainees who receive a certification are actually able to perform consistently at the level of expertise the program purports to provide.

Training to a level of expertise is essential for two distinct reasons. First, trainees who cannot perform at the expected level may assert that you failed to provide them with the expertise they anticipated, and were either negligent or fraudulent in your representations to them. Their claims can range from return of their fee to substantial damages for their subsequent loss of a job or opportunity. Second, external organizations that retain or place your certified trainees and find them deficient may assert that you breached your duty of care by falling below the standard for similar certified programs.

Setting Objective Standards

The primary way to avoid potential lawsuits for negligent design or delivery of a certified program is to set clear and realistic objectives for certifying the program. The process begins with understanding the specialized functions that the certification program is to provide.

In designing these programs, you should have a very clear idea of what the training is to accomplish and how this goal relates to the demands of the jobs that participants are being certified to perform. Formulate written objectives that state what skill-based behaviors the training will impart. Such a statement will provide an objective basis for the participants *and* their subsequent employers to anticipate the level at which they will be able to perform.

Skill-based objectives should identify the exact behavior or knowledge (rather than a general area) that the certified trainee will be able to produce. This too will help in objectively evaluating the level of specific expertise to be expected following certification. For example, for a certified emergency response team member, the objective would not simply be to gain a knowledge of chemical exposure injuries. Rather, it would be to be able to recognize the symptoms of toxic exposure, respond promptly under stress, and stabilize patients for transport to medical facilities.

Establish precise performance expectations for participants who achieve certification status. Specify whether they can perform at entry level, next-highest job level, or top level in the particular position, just as the EMT program did in *Falkowski,* discussed previously at pp. 222–223.

Identify content or skill-based performance standards created by government regulations, such as occupational safety laws, industry requirements, or local regulations. Take steps to ensure that the content of the program is adjusted or supplemented as required for changes in production methods, technology, or legal and regulatory changes.

Specify the time frame for anticipated effective performance of participants who receive their certification. If refresher training or other advanced-level training will be required, make sure participants are aware of this requirement before they begin the program. Establish an enforceable system for the follow-up training and evaluation necessary to *retain* the certification.

Provide realistic, objective, job-related standards for achieving the certificate, *and enforce them consistently.* Use effective methods for evaluating participant performance, and make sure the methods are uniformly administered. Nothing is more harmful to the success of a certification program—and more devastating to your defense against lawsuits—than to have unqualified participants receive a certification. For example, if you certify an emergency responder and she fails to perform under realistic workplace conditions, you may be held accountable for injuries caused or made worse by her inability to perform under such conditions. Thus, trainees in a certification program should be candidly assessed, and given candid, constructive criticism. Testing standards should meet all requirements (set forth in Chapter 7, pp. 174–182) to ensure equal opportunities for all participants.

Because certification is a specialized designation, the desire to enter and complete the program may be very high. Candidates for the certification program should be objectively screened, and the program should have very objective qualification standards to prevent a discriminatory selection process. See the detailed discussion in Chapter 6, pp. 129–134 and 136–141.

Finally, conduct pilot tests of the program, and regularly evaluate the effectiveness of participants who receive their certification.

Evaluating Your Course Description

When you are required to write a course description for your certification program, you should recognize that potential applicants will rely on your description. The description may also be used as evidence in a later lawsuit over the efficacy of the program. Whether it is evidence introduced for you or against you will depend upon how carefully and completely you describe the program. Consider the following guidelines.

- Describe the overall purpose or function of the job for which the trainee is being certified—the what, how, and why it is done—as well as the organizational structure of the program—how many modules, hours, or other educational units are included and the participant's responsibility to meet all course requirements.

- Make the description as factual and concise as possible. It must be easily understood and must cover the subject offered.

- The terminology should be standardized for uniformity and clarity. The language should be clear enough to eliminate any confusion about the anticipated level of expertise following certification.

- The course description must be well organized, describing every area of content in the correct order. Provide a step-by-step breakdown of the content. Each statement should relate to an end result or objective that must be accomplished for successful completion and certification. Alert candidates when any follow-up training or on-the-job apprenticeship will be required.

- Specify minimum requisites for formal education or on-the-job experience and training. Determine whether qualifications standards affect legal protections for disabled participants, and ask candidates to specify what reasonable accommodations they may need in order to fully participate.

- Make sure that the objectives set forth for knowledge- or skill-based performance by certification candidates are attainable, realistic, and clearly tied to job demands and that they contribute to quality and productivity.

Special Considerations for Certification Programs Involving Hazard Training

Identify the person or people responsible for ensuring that the objective standards established by the certification program are followed by all instructors and participants. Establish a system for identifying and evaluating necessary content, methodology, refreshers, and recertifications for high-risk jobs or hazardous work environments. Provide detailed procedures and methods for correcting unsafe or unhealthy conditions in a timely manner, including how the hazards will be controlled or eliminated and the time frame involved.

When a certification program involving health and safety standards is implemented, all trainers should be trained about the safe practices, and all new employees and current employees given new job assignments must receive training on safe practices. When any new equipment, substances, or procedures are introduced into the workplace that represent a new hazard, you must provide training and include appropriate provisions concerning the new condition and how it affects existing practices. Similar action must be taken if the employer receives information or notification of a new or previously unrecognized hazard.

Chapter 2, pp. 39–45 and 60–63, describes the content and delivery of hazard communication training, regardless of whether the program leads to certification of participants.

Protection of Training Materials With Proprietary Value

Some training programs involve proprietary processes and procedures that require significant time and expense to create. These may be protected as trade secrets. A *trade secret* is a compilation of valuable technical information and procedures, generally created at great expense, and useful tools for technical employees in performing specialized work for your company. The unauthorized disclosure of such proprietary materials can place your company at a competitive disadvantage or devalue its products and services.

For example, certification programs for technical employees—such as computer technicians, field service engineers, and unique service providers—frequently focus on ongoing maintenance and repair of specialized equipment sold by the company. The consequences of such competitive and costly information being misappropriated may be devastating.

Certified trainers should be mindful of the need to protect this valuable information during and after training. At a minimum, trainers should honor, and remind trainees to honor, any confidentiality agreements concerning the training materials. Trainers should also take great care in limiting access to proprietary training materials, in accordance with any company policies they create. Chapter 19, pp. 400–413, contains a detailed explanation of these issues and provides a comprehensive checklist for ensuring confidentiality and protecting valuable training materials.

Evaluating External and Public Certification Programs

Your organizations may not be in a position to design and deliver comprehensive in-house certification programs. Accordingly, you may wish to evaluate outside programs to send your employees to, or from whose ranks you can hire previously certified employees. The following guidelines are useful.

1. Consider available programs in light of your clearly defined corporate training objectives.
   - Will the program help employees acquire or perform job-related skills?
   - Is outside training needed for employees to keep up with technological changes, to learn new skills or technologies, or to develop professionally?
   - Is outside training the best approach to meeting corporate training objectives?
   - Can the program be customized to the needs of the organization?
   - Are industry-specific standards applicable and, if so, are they addressed?

2. Evaluate the program content.
   - Are the course content, design, and emphasis in line with corporate needs?

- Are written materials consistent with your corporate training objectives? Do they conflict with important policies and procedures within your organization? If so, can the conflict be reconciled?
- What is missing that should be part of a customized course?
- Are the approach and the teaching methodology appropriate for the employees who will attend the course? Is the appropriate level of specialization included?

3. Evaluate the provider's credentials.

- Is appropriate training available that will also count toward a professional certificate or degree for trainees?
- Have any training providers been recommended highly?
- What training programs are other, similarly situated companies using?
- Has the provider supplied a list of corporate clients that are willing to share their evaluations of the provider and the expertise of the instructional designers and presenters?
- Do clients randomly selected from this list endorse the certification training program?
- Did the selected clients have similar training objectives?
- Do instructors have the appropriate credentials? What level of qualifications, education, experience and skills do they have? Obtain as many references as you can, with a focus on programs in similar industries.

4. Consider scheduling for your employees.

- Must the training occur before participants can be placed on the job? Is there a regulatory requirement that prohibits you from placing an uncertified individual? (Remember "Murphy's Law": An accident or injury caused by an uncertified individual can happen any time; it is bad luck, but not unheard of, for such misfortune to occur prior to formal certification.)
- Will it be more expedient to hire precertified individuals, or is there time to send your existing employees for certification?
- Do the workload and the pace of the program coincide with corporate objectives?
- Is there a business imperative to complete the program quickly? Is there a regulatory imperative?
- Are the course length and the depth of coverage consistent with your needs?
- Will trainees have difficulty fitting the program into their work schedules?

5. Examine the methodology used by the provider to test, evaluate, and confer certification on participants.

   - Is it objective?
   - Is it consistent with performance expectations?
   - Is it rigorous but fair? Does it allow your organization to maintain the highest realistic standards for performance while still complying with equal employment opportunity requirements? (See the discussion in Chapters 6, pp. 122–129, and 7, pp. 158–163.)
   - Will it realistically produce successful job performance as well as knowledge?
   - Are all tests validated and administered in accordance with applicable legal standards? (See Chapter 7, pp. 163–167 and 174–182, for a comprehensive discussion of the legalities governing posttraining testing.)

6. Evaluate the program again after training is complete.

   - Did the provider deliver as agreed?
   - Were trainees asked for their evaluation of the content, methodology, coaching, feedback, and assessment standards? Was the program sufficiently relevant and job-related?

     Did trainees rate the manner of presentation highly?

     Was the training relevant to their work?

     Would they recommend that others like themselves receive such training?

References

1. *Falkowski v. City of Baton Rouge,* 637 So.2d 522 (1993; released for publication May 5, 1994).

2. *Falkowski v. City of Baton Rouge,* 637 So.2d 522, 527 (1993; released for publication May 5, 1994).

3. *Simpson v. Sisters of Charity of Providence in Oregon,* 284 Ore. 547 (1978).

4. *Journal of the American Medical Association,* March 19, 1996.

5. *Journal of the American Medical Association,* April 19, 1995.

11

Terror, Violence, Sickness, and Stress in the Workplace

The Role and Responsibilities of Training

Workplace Security, Violence Prevention, and Crisis Management Training: Where to Begin

Trainers cannot ignore the real threat of workplace violence. We read and hear about it all the time, as Figure 11-1 reflects. And where violent episodes have occurred, litigation has followed. Figure 11-2 provides just two examples.

The costs of even one violent incident in the workplace can be significant. In addition to liability lawsuits, workplace violence results in medical and psychiatric care, long-term disabilities, property damage, impaired productivity, and lost business. Indeed, the North Carolina–based National Safe Workplace Institute calculates the dollar cost of a single episode of serious workplace violence at $250,000.[1]

Violence by Disgruntled Employees

- In 1993, an adjuster fired eight months earlier returned to St. Paul Fire and Marine in Tampa, Florida, killing three executives and injuring two more.

- In 1993, a disgruntled employee in California, complaining about a late $150 paycheck, doused the bookkeeper with flammable liquid and set her on fire with a cigarette lighter.

- In 1992, a General Dynamics employee fired for poor attendance returned to work with a gun, killing an employee and injuring a supervisor.

- In 1994, a fired technician of Elgar Corporation went on a rampage, setting off bombs, shooting out the switchboard, looking for specific targets, and killing two executives.

Violence by External Services

- In 1994, a dissatisfied litigant returned to a San Francisco law firm with an automatic weapon and killed nine people, before turning the gun on himself.

- In March 1996, a customer in a Georgia deli rescued a female employee who was being attacked by a knife-wielding former boyfriend. The attacker was shot and killed.

- In January 1993, a gunman stormed the emergency room at USC Hospital, shooting three emergency physicians and holding a nurse hostage for several hours.

Figure 11-1 Examples of High-Profile Workplace Violence Incidents.

When Violence Prevention Training Is Mandated by Law or Regulation

When a violent incident occurs in the workplace, there are several potential bases for legal responsibility involving training. These include regulatory penalties for violation of the OSHA general-duty clause, state-imposed training requirements, or industry-specific training requirements. Chapter 2, pp. 39–46 and 60–63, contains a detailed discussion of these requirements.

FED-OSHA has used the general-duty clause to encourage employers to take steps to prevent injury to employees, and has developed

> - An employee who was sexually assaulted by a coworker outside the workplace successfully sued her employer for failure to warn her about the assailant's previous convictions for kidnapping and sexual assault, even after she had complained that the man had sexually harassed her. The court held that the employer's awareness of the danger, and of a specific potential victim, created a duty to warn her. [*Duffy v. City of Oceanside* (1986).]
>
> - A hotel operator was held liable for over $100,000 in damages after a supervisor threatened a security agent with a gun, causing the agent severe emotional distress. The court allowed the injured employee to bypass the state workers' compensation remedy, because the employer had ratified (permitted) the willful assault by its supervisor. The court based this finding on evidence that the employer was aware that the supervisor maintained guns at work, and that he had been arrested—though not convicted—of assault. The hotel operator failed to discipline or terminate the supervisor, and *did not take steps to warn or train its workforce* on appropriate behavior in the workplace. [*Herrick v. Quality Hotels, Inns, and Resorts, Inc.* (1993).]

Figure 11-2 Examples of Lawsuits Stemming From Workplace Violence.

workplace violence guidelines that focus on preventing workplace violence in several industries. Characterized by OSHA as "advisory in nature, informational in content," these violence prevention guidelines are directed at health care and social service employers and providers. The reason for this direction is simple: These are the industries in which the most assaults occur.

Other guidelines directed at occupations that have also proved to be significantly at risk—such as night retail operations—are expected. Many of the fundamental elements in this preventive effort, however, are sufficiently "generic" that they can be useful to employers in any industry.

Several states have also enacted training requirements in specific industries, including hospitality and health care. California, Minnesota, and Washington State lead the way in mandating violence prevention training.

FED-OSHA emphasizes the importance of training when potential assailants have an employment-related involvement with the workplace, such as current or former employees, supervisors, or managers. If your employer learns that a current or former employee has threatened violence against managers, supervisors, or other employees, the company may be required to take preventive steps to ward off a violent incident. Recognizing the signs of violence is considered to be within the general requirement of providing a safe and healthful work environment. Thus, if your organization doesn't have a workplace security or violence prevention plan that includes training, you should consider proposing one to management. Training for managers on recognizing potential signs of violence, and for all employees on preventing violence, may be the best investment your organization makes.

Who Can Sue You After a Violent Incident and What Can the Injured Party Recover?

Historically, employers were held responsible for unlawful or improper acts of their employees under the doctrine of *respondeat superior*. In plain English, this meant that employers were liable for acts of their employees only if those acts fell within the scope of their employment. Taken to its logical conclusion, the doctrine normally did not hold an employer liable for an employee's act of violence, since such an act was considered outside the scope of employment. This general principle has been eroded by state common law theories such as negligent hiring and retention, which have been used to hold an employer responsible for acts of an employee that clearly occur outside the scope of the latter's employment but that are somehow connected to the workplace.

The courts in 30 states have recognized a common law liability for negligent hiring or negligent retention of an unsafe employee. These claims are established when the employer knows, or through a reasonable investigation should know, of the employee's unfitness for the job (including his or her lack of training), but fails to take preventive action to reduce the risk of foreseeable harm. In these situations, the employer owes a duty of protection to the person injured and to the unfit employee causing the injury. See the discussion of how legal duties are established in negligence lawsuits in Chapter 3, pp. 70–76.)

Claims for Physical or Mental Injuries by Employees.   In most states, recovery for injuries incurred on the job are limited to workers' compensation benefits. In many states, in order for an injury to be compensable under the workers' compensation system, the injury must occur in the course of employment and must arise out of employment. If these conditions are met, the workers' compensation benefits will be the exclusive source of recovery, and the employee will be unable to sue the employer in any other forum.

If there is a finding of willful or intentional disregard for the safety of employees, an injured employee may also file a lawsuit for damages. Typically, such claims allege gross negligence or reckless disregard for employees' safety by failure to train and/or supervise effectively. Injured workers may also make claims for damages against a coworker if the injury was caused by a willful and unprovoked act of aggression or if the other employee was acting outside the scope of employment at the time of the injury. Consult your specific state workers' compensation statutes to determine what is and is not compensable.

Third-Party Lawsuits. Workers' compensation is available only for employees' injuries. Injury lawsuits by third parties focus on whether the company has met its legal duties to protect visitors, vendors, and bystanders (as well as employees) from the foreseeable risks of harm from violent incidents. The civil court will determine the applicable standard of care imposed on reasonable businesses in the community. A detailed discussion of negligence principles and the issues of legal duty is set forth in Chapter 3, pp. 70–78.

In the wake of a violent incident, courts have not been reluctant to pin the blame on an employer's failure to train. For example, in *Gonzales v. Southwest Security & Protection Agency, Inc.,*[2] an employee of a security firm injured a bystander through negligent use of a nightstick. The New Mexico court of appeal found that if the employer supervises employees who have the tools to commit violent acts, the employer is legally responsible for an injury if it fails to train employees adequately in the use of the tools. The court concluded that the employees had not been properly trained in the use of the tools (nightsticks), and in how to detain suspects properly.

In other states, juries have found companies at fault for the acts of violent employees, particularly when the signs of potential violence were ignored. The finding reaffirms the value and necessity of training managers, line supervisors, and coworkers to be alert to the signs of violence or instability, and to report the facts to management, which can then evaluate appropriate precautionary actions consistent with the rights of all employees.

In order for legal duty to be established, the risk must be foreseeable and the victim identifiable. For example, if the victim informs the employer that the violent coworker had engaged in harassment, stalking, or threats, a court would be more likely to consider the victim to be within the foreseeable zone of people who might be potential victims.

There is a definite trend toward notifying prospective employers about a potentially violent employee when they call for an employment reference. Two examples from opposite coasts reflect the concern. In Tampa, Florida, a disgruntled former employee of St. Paul Fire and

Marine Insurance Company returned to the work site and killed several executives who had participated in his termination. The families of the survivors sued the shooter's former employer, Allstate Insurance Company, for wrongful death because it had failed to disclose to St. Paul during a preemployment reference check that the employee had been terminated for disruptive (and potentially violent) behavior. The appellate court allowed the case to proceed to trial, with a request for both compensation and punitive damages.

St. Paul Fire and Marine was legally exposed to damage claims. Eight months earlier, the fired employee had warned management that he would "be back." This single piece of evidence established liability for negligence, because the company ignored the sign of potential violence and took no proactive steps to prevent harm to foreseeable victims.

On the other side of the country, the California Supreme Court ruled in 1997 that an employer has a duty when providing an employment reference to provide the entire story: the good, the bad, and the ugly, including violent behavior or tendencies. The failure to do so may result in liability to third parties for injuries caused by the prior employee. The case arose after a school administrator was accused of sexually molesting a 13-year-old girl. It turned out that a prior employer had provided a reference in which only the positive aspects of the administrator's performance were disclosed. The omission: almost identical allegations of molestation by a student. In fact, the prior employer had provided a "detailed recommendation" with the knowledge that it would be passed on to prospective employers, despite the knowledge of the employee's prior sexual misconduct with female students.

In *Randi W. v. Muroc School District*,[3] the California Supreme Court stated that employers have no obligation to provide a reference at all; but when they do, they must provide complete information. In fact, the court strongly noted that although an employer will not generally be accountable for failing to disclose negative information about a former employee, there are legal risks when, as here, the employer's letter "amounts to an *affirmative misrepresentation*, presenting a foreseeable and substantial risk of physical harm to a prospective employer or third person" (emphasis in original). Half-truths become unlawful misrepresentations. One key to minimizing these legal risks is to effectively train all personnel responsible for providing references.

Eight Practical Strategies for Preventing Workplace Disasters

If your company does not have a workforce security or violence prevention program in place, you should seriously consider proposing one to senior management. In order to make practical, concrete, and legally defensible recommendations, consider the following guidelines.

1. Make violence prevention a priority.

Prevention is a dual issue: preventing violent incidents and preventing disruption or further harm in the event of a crisis. Identify a management team to handle issues before they swell into a crisis. Team members should be drawn from several departments, including executive, security, risk management, human resources, training, and legal. Conduct a thorough analysis of all training and management requirements that you will face in the event of a crisis.

2. Obtain management commitment of interest and resources.

Develop a clear policy of zero-tolerance for workplace violence, verbal and nonverbal threats, and related actions. Such a policy requires enforcement by visible involvement of senior management. Experienced trainers can use your skills in needs assessment to help develop a program of clear goals and objectives tailored to the workplace and communicated to all staff. There must be assignment of responsibility and accountability for various parts of the program, and an appropriate allocation of resources.

Your employer should also establish and enforce written policies and procedures, including disciplinary action for employees who threaten others or engage in inappropriate behaviors. All employees should be trained on the substance of these policies, and supervisors need additional skills training on how to enforce the policies consistently without fear of discrimination claims. For example, in *Marino v. U.S. Postal Service*,[4] the U.S. Postal Service was held not to have violated the federal Rehabilitation Act when it discharged an employee with an anxiety neurosis after he acted insubordinately and punched his supervisor in the face.

Likewise, in *Fenton v. Pritchard*,[5] a court in Kansas held that an employee fired for disruptive or menacing behavior toward coworkers was not entitled to legal protection. The employee stalked a female colleague, slapped her when she tried to end a romance, and threatened another coworker who honked at him in the parking lot. Claiming that the employer fired him because management "regarded him as being mentally or emotionally impaired," the employee sought relief under the Americans With Disabilities Act. The court upheld the discharge, with the trial judge concluding that "people who become easily angered are commonplace. His low threshold of tolerance is not unique, nor does it merit recognition under the Americans With Disabilities Act."[6]

3. Encourage employee involvement at all levels.

Employees need to understand and comply with the program and with related safety and security measures. Provide opportunities for them to express their concern. Make sure that violent incidents are reported promptly and accurately, and allow employees to make recommendations for corrective strategies. Teams may be encouraged to participate in incident investigation and workplace inspections.

Every employee should be trained on how to handle threats of potential violence, and how to react during and immediately after a violent episode. They should know precisely how to report any concerns and should not fear being ignored or subjected to reprisals for raising their concerns.

4. Conduct a work-site analysis.

According to OSHA, work-site analysis involves "a step-by-step commonsense look at the workplace to find existing or potential hazards" relating to violence—including procedures, operations, or specific locations that may be a source of such hazards. OSHA suggests a "threat assessment team" or similar task force comprised of representatives from senior management, operations, employee assistance, security, occupational health, legal, and human resources. Tools that can be used for this process include:

- *Records analysis and tracking.* Trained personnel should review medical, safety, workers' compensation, and insurance records to pinpoint instances of workplace violence. The objective is to identify, tabulate, and analyze any *trends* that are revealed, since they may relate to particular departments or units and their activities, job titles, workstations, or even time of day.

- *Monitoring trends.* Contact similar local operations, trade associations, and community or civic groups to learn about their experiences with actual or potential workplace violence. Monitor trends or patterns.

- *Screening surveys.* Input from employees, by means of a survey or questionnaire, on potential violence hazards and the effectiveness of security measures can be very valuable. When repeated periodically, these surveys can help identify risk factors not previously noticed and assess the effects of changes that have been made as part of the program. Reviews by outside professionals in such fields as law enforcement, security, insurance, and safety can contribute useful perspectives and suggestions.

- *Workplace security analysis.* Periodic workplace inspections and task evaluations can identify operations or situations and conditions that could lead to violence. Consider characteristics of both assailants and victims in an incident, and take into account exact details of what happened before, during, and after the incident. Also take into account the particular jobs, locations, and procedures that have put employees at risk, along with when and how often this occurred.

5. Establish hazard prevention and control procedures.

The hazard-control component of the violence prevention program involves engineering and administrative controls, work practices, workplace adaptation, and postincident response. Examples include alarm systems and other security devices (panic buttons, private-channel radios, etc.), round-the-clock closed-circuit video recording for high-risk areas, and metal detectors to identify weapons.

Administrative and work practice controls deal with how job functions are carried out and specific tasks are performed. Make clear to employees and the public that violent behavior will not be tolerated. Minimize the number of employees working alone at night or in areas of particular risk (e.g., elevators, stairwells, drug storage or pharmacy areas). Use the "buddy system" whenever possible. Consider providing employees with security escorts to parking areas, especially at late hours.

6. Design and deliver effective training on workplace security and violence prevention.

The delivery component of the program ensures that *staff members at all levels* are aware of potential security hazards—and of how the established policies and procedures can help them protect themselves and coworkers from these hazards. New and reassigned staff and visiting staff should receive the training, along with periodic refreshers. It should be conducted by qualified trainers and, in OSHA's words, "should involve role playing, simulations, and drills."

Topics to be covered include your company's workplace security and violence prevention policy, factors that create or contribute to the risk of assault, and how to recognize escalating behavior or warning signs that may predict a possible violent incident. Effective training also addresses methods of preventing or defusing a volatile situation, managing anger, and using medication appropriately as a chemical restraint; how to enforce a standard response action plan for violent situations; and policies for recording and reporting incidents and obtaining medical, legal, and insurance assistance after a violent episode.

One of the leading experts on workplace violence is S. Anthony Baron. According to Dr. Baron, the following components are crucial to an effective training program:

- Training should cover the identification of potential sources of violence. Familiarize employees with the profile of potentially violent people.

- Train employees to be alert to the warning signs and to avert violence by reporting any threatening remarks or situations.

- Train employees and managers to be observant, particularly to recognize the signs of stress.

- Train managers and supervisors on the practical skills involved in hiring, downsizing, and terminating employees. Other programs recommended for supervisors are stress management, effective communications, conflict resolution, dealing with difficult people, managing change, and conducting effective discipline and termination actions.[7]

7. Assess which employees are at high risk for violence.

Take steps to provide protection to employees who are foreseeably in harm's way: receptionists, bank tellers, security guards, fast-food personnel, and others on the "front line" of potential external threats. In addition, consider human resources personnel, managers, or others who may be targeted by a disgruntled employee following adverse employment actions.

8. Develop programs to help former employees.

Be sensitive to the stress, helplessness, and anger felt by employees who lose their jobs or suffer an adverse employment action. This is a critical component of violence prevention. Make resources, including employee assistance programs and appropriate counseling, available to employees. Develop consistent out-placement services to help employees find new jobs.

Training is key in this area as well. Supervisors should be trained on how to deliver "bad news" as a part of performance reviews, how to respond if an employee reacts with a threat, and how to carry out large downsizings or reductions in force.

The Critical Role of Training After a Crisis

The Bureau of Justice Assistance cites the case of a major manufacturing company with over 300,000 employees as a good example of the value of training in preparation for dealing with violent incidents at work. The company had developed a coordinated management plan for preventing and dealing with workplace violence.

During one incident, an employee shot his lover and wounded another individual before shooting himself. The incident occurred at a plant where training had recently been received and an action plan developed. Although the death and injury could not have been prevented, the planned system for coping with the aftermath worked flawlessly. The police were called immediately, the families promptly notified, the facilities temporarily closed, and the relatives and remaining employees counseled. The company also dealt effectively with the media. The Department of Justice concluded that "only thorough training and advanced planning could account for the excellent manner in which the aftermath was handled."[8]

Designing and delivering training to cope with the aftermath of a violent incident in your workplace is indispensable. These are programs you design with great care, hoping you will *never* need to use them. It's like life insurance. Management and risk managers need a comfort level (a feeling that your company will be able to deal quickly and efficiently with a recovery) from a violent episode. It is difficult to do so without advance planning, preparation, and training.

The training department can and should serve as a critical component of any workplace security and crisis management team. Experienced trainers should be involved at the earliest stages to help develop awareness training for the entire workforce, specialized training for managers and supervisors on detecting the signs of potential violence, and most important, crisis management instructions for employees who will be on the front lines for coping with the aftermath of a crisis.

The human and productivity consequences of a violent incident—particularly when coworkers are killed or injured—can have serious long-term repercussions. Disruption should be minimized, so that workers can return to normalcy. The issue is not simply productivity. The more quickly the workplace resumes regular schedules, the easier it will be for employees to cope with their natural feelings of fear, helplessness, or depression. This does not mean, however, that management simply ignores the trauma people have experienced. Quite the contrary.

Thorough training, combined with counseling and other interventions, provides a vital service to employees by allowing them to grieve, discuss, vent their feelings, and reach a resolution of their fury and fear. Don't minimize the danger of "posttraumatic stress disorder" and other illness. For these interventions to work effectively, they must be immediately in place. They will be only when you have planned in advance for a circumstance that you hope will never occur.

Experts who have studied the effects of workplace violence recommend that appropriate counseling begin immediately, since delays can be costly and permanent. In 1991, the Barrington Psychiatric Institute in Los Angeles studied 200 people suffering major psychic trauma. Half were given therapy immediately, and their average recovery time was 12 weeks. The other half, whose treatment was delayed, took an average of 46 weeks to recover. The human toll is obvious.

More interestingly, the overwhelming majority (94 percent) of the second group brought lawsuits, while only 13 percent of the first group chose litigation.[9] The legal consequences are equally plain.

Specific case studies bolster the value of immediate counseling and intervention. When a part-time postal employee killed 14 people in Edmond, Oklahoma, the U.S. Postal Service began counseling and therapy for the families and employee survivors within hours. Quick intervention helped ease the trauma and demonstrated a caring approach by management. Although the effects of an ordeal of such magnitude may remain for years, fixing the problem rather than fixing the blame helps ease a difficult situation.

Most authorities on workplace violence agree that managers and line supervisors must be prepared to handle both the violent incident and its aftermath. The tools and skills they acquire in training must address how to handle employees who have witnessed an act of violence; how to recognize clues that might previously have been ignored and, more important, what to do when they see these clues; where to go for help; and how to handle their own feelings of helplessness, fear, loss, and anger.

Implement a Crisis Plan

The crisis management team should be prepared to handle issues consistently and respond affirmatively. Your training should directly address these concerns. Identify procedures and make assignments in advance for calling the police or an emergency response team, for identifying avenues for egress from the work site, and for assessing safety issues surrounding evacuation of the area. (Generally it is prudent to defer to local law enforcement or emergency responders.)

You should also train personnel responsible for contacting family or friends of injured employees and for calling your employee assistance program or notifying the workers' compensation carrier. (These services will often have immediate access to trained crisis counselors.)

The victims of a workplace assault suffer other effects. Among these are short- or long-term trauma, fear of returning to work or of criticism by supervisors, and feelings of guilt, incompetence, and powerlessness—all of which can affect witnesses as well. These effects must be dealt with promptly, professionally, and compassionately, if the overall program is to be successful. In addition to certified counselors and other specialists, peer counselors and other support groups can play a useful role in postincident response.

Plan to Deal With the Media

High-profile stories of deaths or serious workplace incidents can cause severe damage to a business and adversely affect the morale and wellbeing of existing employees. It is critical to get back to some level of normalcy as quickly as possible. Training, crisis counseling, and other appropriate interventions may be less successful if employees are bombarded with repeated images on the nightly news.

In addition, media accounts may fuel litigation. Plan to train your managers or public affairs representatives to explain the company's precautions, management training, and security measures to the media. However, remember that if there is litigation, all such statements— which are undoubtedly recorded during times of stress—will be available during discovery and throughout later stages of litigation. (See the discussion of the civil discovery process in Chapter 1, p. 33.) Few things are more harmful to defending a case than well-intentioned but ill-considered statements about the content and specifics of your training and prevention plans. Thus, those expected to be on the "front line" for media coverage should be separately trained or briefed on the specifics of your training and prevention.

References

1. Associated Press business wire, March 24, 1997.
2. *Gonzales v. Southwest Security & Protection Agency, Inc.*, 665 P.2d 810 (New Mexico 1983).
3. *Randi W. v. Muroc School District*, 14 Cal.4th 1066 (California Supreme Court January 27, 1997).
4. *Marino v. U.S. Postal Service*, No. 93-1958 (1st Cir. May 27, 1994).

5. *Fenton v. Pritchard* (Kansas, May 30, 1996). Source: *BNA Discrimination Reporter.*

6. *Fenton v. Pritchard* (Kansas, May 30, 1996). Source: *BNA Discrimination Reporter.*

7. "Violence in the Workplace," *ASTD Infoline,* July 1993.

8. Bureau of Justice Assistance, *Combatting Workplace Violence: Guidelines for Employers and Law Enforcement,* Washington, D.C., 1995, p. 14.

9. "Violence in the Workplace," *ASTD Infoline,* July 1993.

12
Training to the Rescue

How to Use Training to Improve Performance and Prevent Liabilities

Why Performance-Based Training Is Key to Limiting Legal Liabilities

Minimizing the risk of litigation is critical in today's legal climate. In addition to the whopping fees for attorneys, investigators, and expert witnesses, there is a hidden cost to litigation: lost managerial time giving testimony, lost staff time compiling defense data, lost administrative and management time combing the files for production in court, reduced executive and line manager productivity, and diminished morale among the remaining population of workers.

Performance-based training and documentation or certification of training programs are extremely useful in preventing liabilities, because the criteria focus *specifically* on job-related skills. This serves three functions. First, it increases the likelihood that the trainee will learn to handle hazardous situations properly on the job; second, it facilitates consistency in training; and third, it minimizes the possibility of designing subjective and discriminatory program content.

There are literally hundreds of federal and state statutes regulating the content of training programs—from environmental to health and safety codes. Greater awareness of legislative enactments and judicial precedents and better understanding of administrative regulations will help minimize liabilities. "How to" training for those responsible for the design and implementation of legally defensible training programs is also a must. It is here that trainers can add the greatest value to an organization by recognizing the need for compliance training, recommending implementation to management through systematic analysis of training needs, and then designing effective programs to meet those needs.

In every legal context, your training program will be examined to determine whether it is based on performance and linked to expected job outcomes:

- In the regulatory arena, OSHA views the hazard communication standard as performance based. Inspectors will examine your program from the perspective of whether it was designed to allow employees to perform safely in the work environment. (Chapter 2, pp. 52–54.)

- In the civil courtroom, an injured party will allege that your training was deficient because you knew or reasonably should have known what training would be necessary to prevent the injury. The jury will be asked to determine whether the human error was foreseeable and whether your training met the requirements for allowing employees to perform safely in the work environment. (Chapters 3, pp. 69–78; 4, pp. 93–100; and 8, pp. 186–188.)

- In a civil rights or discrimination lawsuit, the aggrieved party will allege that she was excluded from opportunities for training on grounds that were not reasonably job related. The trier of fact will focus on whether your selection process was based on skills and qualifications reasonably related to anticipated job performance. (Chapter 6, pp. 122–131 and 141–150.)

- In a discrimination claim involving a lack of objective performance standards on an improperly designed test instrument, once again the jury will look directly at your analysis of objective job-related performance standards that may be consistently applied. (Chapter 7, pp. 158–163.)

- When you adopt nontraditional training methods, such as new-age (Chapter 9) and adventure training (Chapter 8), the determination will be whether the objectives of the program are reasonably necessary to develop a job-related performance skill. If not, the court may conclude that the objectives do not justify the intrusion on religion or privacy (Chapter 9, pp. 206–210 and 212–213) or the physical or emotional risk (Chapter 8, pp. 186–188 and 191–195).

In each instance, the focus is on the link between performance and training. Indeed, by focusing on performance-based technologies to design and deliver your training, you will provide the basis for a solid defense to any claims of wrongdoing. This is because performance technology is a *systematic approach* to analyzing, improving, and managing performance in the workplace through appropriate and varied training interventions.

How to Use Performance Technologies to Keep Your Company Out of Court

The goal of a systematic analysis is not simply to marshal information, but to establish a course of action. A jury in a personal injury lawsuit will want to know how your organization addressed the foreseeable factor of human error, and what steps you took—through training—to minimize the risk. Under a negligence analysis, this is a powerful defense: You did everything you could to reduce the risk of harm. You don't even have to be 100 percent right if you took the most prudent action available on the basis of your knowledge *at the time* you designed and delivered the training.

Your performance interventions are rarely a single, isolated solution. Several levels of the organization may be required to achieve maximum results. Executives and high-level managers must support the need for the training. Line supervisors must model the skills and behaviors desired for their workforce, and must also support the time for workers to attend training and then practice their new skills on the job. Trainees must be motivated to learn and apply the skills or work methods, because they are provided with relevant information on *why* the training is necessary, *how* it will make them better and safer employees, and *what* the consequences will be for not applying the information on the job.

It is critical to understand that in an injury lawsuit for damages the *organization* is the target defendant, not the training department or the HR department or the plant floor, or even individual trainers. It doesn't help—indeed, it may devastate—the defense for different departments to point the finger at one another.

Consider a hypothetical example. A poorly performing trainee is scheduled for further instruction. When he fails to pass the posttraining evaluation, the trainer notifies the line supervisor and recommends further training. The employee goes back to the work site and later makes a mistake that causes a fire, seriously injuring three employees. The supervisor claims that the training was deficient. The trainer says, "Not me. Here's my documentation that he failed posttraining tests and

I told the supervisor not to put him back on the job." Human resources weighs in with the caveat: "We told senior managers we had a problem on the manufacturing floor, and they said they'd budget next year for more training." The jurors conclude that one department doesn't know what the other is doing. Verdict: company liable for monetary damages.

Consider a second example which is drawn from an actual case. Maintenance workers in a metropolitan hospital work only on the first two floors. Patients with infectious diseases are on the fifth floor. The training department designs a comprehensive program for physicians, nurses, aides, and others working on the fifth floor (including maintenance) on universal precautions and blood-borne pathogens. There is no communication with line supervisors in the building maintenance department about the training or their practices in making assignments.

A 22-year-old, limited-English-speaking janitor reports for work and is assigned for the night to the fifth floor because two regular workers called in sick. Unaware of the blood-borne hazards, untrained on universal precautions, and unsure about using protective equipment, the janitor is accidentally pricked by a needle and later tests positive for the virus that causes AIDS. It is counterproductive for the training department to point fingers at the maintenance department and vice versa; the organization is found legally responsible for ineffective training and supervision procedures. A performance technology approach would have minimized or prevented this tragic incident by focusing on an analysis of all aspects of performance that could put employees foreseeably at risk of harm.

The training department can come to the rescue by serving as an internal coordinator of all diverse departments within the company, conducting practical needs assessments, recommending specialized instruction as warranted, managing communications relevant to the training programs and employees in need of training, and developing training solutions to be implemented. Effective interaction with managers and supervisors is critical. Instead of waiting for managers to request specific training, you can—and should—add real value by offering your expertise.

A systematic performance assessment identifies gaps between the actual and desired performance and the problems causing the gaps. It also identifies workplace challenges or obstacles to achieving desired performance. For example, an intervention designed to fulfill the OSHA requirements for an ergonomics program will be of little practical value if the trainees' workstations are poorly configured or inadequately designed. In fact, the failure to coordinate information passed on in training with actual work practices can exacerbate the problem in a later negligence lawsuit.

A hypothetical worker with severe repetitive stress disorder could potentially bypass a workers' compensation claim and head straight for the civil courthouse, alleging "serious and willful" violations of safety practices by an employer whose trainers instruct on how to avoid such injuries, while line supervisors insist that employees must work at unsafe workstations. A performance technology needs assessment would presumably pinpoint such incongruity and save the employer the cost of repetitive stress injuries and a potentially unsuccessful defense to a personal injury lawsuit.

Once you have identified the desired performance, you can evaluate any obstacles to performance and design a training program to address those performance requirements directly. This comprehensive analysis includes determining the following:

- What safety-related performance problems exist currently?

- What is necessary for safer or more effective performance?

- How can training be designed or delivered to address these needs?

- Are there organizational barriers to achieving the desired performance? (For example, line supervisors do not model safe practices, or neglect to use safety equipment.)

- Does the workplace have the right tools and equipment for employees to correctly perform the skills learned in training?

- Do employees know the performance standards and the consequences for failure to meet them?

One of the significant values to this approach is that as a course developer you can design reality-based exercises. In order to do so, you need information about the specific work environment and the actual performance system in place. This requires *both* collaboration with other departments and effective methods for simulating real work conditions, while ensuring that your curriculum is relevant to the real performance needs of your organization.

As an internal performance technologist, you also can positively contribute to your company's risk-management programs by assisting in developing tracking mechanisms to evaluate accident and injury data within the organization. By focusing on which work units have the most frequent or repetitive workers' compensation injuries, you can devise a plan for training on concrete work practices that will reduce these injuries.

Alternatively, if a particular department has very few injuries or lost workdays, a "benchmarking" study of what employees are doing right may become the basis for a companywide refresher training on safe and healthful work practices. Once again, a performance technology perspective is quite helpful in identifying where training will add value and then designing relevant, job-specific instruction.

The next step is to apply the analysis to training design. Using the performance technology approach, you document the direct links between the desired performance and the training curriculum you have designed. These linkages become the framework of a defense to a claim of negligence, because they should demonstrate your direct application of training content or methodology to achieve the desired performance. For example:

1. *Needs assessment.* You are told that the company is experiencing significant numbers of repetitive stress injuries, costing both time (lost productivity) and money (workers' compensation).

2. *Performance analysis.* You determine that some workstations are improperly configured and workers don't know how to minimize the potential for injuries and work safely.

3. *Design and delivery.* You develop a training program to address ergonomics, pinpointing the causes and warning signs of repetitive stress disorders and informing employees how to work safely and what to do if they have problems with their workstations. Line supervisors are also trained to respond effectively to complaints. Employees are informed of the disciplinary consequences of not using carpal rests.

In this hypothetical case alleging repetitive stress injuries, your company is in a positive position to defend itself by establishing that you met your legal duty to employees foreseeably at risk by identifying safe performance needs, working backward to supply training to meet those needs, and then continually evaluating the outcomes in reference to reduced injuries. See Chapter 3, pp. 70–76, for a full discussion of how the courts determine your legal duties.

The next step is implementation. Your organization can have the best plan in place, and still fall short of meeting its legal duty by failing to implement effectively *and consistently.* Your implementation should continually measure results and training effectiveness. Once again, a systematic approach will serve you well, because it reduces the likelihood that safety training will be compliance driven. If, following training, injuries are still occurring or safe work practices are ignored and you have simply dodged the bullet because nobody is yet injured, you are likely falling short of your standard of care. On the other hand, if your follow-up reveals that the problem is not with the trainees, but in the supervision, a performance technology approach would attack the problem at its source. Training for the sake of training may not be the sole answer. Defining incentives—positive and negative—for supervisors and management to develop employees, enhance performance, and maintain high standards for productivity and safety is critical.

Never lose sight of the real objective: It is not to defend lawsuits, but to prevent injuries in the first place. The performance technology approach—by linking instruction on safe work practices with actual on-the-job performance requirements—provides one of the best methods to reduce the errors that cause injury and illness.

Seven Critical Steps to Developing Legally Supportable Performance-Based Curriculum, Certification, and Evaluation Tools

1. Establish performance-based training priorities for compliance with law, regulation, and policy.

Following OSHA's lead, employers should consider regulatory training standards as performance-based requirements. Every program should focus on the essential functions of the jobs that your employees will perform, both under normal operating conditions and during foreseeable emergencies. Consider the entire mix of skills required to perform safely and with the highest quality and then provide targeted training to develop relevant skills.

Your policies should focus on the objective, job-related performance skills that each trainee will need. As the needs of the work environment change, policies should keep pace and training should reflect the new job realities. Then, if your program is challenged in court, you can point to the precise policies your company developed to ensure a continually well-trained workforce, and the steps you took to achieve and maintain those standards consistently. *Caveat:* If your policy calls for more than the minimum training required by statute, you must be prepared to consistently enforce that policy. See Chapter 3, pp. 74–75.

2. Identify organizational systems that impede or affect workers' performance.

Enlist line supervisors as partners in assessing where further training will cut injuries, reduce errors, or bolster productivity. Help them understand where your program will address and resolve impediments to their workers' effective performance. Performance technologists recognize that every training program should have measurable objectives. Trainers, supervisors, and employees should all understand the objectives, and be able to evaluate their individual progress and the ultimate effect on their performance capacities.

Alternatively, if the realities of the workplace impede performance— for example, through lack of performance-related resources or management support—your analysis of necessary training needs may pinpoint the challenge and resolve the problem without additional training.

3. Develop performance standards that are congruent with required or expected performance and make sure that employees know what is required.

One major management challenge is communicating expectations to employees. Many successful discrimination cases arise when employees assert:

- "I didn't know what was expected of me" (performance expectations were not communicated)
- "Nobody told me my performance wasn't acceptable" (performance deficiencies were not communicated)
- "I didn't know this could happen to me if I didn't improve my performance" (consequences of unacceptable performance were not communicated)

Then, following an adverse action—poor appraisal, counseling, discipline, or discharge—employees usually assert that they would have met standards if this information had been effectively communicated. Unfortunately, when you can't point to objective standards, efforts to provide training to address those standards, and timely communication to the workforce, juries often conclude that the "real" reason for the adverse action was discrimination.

You can remedy many of these problems by recommending training that is congruent with the precise standards on which employees will be evaluated. Every training program should encompass both the substantive training and communication with participants about how supervisors will evaluate their new or enhanced skills. Of course, partnership with line management to ensure consistency between the information provided by trainers and the realities of the performance appraisal is critical to your success. Inconsistency breeds complaints ranging from simple unfairness to outright discrimination.

4. Make training job-related and reality-based.

5. Make the learning experience meaningful for all participants, by demonstrating job-relatedness and relevancy.

These two practices go hand in hand. Participants and management should recognize the relevancy of the training to their immediate and long-range needs. Use effective simulations and real-world examples or exercises drawn from the trainees' work environment.

6. Build in opportunities for practice and continuous implementation or regular reinforcement.

As the cases addressed in Chapters 2, 3, and 4 reflect, you risk legal repercussions by failing to build directly into your training opportunities for trainees to demonstrate and practice the skills they will need on the job. Performance technology analyses are highly effective means to develop reality-based methodologies, because they focus on end performance rather than knowledge alone.

7. Obtain management and line supervisors' buy-in and keep the channels of communication open.

Establish a true partnership between training and line managers. It will serve employers well when they are required to justify their employment practices—including training and performance standards—to an external source such as judge or jury.

When Must You Train Your Workforce to Comply With the Law?

Supervisors, managers—yes, even trainers—need instruction to ensure that their behavior does not compromise their own or their employer's legal position relative to employment discrimination laws, labor relations, and personnel management. Because an "employer" can act only through its managers and supervisors, they must understand legal requirements and manage effectively within the law. As a trainer, you are in the best position to recognize when this training is needed, to make responsible recommendations on when and what subjects to cover, and then to design effective—and practical—workshops. Like it or not, the burden of keeping other departments out of legal hot water often falls on the training department.

Mandated Training

Until recently, the primary area of statutorily mandated training has been in health and safety. (See the discussion throughout Chapter 2.) However, some states have begun to mandate other types of workplace training and will impose business penalties for failure to comply. For example, the Maine Human Rights Act requires all employers to take specific steps to ensure a workplace "free of sexual harassment." In a workplace with 15 or more employees, the employer *must* conduct an education and training program for all new employees within one year of commencement of employment—a program that includes information on employees' rights and responsibilities. Additional training for supervisory and managerial employees must include specific responsibilities and methods they must take to address sexual harassment claims.

Another example of a federal statute requiring education of employers on their legal rights is the 1992 Family and Medical Leave Act. It *mandates* that employees be instructed on their rights under the FMLA. This includes posting in conspicuous places on the premises a notice that explains pertinent provisions of the law and information about filing a violation charge. The regulations provide that where a significant portion of the workforce is not literate in English, the employer must provide the required information "in a language in which the employees are literate." The U.S. Department of Labor will impose penalties for each violation for not posting the notice and providing the required information.

A complaint filed in federal district court in Ft. Lauderdale, Florida, in January 1997 against the Ding-A-Ling Telephone Answering Service highlights the need for effective management training on compliance with the FMLA. The lawsuit alleges that a supervisor left a message on an employee's answering machine, informing her that "I just got word...that you pulled out. I'm not very pleased. It is a holiday weekend and of all times in the world you should be here. Uh, I know you said you had a doctor's note but that still does not make me any more pleased." The supervisor allegedly further said, "Now I expect you here tonight. I don't care if you have to drag yourself in."

The employee was suffering from a serious health condition, as defined by the FMLA. The telephone call reflected unlawful supervisor conduct. The result was a claim for bad-faith violation of the FMLA, with the telephone tape recording as Exhibit A. If successful, the employee could receive an award equal to twice her economic damages, which include the wages and health insurance benefits she lost after she was terminated.[1] *The lesson:* All supervisors should be trained on the basic provisions of the FMLA. Anyone who can get the company in legal trouble should understand the legal requirements of the law and the areas of legal risk from their own conduct.

Case decisions also sometimes specify required legal training, which then becomes a common law standard of care. In a California case, for instance, Brown-Forman Distillers Corp. was found liable for failing to train employees on the law as it related to regulatory requirements in the alcoholic beverage industry. When the distillery employees broke the law by moving competitors' displays in retail stores, and an employee was discharged for blowing the whistle, the court concluded the company should have trained its employees on the law.[2]

Training Managers on Their Responsibilities Under the Law

Mistakes by management can be costly. Consider a brief case study. In February 1997, a New Mexico jury awarded a disabled job applicant over $150,000 after a Wal-Mart interviewer asked him an illegal question about his medical problems during a preemployment interview. Up to that point, this was the largest award involving an unlawful preemployment medical inquiry.[3] The EEOC filed suit under the Americans With Disabilities Act, alleging that the applicant was asked "What current or past medical problems might limit your ability to do a job?" Under the ADA such inquiries are flatly unlawful (see Chapter 6, pp. 136–138). Indeed, Wal-Mart's human resources department had issued a company manual citing a nearly identical question as an unlawful inquiry.

Wal-Mart was faced with two interrelated legal problems. First, the interviewer failed to follow corporate policy. Second, and more significant for the company *and its trainers,* the company failed to take all appropriate steps to implement the policy, and employees had not been trained on the ADA and how to enforce company policy. Placing a copy of the manual in the store was deemed inadequate training.

This New Mexico victory for the EEOC against Wal-Mart followed a similar result in Texas in late 1996, in which a woman was awarded over $100,000 in a racial discrimination and retaliation case against the chain. In addition, in December 1996, two employees were awarded over $2 million in a sexual harassment case. The EEOC attorney who tried the 1997 case placed the blame squarely on the absence of management training:

The common thread in all three cases was evidence that *Wal-Mart made little or no attempt to train its managerial employees to comply with the antidiscrimination laws.* There was a copy of the manual in the store, but employees were not instructed on how to use it.[4]

As a trainer, if you determine that your company may be at risk of liabilities because it doesn't have a program for training managers and supervisors on significant legal issues, you can suggest that senior managers evaluate their needs before they encounter a serious problem.

Mandatory Training as Part of a Court Order or Settlement

Many times discrimination cases are resolved by settlement or conciliation orders. Although the parties to the dispute—particularly the settling defendant-employer—typically include language specifying that the settlement is not an admission of fault, they will often agree to make mandated training part of the resolution. Figure 12-1 highlights some recent examples.

In several notable cases, judges also have imposed significant affirmative training obligations. For example, following a 1997 jury trial in which Circuit City was found to have engaged in a pattern and practice of racial discrimination, the judge ordered the retailer to hire a director of diversity and an outside consultant, and to take several remedial steps to address the jury's findings. As part of the formal judgment against the company, the judge issued a unique order mandating that training include content on the "best practices" of other companies regarding race-neutral promotions, mentor training, and the proper way to interview applicants for promotion. The court retained the power to monitor compliance with the training and other remedial and outreach programs. All this was in addition to a hefty award of compensatory and punitive damages.[5]

In addition to court orders following adverse decisions, some employers agree to implement training as part of a settlement. Figure 12-2 provides some notable examples.

Effective Training to Avoid Sexual Harassment

A definite trend is appearing in sexual harassment cases nationwide. Significant liabilities for sexual harassment often arise more from an employer's response to a complaint than from the sexual behavior that triggers the protest. In *Weeks v. Baker & MacKenzie*,[6] for example, the jury

- In 1996, the U.S. Department of Justice and the Louisiana State Police Department reached a settlement of a race discrimination suit filed on behalf of 18 African-American applicants who failed a written examination for the position of cadet. The DOJ claimed that the test violated Title VII by disproportionately excluding otherwise qualified African-American applicants. [*U.S. v. Louisiana* (1996).] The settlement established a fund to provide back pay and related damages. The state police also agreed to train officers in ranks of captain and above and the state police commission authorities about their responsibilities under the consent decree. [Source: *BNA Employment Discrimination Report*, Vol. 7 (September 18, 1996), p. 352.]

- Housekeepers at the University of North Carolina–Chapel Hill settled their race discrimination lawsuit with provisions that included, among other things, a pay bonus and a training program. The university pledged $400,000 over three years in a program targeted at the lowest-paid employees. [Source: *BNA Employment Discrimination Report*, Vol. 7 (December 11, 1996), p. 717.]

- Jacksonville Shipyards, Inc. was ordered to implement and distribute a sexual harassment policy that included formal training on sexual harassment prevention for supervisors, managers, and investigators. [*Robinson v. Jacksonville Shipyards, Inc.* (1991.]

Figure 12-1 Examples of Court-Ordered Training Following Litigation.

awarded over $6 million in punitive damages to a legal secretary who was subjected to a sexually hostile environment for fewer than 70 days. The firm had ignored a series of similar complaints about the same offender over several years. In upholding more than $3 million of the original award, the trial judge found that the firm failed to meet its legal obligation to take immediate and appropriate corrective action to stop the offending behavior. Had the employer done so, new employees such as Ms. Weeks would not have confronted a legally hostile work environment.

Thus, it isn't so much the original behavior—unwelcome verbal, physical, or visual conduct of a sexual nature—that creates massive liabilities. Examples of such behavior occur in workplaces every day. Rather, it is the way management handles the issue, or fails to deal with a complaint, that subjects the employer to significant legal exposure. The underlying conduct merely triggers the complaint. The employer's legal responsibility to conduct an immediate investigation and then to

Figure 12-2 Examples of Settlement Agreements Imposing New Training Requirements Following Litigation.

- A federal court in Los Angeles approved an $11.25 million settlement of a class action lawsuit alleging racial discrimination against Southern California Edison Co., the nation's largest electric utility. Allegations included limitations on career advancement, pay, and training opportunities for African-Americans.

  In addition to the monetary terms, Edison agreed to develop and expand management training programs for all employees, and to develop and provide diversity training to its entire workforce. The settlement will remain in effect for up to seven years and will have the force and effect of a court order. Violations of the order, including failure to provide the training, may result in sanctions. [*Rice v. Southern California Edison* (1996).]

- In another consent decree entered as a formal court order to resolve a "glass ceiling" bias lawsuit—this time for sexual discrimination—Publix Super Markets, Inc. accepted a formal training requirement, in addition to monetary relief and other compliance initiatives. The company will train managers and supervisors regarding equal employment opportunity laws and will establish an internal complaint procedure. The consent decree will remain in effect, with mandatory monitoring by an outside compliance consultant, for seven years. [*Shores v. Publix Super Markets, Inc.* (1997).]

- Still another discrimination action involved allegations of same-sex sexual harassment. The settlement ended five months of litigation in which the EEOC accused a vessel captain employed by Stapp Towing Company of fondling male crew members and demanding sexual favors. A federal judge in Galveston, Texas, signed a consent decree in early 1997 that mandates several remedies, *including extensive training.*

  In order to settle the claims, which were admitted by the employer, the company agreed to post notices of nondiscrimination in a public area of its facilities and to have the EEOC provide all employees, including all managers and ship captains, with training on dealing with sexual harassment on company premises. The training was required to be completed within six months. [*EEOC v. Stapp Towing Co.* (1997).]

take immediate and appropriate corrective action is the focus of many cases today. Accordingly, you may be called upon to design management training that successfully avoids or minimizes these real legal risks.

In *Kathleen Kelly-Zurian v. Wohl Shoe Company*,[7] a California case, a trial judge found an employer automatically liable for sexual harassment committed by a supervisor. A significant consequence of this decision is that even after distributing written antiharassment policies and training employees, an employer can be held liable for harassment by a supervisory employee. For this reason, it is especially important to conduct effective sexual harassment prevention training for managers and supervisors, with the objective of having a positive effect on their behavior.

One of the major challenges you may face in presenting sexual harassment programs is resistance by the participants. Many simply don't want to be there. The best way to gain and retain their attention is to explain the concept of personal liability. (See Chapter 6, pp. 145–148; Chapter 1, pp. 35–36; and Introduction, pp. 2–5.) Begin with your organization's policy, as well as all the pertinent laws and regulations. A review of the range of personal consequences for employees can include potential disciplinary actions for violations.

Sexual harassment is hard to define and even more difficult to explain. You may find some philosophical resistance to government "regulation" of interpersonal behavior. Trainees often have trouble with the legal definition of sexual discrimination in the form of harassment, because much of the behavior is socially acceptable outside the work setting (such as at parties and happy hour).

The notion that discrimination must be motivated by ill-will, malice, or other intentional conduct is hard to overcome. Employees often feel threatened by the fact that unintentional behavior (e.g., joking, compliments) can be unlawful discrimination if it is perceived as such by the person who claims to be offended (in legal parlance, the victim of discrimination). Finally, issues of gender identity, sexuality, and sexual interaction are uniquely personal and emotional, and the differences in reaction perception are compounded by cultural, spiritual, and other life experiences.

Because of the difficulty in defining sexual harassment and the fact that a partially subjective standard (perception of the reasonable "victim") applies, many organizations approach the training from an awareness perspective. This approach is premised on the belief that if employees, supervisors, and managers are sensitized to the issues involved in sexual harassment, they will make efforts to question whether their own behavior or that of others could possibly be construed as offensive or could be found illegal. The following guidelines may prove useful.

1. Carefully consider mixing management and rank and file in the same program.

Cautiously approach the decision to train management and nonmanagement employees together. The advantage to training employees of all levels together is that everyone will be reading the same materials, and nonmanagement employees have the benefit of witnessing firsthand that management has knowledge of how to properly handle such matters. The main disadvantage is the risk that managers in the session will *not* be knowledgeable and will show their ignorance to employees who report to them or even make comments that can exacerbate an environment that is already hostile. Likewise, employees may be intimidated about asking questions, particularly about incidents they feel management may not have handled appropriately.

2. Obtain management support.

Top management must support the programs and make attendance mandatory. Monitoring complete attendance helps make the content available to everyone, and serves the legal purpose of documenting the employer's efforts to prevent harassment in its workplace.

Training alone will be insufficient to shield an employer from liability if it fails to enforce consistent policies, take improper conduct seriously, properly investigate complaints, and take appropriate corrective action as warranted. Training does, however, demonstrate a level of commitment to a harassment-free work environment and may mitigate damages in a subsequent lawsuit.

3. Consider content issues carefully.

Training should reinforce participants' awareness and provide practical examples for development. The following specific content is critical to legal compliance:

- Make sure that management participants understand how to create an environment that encourages recipients of unwelcome behavior to talk with the harasser or employer.
- Clarify the specific differences between compliments and sexually harassing behavior.

- Encourage an environment in which sexual harassment is taken seriously, and men and women are not afraid to interact when addressing the issue.

- Clarify the responsibilities of the employer, management, and employees to create a harassment-free workplace and to take appropriate corrective action if a sexual harassment situation occurs.

- Encourage participation with a nonjudgmental attitude. If a participant's behavior is inappropriate, or if a trainee advocates an action that is unlawful or violates company policy, the trainer must clearly say so and explain why.

4. Use only qualified trainers.

The trainers you select must be professional at all times and take the issue seriously, because they are the role models for how sexual harassment is dealt with in the training program. In addition, the presenters should know the audience—specifically, its jargon, history of sexual harassment situations, sexual harassment policy, complaint process, and any unique issues that may affect the program's effectiveness.

Select and train trainers carefully. Before implementing training, ensure that the trainers themselves are sensitized to the issues that are likely to be raised in sessions, understand the company's strategy, and are well versed in the company's sexual harassment policy and procedures, disciplinary process, and all applicable laws.

The skills, knowledge, and ability of individuals selected to conduct training should include, at a minimum, thorough knowledge and understanding of applicable legal and administrative standards and familiarity with the employer's policies. Trainers should also have a perspective on unique company issues (prior to existing complaints) to avoid stumbling unintentionally on a fact pattern too close to home. Otherwise, disruption or inattention may arise in the workshop as participants "speculate" about who is being discussed.

Trainers should also be sensitive to issues of confidentiality (concerning both knowledge of existing complaints *and* questions raised by participants). This is critical and often dictates the use of an external consultant or otherwise independent trainer. In addition, trainers should be aware of, and sensitive to, gay, lesbian, and bisexual issues. Although federal law does not yet provide a separate protection for sexual orientation, hostile environments created by targeted behaviors are actionable. Some states provide separate protection from all forms of discrimination, including harassment based on sexual orientation.

Finally, presentation of a successful sexual harassment program requires the ability to avoid confrontation and "value judgments" about employees' comments and reactions to the subject area. The goal is to deal objectively and compassionately with emotionally distressed individuals in the context of the training and to answer questions and refer trainees to alternative resources for obtaining further information.

5. Use effective methodology, designed for maximum understanding and application of skills, to enforce legally defensible behaviors throughout the workplace.

Your curriculum design should include lectures, group discussions, small group exercises, and case studies to encompass a variety of learning styles. Role play is also extremely useful for management training. Highly interactive sessions build upon individual attitudes, behaviors, and knowledge. Place emphasis on creating an atmosphere of trust in which women and men are encouraged to communicate openly and with mutual respect. Participants should be encouraged to practice new behaviors.

6. Carefully approach the issue of videotaping sessions.

Since sexual harassment training must be provided periodically, and to all new hires within a reasonable period of time, employers may seek to reduce the cost by videotaping sessions for later use. Carefully consider this decision. Although it is cost-effective, two problems may arise. First, the camera may cause some employees to withdraw or fail to seek clarification of issues they don't understand. The value of interaction and discussion—so important with this topic—is thereby diminished. Second, the law on sexual harassment changes frequently. Unless you assign someone to continually monitor the content, you may find yourself providing outdated (and inaccurate) information.

Training During and After Layoffs

Another area of significant legal risk arises when the workforce is reduced. The variety of euphemistic expressions for a reduction in force (RIF)—downsizing, right-sizing, workforce adjustment, workforce restructuring, and others—is the subject of jokes. Call it what you like, the bottom line is *layoffs*. People who lose their jobs are more likely to sue today than ever before. The claims run the gamut from age discrimination to wrongful termination. Age cases can be brought under federal law (ADEA) or state law. Wrongful termination, emotional distress, and related personal injury actions are typically brought in state court. But the trend seems to be increasing; the number of employees suing their former employers is at an all-time high.

As corporate downsizing continues, so will the lawsuits by employees. You can take steps to minimize the potential for lawsuits, and to defend effectively against those that are unavoidable. In addition to being ready to justify a RIF on economic grounds, evaluate other alternatives such as use of federal job training, voluntary reduced-pay training programs, temporary shutdowns, and shortened workweeks.

The components of a training program for managers, supervisors, and human resources specialists should include how to identify jobs that can be eliminated, how to administer an objective and consistent set of standards for ranking employees for layoff, how to communicate the notification to affected employees and understand their anticipated reactions, and how to document the communications with employees regarding the RIF and individual employee options.

In addition, management training should address how to minimize the anticipated anxiety and speculation about a looming layoff, and how to counsel employees while conducting the actual termination (and define the scope of authority of each participant in that process). Participants should be taught how to identify the potential sources of liability facing the company if employees are treated unfairly or subjected to unlawful discrimination and how to develop consistent and legally defensible documentation of the process.

Training About Company Benefits

Under federal law, organizations with participant-directed investment systems, such as 401(k) retirement plans, must train their employees to invest wisely. The failure to do so may result in significant legal exposure if the untrained investor loses significant sums in the market.

In mid-1994 the U.S. Department of Labor instituted a set of guidelines to relieve the plan provider—the employer—from legal exposure for violations of fiduciary duties to investors. The guidelines specify that the plan provider offer at least three investment options with different risk factors, offer quarterly options to switch investments, *and provide sufficient communication and education.*

Employees must be educated on a variety of subjects, including the investment options they have, the benefits available under the plan, how to determine what their financial needs will be in retirement, how to administer their own portfolios, the role of the company or plan administrator in managing the plan, and how to develop their own investment strategies for short-term profit and long-term security.

There is, however, a significant line between education and investment advice. Crossing the line can result in other forms of liability, including allegations of negligent advice, fraudulent recommendations, and similar breaches of the obligations inherent in a relationship of trust. The required training to educate employees on the benefits, options, and administration of their 401(k) or other retirement plan is just that—general awareness training on the plan itself. Provide the facts about the investment options, but always let the employees make the ultimate decisions by reaching independent conclusions. It is especially important for trainers to avoid giving the appearance of offering individualized advice, such as recommendations on investment strategies.

References

1. CCH, "Human Resources Management," *Ideas and Trends*, No. 399 (February 12, 1996).

2. *Smith v. Brown-Forman Distillers Corp.*, 196 Cal.App.3d 503, 513 (1987).

3. *EEOC v. Wal-Mart Stores*, U.S. District Court, New Mexico (February 24, 1997), Lexis Cite 3188.

4. *BNA Employment Discrimination Report*, Vol. 8, No. 10, (March 5, 1997), p. 319, (emphasis added).

5. *McKnight v. Circuit City Stores*, District Court, Eastern District of Virginia, No. 3:95CV964 (March 13, 1997).

6. *Weeks v. Baker & MacKenzie*, California Superior Court, No. 943043 (San Francisco County 1994).

7. *Kathleen Kelly-Zurian v. Wohl Shoe Company*, 22 Cal.App.4th 397 (1994).

PART 2

Legal Dos and Taboos for Speakers (and Stand-Up Trainers)

13

The 10 Most Common Legal Problems for Presenters and How to Avoid Them

1. Copyright infringement through distribution of written materials or multimedia materials without permission

When you create or distribute written materials in the form of handouts, articles, outlines, or graphic presentations, copyright law applies. All such intellectual property is protected by the U.S. Copyright Act of 1976. The author or creator of the work has an ownership interest from the moment the materials are fixed in tangible form. In order to protect the work from infringement by other presenters, the creator may simply affix a copyright notice on the documents. For example:

> Copyright © 1998 [author's name]. All rights reserved, including the right to reproduce these materials in any form, in whole or in part, without the express written permission of the copyright holder.

Additionally, the author may register the work product with the U.S. Copyright Office, which establishes the date of original use for purposes of seeking damages for copyright infringement. When a proper copyright notice is used, infringers are typically unable to reduce their liability for damages by arguing that their infringement was innocent.

The owner of the copyright has the exclusive right to reproduce, adapt, and distribute textual materials. Speakers who fail to obtain permission to use or distribute such material are subject to liability for infringement. Copyright issues are addressed in detail throughout Chapters 18 and 19.

Presenters who distribute handouts and participant materials that incorporate *portions* of copyrighted work violate the Copyright Act. Infringement entends to photocopying articles without obtaining express permission, citing lengthy quotations, and closely paraphrasing others' work (even with quotation marks, attribution, or "credit"). The defense of "fair use," even for educational purposes, is not usually applicable when the user is a commercial or profit-making venture—which all speakers hope to be. The details of fair use, how to obtain permission, and how to quote fairly are presented in Chapter 19, pp. 380, 387–388, and 400–403.

Speakers on the cutting edge of technology are using computer-based presentation tools, including multimedia. Multimedia products involve multiple categories of content, such as literacy works (text), pictures (moving or still images), audiovisual works, and musical works, all presented via a single medium, such as a CD-ROM or the Internet.

Computer technology has made it possible to combine all forms of content to create a new integrated presentation product that may be used interactively. The copyright laws apply to each separate content element: music, video, sound, animation, graphics, art, and print media. Accordingly, you must obtain separate authorizations from all authors, creators, and contributors (such as audiotape and videotape producers or photographers) before you can lawfully use the multimedia product.

When using printed materials, start from the assumption that they are protected by copyright. First, look for a copyright notice. If there is none, but the materials are printed in a newspaper or periodical, call the publication's copyright permission department. Inquire who owns the copyright and get a complete address and telephone number.

When you obtain material from electronic sources (such as the Internet), look for a copyright notice or a hypertext link to a "legal notices" page. If you cannot locate a notice, do not assume the material is not subject to protection. If you intend to use the material frequently, contact the U.S. Copyright Office, which will direct you to resources for conducting a search. Chapter 19, pp. 400–403, explains how to obtain permission to use copyrighted works in your presentations.

2. Use of music and sound recordings without permission or license agreements

When you enhance your presentations with sound and music, copyright laws apply. A sound recording is subject to copyright protection, giving the copyright holder exclusive performance rights. Playing an audiotape or CD at a speech is as much a performance as singing or playing the music live for the audience.

One common mistake is assuming that music and other sound recordings are in the public domain and freely usable. This can be a costly error when your presentation is built around sound and music created by others and you haven't obtained permission or license agreements. Sound recordings are subject to copyright laws regardless of the nature of the sounds recorded. Examples include a performance of a copyrighted or public domain musical work, a recording of spoken words (such as a drama or speech), sounds of nature, and special effects. Sound recordings are "works that result from the fixation of a series of musical, spoken, or other sounds . . . regardless of the nature of the physical medium, such as disks or tapes, in which they are embodied."[1]

Copyright protection generally extends to two elements in a sound recording: the contribution of the performers and the contribution of the producers—the people responsible for capturing, editing, and processing the sounds to make the final recording. U.S. Copyright Office Circular 56, "Copyright for Sound Recordings 1" (1991), provides that no copyright may be claimed for sounds that are "fixed by mechanical means without any originality of any kind." The required originality must come from the performer or the producer who together create the final creative product.

Many times the producer who records, processes, compiles, and edits the recording operates on a fee, creating a *work-for-hire*. In these circumstances, the client or employer that hires the producer retains the copyright. Many speakers hire professional organizations to help develop and record audiotapes of their speeches. In the absence of a work-for-hire arrangement or other agreement, the recorder may claim some copyright rights. Thus, to protect your own rights when you perform on sound recordings, you should have a clear understanding with these service providers regarding their limitations of rights pursuant to the work-for-hire arrangement. For a further discussion of works made for hire and sample contractual language, see Chapter 19, pp. 388–392, and Appendix C.

Conversely, if you intend to use clips, excerpts, or other portions of a sound recording—even of your own presentations—in which the rights of the recorder are not clearly subject to a work-for-hire arrangement with you or the conference sponsor, you may need to obtain written permission to use the recording again or to incorporate it into other new products. Remember too that live musician-performers at your presentations may have common law copyright protection for their portion of the overall performance, unless they are providing a work-for-hire or you have a specific agreement.

Each recording of a musical work may have several separate parties with rights to the recording: the composer and/or lyricist who creates the piece, the performer, and the producer of the recording itself. A common legal problem confronting speakers is the use of copyrighted music without authorization. Unless the musical work is in the public domain, or is recorded pursuant to a work-for-hire, the speaker who uses it without obtaining permission or negotiating a license agreement risks liability for copyright infringement.

Further, the copyright in a sound recording is distinct from the copyright in the literary, dramatic, or musical work being performed. Copyright in a sound recording is not the same as, or a substitute for, copyright in the underlying work.[2] This is relevant for speakers in the following respects:

- Copyright ownership of the speech itself is separate from the recording of the spoken words, if the speech is reduced to writing.

- When poems, quotations, or other materials are recited in the context of a speech, copyright protections may exist in each of those underlying works. Thus, you must get permission from the author of those words to incorporate them into your speech, and then *for each intended use in an oral program or subsequent sound recording.*

In order to produce a sound recording of a speech containing a copyrighted song or poem, it is essential to obtain permission from the owner of the copyright. Failure to get such authorization not only constitutes copyright infringement, *but will also invalidate the copyright in the sound recording created.* For example, in *Jarvis v. A&M Records,*[3] the court held that "copyright protection for a sound recording of musical compositions must be denied if the copyright claimant of the sound recording has not lawfully obtained the rights to utilize the musical compositions in the sound recording."

In a hypothetical recorded speech to a live audience that is taped for later replays, the following copyright holders all have an interest in the final product: the speaker (for his or her words); the author of quoted poems, words, or expressions; the composer, performer, and/or producer of recorded music or sound effects; the performer of live musical accompaniment; and the recorder and/or producer of the tape. Many of these rights may be handled through work-for-hire. The remainder may be the subject of license agreements or written authorizations for one or a series of replays.

If you have a license to use music or sound recordings, the licensor may request that you specifically state in the written program or course materials that the music is furnished pursuant to a license agreement. Include the name of the copyright holders, the dates the sound recording was made, and a notice that it is used with permission. Such requests are often made when a large audience is anticipated, because copyright holders do not want to give audience members the false impression that the music is in the public domain or otherwise available for them to use or record without permission.

Speakers should make sure that anyone recording their presentation is aware of the limitations of further uses of the recording. For example, distribution of a videotape of a speech, in which a sound recording is used pursuant to a limited license for that live presentation, will violate the rights of all copyright owners to the sound recording. The best way to avoid this problem is to include rights to videotape and distribute your presentations as part of the license agreement for the underlying sound recording. If you don't, you jeopardize your own copyright to the videotape.

Finally, require every employee who creates audiovisual aids or other presentation materials to keep accurate records of all source materials. Provide appropriate forms for obtaining copyright permissions. See Chapter 19, pp. 400–403, and Figure 19-1.

Always seek permission to use music, sound recordings, or videos in your programs or presentations. Obtaining permission includes the following steps:

1. Determine who owns the copyright (or multiple rights in the case of sound recordings). This information may appear on the jacket or promotional materials for the recording. If not, contact the recording studio and/or the performer's agent.

2. Make your request specific, and in writing. Include all pertinent information concerning your anticipated use or uses, the number of times you wish to include the protected work, the geographic areas (if you know them), and any other pertinent information.

3. Anticipate using music or videos multiple times. Accordingly, be prepared to negotiate a fair and reasonable license fee, based on the number of uses. Typical arrangements include:

   - A one-time fixed fee (typically for a limited number of "performances").
   - A flat fee for each separate use. In this case, you need to keep accurate records and report regularly to the licensor.

■ A sliding-scale fee at regular increments. The per-performance fee may go up or down for each use over 25, 50, 75, 100, and so on, depending upon the licensor's receptivity to your multiple uses. Providers in the business of licensing videos tend to make the fees cost-effective for higher-volume licensees. Composers and lyricists may be less receptive to repetitive replays of their work and may try to invoke a disincentive to repeated or long-term use.

4. Include a copy or recording of the work with your written request. This is especially important when you are using excerpts of music or video clips. If written materials accompany the video, and the prose copyright holder is different from the video copyright holder, include in your letter the fact that you are seeking (or have already obtained) permission to use the prose. Figure 13-1 provides an example.

5. Keep a copy of all written authorizations you receive in a well-organized, accessible file.

6. If you are flexible in the music you can use in your speech or presentation, look into music libraries. They are in the business of licensing music recordings, and have the right to authorize the use for all separate owners of the copyright. They will have a complete set of samples for your consideration, and can provide you with an immediate license or authorization. You can often obtain multiple-use licenses quite cost-effectively.

7. If only a *specific* recording will do, leave yourself ample time to locate all the copyright holders—composer, lyricist, performers (musicians and vocalists), and technicians who recorded or produced the recording itself. Then, send a separate written request to each copyright holder. Do not assume that the producer created a work-for-hire. Make the request, and then be happily surprised if you learn that the rights were not individually retained.

3. Use of other proprietary materials, such as visual images, graphics, and cartoons, without permission or compensation

As a professional speaker, you may frequently use visual images to enhance your presentation: in handouts, overhead transparencies, slides, large-scale blowups, diagrams, or other displays. Still images, such as photographs, cartoon strips, pictures, calendars, posters, greeting cards, drawings, and designs, are all subject to copyright protection. So are moving images, such as film, video, and television broadcasts.

November 1, 1997

Master ("Mike") Musician
SPEAKERS RESOURCE RECORDING STUDIO
4000 Keynote Lane
Anytown, USA

Dear Mike:

This letter is to request permission to use the opening two minutes of your 1995 release, "Motivational Mania," in a nationwide presentation I am making to training directors. Enclosed for your information is a complete recording of the proposed presentation incorporating your piece.

I am intending to use this recorded excerpt at the following dates and times: [*list specifics*]. I intend to book additional dates throughout the year, with a total for 1998 expected to be 150.

I am receptive to a reasonable license fee for use of this clip. I will also require written permission from all copyright holders.

Please contact me to discuss the details.

Very truly yours,

SPEAKERS FOR LEGAL COMPLIANCE

Jane Doe
Principal Speaker

JD/tks
Enclosure

Figure 13-1 Sample Letter Seeking Permission and License Agreement to Use Copyright-Protected Sound Recording in Speeches.

U.S. Copyright Office Circular 40, "Copyright Registration for Works of the Visual Arts 2" (1990), provides examples of works that qualify for copyright protection as "pictorial, graphic, and sculptural works." These include cartoons, comic strips, games, puzzles, greeting cards, holograms, computer and laser artwork, logo artwork, drawings, paintings, print advertisements, reproductions, technical drawings, and diagrams—all of which are frequently incorporated by speakers and trainers into their overall presentations.

In addition, photographs are copyrightable in many forms, including prints, blowups, negatives, film strips, slides, overhead transparencies, and machine-readable digital data. In *Playboy Enterprises, Inc. v. Frena*,[4] for example, the court held that making digitized versions of copyrighted photographs available on a computer bulletin board infringes the copyright owner's rights of distribution and public display.

The holder of the copyright is the photographer. Speakers who intend to use photographs or still images should obtain permission and/or license agreements from both the photographer and the subjects featured in the photograph. When the "use" will typically involve more than a single publication, the request for authorization should state the scope of the intended use, specify the anticipated number of times the photo will be used and in what context, and seek written authorization for multiple uses. These steps will prevent later claims that the actual use exceeded the authorization. With multiple uses, you may wish to obtain a license agreement, or fee arrangement, to compensate the copyright holder for the anticipated number of repeated uses of his or her work.

If you have your own home page on the Internet or are marketing materials with photographs taken by other people, determine whether the photos were works-for-hire or the photographer has copyright ownership. Obtain permission to use the photographs in the same way you would written materials and sound recordings. You may need to negotiate a license agreement for multiple or long-term use.

Determining who owns the rights to a photograph can be difficult and time-consuming. If it appears in a print publication, the publisher may have acquired ownership of the copyright. However, photographers often retain their own rights. Many photographers retain the copyright, and sell to the publisher the right to use a print in certain ways. Such agreements often contain restrictions on use and reproduction, including the size, format, time frame, geographic area, and number of copies that may be reproduced.

Once you have obtained permission to use copyrighted cartoons or graphics on your slides or transparencies, include the complete name of the artist, date created, publication (if applicable), and date published and place the copyright notice on the bottom of each slide (e.g., Copyright © 1997 Charles Schulz. All rights reserved). Identify in your handout the overheads you used, and specify that they were used with the permission of the copyright holder. When seeking permission to use cartoons, graphics, animation, or other audiovisual materials, provide a complete description or picture of the materials or an actual copy of your intended final product to the copyright holder. Keep a complete set for your own files, along with the permission or license agreement.

4. Ineffective protection of your own work product and proprietary interests

Speakers invest significant time and resources developing speeches, handouts, and audiovisual or graphic materials. They also develop and market workbooks, instruments, and other products, including audiotapes and videotapes. These materials are proprietary and of substantial value. Yet many speakers don't take the time to protect their own work product from infringement or misappropriation. If you don't protect your own work product, when you learn that a signature story, a unique exercise, or a persuasive message has been used—verbatim or in significant detail—by someone else, you may not be positioned to enforce these rights and obtain redress for losses caused by the misappropriation. Consider the following solutions.

Know Your Rights

As a professional speaker, you should understand which of your products and materials are subject to protection under the federal Copyright Act of 1976 and any relevant state laws. The Copyright Act grants speakers, as creators of intellectual property, a wide range of intangible, exclusive rights over their work. These rights include:

- Reproduction right—the right to make copies of a protected work, including the text of a speech, passages of a poem, or other material recited in a presentation
- Distribution right—the right to sell or otherwise distribute the work publicly or privately
- Right to create derivative work, to prepare new work based on the protected work, or to create adaptations of the original or derivative work
- Display right—the right to display work in public

- Performance right—the right to exclusively perform the work in public (whether or not for a paid fee)

Once you know which products and presentations are protectable, evaluate the extent to which you wish to seek copyright protection.

Preserve Your Rights

Take the steps to reserve and enforce copyright protection. Place appropriate copyright notices on all written materials and audiovisual aids you will reproduce, distribute, display, or publicly perform. Also place copyright notices on all visual aids you use during a presentation, particularly if you intend to distribute or provide copies of your visuals upon request of your client or an audience member. Take the steps to register those products and materials which, if used by others, would impair your business and for which you wish to preserve the right to sue for infringement.

Prepare to Respond to Requests to Use Your Work

Be prepared when someone asks for permission to use, display, or perform your copyrighted work. If you don't want others using your work, politely decline. Although copyright protection is preserved unless you expressly give permission for use, it is prudent to respond in writing to every request. If you don't respond at all, or your record keeping is haphazard, an infringer may be able to assert that a subsequent use was not willful. Keep accurate records of every request and your response.

Consider in advance how you will define the limits of authorization you are willing to provide to those who request a license agreement for use of your handouts, unique presentation products, and related materials. To facilitate negotiations, plan the parameters of any license agreements you will sign. Planning reduces the risk that your initial pleasure at someone's interest in using your work will interfere with your thorough analysis of the financial dimensions of the arrangement. For further amplification on preserving your rights, see Chapter 19, pp. 403–413, and Appendix C.

5. Unlawful content during a presentation

Discriminatory Content

As a speaker, you may often make presentations at employer meetings, conferences, or other professional, trade, or business gatherings.

Audience members attend because the program is mandatory, strongly recommended, or an enhancement to their career. Their attendance is work related, and thereby an extension of their work environment, in which they are protected from discrimination and harassment. These employees have a legal right not to be forced to leave the program in order to avoid hearing unwelcome language or seeing graphics which are sexual, racial, religious, or other inappropriate content that is offensive.

"It Was Only a Joke" and Other Legends That Lead to Liabilities

Ever hear the one about the mermaid and the fisherman? A fisherman asks a magic mermaid to make him smarter. So, the mermaid turns him into a woman. Several hundred employees of the Social Security Administration heard that story during a diversity conference in Miami, when the joke was told from the podium by a senior agency official. The resulting furor from the men in attendance, who perceived it as "antimale sexism," resulted in a demand for an apology from the leader of GMEN (Government Men for Equality Now).

Presenters—both speakers and trainers—love to use jokes to break the ice at the beginning of a program. Often, the objective is to establish immediate rapport with the audience. At the Social Security Administration, not only was rapport broken, but an entire group of participants was turned off to the remainder of the program.

Some humor is just plain inappropriate, particularly in a business context. Wisecracks can backfire in presentations focusing on a serious topic, such as violence prevention, high-risk activities, change management, or downsizing. Jokes at the expense of *any* group can offend participants of training programs on sexual harassment, diversity, or any other highly sensitive workplace issue. Jokes about an aging workforce—when apparently condoned by management—can lead to litigation if later downsizing disproportionately affects older workers.

Speakers and presenters are always looking for techniques to keep the audience engaged and interested. Humor can fulfill this function very well. But once your audiences are turned off, you've lost them. And you may invite discrimination claims personally or against the client who hired you. Consider some examples of inappropriate content that turn audiences off the speaker's message and onto litigation against the sponsor of the program:

- Sexist comments, terms, or stereotypes, such as using females as the brunt of jokes about lack of mechanical skills

- Content of a program containing sexually explicit graphics, words, or gestures, including innuendo

- Off-color or sexually demeaning, explicit, or graphic words, jokes, or other verbal/nonverbal communications, including innuendo and body language by the presenter

- Display or distribution of sexually explicit cartoons, pictures, graphics, or other program materials

- Jokes about sexual orientation or lifestyle preference

- Ethnically charged references ("camel jockey," "potato eater")

- Mimicking accents, particularly Asian or Hispanic

- Fictional names—even in stories or hypotheticals—with a clear ethnic slant ("José," "Leroy")

- Political humor taken to an extreme, through insensitive references to religious groups ("God squad," "religious fanatics")

- Repeated references to older people as "dinosaurs," "the Geritol set," or other dismissive expressions (usually in workplaces where there have been substantial downsizings or other stressful changes)

- Intolerant or patronizing words, gestures, or mimicking of people with sensory impairments, mobility problems, or medical disorders

Don't succumb to the "it could never happen to me" syndrome. Avoid jokes and stereotypes, especially if they relate to ethnic origin or race. Late-night entertainers may be paid to draw laughs with insults, mimicking of accents or physical disabilities, or terms of derision, but professional speakers who target an individual or an entire group during a keynote speech, workshop, sales rally, or retreat are setting themselves and their clients up for litigation. They may be proud of the laughs they do get, but a video or audiotape of their performance may be shown to the jury as Exhibit A in a later discrimination lawsuit, and the jury may not be as amused.

Don't use cartoons, pictures, or other written materials that demean, insult, patronize, or otherwise strip an individual or a group of dignity and respect. Other potential vehicles for discrimination are displays, replicas in the workplace, e-mail messages, and other printed or hand-drawn material. Recent litigation even includes graphic material and animation downloaded from the Internet.

Most presenters make a single appearance before a convention or industry meeting. Legal liabilities arising from one speech are rare. However, the potential for embarrassment, emotional distress, or anger by the audience is real. At a minimum, it can cost the speaker a repeat invitation from the meeting planner, association, or bureau. In more serious cases, it can result in a full-blown lawsuit.

The most significant potential liability from a joke gone awry involves claims of workplace harassment. Harassment based on gender, race, religion, ethnicity, age, or disability is unlawful under federal law and many parallel state statutes. The ramifications of sexual harassment in the training facility or in a training exercise are discussed at length in Chapters 5, pp. 114–116, and 6, pp. 143–150. Can unlawful harassment occur in a single presentation? You bet it can, when the remarks are targeted to an audience member or the content is explicit, graphic, or demeaning. Racial and sexually explicit jokes are especially vulnerable to single-incident claims. Although claims of hostile-environment harassment must usually involve persistent conduct, at least one court has ruled that a single incident of sexually explicit language may violate Title VII. A single incident of egregious nonphysical sexual harassment can violate the law as well. In Massachusetts, a female employee was sexually harassed when a male employee superimposed her face and name over pictures of nude and partially nude female bodies, and then distributed them in the workplace. The court emphatically rejected the harasser's contention that more than a single isolated incident is necessary to create a hostile environment.

Your employer or client is legally responsible for all activities that occur in its workplace or at a company-sponsored event, and you may also be personally at risk of being sued. This is especially true when program attendance is mandated. Your client or the employer sponsoring the program *must*, by law, take action if an employee is subject to harassment by customers, vendors, or others with whom contact occurs on the job. If the meeting planners receive a complaint from someone sent to hear a speech, or if they witness a sexually oriented presentation that is clearly unwelcome to people in the group—even if nobody formally complains—they must take immediate and appropriate corrective action.

Verbal hostile-environment harassment includes jokes, insults, comments of a sexual nature, innuendo, repeated use of terms of affection, gossip, pranks, mimicking of accent or physical disabilities, terms of derision, or other audible communication targeted to an individual or an entire group.

Visual harassment includes cartoons, posters, pinups, written materials, handouts, or graphics that are demeaning, insulting, patronizing, or otherwise strip an individual or a group of dignity and respect. Displays, overhead transparencies, slides, props, or replicas used during the presentation should be monitored carefully. One case involved a presenter who sprinkled slides of bikini-clad women into a technical presentation on fingerprinting analysis. The result: claims of harassment and sexual discrimination by two female employees who were forced to attend the program. The presenter was a guest lecturer. The employer that hired him—and sponsored the program—was liable for the damages.

It is a fundamental denial of equal employment opportunity to say (or imply) to an individual who wants—or is required—to attend your speech, but objects to off-color words, that he should leave if he doesn't like the jokes, "because it's all in good fun." The same behavior in a social setting would be no problem, because an individual who doesn't appreciate the humor is free to leave with no professional or work-related repercussions. This is not always the case at a professional conference or meeting.

Use humor cautiously. What is funny to you may offend someone else. This is not just a matter of being "politically correct." The wrong joke—where age, gender, ethnicity, religion, sexual orientation, or disability is a target—is also unlawful. A poor attempt at humor may result in a very real charge of discrimination, based on hostile or offensive work environment.

Use only victimless jokes and eliminate those that perpetuate a stereotype of any group. Even self-deprecating humor may be inappropriate, if the brunt is your own gender, disability, or similar characteristic. Use this technique only when it is integral to the substance of your presentation, such as stereotypes you have personally dealt with and overcome.

Beyond Politically Correct: Why Neutral and Inclusive Language Is a Legal Necessity

Speakers are increasingly called upon to design and deliver presentations in diverse workplaces. Although diversity encompasses the traditional issues of gender, race, and ethnicity, it also includes a broader range of differences, such as age, physical and mental capacities, economic status, and geographic background. Even differing approaches to work styles are in their broadest sense diversity issues (e.g., military vs. civilian, government vs. private sector, urban vs. rural, "fast paced" vs. "laid back"). Successful speakers are those who use methods and language that are inclusive, so that every member of their audience receives value from the presentation.

Common sense? Of course. Sound business practice? Certainly. Legally required? Yes, when noninclusive language or nonverbal cues become demeaning or exclusionary. When a speaker is retained to present to a group of employees who are expected to obtain and act upon the message or instruction, the employer and the speaker (as the employer's agent) must provide equality of access to the career or job opportunity.

The following guidelines will help you as a speaker (and your client) to avoid embarrassment and will also ensure an equal opportunity for all participants:

1. Use gender-neutral descriptions whenever possible: labor-hours, not man-hours; workers' comp, not workman's comp. Also use gender-neutral terms for jobs: firefighter, police officer, flight attendant, plant superintendent (instead of foreman), food server (instead of waiter). Many trade and professional conferences provide detailed directions to speakers on the use of inclusive language.

2. Avoid using "him" or "him/her." Try alternating. Use plurals (e.g., "employees/their") rather than singulars ("employee/his"). Replace "his" with "the."

3. Avoid examples that stereotype people by age. References to a "young manager" or "old-timer" must go. Use substitutes for old and older, such as seasoned, mature, experienced, veteran, long-standing employee. Avoid sayings like "Old dogs won't hunt" and "You can't teach an old dog new tricks."

4. Avoid stereotyping people on the basis of culture or ethnicity. For example, when discussing free trade with Mexico, avoid using clichéd names like "José" and "Pablo." Avoid gender and racial stereotyping in handouts and visual aids. When using pictures, include examples of men and women of all races and abilities.

5. Avoid mimicking or deriding people with physical challenges. Although most inappropriate humor directed at disabilities is not intended to offend, avoid any verbal or nonverbal communication that may be reasonably construed as targeting the disabled, such as exaggerated body language to signify sensory impairments. This is offensive to people with disabilities and is exclusionary.

In addition to using inclusive language, keep in mind your legal obligations to audience members who have special needs arising from a disability or language barrier. See Chapter 14, pp. 298–305 and 306–307.

How to Avoid Damaging Reputations During Your Presentations

When you tell a story about someone or otherwise refer to a person's abilities, lifestyle, business acumen, or performance during a presentation and that information is false or made with reckless disregard for the truth, you may face a claim for defamation of character. When you customize your materials to include anecdotes or other stories about real people in the organization or industry—past or present—you should be careful to verify your facts, or obtain permission from the subject of the comments. Verification will avoid potential embarrassment or worse.

A single speech to a confined audience is unlikely to generate either negative attention from the subject of the defamatory remarks or damages significant enough to justify a lawsuit. However, when professional speakers make guest appearances on broadcast media, the audience is far broader and the potential for liability far greater.

Defamation of character can be either libel (written) or slander (verbal). Since speakers use both mediums of communication, both theories may apply in any given presentation. The law of defamation is divided into two parts: the state common law elements and the constitutional requirements.

The elements of common law defamation are defamatory language (verbal or written), which is "of or concerning" another person. This means language that injures the person's reputation. The person about whom the statements are made must prove that the statements were published to a third party and that this damaged the person's reputation. Since a speech or media interview is a publication to others, the central issue is whether the content is defamatory.

In most cases, name calling, hyperbole, abusive epithets, and other figurative statements are not defamatory, because, when the language is taken in context, a reasonable person understands that the speaker or author is using it to emphasize a point of view, and not describing facts about the person that would harm that person's reputation. Although such language, when extreme, may subject the speaker—and his or her client—to discrimination or claims of emotional distress, the law of defamation does not apply.

A claim of defamation requires evidence of more than generalized distress over something that was said or written. Statements are "defamatory" if they "tend" to cause injury to people's reputation, expose them to public hatred, contempt, ridicule, shame, or disgrace, or affect them adversely in their trade or business.

To be actionable, the statements must be capable of bearing a meaning that injures reputation, which is a question of law decided by a judge. If the judge finds that the words, in context, are capable of two meanings, only one of which is defamatory, the alleged defamed party must then prove that people hearing the words understood the statement to have a defamatory meaning. This is a question of fact for a jury. See the discussion of the role of juries in Chapter 1, pp. 33–35.

If a reasonable person would understand that the words "on their face" tend to harm a person's reputation, the statement is considered defamatory per se and harm to the subject's reputation is presumed as a matter of law. Even when the words are not defamatory on their face, they may be unlawful if extrinsic facts known to the audience would reveal the defamatory meaning. For example, announcing that Sammy Speaker received an award for his original story presentation could tend to injure his reputation if he is known to the audience to have pirated the story from another speaker.

You may not intend to harm reputations, but that won't matter if you are sued for defamation. In essence, a speaker who makes a false statement of fact about another person in a presentation may be liable for damages if the statement damages reputation, even if the comment is negligent. Figure 13-2 should help you to visualize the required proof of malice to pass constitutional standards when the statements are about public figures or matters of public interest versus a private person.

Many forms of disparaging statements can land a speaker in court. Just one example involves deprecating remarks about food products. For example, an *Oprah!* show on "mad cow" disease faced the first legal

---

Public Official or Public Figure

Fault required: actual malice (knowledge of falsity or reckless disregard as to the truth or falsity)

Damages available: presumed damages under common law rules and punitive damages as appropriate

Private Person on a Matter of Public Concern

Fault required: at least negligence as to the statement's truth or falsity

Damages available: only for proved actual injury; if malice is shown, presumed damages and punitive damages

Private Person on a Matter of Private Concern

Fault required: no fault as to truth or falsity

Damages available: presumed damages under common law rules and punitive damages as appropriate

Figure 13-2 Legal Elements of a Defamation Claim.

action under new laws aimed at protecting U.S. food supplies from defamatory comments. Thirteen states have enacted "food disparagement laws" in the last six years, and eight more have legislation pending. Most give food producers a legal right to sue those who make false statements—verbally or in writing—about the safety of their products.

These state laws go substantially farther than previous judicial precedents. Courts have limited damage awards to businesses whose products are disparaged publicly when the speaker (generally a competitor) intentionally attempts to hurt sales. The emerging trend seems to be to broaden the potential for legal action against any speaker who makes comments about a food product that are false or spoken with reckless disregard for the truth. Most of the state laws would hold speakers liable even for statements they did not know were false.

This trend conflicts sharply with the landmark *New York Times v. Sullivan*[5] standard that applies to public figures or matters of public interest. Because this is a constitutional issue involving freedom of expression, the plaintiff is ordinarily required to prove that the speaker knew the comments were false, or showed reckless disregard for their truth or falsity. These laws appear to relax the standard considerably.

In *Engler v. Winfrey*,[6] a Texas case, Cactus Feeders, Inc. attempted to invoke the 1995 Texas food disparagement law on the basis of comments about "mad cow" disease, and the U.S. beef industry's practices, made on the *Oprah!* show by the host as well as a guest speaker. The show aired on April 16, 1997, and the following day cattle prices plummeted.

Naturally, the broader the dissemination of the words (here, a national television audience), the greater the potential that disparaging remarks will produce enough impact to prompt legal action. However, since the legislation does not require "actual malice," even a nonmalicious statement that tends to injure an individual's reputation may give rise to a claim, particularly when the false statement is made during a presentation to a business, professional, or industry group to which the individual belongs.

This issue will be thoroughly litigated in the courts, with defenses based on public interest, first amendment freedom of expression, and related public policy considerations. At press time for this book, the *Winfrey* case remained unresolved. However, the zeal with which state lawmakers have embraced food disparagement bills reflects an intent to hold public speakers accountable for damages arising from their commentary about products, even when the statements are not malicious and noncompetitive.

The solution is to be careful about disparaging remarks concerning people and/or products. A few safeguards include:

- Be prepared to support statements with specific facts. One of the allegations against the guest speaker in the *Winfrey* case involves the following question-and-answer sequence:

  Q: You say this disease could make AIDS look like the common cold?
  A: Absolutely.
  Q: It has just stopped me cold from eating another burger![7]

- Avoid speculation about practices of specific businesses or industries, unless you have specific data and/or the permission of the subject of the comments.

- Of course, when you have been asked to review and comment upon your client's business issues, you are free to exercise your best professional judgment in giving advice. However, business speakers may wish to make points about improvement of personnel or business practices. Make sure you refrain from using specific names in a negative context—both to avoid defamation and to prevent embarrassment to an audience member.

- Refrain from making disparaging jokes about particular industries or identifiable products. In reality, you never know whether you will offend an audience member. Although the comments may not be unlawful per se, the potential to turn off members of the audience to your message is unlikely to result in positive impressions or repeat business.

A photograph can also be defamatory if it does not accurately reflect the image originally sought to be captured, or it is displayed in a context that suggests a defamatory "fact" about the person depicted. This is especially a problem with multimedia technology, because digital alteration of photographs and images makes it impossible to distinguish the altered image from the original. Alterations of photographs have been held to be defamatory in several instances involving print media. For example, a picture of a woman was altered to make it appear that she was bald,[8] and a photograph of a female model was juxtaposed with a picture of an elderly male holding a "dirty book."[9]

With new technologies, photographs can be scanned and put into digital format, and altered or displayed with offensive or false captions. Speakers should carefully consider the legal ramifications of using photographs either to amuse the audience or to make serious points. The following methods may limit exposure to a lawsuit for damages:

- Always obtain permission from anyone depicted in a photograph before displaying it during a presentation. (This is *independent* of authorization from copyright holders. See p. 278.)

- Take care to ensure that any captions or explanations you use to describe the photo are accurate.

- Don't use technology to distort the picture or alter it without express permission and a clearly appropriate purpose.

- Avoid making the subject of the photo the brunt of a joke, unless you have express permission and it advances a relevant, substantive point in your presentation.

- When using photographs to depict appropriate content (such as explaining a particular skill or highlighting a positive activity), give credit and thanks to those depicted and specify that the photographs are used with permission of all copyright holders.

There are several defenses to a claim of defamation. Consent to the publication is a complete defense. Truth is also an absolute defense. This is especially important with respect to private citizens on a private matter, where the burden is on the defendant (presenter) to prove truth, rather than on the subject of the statement to prove falsity.

When the remarks are made in judicial proceedings, by legislators in debate, or by federal executive officials, an *absolute* privilege exists. This means that even maliciously false statements are not subject to damage claims.

A qualified privilege exists when the speaker reports on official proceedings. Additionally, statements in the interest of the publisher or the recipient are subject to a qualified privilege. Thus, a trainer's statements to a manager about a trainee's performance, or a supervisor's statements to an executive, are qualifiedly privileged when the subject is of mutual interest, such as the evaluation of an employee.

One of the most disturbing aspects of defamation is that the speaker need not consider the statement defamatory, if the subject is convinced that it was false. Even comments that an employee "suddenly resigned" or was terminated for unspecified reasons constituting "unsatisfactory performance" have been considered sufficiently negative to be construed as defamatory statements. Also, discussion about management deficiencies can come back to haunt speakers who can't substantiate their facts. Although the statements may not ultimately be proved defamatory, they raise the odds that a speaker will have to defend their accuracy before a jury.

Public Disclosure of Private Facts: A Privacy Primer for Presenters

A growing trend in state judicial decisions involves invasion-of-privacy claims. The premise is that individuals have a right to expect that their private affairs will remain private. A person, including a speaker, may be liable for invasion of privacy if he or she interferes with an individual's right to be let alone and to be free from unwarranted publicity. The subject of a presentation can bring a claim of invasion of the right to privacy in five specific ways.

1. *Appropriation of a picture or name without consent.* It is necessary to show unauthorized use of the likeness or name for the commercial advantage of the speaker. The commercial advantage would be shown every time the speaker makes a presentation for a fee, however modest. Liability is generally limited, however, to advertisements or promotions of products or services rather than to substantive presentations.

2. *Intrusion on the affairs or seclusion of a person.* The act of "prying" or "intruding" must be objectionable to a reasonable person. More important, the content must be private. Thus, photographs taken in public places are not actionable.

3. *Publication of facts that place the person in a false light.* "False light" exists when a speaker attributes to the plaintiff views that he or she does not hold or actions he or she did not take. The false light must be objectionable to a reasonable person under the circumstances. As with defamation, if the matter is in the public interest, malice must be proved.

4. *Public disclosure of private facts about the person.* Public disclosure of private information about the plaintiff must be objectionable to a reasonable person of ordinary sensibilities. More important, liability exists even when the statement is true, as long as it is not a matter of public record or legitimate public interest.

Special damages are not required to establish invasion of privacy. Emotional distress and mental anguish are sufficient. The legal risk of liability depends on the degree and extent of the intrusion and the justification surrounding the intrusion. The existence of a specific reason to disclose the information in a presentation, evidence of reasonable safeguards taken against abuse of the private information, or permission from the subject to disclose all or part of the information can aid the speaker in avoiding liability in the courtroom.

To avoid invasion-of-privacy allegations, a professional or business speaker should carefully consider the kind of information legitimately needed for the presentation. The speaker should also restrict who can use the information and for what purpose.

5. *Inadvertent disclosure of private employee information during a presentation.* Essentially the courts do a balancing test in assessing the right to privacy, balancing the business justifications of the employer against the employee's reasonable expectation of privacy. If information about

a particular employee is disclosed, even inadvertently, the employer and the presenter may face legal action.

In *Bourke v. Nissan Motor Corp.*[10] a California court of appeal addressed this precise issue. In the course of training employees about the use of the company's e-mail system, a trainer randomly accessed an e-mail message for demonstration purposes. The e-mail message, which belonged to the plaintiff, contained information of a personal, sexual nature. After the incident was reported to management, the plaintiff's e-mail messages and those in her work group were reviewed. All employees who had misused the e-mail system were issued written warnings.

The plaintiff and one other employee sued Nissan for invasion of privacy, violation of criminal wiretapping statutes, and wrongful discharge. The appellate court affirmed a ruling in favor of the employer, because the employees had no reasonable expectation of privacy in their e-mail messages. The court's decision was based on the fact that Nissan's employees were aware that e-mail messages could be accessed and read without the sender's knowledge or express consent.

In rejecting the employees' claims for invasion of privacy, the court relied on the fact that the employees had signed waivers stating that "it is company policy that employees and contractors restrict their use of company-owned computer hardware and software to company business." The waivers saved the day for the employer. Still, presenters should be alert to avoid potential intrusions for which the subject may assert a reasonable expectation of privacy.

6. Ethical lapses, such as knowingly using another person's ideas or original material without attribution or credit (even when the material is not subject to copyright protection)

What if "borrowing" is not actually illegal? Suppose that a presenter knowingly uses original material developed by another speaker, for commercial gain without attribution, credit, or compensation. Is it acceptable if the originator did not take the steps to secure a copyright and the presenter has no license agreement? Although the remedies may not be clear-cut, the conduct is simply unethical.

Some say imitation is the sincerest form of flattery. Not when livelihoods are affected and reputations are on the line. Speakers should heed a simple rule of thumb: Consider whether you would want your own material—which took extensive time and effort to develop—used by another presenter without credit or attribution. Better yet, follow renowned speaker Tony Allesandra's Platinum Rule®, and treat other speakers the way you know they want to be treated. Ask for permission to use material that you know has been developed by another speaker and then acknowledge the source and the authorization during the presentation.

The National Speakers Association publishes a set of ethical guidelines, available from its corporate headquarters in Tempe, Arizona.

7. Failure to honor contractual commitments and/or misrepresentations about qualifications to perform

Most speaking engagements are performed for a fee and pursuant to a contractual agreement. Contracts are essentially promises to perform certain activities or obligations. Most speaking engagements are bilateral, meaning that the parties undertake reciprocal obligations. The client agrees to pay a fee, and the speaker agrees to make a presentation at a specific date and time.

In addition, the client may agree to provide special audiovisual equipment and the speaker may promise a computerized presentation or a specific interactive methodology. To avoid disappointment by either party, the details and mutual expectations should be clearly defined and agreed upon. Once agreed, the written memorialization may take many forms, from a simple letter agreement, to a memorandum of understanding, to a formal contract. The method of documentation is less important than the substance of the agreement, although the more specific and objective the written agreement is, the easier it will be to enforce.

Speakers can enter into three types of contractual arrangements: directly with the organizations engaging them, with meeting planners, or with speakers' bureaus. Bureaus maintain the direct relationship with the client (meeting planner or organization). When they book an engagement for a speaker, they bill the client and pay the speaker, deducting the agreed-upon percentage for commission. Bureaus earn their commission by establishing the client contact, undertaking all the marketing and related work, and cultivating further bookings. Booking agents work in similar ways, but they sometimes allow the speaker to bill the client directly and then to pay a separate agency fee, which is typically a percentage of the entire fee.

One significant contractual issue with bureaus is the concept of "spin-off" business. If a speaker whose booking came from a bureau receives a further speaking engagement directly from the client or association, or as a referral from someone who heard the speech, the bureau is owed a percentage of that business—because it arose directly from the original booking. In addition, the bureau is entitled to a percentage of the sales of a speaker's product (video, audiotapes, or workbooks) to members of the audience at a bureau-booked engagement or as a result of spin-off sales.

The percentages and nature of spin-off business is a matter of contractual negotiation between the speaker and the bureau, and once agreement has been reached, the speaker's failure or refusal to keep track of and report spin-off business is a breach of contract. Sample agreements are provided in Appendix C.

A contract is a promise or set of promises. It may be express (communicated by language) or implied (communicated by conduct indicating the parties' assent to be bound). The failure to perform contractual obligations is a breach, giving rise to legal remedies. The law recognizes performance of an enforceable contractual promise as a legal duty.

Contracts do not have to be formal to be binding. Everything from a simple letter agreement to a lengthy document qualifies for protection so long as there is mutual assent and legally effective "bargained-for exchange." Enforceable contracts include several concrete elements:

1. A specific *offer,* which is a promise or commitment with definite and certain terms communicated: "The association would like you to make a presentation on coping with change in our industry."

2. *Acceptance* of the offer before termination by revocation or rejection: "The speaker will be happy to make this presentation."

3. *Bargained-for exchange* of something of legal value, involving a determination of whether a party incurred an obligation to do or pay something of value, or refrain from doing something he or she was legally entitled to do: "The association will pay $2000 for the speech, plus airfare and one night at a hotel, and the speaker will agree to reserve the date and appear on time."

4. *Concrete terms to measure performance,* including the date, time, location, and other material terms.

These four elements are the basis for an enforceable contract. Naturally there may be additional material terms, such as allocation of additional expenses, types of materials to be provided, opportunities for the speaker to sell various products at the conference, and levels of customization required. These details should be negotiated and spelled out in the agreement, to ensure mutual satisfaction.

Many states will enforce verbal agreements, if they contain the basic elements of an offer, acceptance, and consideration (bargained-for exchange). For example, a client may invite a speaker to present a keynote address on the topic of sexual harassment prevention at a future conference for a fee of $2000 (offer). The speaker accepts by telephone. No writings are exchanged. At this stage, the first three basic elements are present, but the contract is too vague as to completion date and location to be capable of performance. If the client says: "We want you at our next convention in April at the Disneyland Hotel," and the speaker responds "You've got me!" the deal is complete and failure to perform may result in a breach-of-contract claim, even though the conversation is entirely verbal, and other key terms have not been discussed. To avoid potential misunderstandings and confusion, it is good business practice to reduce the basic agreement to a writing, such as a letter agreement.

For an agreement to be enforced as a contract, there must be mutual assent. In plain English, one party must accept the other's offer. When the offer is not accepted in its entirety, or new conditions or terms are suggested, it becomes a counteroffer. The process of negotiating a final agreement acceptable to both parties may encompass a series of offers and counteroffers. The final agreement must then have a definite offer, acceptance, bargained-for exchange of obligations, and sufficient terms to render it enforceable.

In distinguishing between preliminary negotiations and promises (offers), the courts consider the language used, the surrounding circumstances, the method of communication, the prior relationship of the parties, the custom and practice in the industry, and most significantly the degree of definiteness and certainty of terms.

As a speaker, you may breach contractual obligations in a number of ways, including failing to appear when scheduled, failing to provide the agreed-upon content, or failing to produce written materials. In addition, when your client requires you to represent that you own the right to use graphics, materials, or other presentation tools, any violation of copyright law may also lead to breach of contract—particularly when your client is included as a codefendant in an infringement action.

Finally, you risk legal exposure if you inaccurately represent yourself as experienced in a particular industry or subject area. "Puffing" or exaggeration may result only in damaged credibility, but outright misrepresentations about education, specific certifications, or experience can lead to breach of contract and in extreme cases to fraud actions. At best, such representations when made to speakers' bureaus or clients can tarnish your reputation. At worst, they can lead to legal action for return of fees or damages based on your client's detrimental reliance on your representations.

Further specifics on bidding, contracting, and follow-through, as applicable to speakers and consultants, are addressed in Chapter 16.

8. Failure to protect your own rights through negotiation and enforcement of effective contracts

Meeting contractual commitments is a sound business practice. It is also legally required to avoid the risks of breaching contracts. It is equally important for speakers to enforce their own contracts. A common legal problem is the inability to quickly and effectively collect fees and enforce clients' promises. Professional speakers should be prepared to pursue appropriate legal action to enforce their contracts, including negotiating and memorializing enforceable agreements so the contracts will hold up in court.

The details of negotiating and enforcing contracts are addressed in Chapter 16, pp. 324–334. Appendix C provides sample contracts for speakers and consultants, including letter agreements, contracts with clients, and a contract between speaker and bureau.

9. Negligent advice or instruction in the context of a presentation that causes business harm to a client

Speakers make presentations on a wide range of topics, including skills that are essential for their clients' business practices. Often, clients rely on the speaker to provide the audience (usually employees) with essential information and to develop important skills. For example, speakers who present skill-based programs on technology, financial management, or other core business issues must provide both appropriate content and methodology to ensure that their audience members apply the information as intended. When a speaker provides inaccurate information, and the audience makes mistakes on the basis of that information, the speaker may be sued for subsequent business losses.

A more significant potential for liability rests with speakers who provide public seminars on matters of interest to a wider audience. Presentations on investment tactics, how to make money in real estate, or other financial or self-improvement methods are ripe for claims of negligence, and even fraud, when an audience member suffers losses as a result of the "advice."

Negligence claims arise primarily under state laws. In a damage lawsuit, legal duty is based on the applicable "standard of care" for speakers in a particular industry. Standard of care is often defined as the level of conduct expected of similarly educated or experienced professionals in a given field. This subject is fully discussed in Chapter 3, pp. 70–76.

The determination of whether a duty of care exists is generally a question of law for the courts to decide; whether the speaker breached this duty of care by giving unreasonable advice under the particular circumstances is a question for the trier of fact.

10. Ineffective or nonexistent documentation

Documentation is a written record of an event, discussion, or observation by one or more individuals. Most organizations rely on documentation to record their activities and those of their employees. Any written information, whether formally or informally generated, can be considered documentary evidence if it is pertinent to a legal action or a regulatory proceeding.

When called upon to defend against a legal claim—copyright violation, discriminatory content, or breach of contract—speakers must be able to provide credible information to reconstruct events, to explain what occurred, or to substantiate their efforts to comply with applicable legal requirements. Haphazard record keeping is both frustrating and potentially devastating to the successful defense.

The issues surrounding documentation, including when and how to effectively document your activities, are addressed in Chapters 19, pp. 400–403, and 20, pp. 419–431.

References

1. Copyright Act, Title 17 of the U.S. Code §101.
2. U.S. Copyright Office Circular 56A, "Copyright Registration of Musical Compositions and Sound Recordings."
3. *Jarvis v. A&M Records*, 827 F.Supp. 282, 292 (D.N.J. 1993).
4. *Playboy Enterprises, Inc. v. Frena*, 839 F.Supp. 1552 (M.D.Fla. 1993).
5. *New York Times v. Sullivan*, 376 U.S. 254 (1964).
6. *Engler v. Winfrey*, 2-96-CV-233 (Texas 1997).
7. *National Law Journal*, May 5, 1997, p. 21.
8. *Carlson v. Hillman Periodicals, Inc.*, 3 A.D.2d 987, 163 N.Y.S.2d 21 (1957).
9. *Russell v. Marboro Books*, 18 Misc.2d 166, 183 N.Y.S.2d 8 (1959).
10. *Bourke v. Nissan Motor Corp.*, Los Angeles trial court, No. B068705 (California 1993).

14

How to Meet Your Legal Responsibilities to Participants With Special Needs

What Disability Discrimination Laws Say About Reasonable Accommodations and How to Comply

Disability discrimination is a major issue for many employers and, in turn, for the speakers and consultants they hire. The subject crosses a number of substantive areas, including special needs to ensure workplace safety (Chapter 2, pp. 57–59), selection for training (Chapter 6, pp. 141–143), testing and evaluation (Chapter 7, pp. 163–171), and equal opportunities during adventure training (Chapter 8, pp. 192–195). This chapter focuses on when presenters are obligated to make reasonable accommodations for the special needs of their audiences and how to do so.

The Americans With Disabilities Act defines disability very broadly to include having a physical or mental impairment that substantially limits one or more major life activities, having a record of such impairment, or being regarded as having the impairment. Although the ADA does not specifically list all the conditions, diseases, or infections that constitute a physical or mental impairment, the developing case law suggests that audience members will be protected by the ADA when they have sensory impairments, including impaired sight, speech, and hearing; learning disabilities, such as dyslexia and attention deficit disorder; mobility impairments that affect the ability to walk, stand, move, or manipulate, such as cerebral palsy, epilepsy, muscular dystrophy, and multiple sclerosis; chronic illnesses, such as cancer, heart disease, and diabetes; and certain mental disorders, such as clinical depression.

Because most audience members attend your presentation as part of their employment, they are protected by the employment provisions of the ADA and by legislation in many states (see Appendix B). Typically, your client, as the employer, has the obligation to satisfy the ADA and applicable state laws. However, you are retained to provide the highest-quality presentation, and you should avoid any act or omission that may cause your client to be liable for disability discrimination. In order to ensure equal opportunities, you must also accommodate the reasonable needs of these individuals when such accommodation can be made without incurring significant difficulty or expense.

When you offer a public seminar, you are required to comply with the public accommodation provisions of the ADA, because you are offering a service or product to the public. Even though you may share responsibility with the owner of the public facility (for physical access issues) as the sponsor of the program, you are primarily accountable to ensure equal opportunities for all participants, unless doing so would create an undue hardship. The essence of a reasonable accommodation is its individuality. You can't generalize about what type of accommodation may assist participants with particular disabilities. In fact, two people with the very same disability—for example, visual impairment—may have different needs and therefore benefit from different accommodations, depending upon the type of presentation or other program-specific variables.

Identify the Need for an Accommodation

You may learn of the need to reasonably accommodate a participant from a variety of sources: the meeting planner, the participant's supervisor, the registration form, your preprogram questionnaire, or the participant herself. The further in advance you identify the need, the more individualized you are able to make the accommodation, while still achieving your presentation objectives. This is particularly important when you plan interactive activities or significant visual components in your presentation.

In other situations, you may not realize until the presentation has begun that an accommodation is in order. For example, you may immediately see the need to provide better access or seating position to a person with a mobility impairment. You may also observe people with sensory challenges who are unable to see or hear portions of your planned program. Other disabilities may be more subtle. Behavior patterns common to people with learning disabilities are fidgeting, asking questions about material you have not covered, asking complicated questions about a subject you have just covered, and aversion to reading and testing.

You should mirror your client's strong EEO commitment in all interactions with participants. Continually encourage full participation by everyone. Without embarrassing reluctant participants, encourage them to tell you when they have questions, cannot follow the material, or need a physical change in their surroundings. Follow up privately during breaks, if necessary. Provide a safe environment in which individuals are able to disclose their special needs.

How to Make Reasonable Accommodations

Program Publicity.   First, make sure that all publicity is posted in a manner that allows equal distribution and access. Consider alternative formats to written e-mail or printed notices. Encourage program sponsors or meeting planners to provide the information in a variety of formats. Registration forms should solicit special learning, environmental, or other individual needs.

Caution: Your preprogram publicity should solicit only the information necessary to make the reasonable accommodation. Questions on the registration form, or in a follow-up conversation, about the disability itself are always unlawful, as depicted in Figure 14-1.

Special Considerations for Learning-Disabled Participants.
Include an assortment of methodologies, beyond just written materials. Although written handouts will often be used, provide critical information in an alternative format, where appropriate, for dyslexic or sight-impaired participants.

Consider a variety of learning tools for retention of complex material. Try analogies and pictures or graphics to make a point. For example, the

Appropriate:	"Will periodic breaks help you concentrate?"
Unlawful:	"Do you have attention deficit disorder?"
Appropriate:	"How frequently will you need a break?"
Unlawful:	"How long can you concentrate at a time?"
Appropriate:	"Will graphics assist in your comprehension?" or "How can we make this learning experience more beneficial to you?"
Unlawful:	"Do you have dyslexia?"
Appropriate:	"Is there a need to accommodate you in any way? If so how?"
Unlawful:	"Do you have any learning disabilities?"

Figure 14-1 Examples of Appropriate and Unlawful Inquiries When Considering Reasonable Accommodations for People with Learning Disabilities.

skull and crossbones is a universal symbol of danger. Consider incorporating the graphic into written course materials, as an adjunct to the printed word. If games and activities are used to reinforce learning, adapt them to the needs of participants with motor coordination limitations.

Plan a logical flow for the presentation of material. Break complex information down into smaller modules as appropriate. Provide an alternative method to reinforce the material for individuals with reading or attention disorders. Build into the program the opportunity for small group tutorials to teach job skills, as appropriate to the learning. Stay focused on the end objective: to transfer complex or technical information in a manner that will ensure safe application of knowledge or skills on the job.

If you use computers or on-line graphics, determine whether modifications to video displays will extend participation to all participants.

Handout Materials. For written materials, select print that is large and clear enough for letters to be easily distinguished. Allow sufficient spacing between lines. Avoid script and other hard-to-distinguish fonts. Make ample use of graphics, as appropriate to the subject matter. Label illustrations and place them close to the text they support. Use off-white or other lightly colored paper, instead of pure white paper, to reduce contrast.

Include copies of all overheads and other visual material used during the presentation. If you use multimedia displays, be sure that they are visible to everyone in the room. Print copies of all relevant computer screens, and add appropriate visuals to aid a dyslexic participant. With video or slide presentations, include an outline or cross-reference to the picture.

Program Presentation. Use a variety of presentation methods, including auditory, visual, and kinetic. Make available one-to-one and small group tutorials to teach specific job skills, such as use of protective devices. Always try to explain complex written materials, diagrams, or other materials to aid sight-impaired employees as well as those with learning disorders. With complex subject matter, devote extra attention to pronunciation, speed, punctuation, and voice inflection.

Avoid communicating in any way to people with learning disabilities that they are dumb or lazy, or can do better if they just work harder. In seminars or workshops, when you intend to have employees read a portion of text and then discuss it in class, provide the material in advance as part of your accommodation. If prescreening is unrealistic, provide extra assistance to the participant during class. A full discussion of reasonable accommodations in the testing process appears in Chapter 7, pp. 167–171.

Special Considerations for Hearing-Impaired Participants. For remote teleconferences or satellite presentations, make sure that telecommunication devices for the deaf (TDDs) are available to facilitate interaction. Consult in advance with the hearing-impaired participant or the meeting planner about the need for an interpreter. If one is needed, provide a qualified interpreter who can translate into American Sign Language (ASL). For technical programs, you might supply a glossary of key terms in advance to the interpreter. Also provide handouts to the interpreter in advance.

Take sufficient breaks to make sure that the interpreter is not fatigued. If time is tight, consider two alternating interpreters. Cost will be a factor in balancing whether a reasonable accommodation can be made for a hearing-impaired participant; however, for existing employees who are performing all essential job functions and must satisfactorily complete mandatory health or safety training, the expense may be essential. If the cost of an interpreter is too burdensome, you may be required to provide follow-up training for the employee or to put more of the material in writing, and to work individually with the employee to ensure comprehension.

Allow the interpreter to "reverse-interpret" so that the hearing-impaired participant is fully engaged in all interactive portions of the training. This means relaying the participant's questions and your answers. If the room must be darkened to show slides, make sure there is sufficient light for the interpreter to be seen.

If individual computer workstations are being used, allow sufficient time for the participant with special needs to devote attention to both the screen and the interpreter. Be sure to include copies of all relevant computer screens in this participant's materials.

Because employees with hearing impairments must depend on vision to benefit from the training, they may not be able to take notes concurrently. Ask if a note taker would be helpful and identify another member of the group who has legible handwriting to provide a copy.

Always document the steps you have taken to accommodate participants with special needs. If challenged, you will then have a basis to explain the procedure you followed to provide effective, complete, and accessible training for everyone. You will earn the respect of your audience, help your client abide by legal requirements, and justify both your fee and possible repeat business.

Speakers and the ADA: How to Determine Who Is Responsible for Ensuring Equal Participation by Every Member of Your Audience

Participation in employer-sponsored training, conferences, and other activities is part of the entire equal employment opportunity. Disabled participants who attend your presentation are likely to be there as a result of their employment and will be seeking an equal opportunity to learn, participate, and contribute. Thus, your client (the sponsoring organization for your presentation) is required to provide reasonable accommodations that enable qualified disabled employees to enjoy all the benefits of employment, including attendance at and full participation in your presentation.

When you offer a public program, the facility you choose has concurrent obligations to satisfy the public accommodation provisions of the ADA. (Again, broader state law may control; see Appendix B.) This does not, however, relieve you—as the program sponsor—from selecting a fully accessible facility or working with the site personnel to ensure complete and comfortable access for all participants.

Making Facilities Accessible

The primary obligation for making reasonable accommodations rests with the employer that sends a participant to your presentation. This is so even when the program takes place in your facility, or at a location you have selected. Your registration forms for the program should inquire about any special needs that your registrants may have for physical access.

If you are not selecting the facility, your primary obligation is to arrange the room for maximum involvement by all participants, especially if you plan interactive exercises or any movement of participants during the program. The most practical approach is to discuss with the program sponsor the best method to determine special physical access needs of employees. Often, the information will be readily accessible—and the employer does have the primary obligation. Assist your client by reinforcing this responsibility and seeking out information about any reasonable accommodations that will be required.

Find out if any participants will need interpreters. If so, discuss with the meeting planner or other employer representative the physical layout that will maximize the success of this accommodation. If you have never spoken with a sign interpreter, make an effort to learn how to adapt your presentation to make full interpretation easier. For example:

- If you use nonverbal (body) language, tell the interpreter for a sight-impaired participant where a description of these cues may aid in understanding. It is terribly frustrating for a sight-impaired participant to listen to audience laughter, and not be able to relate it to the spoken word. An experienced interpreter, notified in advance, can aid in this process.

- If you are using computer graphics or visual aids, make it a practice to describe verbally the materials being displayed. Better yet, provide the sign interpreter with copies in advance.

- When planning experiential activities, consider the needs of disabled participants. Use preprogram planning questionnaires and other data collection methods to determine whether reasonable accommodations will be required. *Caveat:* Don't ask meeting planners if disabled employees will attend. They are precluded by law from classifying employees or conference participants in this manner. Instead, ask whether any physical accommodations will be required for room setup or audiovisual tools. You can then discuss specific needs from the framework of making an accommodation to *include* all participants rather than to identify or exclude on the basis of disability.

When appropriate, use more visuals to overcome language barriers. Pictures, graphics, and industry diagrams can help. If you can, schedule additional question-and-answer sessions during a break or after the program. The sessions will encourage those from different cultures to let you know in a more private way when they are having difficulty understanding.

Avoid Those Assumptions! What the Law Says About Unintentional Bias

Some stereotypes about disabled individuals in the work environment, when used negatively in the employment or presentation setting, may give rise to a claim of discrimination. It is important to dispel the fiction that disabled participants present an unacceptable risk to their own safety or the safety of others during emergencies (such as fire or earthquake), or the myth that disabled employees should be excluded to protect them from being made uncomfortable by the reactions or attitudes of other participants, facilitators, or personnel over whom you have no control. These assumptions are inappropriate and become unlawful when they undermine the learning experience.

Another frequent source of complaints by program participants is the assumption that they are unable to perform or fully participate because of linguistic differences. Frequently, the communication issues are raised because of a noticeable accent. Many of these assumptions are flatly unlawful. Denial of employment opportunities because of an individual's foreign accent or inability to communicate well in English violates Title VII of the Civil Rights Act of 1964.

To meet your legal obligations and avoid having unlawful assumptions invade your presentation, steer clear of inaccurate stereotypes that employees with accents are slow, unintelligent, or unable to learn English. Demonstrate respect to all participants in your program. If you bring staff members to your speech to sell products, encourage them to make their communications as understandable as possible without belittling, patronizing, or creating a hostile or offensive environment.

Call on a representative cross section of the audience to participate in exercises and discussion. Do not "assume" that Asian participants will not wish to take part. Don't "assume" that English-limited participants will be unable to communicate their thoughts or that disabled participants will be uncomfortable taking a lead in participative exercises.

Be sensitive to nonverbal cues. For example, if someone repeatedly smiles and nods, he or she may be overcompensating for a lack of understanding. Do not assume understanding; recognize that the participant may simply be showing deference and respect to your status as presenter.

How to Recognize When Your Workshops May Be Culturally Biased and What to Do About It

English language barriers and cultural differences in learning style can impede the effectiveness of any presentation. In extreme situations, they may actually deprive participants of an equal employment opportunity. Because of the legal ramifications of Title VII's strictures against discrimination based on national origin, all presenters should exercise great care in designing and delivering training to multinational audiences. Caution is especially important when the learning is mandatory for full, fair, and safe performance in the workplace or for safety considerations.

When some of your participants nod without really understanding the instruction, communicate that they will be expected to demonstrate their knowledge. Ask participants if they will benefit from language translation services. You may be able to get a proficient coworker to translate. If not, consider hiring a translator. An alternative is to provide comprehensive written materials in a language the employees can understand.

Most training seminars and presentations focus on the substance of the program. In multicultural work environments, the substance of the program may be lost to many participants if you neglect to adapt to cultural variables in learning styles. Instructional systems design (ISD) is a systematic process that includes analyzing, designing, and evaluating instruction. In the September 1996 issue of *Training and Development Journal*, Zhuoran Huang recommends that ISD principles, when applied to multicultural training situations, be modified to make the training friendly and effective for multiple cultures. Huang suggests the following steps:

1. Conduct a thorough training needs and audience analysis. The presentation should be adapted to be relevant, interesting and meaningful to a variety of participants.
2. Conduct English classes—both before and during training.
3. Include international members on the design team.
4. Make task analysis meaningful to trainees.
5. Survey prerequisite skills before each training class.
6. Clearly state and explain program objectives to the trainees.
7. Ensure that the information presented is suitable for multicultural trainees. Huang recommends simpler language, slower delivery,

and glossaries or written explanations of unfamiliar terms. Pause frequently, provide breaks, and summarize regularly.

8. Schedule a question-and-answer session during a class break or after class.

9. Use more visuals to overcome language barriers.

10. Provide more group exercises and activities to encourage teamwork and full participation by everyone.

11. Ensure that the training evaluation is appropriate to multicultural trainees.[1]

Presenters who focus on advanced technology should also avoid assumptions or biases about older participants. These include perceptions that older workers are inflexible, unreceptive to new technologies, or hostile to rapid workplace changes. (See the discussion in the context of selection for training in Chapter 6, pp. 135–136 and 141–143.) It is equally clear that presentations based on these assumptions may be discriminatory if they isolate, segregate, or exclude participants on the basis of age.

Reference

1. Zhuoran Huang, "Training 101: Making Training Friendly to Other Cultures," *Training and Development Journal,* September 1996, p. 13.

PART 3

Legal Dos and Taboos for Consultants

15

The 10 Most Common Legal Problems Facing Consultants and How to Avoid Them

1. Failure to honor contractual commitments and/or misrepresentation about qualifications to perform

Most consulting engagements are performed for a fee and pursuant to a contractual agreement. Contracts are essentially promises to perform certain activities or obligations. Most speaking engagements are bilateral, meaning that the parties undertake reciprocal obligations. The client agrees to pay a fee, and the consultant agrees to provide services at a specific time. Consulting projects range from diversity scans, to curriculum design for technical training, to facilitation of nontraditional programs. Typically, the consultant agrees to provide specific deliverables.

In addition, the client may agree to provide special audiovisual equipment and the consultant may promise a computerized presentation or a specific interactive methodology. To avoid disappointment by either party, the details and mutual expectations should be clearly defined and agreed upon. Once terms are established, the written memorialization may take many forms—from a memorandum of understanding, to a simple letter agreement, to a lengthy formal contract. The agreement qualifies for enforcement so long as there is mutual assent and a legally effective commitment by each party. The method of documentation is less important than the substance of the agreement, although the more specific and objective the written agreement, the easier it will be to enforce.

A contract may be express (communicated by language) or implied (communicated by conduct indicating the parties' assent to be bound). Contracts don't have to be formal to be binding. The law recognizes performance of an enforceable contractual promise as a legal duty. Failure to perform contractual obligations is a breach, giving rise to legal action to enforce the terms of the agreement or receive damages.

Many states will also enforce a verbal agreement if it includes the basic elements of an offer, an acceptance and a bargained-for exchange (consideration). For example, a client may invite a consultant to conduct a diversity audit, issue a report, and recommend effective management training. The consultant accepts by telephone. No writings are exchanged. At this stage, the first three basic elements are present, but the contract is too vague as to completion date and location to be capable of performance. If the client says "We need the audit completed by the end of the second quarter to satisfy an EEOC conciliation order," and the consultant responds "I'll arrange my workload to meet your needs," the deal is complete. Failure to perform may result in a breach-of-contract claim, even though the conversation is entirely verbal and other key terms have not been discussed.

Legal problems arise for consultants when they breach contractual obligations by failing to appear when scheduled, failing to produce the required deliverables, or violating a confidentiality agreement. In addition, when the client requires the consultant to represent that he or she owns the right to use specific tools or instruments—such as tests or performance aids—any violation of copyright law may also lead to breach of contract, particularly when the client is also sued for infringement. Appendix C contains sample language regarding copyright ownership representations in contracts.

The best way to avoid breaches of contract is to make realistic commitments and to proactively manage your performance of contractual commitments. If you promise a rapid turnaround of work product, you should plan for foreseeable contingencies that may interfere with performance. Address these issues at the outset. Then, if unforeseen circumstances occur, immediately discuss with your client reasonable modifications of your commitment to meet the changed circumstances. Unfortunately, the most frequent source of contractual disputes involves failure to meet commitments *on time*. Typically, open communication will alert the client to the reasons for any delays and avoid misplaced expectations. The details of making and keeping contractual promises are addressed in Chapter 16, pp. 324–334, and Appendix C.

You also risk legal consequences if you inaccurately represent your experience in a particular industry or subject area. Outright misrepresentations about education, specific certifications, or experience can lead to breach of contract and in extreme cases to claims of fraud. At best, such representations can tarnish your reputation when you fail to meet a client's expectations. At worst, they can lead to legal action for return of fees or additional damages to the client's business interests.

As you market and negotiate consulting agreements, you will discover that your qualifications to perform the contemplated services are a critical factor to prospective clients. In selecting effective consultants, an industry client will evaluate a variety of items, including credentials, background, experience, past performance and outcomes, availability, and cost-effectiveness. Naturally, the consultant who aspires to a particular job wants to convince the client that she or he is best suited to perform the work.

Whether you call it bragging, puffing, exaggeration, hyperbole, overstatement, stretching, enhancement, or embellishment, you are making affirmative representations about your qualifications to perform particular work upon which the client will rely. Indeed, in this situation you *intend* for the client to rely on your representations and hire you for the consulting project. If it turns out that your representations about qualifications were significantly exaggerated—or outright falsehoods—you could find yourself defending an action for "fraud in the inducement of the contract." As the name implies, this type of civil fraud action is premised on a false statement of material fact, made with the specific intent of inducing the promisee (the prospective client) to rely upon the statement in agreeing to the contract. Consider these examples:

- You represent that you hold a specific educational degree, license, or certification. One case involved a consultant who was four units away from coursework completion, but didn't have the degree at the time of contracting or performance.

- You represent that a noncredit community college extension course was a certification program.

- You represent that you have conducted "many" or "hundreds" of such programs, when in fact you have completed fewer than 10.

- You brag that your performance evaluations from clients and trainees have been "universally excellent." (We all know you can't please everyone all the time, no matter how good you are!)

- You represent that you have saved similar organizations "millions of dollars" or have "turned their business around," when in fact you have no specific facts to support this claim if asked—under oath—to substantiate it.

- You represent that you have "highly experienced" staff, when in fact you intend to hire someone as soon as you receive this retainer and have not yet verified the employee's references or experience. *Note:* This may be a "negligent misrepresentation" too, if you have no reasonable basis for believing your representation to be true.

- You represent that you are a "diversity expert," when in fact your experience is limited to conducting general sexual harassment awareness training.

- You represent that you have been "court-qualified" and have served as an expert witness, when in fact you were retained in a case that was actually settled before it got to court. This is a technical misrepresentation, because you can be court-qualified only after a judge has ruled that you can testify to expert opinion.

Most consultants who use exaggerated or imprecise language are never called on it. Likewise, many clients don't make the time or effort to check all references or educational transcripts. Embellishment or exaggeration may never come to light, and probably will not materially affect the outcome of most consulting projects. The sad reality in today's legal climate, however, is that if the project goes astray—for any reason—evidence of your misstatements of material fact may loom large in the minds of both the client and the jury in a later legal action. See Chapter 1, pp. 33–35, for an explanation of how the jury system operates.

In order to avoid being confronted with earlier misstatements, follow these simple guidelines. Never represent that you have a degree, license, or certification when you can't produce a transcript or certificate to back up the claim. If you are a degree candidate, just say so and describe how your experience or skills independently qualify you for the particular job.

Carefully and accurately characterize your outcomes with other clients. It helps to obtain letters of reference from extremely satisfied clients, and limit your representations to those specifics. If you intend to rely on specific success stories, be sure your facts are correct and your former clients are comfortable with your disclosures. Don't hide behind "client confidentiality" to avoid providing specifics, since your other clients may be called as witnesses to verify—or refute—your representations.

Avoid sweeping generalizations about the number of projects you have completed, the widespread success of your methods, or the universal acclaim of participants in your programs. Granted the client may discount your claims of "all," "hundreds," "everyone," and "always," but if you find yourself in later litigation, broad statements that can't be substantiated may impair your credibility in the eyes of a jury, judge, or arbitrator.

Be prepared to provide specific work samples, and offer them freely. If you are concerned about confidentiality or copyright protection, openly discuss the issue with the prospective client and reach agreement in advance. Chapter 19 provides detailed information on protecting your rights to intellectual property through work-for-hire or other arrangements.

If you are making claims about the qualifications, experience, or skills of your staff, subcontractors, or other vendors, take the time to investigate the facts in advance. Any representations you make about *their* abilities should be as capable of verification as your own. This is important from the standpoint of both contractual violations and negligence claims if someone is injured during your program. See Chapters 3, pp. 80–82, and 8, pp. 198–202; and 4, pp. 94–96, for a further discussion of when you are responsible for the mistakes of your sub-contractors.

When promising specific results or measurable outcomes, draw upon your actual experience and consider foreseeable delays or external impediments. Even your most well-intentioned expectations can backfire if it later appears that you had no reasonable basis for making the specific commitments or were reckless in your promises. When you will need to use external resources to fulfill your commitments—such as desktop publishing software, multimedia programs, or specific equipment—make sure that you are, in fact, qualified to use those resources. Once again, well-meaning consultants sometimes represent that they "are qualified" and "have used" such materials, when in fact they intend "to become qualified" or "will use" the systems prior to starting the work. These claims become much more than semantic distinctions if your plans are not realized in time to meet your client's performance expectations.

2. Failure to protect your rights through negotiation and enforcement of effective contracts

Meeting contractual commitments is sound business practice. It is equally important for consultants to enforce their own contracts. A common legal problem is the inability to quickly and effectively collect fees and enforce clients' promises. Although litigation is always a last resort, professional consultants should be prepared to pursue appropriate legal action. Make sure that you negotiate and memorialize an enforceable agreement, so the contract will hold up in court. The details of negotiating and enforcing contracts are addressed in Chapter 16, pp. 324–334. Chapter 19, pp. 403–413, provides information on protecting your intellectual property rights.

3. Breaches of client confidences through written and electronic communications

There are several constructive reasons to use e-mail when you work with clients. Electronic communications eliminate telephone tag and permit consultants and their clients to keep current on important items, thereby speeding up decisions and shortening the communication cycle time. The increase in productivity can be dramatic.

In addition, use of e-mail from laptop computers allows you to communicate on a global basis virtually at any time and from any place. You can effectively communicate with clients, send drafts of reports, and exchange other pertinent information, saving both time and paper.

However, you and your clients should keep in mind that e-mail is not always completely private. Sensitive or proprietary information should be exchanged with extreme caution, since your client's employees and your own office can also use e-mail to divulge valuable trade secrets or proprietary client data to third parties (intentionally or inadvertently).

Be mindful of the need to maintain confidentiality over client information received electronically. Remind your staff periodically of this important issue. Consultants and client organizations should establish policies to alert their respective employees that e-mail may be monitored to make sure that confidential business information generated during the consulting project is not being compromised or disclosed. Specific or unique confidentiality issues should be addressed *directly* in the contract. The details of developing such a policy are given in Chapter 16, pp. 344–348; the sample contracts in Appendix C provide language on confidentiality obligations.

4. Negligent advice or instruction that causes business harm to a client

As a consultant, you provide advice on a wide range of topics, including skills that are essential for your clients' business practices. Clients rely on you to render advice or provide information on essential business issues, such as development of test instruments, initiation of team building, diversity or organizational development, and other human performance interventions. Your client's legal and regulatory compliance may be affected, so that reliance on inaccurate advice may result in significant legal risks and potential financial harm.

Likewise, if you present skill-based training programs on technology management, diversity, financial management, safe work practices, or other core business issues, you must provide both appropriate content and methodology to ensure that your client's employees apply the information as intended. When your client's employees make mistakes on the basis of information you provide, you may be sued for subsequent business losses.

Negligence lawsuits against consultants are essentially like malpractice claims. Errors and omissions by an experienced or educated professional run the gamut from personal injury claims (such as participants injured during a program facilitated by a consultant) to breaches of professional standards for similarly situated consultants (a form of malpractice) to claims for indemnification (in plain English, reimbursement) by a client who is sued and found liable because of a consultant's advice on how to design and deliver safety training.

Negligence claims arise primarily under state laws. In a damage lawsuit, legal duty is based on the applicable standard of care for consultants in a particular industry. Standard of care is often defined as the level of conduct expected of similarly educated or experienced professionals in a given field. The determination of whether a duty of care exists is generally a question of law for the courts to decide; whether the consultant breached this duty of care by giving unreasonable advice under the particular circumstances is a question for the trier of fact, which is usually a jury. Chapter 3, pp. 70–76, defines, in detail, the six ways that legal duties are established in negligence actions.

The best ways to avoid legal exposure are to understand your duties and responsibilities to clients under the applicable standards for similarly situated consultants, to keep accurate records and to follow the steps outlined in Chapter 17, pp. 353–358. For a fuller discussion of negligence and malpractice liabilities for programs you design or facilitate, see Chapters 3, pp. 67–68; 4, pp. 93–100; 8, pp. 186–196; and 17, pp. 353–359.

5. Use of discriminatory training materials and curriculum in client projects

The courts hold external consultants to the same standards of care as that applied to in-house trainers. Just as internal curriculum designers may create a legal liability for their employer if their methodology doesn't meet appropriate standards or the content is discriminatory, so too can external facilitators. Negligence in your curriculum design will result in liability for the sponsoring organization—the employer or client. If your content or delivery discriminates, you may have personal liability as well.

Discrimination in Diversity Training

In addition to the various employee relations problems they pose, diversity training programs may have adverse legal implications for employers (your clients) in defending employment discrimination lawsuits. The primary danger of diversity programs from a legal standpoint is that racial, ethnic, or sex-based remarks made during the sessions may be used in later employment discrimination litigation as evidence of management bias.

When an employer's diversity training materials contain candid remarks by managers that could be construed as racial or sexual bias, or when a "diversity scan" reflects unfavorably (statistically or through anecdotal evidence) on the employer's record with minorities or female employees, admission of such information as evidence in a subsequent discrimination lawsuit can damage the employer's case.

One example is *Stender v. Lucky Stores, Inc.*[1] In 1988, Lucky sought to determine the cause of the glaring lack of promotions among women and minorities within the organization. In an attempt to remedy the situation, the company conducted an in-house diversity training session for all store managers. The managers took part in an exercise that is commonplace in many diversity training seminars—they were asked to list various stereotypes that they had heard about women and minorities. The resulting lists proved compromising for the company. Chapter 5, pp. 112–114, has a full discussion of these issues.

Training Methodology

Your curriculum design and training methodology must be appropriate to meet the learning objectives of your client and must not in itself create a separate basis for significant legal culpability. The most widely publicized problems with diversity training methodology stem from a program conducted throughout 1994 by the Federal Aviation Administration. The confrontational sexual harassment exercise, which was part of a much larger program on diversity, included an exercise drawn from the Navy's Tailhook episode. During the exercise, men were subjected to a one-minute trip through a gauntlet of women, who teased, taunted, and fondled them. The stated purpose: to turn the tables on the men and give them a blunt lesson on what many women regularly experience. The case is discussed in detail in Chapters 5, pp. 114–117, and 6, pp. 146–147.

Presentation Content

Even when your training doesn't focus directly on controversial or emotional topics, your content can result in troublesome legal problems for both you and your client. Jokes, graphics, and other "icebreaking" material sprinkled throughout the program may be designed to engage the audience and generate interest. When used appropriately, these tools enhance the professional presentation, but when the content strays into an inappropriate area—sex, race, or religion—the consequences range from embarrassment (for both the presenter and the client) to discrimination claims.

To minimize the risk of legal exposure for discrimination, consultants should be well versed on the various forms of discrimination and take proactive steps to avoid inappropriate methodology. (Further direction is provided in Chapters 5, pp. 112–117; 6, pp. 143–150; and 9, pp. 206–217.) Although most consultants are not in a position to provide legal advice—and should never attempt to do so—they can provide appropriate direction to clients who may be in danger of violating regulatory standards or other legal responsibilities in the discrimination arena.

6. Copyright infringement by incorporating protected work into reports and materials without permission

Consultants frequently create and distribute written materials in the form of handouts, articles, outlines, and graphic presentations. All are forms of intellectual property protected by the U.S. Copyright Act of 1976. The author or creator of the work has an ownership interest from the moment the materials are fixed in tangible form.

Handouts that incorporate portions of a copyrighted work without written authorization from the author violate the Copyright Act. Included here are direct photocopies of articles or passages, lengthy quotations, and close paraphrasing (even with quotation marks, attribution, or "credit") that does not constitute a "fair use." Fair use, even for educational purposes, is not usually applicable when the user is a commercial or profit-making venture—which all consultants hope to be. Common copyright problems are addressed in Chapter 18. The details of fair use, how to obtain permission, and how to quote fairly are given in Chapter 19, pp. 387–388 and 393–395.

7. Ineffective protection of your own work product and proprietary interests

As a professional consultant, you invest significant time and resources developing speeches, handouts, and audiovisual or graphic materials to enhance your presentations. In addition, you develop and market workbooks, instruments, and other products, including audiotapes and videotapes. These materials are proprietary and of substantial value. Yet many consultants don't take the time to protect their own work product from infringement or misappropriation. When you learn that an exercise or technique you developed has been used—verbatim or in significant detail—by someone else, you may not be in a position to enforce your rights and obtain redress for losses caused by the misappropriation. Chapter 19, pp. 403–406 and 409–412, provides complete details on how to recognize and protect your rights in this area, including special considerations for consultants (Chapter 19, pp. 412–413).

8. Inappropriate behavior, particularly sexual harassment, toward clients' employees

Extensive contact with clients' employees is inherent in your professional relationships. Both federal law and the laws of several states require all employers to maintain harassment-free work environments. In essence, your clients can be held liable when *their employees* are harassed by supervisors, coworkers, or *third parties that regularly interact with them.* As an independent consultant, you fall into the last group. Workplace harassment, based on sex, race, nationality, age, or disability, is unlawful discrimination. This is one of the few areas of discrimination law where the individual "harasser" can have personal liability. Individual liability is *independent* of the liability imposed on the employer (perhaps your client) for failing to take appropriate steps to stop the harassment of its employees by outsiders.

Most sexual harassment cases involving consultants or other third parties are based on claims of a "hostile work environment." Actionable harassment occurs when an employee is forced to work in an environment that is offensive, intimidating, hostile, or abusive because of sexually explicit or demeaning behavior. The behavior may be verbal, physical, or graphic (visual), or a combination thereof.

Consultants who tell unwelcome off-color stories—even those intended as jokes—invite sexual harassment claims. Graphic or visual materials—including e-mail messages, cards, cartoons, or other sexually suggestive written communications—are also off-limits for consultants who want to maintain professional relationships and avoid costly (not to mention embarrassing) lawsuits.

The potential for personal liability is real. In addition, consider this: Once your client (an employer) learns of behavior in its work environment that is unwelcome and offensive to its employees, it is *legally required to conduct a thorough investigation and then to take immediate and appropriate corrective action.* The corrective action can range from a strong warning to cease the offending behavior, to asking the "harasser" to leave the premises and not return. The level of corrective action required by federal law (and by many states too) is what is sufficient to end the harassment. In extreme situations, it may mean terminating the business relationship. Further discussion and examples of hostile environment sexual harassment as it applies to consultants appear in Chapters 6, pp. 145–148, and 13, pp. 281–285.

Quid pro quo conditional harassment (e.g., "sleep with me…or else") is less common with nonemployee harassers than with fellow workers. Still, some states have passed specific legislation addressing such behavior in professional relationships. California provides a useful example. In September 1994 Governor Pete Wilson signed into law an amendment to the state civil rights act making sexual harassment that occurs as part of a "professional relationship" unlawful.[2] This legislation does not alter an employer's (your client's) responsibilities and liabilities for sexual harassment in its work environment. The act provides that a person is liable for sexual harassment when the offended party proves that:

- A business, service, or professional relationship exists between the victim and the accused.
- The victim cannot "easily terminate the relationship without tangible hardship."
- The professional has made sexual advances, solicitations, sexual requests, or demands for sexual compliance.
- The professional's conduct was unwelcome and persistent or severe.
- The conduct continued after a request to stop.
- The victim "has suffered or will suffer economic loss or disadvantage or personal injury as a result" of the professional's conduct.

The law was intended to affect lawyers, physicians, accountants, and *other professionals who have ongoing relationships with clients and their employees.* Consultants, particularly those with continuing professional relationships with the client organization, fall well within the statutory definitions. One significant advantage for the professional is the requirement that the victim specifically request the harasser to stop the behavior. Under Title VII or state law, when the harasser is a coworker or supervisor, a request to stop is not required and the "victim" can go to someone else in the organization to complain.

The bottom line: Sexual harassment of your clients' employees is both bad business and legally risky. The solution is to understand the legal and practical circumstances under which liability may arise and to avoid any behavior that is inappropriate.

9. Misclassification of independent contractor status

Consultants who provide ongoing extensive services to a single client are often classified as independent contractors when in fact they are operating as employees. An independent contractor is an individual who renders service through an independent business and generally contracts for an end product or specific result. Independent contractors are self-employed, and pay their own income taxes, unemployment taxes, and state disability insurance contributions. They are also responsible for securing and maintaining their own workers' compensation, medical, and related insurance benefits.

Misclassification of a service provider as an independent contractor strips that individual of valuable benefits, and risks significant exposure for unpaid payroll taxes, including penalties and interest. The details of independent contractor versus employee status are addressed in Chapter 16, pp. 339–342.

10. Ineffective or nonexistent documentation

Documentation is a written record of an event, discussion, or observation by one or more individuals. Most organizations rely on documentation to record their activities and those of their employees. Any written information, whether formally or informally generated, can be considered documentary evidence if it is pertinent to an administrative proceeding or lawsuit.

When called upon to defend against a legal claim—copyright violation, discriminatory content, negligence or professional error, breach of contract—consultants must be able to provide credible information to reconstruct events, to explain what occurred, or to substantiate their efforts to comply with applicable legal statutes.

Haphazard record keeping is both frustrating and potentially devastating to your successful defense. The important issues surrounding documentation, including when and how to document your activities effectively are addressed in Chapters 2, pp. 51–52; 8, pp. 195–197; 19, pp. 400–403 and 404–409; and 20, pp. 419–425 and 429–431.

References

1. *Stender v. Lucky Stores, Inc.*, 803 F.Supp. 259 (N.D.Cal. 1992).
2. California Civil Code, §51.9.

16

Bidding, Contracting, and Follow-Through

Essential Elements of a Successful Consulting Contract

When consultants and their clients enter into a contract, they anticipate a successful and mutually beneficial project. They don't necessarily focus on potential areas of conflict. Consulting agreements, like other business arrangements, should be carefully planned and the essential terms of the relationship memorialized. These safeguards minimize ambiguities while the relationship is ongoing and prevent breach-of-contract charges when it ends.

The specific format of consulting contracts varies widely, from a simple letter agreement, to a memorandum of understanding, to a lengthy consulting contract. There is no single approach required to pass legal muster. Even an oral contract is enforceable in most states if it contains the essential terms necessary to establish a meeting of the minds by the parties involved.

The objectives of the parties, their working relationship, and the scope of the project will generally dictate the complexity of the written agreement. There are, however, several essential elements required in every consulting relationship, elements that are critical to enforcement in a breach-of-contract action.

A contract is a promise or set of promises for which the law provides a remedy when they are unmet. Alternatively, courts recognize performance of the promises as a legal duty. Contracts are classified by how they are formed and how they can be accepted. They may be express, by promises communicated through language, or implied, by conduct reflecting an intent to be bound. They may be bilateral, which requires an exchange of promises, or unilateral, with acceptance conditional on performance (e.g., a public offer of a reward for information). Most are expressed in writing and require performance by both the consultant and the client.

Mutual assent of the parties is reflected by an offer, which is a promise or commitment with definite and certain terms communicated to the client, and by acceptance of those terms without conditions. If the client proposes conditions, they form the basis for a counteroffer, which may then be negotiated until agreement is reached on the final terms. You must have enough essential terms to make the agreement capable of enforcement through a court order specifying performance.

The mutual promises encompassed in the offer and acceptance must be sufficiently definite to be capable of enforcement. These generally include the basic scope of the work (what is to be performed), the time frame involved (when the work is to be performed), and the amount of the fee or compensation and the timing of payment (e.g., advance retainer, installments based on defined progress or phases, or end-of-project payment).

In addition to mutual assent, there must be something of legal value bargained for and exchanged. The legal term for this exchange is *consideration,* and it may consist of either an affirmative obligation (such as payment of fees) or an agreement to refrain from doing something the party is legally entitled to do. A release of potential legal claims and agreement not to sue in exchange for payment is bargained-for consideration, since one party is paying and the other is agreeing to refrain from something it is entitled to do. The majority of courts require that a party incur some detriment, but a court will not address the adequacy or fairness of the consideration, unless it is entirely devoid of value. (Lawyers call this "illusory.")

Given the complexity of most consulting projects, you may find that the bare essentials—mutual assent and basic bargained-for exchange—are insufficient to ensure a successful relationship and satisfactory enforcement should disputes arise. You may encounter foreseeable complications, as well as those completely beyond your expectations. These complications can be extremely expensive if the agreement is not structured in a way that protects both parties' interests.

To be proactive in managing your contractual agreements, you should discuss with the client and build into the final agreement terms that provide focus for your mutual obligations and reciprocal accountability, as appropriate. These terms protect you and your client in the event of future disputes.

Other Significant
Contractual Terms

Other contractual terms, while not legally required for enforceability, will help define the relationship and aid in the resolution of conflicts. When negotiating a contractual agreement with a client, you should consider all of the following.

1. Allocation of responsibilities

Since most consulting contracts involve reciprocal obligations, the contract should specify the required scope and timing of obligations by both the client and the consultant. Address directly the division of responsibility between you and your client on all essential responsibilities, including data collection, follow-through, and performance of key activities.

For example, a diversity consultant who agrees to conduct an audit and develop a hiring or placement plan will require collection of specific data from the client's employment records. Gathering of the data, and excising of any confidential information, may require significant time by the client's employees. If the necessary data are not forthcoming, the consultant may miss the agreed-upon deadline for project completion. The consequences can range from embarrassment to relinquishment of the fee for failure to meet the deadline.

One way to avoid this problem is to determine in advance the division of responsibilities among all parties to the agreement—generally you and your client. Allocate assignments, set specific time frames for reciprocal performance, and address mutual accountability. Make every effort to consider foreseeable impediments to performance by either party, and decide *in advance* how you will handle them or modify your agreement.

2. Scope of the work

The contract should specify the work product you are expected to generate. Although a written report or other deliverable may not be required at the conclusion of the project, if it is desirable, build it into the contract.

The contract should specify the time for performance. For example, a diversity consultant may be asked to prepare an audit and make recommendations about a diversity training program. The client organization may wish to build this project into a larger diversity program, or it may be part of the resolution of a discrimination charge. If a concrete deadline exists for the rollout of other activities in the workplace, the contractual schedule should reflect the place that the project has in overall workplace activities.

You may benefit from a clause limiting the scope of services, in order to precisely spell out what you will—and will not—accomplish. A provision limiting the scope of services is a useful complement to the scope-of-work clause. The limitation provides a further indication to the client that the particular work is not all-inclusive, but is limited by time, resources, or other objective factors.

Consider a practical example. As a curriculum designer for specialized software training, you may have opened the negotiations with an offer to provide comprehensive services in accordance with the custom in the industry for similar technical projects. During negotiations, you discover that the client's budget is limited, or the time frame is too tight to provide the entire customary package. In order to get a start on the project, you may agree to narrow the scope of work to fit the client's current limitations. The scope-of-work clause should list any items that are commonly done as part of the type of work, but that are being omitted (or delayed) by express agreement of the parties. The written record prevents disputes when the final work product is narrower than customary for similar projects, and limits the damage from any selective memory the client's agents may have about your earlier discussions.

Conversely, be very careful about assuming that the contract will be expanded once performance commences. Sometimes consultants who know that their work will be extremely valuable to the client are tempted to agree orally to a limited scope of work, expecting that they will be authorized to expand to all appropriate services during the life of the project. Don't count on it. Budgetary considerations, corporate restructuring, economic downturns, or other external variables may prevent expansion of the project. If you haven't specified the limitations of your final agreement, you may be confronted by differing interpretations of what was expected.

Worse yet, the same external variables may require narrowing or terminating the project. You will be in a better position to obtain payment for work already completed if you have specified the scope of work in stages, with defined services and accompanying payment for each phase. Appendix C includes samples of contractual scope-of-work clauses for consultants and speakers.

3. Foreseeable delays

During your contract negotiations, address how foreseeable delays in project completion will be handled and allocate accountability. Delays by either party that can hamper further performance should be addressed in both schedule and payment provisions. Once you reach agreement, memorialize the terms or parameters in your contract. Appendix C provides examples.

4. Consultant's standards for performance

In most situations, there are no absolute legal or professional standards for consulting. The standards vary by industry, project, and certification. In the absence of independent guidelines or industry standards, your consulting contract should contain explicit standards against which your performance may be judged. A set of standards not only provides your client with recourse for inadequate performance, but is also in your best interests as a careful consultant. Objective standards by which to assess the quality, value, and timeliness of your work minimize the potential that subjective judgments will interfere with what was clearly contemplated at the outset of the relationship. They also preclude your client's subjective dissatisfaction or resistance to your advice from jeopardizing payment of your fees.

Under the laws of most states, you will be held to the ordinary level of care exercised by consultants in the same locality under similar circumstances. Of course, you may raise your standard beyond industry norms by contractual agreement. As a conscientious professional consultant, you always attempt to provide clients with the highest-quality work possible. As such, you may certainly agree by contract to be held accountable to the most stringent performance standards. Some consultants even agree to a provision limiting or relinquishing the negotiated fee in the event that the final work product fails to conform to the highest standard of care.

Whatever standard you agree upon, be acutely aware of the obligations you are undertaking, particularly when the language can be used as evidence in both a breach-of-contract action *and* a negligence action. In the latter case, the client—or other injured party—may use the terms of the contract against you, by arguing that you intended to be held to a higher standard than that required by the state common law of negligence. (See Chapters 3, pp. 70–78; 8, pp. 186–191; and 17, pp. 353–357, for a complete discussion of standard of care.)

Figure 16-1 provides two samples of contractual language on the standard of care, one broad and one limited.

5. Client's responsibilities

It is critical to the successful consulting contract to specify the reciprocal obligations your client's organization will undertake. These go far beyond the ultimate obligation to pay the consulting fee. You should

---

Broad Description of Standard of Care

Consultant is knowledgeable, skilled, and experienced in providing technical consulting services comparable to the services enumerated in this Agreement. Consultant represents that the services will be performed in a manner consistent with the highest standards of care, diligence, and skill exercised by nationally recognized consulting firms providing similar services.

Limitation on Applicable Standard of Care

Consultant's services pursuant to this Agreement will be performed in a manner consistent with the level of care and skill ordinarily exercised by members of the consulting profession in the same locale and acting under similar circumstances and conditions. Consultant makes no other representation, guarantee, or warranty, expressed or implied, concerning the services that are furnished to [Client].

Figure 16-1 Sample Contract Clauses Relative to Consultant's Legal Duty and Standard of Care.

consider and build into your agreement all activities for which the client is responsible, including gathering internal data, making files and records available, allocating appropriate staff services, providing meeting rooms, conference space, or training facilities, ensuring medical or related services for off-site training, and providing related services necessary to the complete fulfillment of your work.

In addition, many consultant contracts require the client to represent that information provided to the consultant for purposes of the services is accurate and complete. Your client may wish to include limiting language specifying accuracy "to the best of [the client's] knowledge at the time of contracting." This is a matter for negotiation, but the best approach is to obligate each party to provide true and correct information that may be relied upon by the other party, and to require disclosures during the terms of the agreement, as necessary, if further information comes to light. Figure 16-2 provides an example of language that helps the consultant.

6. Consultant's compliance with applicable laws

The contract should also require strict adherence to all applicable laws, as reflected in the sample language of Figure 16-3. (See also Appendix C.)

Client shall provide Consultant with all information, known or readily accessible to Client, that may be reasonably necessary for completion of the services to be performed. Such information includes [*specify, in accordance with the nature of the consulting project.*]

Prior to the commencement of services, or at any time thereafter when new information becomes available to Client, Client shall provide prompt, full, and complete disclosures to Consultant of new information that could affect Consultant's performance of its services or could pose potential hazardous conditions or risk to the health or safety of Consultant's employees, agents, and subcontractors.

Figure 16-2 Sample Consulting Contract Provision Addressing Client's Reciprocal Obligations.

This is especially important when you perform work on the client's premises, and are responsible for any aspect of consulting or training on safety and health issues, environmental compliance, EEO compliance, or related regulatory standards.

Consultant, its representatives, and subcontractors shall at all times comply with any and all applicable foreign, federal, state, and local government laws, ordinances, statutes, standards, rules, regulations, and guidances, including but not limited to those relating to working hours, working conditions, safety and health, equal employment opportunity, and fair employment practices.

Consultant shall obtain all required permits, licenses, agency approvals, and other necessary documentation in order to provide and complete the services required under this Agreement. Should Consultant fail to comply, Consultant shall indemnify [*Client*] for any fees, penalties, or fines assessed against [*Client*].

In the event Consultant determines that its employees, agents, or subcontractors have not complied with the applicable law or with contractual specifications, then Consultant shall stop the noncomplying work immediately, provide prompt written notice to [*Client*], and instruct its employees, agents, and subcontractors, as appropriate, to take appropriate corrective action.

Figure 16-3 Sample Contract Language Requiring Consultant to Comply With All Applicable Laws.

7. Indemnification and liability limitations

In plain English, indemnification is a contractual promise to reimburse or pay the costs of any liability incurred by the other party. Indemnity usually arises when a party (e.g., the client) is held legally accountable to a third person (e.g., an employee, trainee, or bystander) for injuries or damages caused by the other party's (e.g., the consultant's) negligence. For example, in an adventure training program, the employer that sponsors the outing will be legally responsible for any injuries to employee participants, even if the program is under the direction and control of a consultant. The employer, as client, will want to contractually require the consultant to indemnify it for amounts it must pay in a lawsuit or settlement involving losses, damages, or liabilities to employees.

It is critical to understand that indemnity *never* shifts the primary legal risk to an injured party. The client will always remain obligated to the employee, and can be reimbursed (indemnified) only if the consultant was negligent. The client, as employer, may never avoid this primary liability or shift it directly to the consultant. See the discussion of *Leno v. Young Men's Christian Association*,[1] in the Introduction, pp. 5–6, and Chapter 4, pp. 95–96.

Some state courts have ruled that contractual provisions attempting to limit liability for a party's own negligence are contrary to public policy and not enforceable. Particularly in the case of employers, the client cannot contract away these direct obligations to its own employees, nor can it relieve itself (in legal parlance of case law, "exculpate itself") of liability for its own negligence, such as negligent hiring of the consultant or inadequate supervision. However, when the consultant's negligence is the sole source of the liability, a contractual indemnification agreement may require the consultant to completely indemnify the client for all losses or damages.

At a minimum, most clients will seek to require the consultant to indemnify them for claims arising out of the consultant's negligence, breaches of the standard of care for similar consultants, and failure to comply with applicable laws. Figure 16-4 highlights sample language, with further examples in Appendix C.

If you are especially concerned about the role your client or its personnel play in joint activities—such as high-risk safety training, management of hazardous training facilities, or nontraditional training programs—you may wish to negotiate a reciprocal indemnification agreement by which the client will indemnify you for liabilities you may incur as a result of the client's sole negligence or breach of the agreement. You can use the same language, reversing the indemnity requirements.

Consultant agrees to indemnify and hold harmless [*Client*] and [*Client's agents and employees*] against any and all claims, damages, demands, liens, claims of lien, losses, actions, or liability of any kind that may be imposed on them, including without limitation, reasonable attorneys' fees and litigation costs arising out of or in connection with (a) any negligent acts, errors, or omissions, or willful misconduct of Consultant in performing the services pursuant to this Agreement; (b) injury or death of any persons resulting from any negligent acts, errors, or omissions, or willful misconduct of Consultant; and (c) negligent or willful nonperformance or breach by Consultant of any duties, obligations, or representations under this Agreement.

Figure 16-4 Sample Indemnification Clause to Consulting Contract.

In addition, you can ask the client to hold you and your consulting organization harmless for damages arising out of the acts, errors, or omissions of any individuals not affiliated with your organization, when they are the sole or substantial cause of the harm. Most clients, however, will limit this provision to people whose actions are under their exclusive direction and control and not the consultant's. The result is to hold the client responsible for its agents and employees, and the consultant culpable for the acts of vendors, suppliers, and others under the consultant's direction and control. In fairness to both parties, limitations on any indirect damages—damages not caused by either party—may be borne equally by the consultant and the client.

8. Insurance

Insurance is essential for any off-site training activity. Your consulting contract should specify acceptable types and levels of insurance coverage to be obtained by both you and your client. When purchasing insurance, be sure to cover workers' compensation for all your staff, professional errors and omissions for yourself (if available and not cost-prohibitive), comprehensive general liability, and appropriate umbrella or excess liability coverage. A new trend is employment-related insurance, covering harassment and discrimination. Although such coverage can be valuable in some settings, it is very expensive.

Append certificates of insurance to your consulting contract, showing the type and amount of coverage and all parties insured (primary policyholder and additional named insureds). The contract should also require that all parties obtaining insurance provide copies of the complete policies upon demand. "Additional named insured" coverage, available for a modest additional cost, allows you to add your client as a direct insured party under your coverage, and vice versa. The benefits are significant: The insurance company *must* provide a defense to covered litigation (e.g., personal injury negligence lawsuits) for *all* insured *and* additional named insured parties, which means that the ongoing costs of attorneys' fees, court costs, and litigation expenses are paid directly by the insurance carrier, rather than being paid by the party and later reimbursed. This can be a tidy sum.

9. Termination

As with a marriage or personal relationship, the professional relationship rarely starts out by considering the "unthinkable": a breakup. However, during contract negotiations you should discuss when and how the consulting agreement may terminate. Typical circumstances are when the project ends by its own terms; when one party breaches its obligations, thereby excusing further performance by the nonbreaching party; and when external conditions not caused by either party call for early termination.

In the first two situations, the more clearly the contract defines acceptable standards for performance, the easier it will be for the nonbreaching party to enforce contractual rights. When external forces— economic downturn, client restructuring, death or disability of the consultant—force the premature termination of the contract, the contract should specify a fair and equitable resolution. If the scope of work is well defined, the parties should be able to wind up their relationship, allowing the consultant to be paid for work completed and the project to end with minimal disruption to the client's ongoing business. Appendix C contains examples of detailed termination provisions.

10. Recovering attorneys' fees

One of the biggest myths about the legal system is that the prevailing party in a dispute will be "made whole." Often, the costs of pursuing litigation—attorneys' fees, court costs, lost time—exceed the value of what is ultimately recovered. For this reason, the decision to proceed with litigation should be very carefully considered and limited to those situations where no alternative dispute resolution is available.

In most states, the prevailing party can't recover attorneys' fees, unless they are specifically provided for in the contract. A clause providing for the court to award reasonable attorneys' fees to the prevailing party is valuable because it brings the prevailing party closer to being made whole and it limits the potential that an adverse party will assert frivolous claims or defenses. The language is very straightforward:

> Should litigation be necessary to enforce rights under this Agreement, the prevailing party shall recover its reasonable attorneys' fees and costs, to be determined by the court in accordance with appropriate community and/or industry standards.

11. Alternative dispute resolution (ADR)

The traditional forum for resolution of contractual disputes is a court of law, where the claims and defenses of the parties may be considered by a judge or jury. However, the judicial system is crowded, delay-prone, and expensive. In many state courts, a civil action for breach of contract can consume two or more years, gobbling up your resources and trying the patience of all parties.

Viable alternatives include mediation, conciliation, and arbitration before a neutral panel or single arbitrator. Arbitration typically involves a hearing, but with relaxed rules of evidence. You can select a panel of arbitrators from your industry or from the American Arbitration Association, or agree upon a single arbitrator. An emerging trend in ADR services is to use retired judges as hearing officers and arbitrators. The parties split the hourly fee, but receive a much faster resolution without the burden and expense of protracted "discovery." See Chapter 1, p. 32, and Chapter 20, pp. 421–425, for an explanation of the discovery process.

The disadvantages of arbitration are twofold. If it is nonbinding, it generally delays the inevitable litigation and actually increases costs, because the losing party at arbitration will invariably seek judicial resolution. If arbitration is binding, the parties waive their right to a trial by a jury of their peers. This can be helpful when the issues are technical or complex, but when credibility or "fairness" is involved, arbitrators are less swayed than jurors.

When you and your client agree in advance to an alternative method of resolving disputes under the contract, you *must* specify the form of ADR you will use. Unless there is an unequivocal waiver of the right to judicial relief, either party may later claim that it did not intend to relinquish the right to a jury trial. In these situations, the claimant is likely to be the party that is in the best financial position to absorb the costs and inherent delays of a civil lawsuit. Independent consultants may be on the losing end of the equation.

Will Your Consulting Contract Hold Up in Court? A Checklist

With precontract planning and thorough discussions, you should be in a position to complete your consulting assignments to your client's satisfaction, collect your fee, and move on to new work for this client or excellent referrals. There are times, however, where despite your best efforts to anticipate every contingency, your client may not perform its obligations or may fail to pay your fee. In those situations, you will need a consulting contract that is capable of enforcement by a court.

The following checklist will help you focus on relevant issues when negotiating and seeking to enforce contracts with your clients.

1. Is there a defined offer? Does it contain the essential elements of time for performance, a definable scope of work with logical phases consistent with the contemplated schedule, and a specific fee and payment schedule?

2. Has the offer been accepted? Are there conditions on acceptance or a counteroffer?

3. Is there bargained-for exchange? Are all parties making promises to perform by payment or refraining from lawful actions?

4. Are the divisions of responsibility clear and capable of being enforced? What is your client to do, and when? What are you to do, and when? Are conditions placed upon performance, such as the need for information or data from external sources? If so, who is responsible for obtaining the information and within what time frame?

5. Are standards for evaluating your performance unambiguous? By what standards will your performance be measured—national, regional, local, or a particular industry? Have you placed relevant limitations on your standards?

6. Are performance measurements built directly into the fee agreement? If so, are the standards reasonably capable of being enforced objectively? If acceptable performance is required prior to payment of fees, have you covered yourself in the event that performance is affected by foreseeable and/or unanticipated external forces?

7. What division of responsibilities will exist for training or other activities contemplated by the contract? Whose facilities will be used and who will absorb the cost? Is audiovisual equipment

required, and who will provide it? How will the cost be allocated? If other technology will be used, how will it be obtained, installed, and serviced? Who is responsible—by cost, effort, and consequence—for technical "glitches"?

8. If third-party contracts with vendors or subcontractors are required, who will sign them? Whose insurance will cover the facilities to be used? Does the insurance cover workers' compensation? Premises liability? General liability? Errors and omissions? Professional liabilities? Sexual harassment or employment-related liabilities?

9. How will you and your client handle foreseeable delays in receipt or collection of data? In performance of activities required by the client's employees or external third parties? Have you accounted for all unforeseen variables in performance by either party? How will changed circumstances be handled during the performance of the agreement?

10. What written work product is contemplated by the agreement? Who will own the work product, including project reports, audits, or other data collection materials? Who will own the copyrights on any final publications, instruments, or training manuals?

11. Will you and your client have potential joint liabilities to third parties? Is there a risk of physical injuries or property damage to employees or third parties arising from the activities contemplated by the contract? Is an indemnification clause desirable? Will it be a unilateral agreement (consultant indemnifies client) or reciprocal (each indemnifies the other)? Do you or the client have applicable insurance to cover the foreseeable risks, and how will the costs of the premiums be allocated?

12. Have you and your client considered potential reasons for termination of the contract? How will you handle external forces or breaches by either party?

13. If a dispute arises, how will you adjudicate your rights and responsibilities—by judicial action (civil lawsuit) only, by arbitration (binding or nonbinding), or by other ADR? Do you need a clause for attorneys' fees and costs to be recoverable by the prevailing party?

14. Do government or regulatory agencies have jurisdiction over any aspect of your work? Are health and safety training issues involved, for which OSHA governs? (See Chapters 1, pp. 24–25; 2, pp. 39–54 and 60–63; and 3, pp. 72–73.) Are equal employment opportunity issues involved, for which the EEOC or state enforcement agencies have jurisdiction? (See Chapter 6, p. 122–148.) Are affirmative action obligations of federal government contractors involved, for which

the Office of Federal Contract Compliance governs? (See Figure 1-1.) Have you addressed or allocated responsibilities for managing a regulatory audit or inspection involving your work? (See Chapter 2, pp. 52–54.)

15. Are your written communications during the negotiations clear and accessible? It is extremely important to print a hard copy of any e-mail communications you have with or on behalf of your client. Although electronic communications are valuable for exchanging business information, most courts will require a "hard copy" as evidence in any subsequent litigation.

How to Determine If You Are Acting as an Independent Contractor or an Employee and Why It Matters

Consultants and contract trainers frequently work extensively for one client or a small group of clients. They may spend entire days or weeks—even months—on long-term projects. The work is frequently done at the client's premises. The compensation arrangement may be a daily rate, a per-course fee, or a flat retainer. There is no promise of continued work and no company benefits. Taxes are not withheld from checks, and at the end of the tax year the consultant's compensation is reported on a 1099 form. Clearly an independent contractor? Not necessarily.

Although you may be flattered when your client's staff refer to you as "one of us," there are legal pitfalls to such long-term relationships. The most prominent is when you are deemed an employee rather than a contractor. The consequences of misclassification are serious.

- The IRS may seek penalties and interest from the "employer" (your client) dating back to the time the relationship commenced—even if you have paid all personal income taxes. In this situation, the employer's matching payroll taxes (FICA) have not been paid. Penalties can be as much as 28 percent of the social security (FICA) owed, plus 1.5 percent of your "wages." These figures double if the employer has not filed a 1099 form for you as an independent contractor.

- State taxing authorities will be next in line for their share of back taxes, disability, and unemployment tax contributions, as well as penalties and interest.

- You—as the consultant who is actually an employee—may be entitled to benefits retroactively. Retroactivity is uncommon with health insurance, but the client's 401(k) plan, pension plan, and other deferred compensation systems may be implicated. It is an understatement to say that this is undesirable from your client's perspective.

One high-profile case involved computer giant Microsoft Corporation. In *Vizcaino v. Microsoft Corp.*,[2] a federal appellate court ruled that Microsoft had misclassified software engineers as independent contractors when they were actually serving functions equivalent to employees. The litigation arose after an IRS audit found that certain types of "freelancers" were actually regular employees. Microsoft paid overdue taxes and converted some to regular employee status. Others continued to work at Microsoft, but as employees of a temporary agency.

Although hired to work on specific projects, seven of eight "freelancers" worked on successive projects for a minimum of two years. They served as software testers and production editors, and performed other consultative work. Microsoft fully integrated the freelancers into its workforce, where they often worked on teams with regular employees, shared supervisors, and performed similar functions. Two critical factors were that the freelancers also worked on site and reported the same core hours as regular employees. They also used company equipment and office supplies.

Other so-called independent contractors then sued Microsoft, claiming that they should be given retroactive retirement benefits. The federal court agreed, finding them eligible for these lucrative benefits. The court held that their "common law employee" status made them eligible to participate in the company's 401(k) and stock purchase plans.

Ownership interests in handouts, training materials, and other resources you create may be affected by your employment status. The author or creator of a work owns the copyright from the moment the material is fixed in tangible form. Unless you have an agreement in writing specifying that your creation is a "work-for-hire," it is presumed to be your own. But employees who are compensated for full-time work are presumed to provide work-for-hire, and the company owns the rights to secure copyright protection. Thus, a retroactive change in status may have profound effects on existing and future intellectual property rights. When those materials have been used or made part of derivative works for which you have registered additional copyrights, this later ownership may be invalidated. Just tracing who owns what may be a nightmare.

In most cases, an independent contractor is not covered by the employer's workers' compensation insurance. Thus, if you are properly classified as an independent contractor, you should obtain insurance to provide medical and disability benefits for on-the-job injuries. Clients may require you to state in your contract that you have obtained and will maintain such coverage for yourself and your employees through the life of the consulting agreement.

The definitions of independent contractor are not uniform. Who is—and is not—an independent contractor depends upon tax, labor, and workers' compensation laws, not solely on the characterization of the parties to the consulting contract. Thus, it isn't enough for the consulting contract simply to include a clause identifying you as an independent contractor, using language like the samples in Appendix C. This is a start, but is not ultimately determinative.

Basic Definition of Independent Contractor

An independent contractor renders service in the course of an independent occupation and generally contracts for an end product or a specific result, not for the means by which the service is regularly accomplished. Independent contractors are self-employed, and pay their own income taxes, unemployment taxes, and state disability insurance contributions. They are also responsible for securing and maintaining their own workers' compensation, medical, and related insurance benefits.

In considering whether an individual is an independent contractor or an employee, the employer must evaluate the extent of the individual's investment, equipment, and facilities, the individual's opportunities for profit or loss, the degree of control exercised by others over the individual's work, the permanency of the relationship between the individual and the organization for which the individual performs work, the skill required of the individual in performing his or her work, and the extent to which the work is an integral part of the alleged employee's business.

The courts have generally relied on the degree of control exercised over the worker, in addition to the other factors established by the IRS, to determine whether an individual is an independent contractor or an employee. IRS Bulletin No. 15 (*Employer's Tax Guide*) provides an explanation of the factors that may be considered. No one factor is controlling, and the foregoing list should not be considered complete.

The 20-Factor Test

In Revenue Ruling 87-41, the IRS developed a 20-factor test to classify employee vs. independent contractor status. The factors and considerations pointing toward independent contractor status are as follows:

1. *Degree of control.* The client organization should not have the right to control the method or manner of the job to be performed.

2. *Right to discharge.* The organization cannot terminate the contractor as long as he or she meets his or her obligations under the contract. Any contractor who fails to meet expected quality, timeliness, or other specified performance criteria may be subject to a breach-of-contract claim.

3. *Right to delegate work.* The contractor can bring in whomever he or she wants to accomplish the purpose of the contract. The contractor is exclusively responsible for compensation and benefits for all such workers.

4. *Hiring practices.* The contractor has the right to hire and fire any assistants used in performing the contract. Any degree of control exercised by the client organization would mitigate against a finding of independent contractor status.

5. *Payment practices.* An independent contractor is paid by the job as opposed to by the hour, week, or month. Although a fixed-retainer contract will not automatically defeat a finding of independent contractor status, it is an indication that full-time—or regular—hours of performance are expected. True independent contractors are project driven.

6. *Furnishing of training.* The organization should not provide any type of training for inexperienced contractors. This factor may be modified by contract, in which the parties contemplate that the consultant will take specialized training to become acquainted with industry issues on behalf of the client organization. In these situations, the consultant-contractor should be responsible for payment of any registration fees and books or course materials.

7. *Skill.* Independent contractors are generally viewed as skilled individuals. The more specialized the expertise, the more likely it is that the client organization will not have employee positions for the consultant, necessitating an independent contractor agreement.

8. *Duration of relationship.* The contractor is hired for a particular project or a specified time period. Continuous work implies an employee relationship.

9. *Control over hours of work.* An independent contractor is allowed to set his or her own hours.

10. *Independent trade.* The contractor is free to work for any number of clients or firms simultaneously, so long as the work is completed properly and on time.

11. *Furnishing of tools and equipment.* The contractor is able to provide his or her own tools and equipment, including office supplies and laptop computer. Consultants and contract trainers who use the client organization's audiovisual equipment, training facilities, and/or specialized computers and software may build this into their independent contractor agreement.

12. *Place of work.* Independent contractors often perform work off the organization's premises. As noted above, use of the client organization's specialized training facility or audiovisual equipment may be most cost-effective. This by itself will not preclude a finding of independent contractor status, if other significant factors in the 20-factor test are met.

13. *Profit and loss.* The contractor should have the opportunity for profit and the burden of loss. For example, if a project goes over the established budget or exceeds the anticipated time frame, the contractor generally bears the business loss (which may be deductible for tax purposes). Conversely, when through the contractor's skill and expertise, the project is completed faster or more economically than anticipated, the contractor's established fee should remain intact. Exceptions may be built directly into the contract.

14. *Intent of the parties.* The parties' intent to create an independent contractor relationship should be documented in writing. Although written intent will not be dispositive in the absence of other significant factors, it is relevant evidence to establish the parties' expectations.

15. *Principal in business.* The contractor is usually a principal in his or her own business. Evidence of a separate business license, employer tax identification number (federal and state), and other indicia of independent business status have helped establish independent contractor status. All checks to the contractor should be payable to the independent business with its employer ID number, rather than to the contractor personally with his or her social security number.

16. *Sequence of work.* The contractor should be able to determine the sequence of the work performed on individual projects outside of the client's control. Any degree of control by the client organization may defeat a finding of independent contractor status. Control refers primarily to the sequencing of tasks on discrete projects. If sequencing is a critical component of the consulting relationship, it should be specified in the independent contractor agreement.

17. *Reports required.* The contractor should not be required to submit regular oral or written reports or to attend organization meetings,

unless they are built into the consulting agreement and are a defined part of the project.

18. *Same work as regular employees.* The organization should not have the independent contractor do the same type of work as its regular employees. This is primarily to assure the IRS that the employer is not using so-called independent contractors to perform overload work, rather than hiring additional employees. Consultants and contract trainers with specialized expertise have a relatively easy time establishing the uniqueness of their work.

19. *Integration.* The organization should not engage an independent contractor to do something that is part of the day-to-day operations of the company. Here too, the more specialized the work, the more likely that an independent contractor or consultant is required.

20. *Industry customs.* The industry should have a definite custom regarding worker classification.

How to Be Sure Your Clients Pay Your Bill and What to Do When They Don't

One of the most difficult challenges facing consultants is keeping abreast of billing and collections. You may be reluctant to push for payment if your client falls behind, fearing disruption of the working relationship. So you keep on working, hoping that the bill will soon be paid. Too often the result is a serious drain on cashflow and pressure while work is in progress.

When your contract calls for payment on a specified schedule and your client doesn't meet its obligations, you may have grounds for a breach-of-contract action, which excuses your further performance. However, if you are working under a tight deadline for meeting your client's obligations to an outside regulatory agency (such as OSHA, OFCCP, or EEOC), or if a delay could jeopardize your client's business, you may be compelled to complete work in progress even though payments are late.

There are two ways to minimize this problem. First, build into your contract a specific statement about how ongoing work will be handled if the payment schedule is not met. Will you complete the project, or will there be an agreed-upon suspension of consulting services? If you handle the issue "up front," you will limit the potential for business damage to both yourself and your client.

Second, if your contract is silent as to payment schedule, gently raise the issue with the appropriate client representatives. Determine whether you can amend the contract to extend the fee schedule, or otherwise adjust the schedule for continuing services to accommodate the client's (hopefully) temporary cashflow problems. If you don't address the issue at all or seek to hold your client to a specific schedule (even as modified), you risk a later assertion that you waived your rights.

You should also determine the applicable "statute of limitations" for filing a legal action in your state's civil court. Some states allow up to two years (for breach of an oral agreement) to as long as four years (for breach of a written contract). Others set significantly shorter limits. In most states, unless you extend the statute of limitations or raise that defense—in writing—you will irrevocably lose rights to legally enforce your agreement if the relevant statute of limitations expires. Consult legal counsel early to avoid completely forgoing your rights while you are "negotiating" with your client.

These steps will maximize your potential for maintaining excellent client relationships while preserving the integrity of your work product. If you don't address the issue at all, and the client falls hopelessly behind on your fees or refuses to pay, you may find yourself having to pursue a breach-of-contract action. Litigation is time-consuming, expensive, and rarely helpful in preserving client relationships. Sometimes it is unavoidable.

The following steps will maximize your potential for success in recovering fees you have earned.

1. Review your contract to determine whether all essential elements to enforceability are present (see pp. 324–325 of this chapter).

2. Talk to your client first, referencing its obligation to meet the payment schedule and providing documentation of your completed work.

3. Write a letter, on your own letterhead, asking for payment within a short time frame. While this is technically a "demand letter," the tone should be business-like and professional. Set forth the chronology of events and your attempts to obtain the client's adherence to the contract. If your contract contains a provision granting reasonable attorneys' fees to the prevailing party, mention it and state that you wish to resolve the matter without necessity of litigation.

4. Some consultants feel that this is the time to get a lawyer. Practically speaking, if you can resolve the matter personally, you will save time and fees, and possibly the client's goodwill. Once lawyers get involved, it may be harder to reach a prompt conclusion. However, if the client's representatives have flatly refused to discuss the matter, you may have no choice. It will certainly help if you have negotiated a clause for recovery of attorneys' fees by the prevailing party; but

remember, this cuts both ways. Evaluate the strengths and weaknesses of your position—realistically—before plunging into litigation. Advice of good legal counsel at this stage can help direct you to the most cost-effective solution.

5. Breach-of-contract actions are brought in state civil court. The time frame involved can be anywhere from one year to four years, depending upon the jurisdiction. Because of inherent delays, and the fact that a recovery of your fee several years later will be worth far less than it is today, be prepared to negotiate a cost-effective resolution at every stage of the process.

6. Provide your legal counsel with accessible, well-organized files. At a minimum you should provide a complete copy of the contract (with all relevant signatures), any supporting documentation concerning the contract terms, copies of all correspondence between you and the client, copies of work you generated on behalf of the client, and a chronology of events during your consulting project. Your thoroughness will reduce the time your counsel has to spend (with the fee meter ticking) learning the basic facts of the dispute.

7. If you have insurance for any part of the work, your counsel will want to see the policies at the earliest time.

8. Remember that the client has the opportunity to raise defenses to your claim. These range from alleging that the contract is unenforceable to claiming that you breached the contract in some manner. Thus, you should be prepared to defend your work as meeting both contractual provisions and the ordinary standard of care for similar consultants in your area.

9. Always consider alternative dispute resolution (ADR), such as mediation, arbitration, or some less formal settlement discussion. Hopefully, you will have addressed these alternatives in your contract negotiations. ADR reduces costs and provides the best opportunity to ensure that litigation doesn't interfere with your ongoing business and good relationships with your clients.

Confidentiality Agreements: What Works, What Doesn't, and What's Absolutely Essential

During the course of your work, you may have access to, acquire, or become acquainted with trade secrets, confidential information, and property relating to your client and its customers' businesses. All information obtained in the course of your employment is to be used only for the purposes of your specific project. Never discuss or disclose such trade secrets, confidential information, or intellectual property, either directly or indirectly, with or in the presence of people outside the company, either during your engagement or at any time thereafter, except as requested by your client.

Information in any form—including, but not limited to, documents, tapes, lists, computer printouts, studies, reports, drafts, pictures, charts, maps, drawings, programs, equipment, scrap, blueprints, vendor lists, customer lists, client billing information, all financial reports, all payroll information, records, files, and other materials pertinent to client or its customers—may be subject to confidentiality agreements. Your client may require you to sign a nondisclosure of confidential information agreement. Figure 16-5 provides a sample confidentiality agreement.

This same level of confidentiality must be maintained regarding coworkers, employee relations matters, and company operations.

The issues of confidentiality and company security are becoming increasingly critical to many client organizations, particularly when their consultants are involved in such highly sensitive areas as finance, legal, technology, and sales/marketing. Additionally, clients frequently retain consultants to help them with work for their own customers, and they have similar responsibilities to safeguard confidential data. Customer information leaked to others through a consultant can damage the client relationship and ruin the consultant's reputation.

The following safeguards will minimize security exposure. Limit access to your own computer network to staff specifically working on the project. Maintain secure areas for all client files, proposals, pricing, and client data. It is not necessary to formalize all aspects of day-to-day behavior, but it is important that you use common sense and think about what to say, whom you say it to, and what written information you pass on to others about client information.

Privileged Information in Litigation

You should always maintain confidentiality over all client information you receive in the course of a project. In most situations this is simply good business practice, since the client organization will be reluctant to have its personnel policies, business practices, procedures, and other proprietary data disclosed to your other clients, particularly in competitive industries. Thus, for ethical reasons alone, you should maintain confidentiality, whether or not it becomes a specific provision of your written agreement.

Figure 16-5 Confidentiality and Nondisclosure Agreement.

Confidentiality of Information:
Nondisclosure and Protection Agreement

I, _____, understand and agree that as a condition of my retention as a consultant at [COMPANY NAME], I am prohibited from disclosing confidential Company information to anyone other than clearly authorized individuals. I understand that this Nondisclosure Agreement applies regardless of how much information may become known to me. I also agree that I will bring to management's attention any violation of confidentiality that I observe of which I become aware, through whatever means. I also agree that I am accountable for the safekeeping of all confidential information in my possession or under my control, including without limitation, computerized or manual records.

Confidential information relating to [COMPANY NAME]'s business shall be used by [consultant's organization] only in the performance of [his or her] work for the Company. Confidential information includes, but is not limited to, the following: training manuals, test instruments, employee test results, curriculum outlines, business strategies, financial data, statistical employment data, unannounced training product information, software programs, pricing practices, promotional plans and advertising, the identity of contractors and the specifications they supply to [COMPANY NAME], and any other information designated from time to time by [COMPANY NAME] management as confidential training, employment, or related materials. Furthermore, I agree to return to [COMPANY NAME] management all confidential information obtained by me during my retention as consultant with the Company.

If the Company determines after an investigation that I have breached any part of this Agreement, immediate cancellation of the consultant contract without prior warning can result. Legal action to recover any damages incurred by the Company owing to my breach-of-confidentiality agreement may also result. The party that prevails in any legal action shall be entitled to recover reasonable attorneys' fees and costs resulting from the legal action.

Consultant Signature _____

Client Signature   _____

In some consulting assignments, the issue of confidentiality becomes a legal imperative. For example, diversity and employment practices consultants frequently receive sensitive information about employees or practices, or employee test results, which may be the subject of pending or future litigation. In these situations, confidentiality is critical to protect the client's interests.

When litigation is pending or contemplated against your client, your work product may become relevant, and the client will want to take all appropriate—and lawful—steps to shield that work product from discovery by adverse parties to the lawsuit. (The discovery process in civil litigation is addressed in Chapter 1, p. 32, and Chapter 20, pp. 421–425. In order to maximize the confidentiality of communications between you and your client, you should have the consulting contract prepared by legal counsel, and all communications between you and your client should go through the attorney.

The issue here is protection of the attorney-client privilege. If you are retained by your client's legal counsel to gather data, render opinions, make recommendations, and possibly testify as an expert witness, you are being retained to assist counsel in preparation for the litigation. The underlying data are not protected by the privilege, but your communications with the client's attorneys may be shielded by this important privilege, since you have become an essential agent of the attorneys. The attorneys need not be intimately involved in all aspects of your work, decision making, or analysis. The appropriate extent of counsel's involvement is in directing the scope of your work as it relates to the appropriate aspects relevant to the litigation.

Because the disclosure of attorney-client confidential communications to third parties may destroy the privilege and prejudice your client's interests, your consulting agreement may contain a confidentiality provision that clearly identifies who is bound—including individual consultants, other personnel of your consulting organization, and subcontractors—and precisely what information must be kept confidential.

Other Confidentiality Issues

The confidentiality provisions should also address such issues as where the documents are kept, who has access to them, the procedures for submission of written communications, and the maintenance of earlier drafts after you submit a final report. As an additional protection, your contract should state that the work product generated during the project becomes your property and that upon termination of the agreement, all documents, data, and notes you have generated are to be relinquished to the client.

You may be justifiably concerned about balancing your contractual obligations to your client with your ethical or legal requirements for disclosing pertinent information to government agencies. If you perform safety audits or EEO/affirmative action compliance reviews, you may feel compelled to disclose adverse information to the Occupational Safety and Health Administration (OSHA) or the Office of Federal Contract Compliance Programs (OFCCP), if requested.

Noncompete Agreements: The Good, the Bad, and the Unenforceable

The issue of noncompete agreements arises when an internal trainer or consultant leaves the company to become an independent consultant or when an employee of a consulting organization leaves to work for another consultant or to work independently for clients that he or she cultivated as an employee.

Internal trainers who begin their career as employees and then leave to enter the world of consulting may be asked to sign an agreement promising not to compete with their prior employer in the development of consulting materials or the conducting of consulting projects. Because these agreements tend to significantly limit an individual's opportunity to earn a livelihood, the courts in most states are conservative in enforcing them.

In a civil lawsuit by the employer against a former employee alleging breach of a "covenant not to compete," a court will strictly scrutinize the agreement to ensure that it is reasonably limited in time (one to two years maximum), geographic reach (within a small radius of direct competition, although for industry-specific consultation services the reach may be wider), and areas of competition (usually limited to the former employee's direct use of processes, procedures, or materials that were acquired solely by reason of the employee's past association with the employer).

Enforceable noncompete agreements are typically limited to those situations where the internal trainer or consultant has acquired during employment a unique area of expertise, accompanied by development of substantial materials that belong to the employer. When the trainer leaves and offers similar services to clients in the same industry— perhaps even competitors of the former employer—a limited agreement not to compete may be enforceable. Of course, the former employee who developed materials as "works-for-hire" will be liable for copyright infringement if he or she uses those materials owned by the employer without express permission. For a complete discussion of this topic, see Chapter 19, pp. 388–393.

The issue becomes more complex when a consultant leaves one organization to compete directly with the prior employer as an employee of another organization or as an independent contractor. Most organizations expect that departing consultants will adhere to appropriate ethical standards respecting the confidentiality of *client information* they have gained during employment. But what about taking the unique information learned during an engagement—such as procedures, unique approaches to report writing, and marketing strategies—and using it to compete directly for the same or new clients?

Once again, the courts will strictly scrutinize noncompete agreements to be sure they do not inappropriately limit the ability of an individual to engage in professional pursuits and to earn a living. The best opportunity for successful enforcement of a noncompete agreement is to require that it be signed by all employees at the beginning of their employment with the organization, *not* when they are departing.

Because a covenant not to compete is a contract, it must have the same essential elements of any contractual agreement—mutual assent and bargained-for exchange. This means that something of value must be given by the employer in exchange for the employee's signing the agreement, such as additional compensation or a one-time fee. If there is no evidence of such value, the contract may later be deemed illusory and unenforceable. Thus, the agreement should precisely define what substantive areas are covered, such as conducting diversity scans using the XYZ Consultancy Corp. process, or developing customized course materials for a specific software program.

Further, the agreement should be limited in duration, such as one year from the date of separation. Finally, it must be circumscribed in geographic or regional scope, to limit direct competition but still allow the consultant to earn a living during the period that the agreement is in effect. Agreements that prevent employees from competing in entire industries or entire states are probably unenforceable.

References

1. *Leno v. Young Men's Christian Association,* 17 Cal.App.3d 651 (1971).
2. *Vizcaino v. Microsoft Corp.,* 105 F.3d 1334 (1997).

17

How to Protect Yourself From Malpractice Lawsuits

Most clients who are dissatisfied with a consultant's work simply choose to end the business relationship. If the client suffers damages from the consultant's work, the most common remedy is a breach-of-contract action. In a civil action for breach of contract, your client is limited to damages flowing directly from the breach itself, which may be the amount of your fee, business-specific losses contemplated at the time the contract is signed, or reimbursement (indemnity) for damages that the client is required to pay to a third party because of your negligence.

Only in extreme situations do clients resort to another form of civil lawsuit: a tort action for professional malpractice, based on alleged errors and omissions in performing the work. The distinction between a contract action and a tort action are significant in one major respect. In a contract action the damages are limited to those flowing from the breach itself; in a tort action the client may recover "all damages proximately caused" by your errors. The latter is a much broader form of relief and is more often submitted to a jury.

Professional malpractice is simply a form of negligence, in which the injured party seeks damages for breach of a legal duty of due care owed by the professional. The client, as the injured party, typically seeks damages either for relying on negligent advice or for lost business because of a consultant's delay in completing work. The ordinary legal definition of negligence is a failure to exercise due care under circumstances in which a legal duty of care is owed to another person. Litigation of consultants' negligence involves an examination of their duty to a client. In a professional relationship, the duty or standard of care is generally higher because of the professional's expertise, special skills, certification, or other unique qualifications. The ways that legal duties are expanded by the courts are fully addressed in Chapter 3, pp. 70–76.

The court is required to determine whether a duty of care exists in the particular circumstance. Claims against consultants typically focus on an alleged failure to provide effective advice, inadequate training design, negligent supervision of training facilities (resulting in an employee's injury), or negligent selection of instructors.

What Unrealistic Promises Can Cost and How to Avoid Making Them

One of the major sources of liability for consultants is a gap between the client's reasonable expectations and the work product the consultant delivers. Several practical situations provide examples.

Situation 1 A client retains you to conduct an audit of employment practices in response to a complaint to the EEOC. You represent that you have extensive experience in the area, and can complete the work and produce viable recommendations within 90 days. The client notifies the EEOC that it is taking appropriate action. You fail to deliver on time, resulting in penalties assessed by the EEOC. In addition, your advice includes design of a performance management system that is itself discriminatory, resulting in further legal risk to the client.

In a contract action, the client could recover fees you were paid and any damages from your failure to deliver on time. With claims of negligence added, the client could try to convince a jury to award the amount of penalties and other liabilities *flowing directly from your mistakes. Note:* Your increased liabilities would stem, not from the client's underlying discrimination in the original EEOC complaint, but only from your failure to comply with the standard of care for similarly situated professional consultants conducting an audit.

Situation 2   You take on a major project to customize a new database software application and develop a training manual to educate your client's employees on how to operate their new system. Relying on your representation that all employees will be functional on the system within 60 days, the client successfully bids a government project that will begin in 90 days. You overstate your experience with the software; the system keeps crashing while employees are on-line, and your client loses both time and data. As a result, the client cannot perform on the government project, and is replaced.

In a breach-of-contract action, the client could seek a reduction (or nonpyament) of your fee and indemnification for any business losses stemming from the lost computer data. With negligence allegations added, you may be responsible for the business losses arising from your client's lost contract, provided it can establish that you failed to meet the applicable standard of care in performing services, and that "but for" your negligence, it would not have lost the government contract. The latter is the essential element of "causation," or legal nexus between the negligence and the harm. Chapter 3, pp. 77–78, describes this in detail, with pertinent case examples.

Situation 3   As an adventure training consultant, you facilitate a physically challenging management retreat, in which an executive is injured. The injury occurs when the protective helmet you provide malfunctions. The executive (who is now permanently disabled) sues you, the helmet manufacturer, and his employer. During pretrial discovery, the client learns that even though you provided safety records and claimed to use only state-of-the-art equipment, you realized on the day of the program that you were one helmet short and decided to use your 10-year-old college football helmet. The client seeks indemnity from you, owing to your negligence, and asks for all damages that it must pay to the executive, together with its own damages for adverse media attention from the accident.

Far-fetched? These factual descriptions are based on real cases, which were filed in state courts and settled prior to reaching a decision by an appellate court. They reflect, more than anything, problems stemming from unrealistic promises or inflated descriptions of qualifications by the consultants.

There are several ways to avoid such problems. Understand your standard of care or legal duty in the project or relationship. Consultants who hold themselves out as "experts" are generally held to a higher standard of care than other consultants, not unlike the difference between cardiologists and general practitioners.

Carefully consider all promises you make to complete projects within a specified time frame. Address all foreseeable delays and contingencies in advance. Build these into your contract and commitments to minimize the potential that your client will make unrealistic business commitments in reliance on your completion date. (See the discussion in Chapters 15, p. 312, and 16, pp. 325–330.) Discuss at the outset contingency plans based on unforeseeable external sources of delay.

If unforeseen circumstances (such as unworkable or unavailable equipment) make it unsafe to continue your project, advise your client and take appropriate action. Never allow unsafe practices to continue, even at the insistence of the client. You can find more detail on consultant liabilities for negligence and how to avoid them in Chapters 3, pp. 70–79; 4, pp. 93–103; and 8, pp. 185–192.

When a Project Goes Astray: How to Avoid Liability If Your Client Claims Your Advice Caused Harm

A letter from your client's CEO claiming that your advice harmed the business can ruin your whole day. Some consultants react defensively; others are so anxious to retain the relationship that they immediately offer to "fix" the situation. Resist the urge to react immediately. This is particularly so if the letter comes from the client's attorney rather than from your direct client contact.

You should determine the circumstances under which you might receive such a letter. Typically, clients make claims of bad advice in two circumstances: when they have been sued and when they are being pressed to pay delinquent consulting fees.

In the first situation, the allegation may not come as a complete surprise, since a malpractice lawsuit generally arises out of an underlying incident that may have occurred months earlier. If you have conducted an adventure training program in which a participant was injured (Chapter 8, pp. 185–192), provided safety training that allegedly didn't meet regulatory standards (Chapter 2, pp. 40–52), designed a diversity program that generated internal controversy and chaos in the client's organization (Chapters 5, pp. 112–117, and 9, pp. 206–215), or used discriminatory methodology or test instruments (Chapters 6, pp. 143–157, and 7, pp. 163–167 and 171–174), you will undoubtedly be aware of those issues. Your files and records of the incident and its aftermath should be readily accessible. That documentation will help you and your own legal counsel determine the strengths and weaknesses of your position and dictate how you respond. See the detailed discussions about documentation techniques in Chapters 2, pp. 50–54; 8, pp. 195–197; and 20, pp. 419–425 and 429–431.

When "bad advice" is raised in a defensive posture to your invoice for services rendered, you may be tempted to write off a part of the bill. Such an offer may later be construed as an admission that you erred in your advice and may also cost you a fee that you have properly earned. Once again, take some "cooling off" time to evaluate the strength of your documentation and decide on an appropriate, measured response.

The following guidelines should help dictate your response. Find out as much as you can about the factual circumstances and specifics of the allegedly bad advice.

- What happened?
- Which aspect of your advice is in question?
- Identify each person who used or relied on the advice.
- Was the advice followed exactly, or was it modified by the client?
- What type of "damage" has occurred and why does the client believe you are responsible?
- What documentation is the client relying on?

Don't react defensively and don't admit anything until you learn the details. If you respond too soon, you may miss important information about the context in which the allegations have arisen. Get as much information as possible about each employee or contact who received and acted upon the advice you provided.

If your client has been named as a defendant in a lawsuit, ask for a copy. If the client refuses, find out what court the claim is filed in and secure a copy from the public records to determine whether you are named as a defendant and have not yet been served. If you are named, the party that brought the lawsuit must serve you personally with a "summons and complaint." If you have not been named, your client may sue you as a "cross-defendant." In either situation, if you are served with a lawsuit, there will be a limited time to respond (usually 30 days), so you should immediately seek legal advice and secure all your files and records. Make copies of any original documents, especially those with ink signatures or handwritten notations, and store them in a safe, dry place. Provide copies to your legal counsel until the originals are required. For further discussion on what to do when legal trouble strikes, see Chapter 20, pp. 417–419 and 431–433.

How to Protect Yourself When Your Advice Is Not Followed: A Checklist

Few things are more frustrating than providing honest, good-faith advice to a client that is not ready to accept the information. The question is frequently asked: "Why was I hired if the client isn't willing to listen to my recommendations?" In today's climate, consultants are retained for a variety of reasons, most of them stemming from a genuine desire to implement valuable programs.

But there are times when your contact leaves and a new manager is less enthusiastic about the project, business circumstances change, or external events compel a change in corporate culture. Initial receptivity to your proposal—team building, technology, change management, diversity, or organizational development—may evaporate. At other times, you may be brought in to serve as a wedge between differing management positions or to comply with a regulatory requirement. Examples include comprehensive safety or environmental programs, diversity initiatives, and sexual harassment prevention programs. If management decision makers are philosophically opposed to your recommendations, you may confront considerable hostility. In still other instances, you may be retained solely to satisfy a perceived internal political issue, and then meet resistance to your substantive recommendations.

Finally, management may be defiant when faced with advice reflecting its ineffective—or unlawful—business and/or employment practices. The practical ramifications of such defiance range from frustration, to projects canceled midstream, to inability to collect earned fees. More serious repercussions can occur when failure to follow your advice results in penalties or genuine legal risks.

Sadly, the same client that refuses to take appropriate direction is usually the first to attempt to shift the blame to you for a later penalty or liability. The claim will often be your alleged failure to provide accurate, timely, or appropriate advice. Yet, like most consultants, you will be reluctant to get "heavy-handed" with a client with which you wish to maintain a positive future relationship. What do you do?

Some general guidelines provide an approach to handling these delicate situations tactfully, while still adequately protecting your own legal position. First, make every reasonable effort to provide guidance on why the client should accept your advice. Be realistic and unambiguous about potential adverse consequences of the client's current practices. Provide backup support for your positions, through appropriate client data, articles, and other resource materials.

Be flexible and creative in considering compromise positions. But if the bottom line is a legal or regulatory risk to your client, be professional and forthright. If you fail to advise the client of all relevant ramifications, you may be faced with a claim that you didn't provide complete contextual advice. Carefully avoid giving "legal" advice.

You may wish to provide a written explanation of the potential consequences to the client's business interests. Remember, however, that all your written communications with the client may be "discovered" by adverse parties in subsequent litigation unless you have been retained by their legal counsel to provide confidential communications in anticipation of specific litigation. (See Chapters 1, p. 32, and 20, pp. 421–425 and 426–428, for explanations of the civil discovery process in litigation.) If you choose to provide a verbal explanation to the client, take accurate notes of your conversation and then memorialize what occurred as quickly as possible. Make detailed, legible, and accurate records of all conversations. Keep logs of your telephone calls, including any phone bills that will substantiate the date and length of time you spoke with the client (assuming you placed the call).

It is unwise to tape-record such communications, for several reasons. First, the tape itself will be subject to disclosure through discovery, just as documents are. Heated discussions may come back to haunt both you and the client if the tape is played by an adversary or by the client in a subsequent fee dispute. Second, in some states tape-recording a telephone conversation without the express permission of the other party is a crime. Third, even when you get the client's permission to record, you are creating a more adversarial setting, which is typically not constructive. Your notes should be sufficient to document the content and timing of the contacts.

Avoid express or implied threats to withdraw from the project. When some of the client's representatives are hostile, you may simply reinforce their position. Then, if the adverse consequences do occur, you will appear to have abandoned the client without adequate advice. Make every effort to provide reasoned information, and ask to present your recommendations to a larger group of managers, or to an executive committee, when appropriate.

If you are discharged, provide a final written report summarizing the areas of disagreement and specifying the nature of your advice; but again, remember that you or your client may be compelled to produce the report later in litigation, even with a third party.

Don't hesitate to send a final billing for your earned fees. If your contractual agreement does not specify a protocol for premature termination, bill your client for reasonable fees and expenses earned to the date of termination.

When you anticipate a fee dispute, keep your correspondence on this issue separate from communications about the advice that the client is rejecting. This may help you in later litigation over the quality and timing of your advice, and minimize the potential that jurors (who are, after all, Monday morning quarterbacks) will perceive your warnings to the client as a method to coerce payment of your fee.

Avoid breaching the confidentiality of these discussions, even when you have no specific confidentiality agreement. It is counterproductive to discuss your disputes with the client's employees, and you may inadvertently trigger litigation into which you are later drawn as an adverse witness.

Finally, keep complete documentation. Maintain copies of all written communications, including drafts, notes, e-mail, and other documentation that may assist you in reconstructing the content and timing of your communications on the subject of the advice. Further information on documentation and record keeping is given in Chapters 16, pp. 344–348, and 20, pp. 419–426 and 429–430.

What to Do When Your Consulting Work Lands Your Client in Court

Despite your best efforts to keep yourself and your client out of legal hot water, your client may be sued as a result of your work. This happens most often with negligently designed or discriminatory training. If a lawsuit arises, you may be called as a fact witness (as distinguished from an expert witness) to testify under oath about your involvement in the work and your communications with your client.

Prepare your documentation throughout the project as if you will be questioned about it years later. Avoid all but the most common abbreviations. Make sure your handwritten notes are complete and legible. Always date your documentation with the month, day, and year. Even though you may know when you make the entry that it is January 10, 1998, you may not be sure of that if you are questioned at trial in the year 2002 (an entirely realistic time frame in most states).

Keep your documentation simple and objective. When you must use subjective criteria (other than test scores) to evaluate trainee performance, avoid such relative terms as frequent, excessive, too many, or too few. Stick to the objective facts: "six times out of ten," or "30 percent of the affected employees."

When giving testimony under oath about your documentation, don't speculate. If you cannot remember, and you cannot reconstruct events from other documentation, don't be afraid to respond truthfully with "I don't know." If the answer is yes or no, provide it without further explanation, until asked. Silence is far better than being confronted with inconsistencies. Stick to your personal knowledge. Don't guess, "interpret," or "sanitize" what may have occurred. If you cannot remember, and cannot refresh your memory from documentation you created or are personally familiar with, just say so.

If you have any question about your own legal rights, consult independent counsel. Although it is in your client's interest—and yours as well—to cooperate with the lawyers, it is prudent to be sure that there is no actual or potential conflict of interest before you have any detailed discussion. A conflict can occur if your interests are potentially adverse to those of your client, either because the mutual opponent will later make claims against both of you or because a probable claim for indemnity will arise between you and the client. (See Chapter 16, pp. 331–332.) Although it is generally valuable to put forth a cohesive defense to a mutual adversary, you should be aware of any potential for adverse positions. Undoubtedly, the client's attorneys will consider the same issues prior to any detailed discussions and may delay meeting with you until you are properly represented.

Remember that unless you retain counsel jointly with your client, your communications with your client's counsel are *not* protected by attorney-client privilege—except when you were originally retained to provide consulting services in anticipation of litigation. (See Chapter 16, pp. 345 and 347.) Thus, always consult your own attorney to obtain advice on how to proceed.

Consultant to the Rescue— When You Can Help Your Client as Expert Witness: Guidelines for Preparation

In injury cases involving claims of inadequate hazard communication or negligent supervision of the training facility, the parties frequently turn to expert witnesses who can address the clarity of warnings and effectiveness of the instruction. Likewise, when employees claim discrimination, experts frequently assess the facts and then testify to the reasonableness of the employer's personnel policies. For a complete discussion of factual and legal proof required in such cases, see Chapters 6, pp. 122–141, and 7, pp. 158–163 and 174–182.

Experts may serve critical roles in both the pretrial and trial phases of an injury or discrimination lawsuit. In the pretrial phase, experts are particularly helpful in identifying the employer's required duties and assessing its compliance. The expert can determine and testify about what standard of care applied. An expert with direct, hands-on experience in the particular industry is uniquely positioned to provide credible testimony regarding the client's conduct, policy development or enforcement, and response to workplace situations.

Who is better suited than a consultant with the same or equivalent experience? As an independent expert with appropriate experience, you can review the documentary records, assess the relevant underlying activities, and reach a conclusion concerning the issues in the litigation. The best experts are people who are full-time practitioners in the relevant field. As witnesses, practitioners are especially convincing when they testify about their own observations and experience.

For example, a consultant who designed and administered particular test instruments is uniquely suited to testify in an action involving allegations of discrimination in testing. Likewise, a diversity consultant may be in the best position to testify to the comprehensive steps that the client took to develop an effective—and legally compliant—diversity initiative. So too, a consultant who develops workplace security, violence prevention, and crisis management plans may be an extremely credible witness in describing how the client's proactive plan put the organization in the best position to minimize the pain and disruption of a violent episode and its aftermath. See Chapter 11, pp. 240–247.

During the trial phase, experts move beyond their roles as advisers and educators. They become responsible for interpreting and clarifying technical information and for providing opinions on central issues of liability. The weight that the jury or judge gives to an expert's testimony often hinges on that expert's credentials. Many injury lawsuits, particularly those arising from exposure to chemicals, dangerous conditions, or hazardous activities, become literally a battle of the experts. Thus, in addition to objective qualifications such as degrees, licenses, relevant publications, and eminent professional accomplishments, the expert's direct experience in a comparable work environment will often affect credibility. The value of an independent expert is precisely that the witness serves as a neutral evaluator of how trainers or their organizations performed. Most consultants who serve as experts are professionals from the same or similar industries, but they are neither employed by a party to the lawsuit nor have a direct stake in its outcome.

As long as your own work will not be the source of legal challenge or factual dispute in the lawsuit, your client may benefit significantly from your services as an expert. Although you may not be perceived as completely independent, since you will have received compensation or had an ongoing business relationship, your *objective testimony* about the steps your client took to maintain a safe and effective work environment may be persuasive. Serving as an expert witness can be a valuable and substantively challenging exercise. Additional benefits include enhanced professional recognition and, of course, financial compensation.

Hold-Harmless Agreements Between Consultant and Client: What Works and What Doesn't

Hold-harmless agreements are essentially contractual arrangements in which a party passes its liability for an accident or injury off to another responsible party. Typical language provides:

> [Consultant] agrees to indemnify and hold harmless [client] from any and all claims, liabilities, judgments, expenses, and or other damages of any kind that may arise out of [description of the consulting project], and that are due to the negligence or breach of duty of [client and its representatives].

Most states will uphold a hold-harmless or indemnification agreement if it is the product of mutual consent and bargained-for exchange. (See the discussion in Chapters 15, pp. 311–314, and 16, pp. 331–333.) The party obtaining the hold-harmless arrangement is indemnified for liabilities that arise vicariously—that is, not through his or her own negligent acts. Most liabilities for accidents arising out of programs that an employer mandates or sponsors are at least vicarious, with additional liabilities for independent negligent acts by its employees. (See Chapters 3, pp. 70–78, and 4, pp. 93–100.)

Hold-harmless agreements are useful as a starting point for allocating responsibilities. But keep in mind that, in all states, a party cannot absolve itself from its *own* independent negligence through a hold-harmless agreement.

PART 4

Copyright Issues: What Every Trainer, Speaker, and Consultant Must Know

18

The 10 Most Common Copyright Problems and How to Solve Them

Whether through handouts, audiovisual aids, multimedia presentations, videos, or sound recordings, information and education professionals use a variety of formats to express ideas and exchange information. Those who are most successful draw upon a wide variety of materials to research, design, and deliver effective presentations. Presenters—stand-up trainers and speakers—inform, instruct, persuade, and entertain. Consultants and trainers also develop tools for skill development. Instructional designers create processes, develop instructional technologies, and package materials for use in training and as ongoing job aids.

Whether you are a speaker, consultant, or trainer, your work inherently involves the design, distribution, and display of information. Much of the content comes from researching materials developed, published, and created by other people. When those materials are copyrighted, you must obtain written permission or a license agreement to use or adapt the materials. Without such authorization, the risk of copyright violation is significant. The unauthorized use of copyrighted material gives rise to a claim for infringement. The remedies in this context may also be civil or criminal.

A copyright is a legal device to provide the creator of a work that conveys information or ideas with the right to control how the work is used. The U.S. Copyright Act of 1976 grants authors a wide range of intangible, exclusive rights over their work. These rights include:

- *Reproduction right*—the right to make copies of a protected work
- *Distribution right*—the right to sell or otherwise distribute the work publicly or privately
- *Right to create derivative work*—the right to prepare new work based on the protected work or to create adaptations of the original or derivative work
- *Display right*—the right to display the work in public
- *Public performance right*—the right to perform, act, or recite the work before a public audience

You must obtain written permission to use a copyrighted work when (1) you take an author's words or the particular sequence of words that comprise the author's expression, (2) the work is not in the "public domain," and (3) the intended use goes beyond the bounds of "fair use." Under the fair use privilege, you are permitted to make *limited use* of another author's work without asking for written permission. All authors and other copyright holders are deemed to give their automatic consent to the fair use of their work by others, so long as proper acknowledgment is given and a full citation to the copyrighted material is set forth.

Copyright violations occur with any unauthorized use of written, sound-recorded, videotaped, or electronically stored materials without the express permission of the copyright holder. When the materials have been registered with the U.S. Copyright Office, the copyright holder may bring an infringement action against unauthorized users. Penalties for copyright infringement can be severe, including a mandatory court order to the infringer to immediately stop using, publishing, selling, or displaying the copyrighted materials, along with actual damages or special statutory damages under the Copyright Act.

Trainers, speakers, and consultants frequently face the following problems when using the work of others and protecting their own creative expressions.

1. Copying passages, sequences of words, or other creative expressions without express permission of the copyright holder

The Copyright Act gives the copyright holder the exclusive right to reproduce, and to authorize others to reproduce, the copyrighted work.

It is the author's creative expression that is protected, rather than the ideas and facts encompassed in the expression. The owner secures a copyright from the moment the work is fixed in tangible form, regardless of whether the work is officially published and independent of registration with the U.S. Copyright Office. Thus, even unpublished handout materials are subject to protection. The copyright owner secures additional rights to pursue damages in an infringement action by officially registering the work.

The Copyright Act defines a copy as any material object "in which a work is fixed by any method now known or later developed, and from which the work can be perceived, reproduced, or otherwise communicated, either directly or with the aid of a machine or device." This definition includes text incorporated into a larger document—such as a training manual—as well as photocopies of entire magazine articles or book chapters. A CD-ROM containing copyrighted text or pictures stored in digital form is also considered a copy.

Even when you give credit through quotations, citations, and/or direct attribution, if you fail to obtain permission to reprint copyrighted text that exceeds the bounds of fair use, you violate the law. Likewise, the copyright owner retains the exclusive right to create derivative works and to distribute the work in any form, including sale, lease, lending, or display. Any encroachment on these exclusive rights, without express permission of the copyright holder, may give rise to infringement penalties.

To avoid copyright violations, you should carefully observe all formalities for obtaining permission to use protected materials. There are four specific steps:

- While researching and preparing the materials, keep careful records of the source, as well as complete identification of the copyright holder.

- Seek permission of the copyright holder to copy, reprint, incorporate, or compile any portion of the protected work into your own training materials.

- Once you obtain permission, include a statement that the work is "reprinted with the express permission of the copyright holder" on all copies you make.

- If you can't locate the copyright holder, or are expressly denied permission to use the materials, don't use any more than a citation to the original source.

Detailed guidelines for quoting lawfully, securing permission, and using copyrighted materials are provided in Chapter 19, pp. 387–388, 393, and 400–403.

2. Using training instruments or materials, including questionnaires, exercises, games, tests, checklists, forms, or related instructional aids, without permission or a license

All tangible training tools, including those in electronic format, are subject to protection under the Copyright Act. You can step over the legal line by assuming that materials not derived directly from published books or magazines are freely usable. Don't assume that the fair use doctrine will shield you from copyright infringement simply because you use the material for educational purposes. Although fair use is the primary exception to the author's exclusive right of reproduction, it applies only in narrowly defined circumstances. In most situations involving internal corporate training or commercially presented workshops, the fair use doctrine doesn't apply. The fair use doctrine is also thoroughly addressed in Chapter 19, pp. 378–380.

Another misconception is that an exercise, game, role play, case study, or simulation created by another person may be used freely, so long as tangible copies are not distributed. So, instead of making copies, misinformed trainers display the instrument on overhead transparencies, post it on the wall, or read the instructions verbally to the group. All these activities violate the copyright holder's exclusive rights to display, use, and perform protected work. Performance includes reciting directions, and the copyright holder has exclusive performance rights. The mere absence of additional copies is not controlling.

Remember that the protected work need not be formally registered or even published, so long as it meets the requirements of creative expression in tangible form. Even handwritten instructions and rules for a creative simulation or game are entitled to protection when they contain a copyright notice as simple as "copyright © 1998 Jane Author. All rights reserved." Trainers who usurp or adapt these tools violate copyright law.

Owners of written materials like books and articles typically grant permission to reproduce all or part of their work in exchange for full citation and reference to their express authorization. In contrast, with instruments, games, or other training tools integral to interactive presentations, copyright holders frequently request a license agreement for multiple uses. The terms are subject to negotiation at the time permission is granted, and the licensee must keep records of all uses and provide an accounting to the owner when requested.

Whenever you want to use, explain, publicly perform, or otherwise employ a training instrument during any portion of your program, follow the four steps listed above to obtain express permission. In addition, be prepared to sign and then honor the terms of any license agreement you negotiate. Failure to do so gives rise to both copyright infringement actions and lawsuits for breach of contract under state laws. Practical approaches to crediting and obtaining permission are provided in Chapter 19, pp. 387–388 and 400–403.

3. Using music, sound recordings, or videos during a presentation without permission or a license

Trainers and speakers frequently use music, videos, and multimedia to enhance their presentations. These works are subject to copyright protection, and unauthorized use of protected materials infringes the performance and display rights of the owner. The Copyright Act defines performance to include the exclusive right to recite, render, play, dance, or act, either directly or by means of any device or process. Performance may be either a live staging or a reenactment by means of a device or process such as videotape, teleconference equipment, or other methods for amplifying sounds or visual images. H.R. Report No. 1476 provides the specific example of using a CD player and an amplifier to play a song recorded on a compact disc at a seminar or conference.[1]

In authorizing the use of audiotapes, video productions, or CD versions of training vignettes, copyright owners frequently request payment of a license fee. Arrangements vary from a one-time fixed fee to a per-performance charge or per-copy calculation for multiple or repeated uses. The terms and conditions of license fees are subject to the agreement of the parties.

Sound recordings frequently have multiple potential copyright holders, as explained in Chapter 13, pp. 273–276. Copyright protection for musical works and sound recordings generally extends to the composer, lyricist, and performers, as well as to the producer or recorder—that is, the person responsible for capturing, editing, and processing the sounds to make the final recording.

Copyright protection for videotaped training vignettes may be secured individually by all contributors, including the scriptwriter, storyboard editor, actors, musicians, videographer, and producer. Fortunately, with most commercially available productions, the performers and technicians are paid for their work, and thereby relinquish their rights through a work-for-hire arrangement. In these situations, the products are also invariably registered with the U.S. Copyright Office, and the owner sells the products with express license documents. Accordingly, locating the owner and obtaining authorization for use is rarely difficult. Chapter 19, pp. 388–393, addresses the availability and limitations of work-for-hire arrangements.

If you elect to use protected material, it is your responsibility to identify the copyright owner or licensor and obtain express permission to use the materials, once or many times. In the absence of a single registered owner or clear-cut evidence that one or more contributors to a finished product were compensated as a work-for-hire, the permission of only one party is insufficient to shield you from infringement claims by joint copyright holders.

4. Using photographs, cartoons, visual aids, animation, or other graphic materials without authorization

The use of cartoons, comic strips, and other graphics clipped from a magazine or newspaper and displayed via overhead projector is one of the most common sources of copyright infringement by trainers, speakers, and consultants. (See Chapter 13, pp. 276–279, and p. 386 of this chapter.) Still images—such as photographs, cartoon strips, pictures, calendars, posters, greeting cards, drawings, and designs—are subject to copyright protection. Use of such materials without authorization—express written permission or license agreement—subjects the user and the user's organization to liability for infringement.

Materials that qualify for copyright protection as "pictorial, graphic, and sculptural works" are frequently incorporated into the overall presentations of speakers and trainers. Copyright Office Circular 40, "Copyright Registration for Works of the Visual Arts 2" (1990), provides these examples: cartoons, comic strips, games, puzzles, greeting cards, holograms, computer and laser artwork, logo artwork, drawings, paintings, print advertisements, reproductions, technical drawings, and diagrams.

The holder of the copyright on a comic strip may be the cartoonist or the newspaper in which it was published, or both. Syndicated cartoonists frequently retain their own rights, and are vigilant about ensuring that their work is not infringed. The work is protected whether or not it is formally registered with the U.S. Copyright Office.

Many creators of comic strips grant permission for limited use of their work for a small fee, or a donation to a designated charity. However, political cartoonists and others with a point of view or specific audience are vigilant about approving the context in which their work is displayed. For example, I once sought permission from the creator of a long-running and popular comic strip to use his work in a management training program on preventing wrongful termination in employment. The creator granted permission on two conditions: first, that the particular cartoon not be used to denigrate workers' rights; and second, that I make a modest donation to a particular charity. In these situations, you should be prepared to honor your commitments and provide appropriate documentation, if requested.

Once you have contacted the copyright holder and agreed upon the terms of use, confirm the agreement in writing and rigorously comply.

Good-faith adherence to the specified conditions ensures compliance with the law, maintains positive relations with the copyright holder, and provides the best opportunity for obtaining future permission for the same or other work.

Photographs are also copyrightable in many forms, including prints, blowups, negatives, film strips, slides, overhead transparencies, and machine-readable digital data. In *Playboy Enterprises, Inc. v. Frena,*[2] for example, the court held that making digitized versions of copyrighted photographs available on a computer bulletin board infringed the copyright owner's rights of distribution and public display. See the discussion in Chapter 13, pp. 278–279.

5. Using multimedia materials or creative expressions contained in electronic documents, portions of databases, and other on-line information or materials without permission

Until recently, most trainers' violations of the Copyright Act involved copying or incorporating the protected work of another person into their own written training materials. With the expanding use of technology for interactive training, new forms of copyright violations have arisen.

Multimedia products are being used increasingly for training purposes. They include on-line interactive modules and presentation displays. The material may include text, graphics, animation, sound, music, video, and scanned images drawn from still photographs. As such, all the underlying works contained in a multimedia product are subject to copyright protection. Each copyright holder must be separately contacted and permission sought.

Just as commercial distributors of training videos acquire the exclusive rights to license their product (by obtaining works-for-hire and permissions of underlying creators), so do vendors who market multimedia products for training. Accordingly, purchase of CD-ROM or other interactive materials for instruction and testing—and adherence to the license agreement—will prevent copyright violations.

Remember that in the absence of a clearly defined licensor, it is your burden to identify all copyright holders and obtain their individual authorizations to use any portion of their protected works. Also, in situations where you intend to make a public performance—such as showing a multimedia work to inform your managers, train your trainers, or prepare a contract facilitator—you must be sure that you are not in violation of the license agreement. Likewise, making a multimedia work available to the public "on demand" via the Internet (or a company intranet or local area network) may be a public performance, and must comply with your license agreement.

6. Copying, using, or displaying software programs in violation of an existing license agreement and without express permission of the copyright holder

You may infringe existing copyrights by downloading and making use of protected intellectual property via the Internet and other public bulletin boards. When your organization selects software for business use, including training, you will typically be required to comply with a license agreement. The agreement provides specifics on the number of copies, the authorized computers, and the limitations on installation beyond the scope of the license. Your company is the licensee of the software itself, and application is usually limited to a specified number of computers.

Software licenses generally provide for limited reproductions of computer software for backup or archival copies, made by owners or licensees of the computer programs. Backups are permitted under Section 117 of the Copyright Act, on the recognition that they are an essential aspect of full use of the program.

The most frequent violation involves copying the software onto laptop or home computers, or displaying the software for training in excess of what the license permits. A secondary, recurrent source of infringement arises when licensees—and their trainers and instructional designers—copy input screens, templates, and help screens from the user manuals for use in internal training programs.

Reproduction of instructional graphics does not come within the framework of most software licenses, particularly when you are developing a separate manual from the user's guide that accompanies the software. You must obtain permission to incorporate these graphic materials into your manual. Once you have received authorization to use the material, the new manual you create may be separately copyrighted. By proceeding without gaining permission to use copyrighted materials incorporated into your product, you jeopardize the validity of your own copyright. These issues are fully addressed in Chapter 19, pp. 393–403.

7. Reciting the work of a copyright holder, including written expressions, word sequences, passages, or creative expressions, without express permission or a license agreement from the copyright holder

If you are a presenter or stand-up trainer, you can violate copyright law simply by reading aloud or reciting from memory passages of a protected work. The most frequent violations are readings of poems and lengthy excerpts from news articles. For example, every Associated Press story, in print media and on-line, carries a copyright notice. Even when you provide full attribution and the recitation is clearly a verbatim quote, you implicate the owner's exclusive performance rights.

Trainers and presenters may take comfort in the fact that the costs involved in bringing an infringement action in federal court discourage a lawsuit for a single or sporadic episode. For instance, if you read from a news account of something very timely in a presentation, you are unlikely to gain the attention much less the ire of most news organizations. Likewise, if you quote a short poem in an invocation to a meeting or dinner, the copyright holder is unlikely ever to find out. However, if the copyright holder does learn of your infringement, you can expect to receive some contact, because the owner will not want to waive rights by failing to assert ownership once he or she knows of an unauthorized use. The copyright holder may elect to send a simple letter requesting that you cease future recitation.

Conversely, if you regularly recite passages from literature, meaningful poems, or relevant published materials as part of a paid presentation without permission, you risk an infringement action. This is so whether or not you provide full attribution. The holder of the copyright may learn of your unauthorized use when members of your audience seek the creator out for permission to quote from the work in other contexts. Thus, your most prudent course of action is to obtain permission from the creator of the work before incorporating it into a larger presentation. Follow the steps outlined above and the detailed guidelines set forth in Chapters 13, pp. 276–279, and 19, pp. 400–403.

Permission is especially important if you develop and market products based upon your presentations. Any audiotape or videotape of a presentation that includes unauthorized materials puts at risk your own copyright for the product. This is discussed thoroughly in Chapter 13, pp. 273–279.

8. Faxing, digital copying, or electronic transmissions of copyrighted materials without express permission of the copyright holder

You can also violate the Copyright Act through fax or on-line transmissions of copyrighted materials, even when such transmission is not part of a presentation. These violations frequently occur in the context of collaborative work on research projects and course development. Direct copying of materials from the Internet, downloading files, and attaching those files to other documents is a common source of copyright infringement. Express permission of the copyright holder is required.

9. Infringement through unauthorized use or violation of an existing license agreement

Infringement occurs in two contexts: use without any authorization at all, and use that exceeds the bounds of the permission granted. The latter is often considered both infringement and breach of contract. A license agreement from a copyright owner is a contract. As such, it is subject to the same enforcement rights as any other commercial agreement. Under state laws, a civil lawsuit for breach of contract may include a wide range of damages. These claims may be raised concurrently in an infringement action in a federal or state trial court.

Much of the litigation for violation of a license agreement is brought against software licensees who make additional unauthorized copies of the software or the program documentation and user's manual. The most common violation seems to be installing software applications on additional computers, or making licensed software available to friends and even clients via on-line downloading. Software makers are vigilant about enforcing their license agreements, both because unauthorized use strikes at the core of their business and because they risk waiving their rights when they knowingly fail to enforce license agreements effectively.

More significantly, the license agreement will reflect on its face the identity of the copyright owner and the limitations of the license. Once you agree to the terms, it will be very difficult to persuade the owner— or a judge—that your unauthorized or excessive use was inadvertent. The Copyright Act provides for significant damages in an infringement action where the copyright owner establishes a willful violation of one or more exclusive ownership rights.

There are a number of penalties for copyright infringement. These include:

- *Criminal sanctions.* Willful copyright infringement is a federal crime. The U.S. Attorney General has the power to prosecute infringers. A person convicted of infringement can be required to pay fines ranging from $10,000 to $50,000 and may be imprisoned for up to two years for a second offense.

- *Criminal restitution.* A convicted infringer may be ordered by a federal court to pay a copyright owner restitution (a form of compensation) to reinstate what the owner lost.

- *Civil penalties.* The holder of the copyright can file his or her own action for damages and an order to cease further unauthorized use of the copyrighted material for commercial or private gain. The lawsuit must be brought by the copyright owner and *must be filed within three years after the owner should reasonably have discovered the infringing act.*

There are several remedies available to the owner who files a copyright infringement lawsuit.

- *Injunctive relief.* An injunction is a court order instructing the infringer to immediately cease the infringing activity. As plaintiff, the copyright owner can often obtain a "temporary restraining order" early in the case to stop the infringing activity while awaiting a trial on the factual issues. Once a trial is held, the court may order a permanent injunction precluding all unauthorized use. However, in the interim (it can be months or even years before a trial is held) you avoid further damages from unauthorized use. Continued use of the materials in violation of a valid court order is punishable by contempt proceedings, including heavy fines and in extreme cases incarceration.

- *Actual damages.* Damages may include the infringer's profits from the unauthorized use. There are also statutory damages set by the copyright law. These are awarded at the judge's discretion and do not require the plaintiff to prove a loss in any specific amount. Absent a finding that the infringer acted willfully or innocently, damages of between $500 and $20,000 may be assessed for all infringements of a single work by a single infringer. With a finding of innocent use, the assessment may be as little as $200. However, if a valid copyright notice is on the work, the infringer cannot support a claim of innocent use. With a finding of willful infringement (where the user knew that he or she had no legal right to use the work), statutory damages may be up to $100,000.

- *Statutory damages.* Under the Copyright Act special damages are available only for work registered with the U.S. Copyright Office prior to the infringement.

- *Other relief.* Other relief may include an order for destruction of all copies of the infringing work as well as attorneys' fees and costs of bringing the lawsuit.

10. Failing to maintain appropriate documentation of license agreements, permission requests, and authorizations

If you find yourself a defendant in an infringement action, your biggest source of frustration may be lack of documentation. Even when the facts would support your position, your success may be hampered by the absence of evidence demonstrating that you sought and/or obtained permission or appropriately concluded that the material in question was subject to fair use or in the public domain.

Documentation is a written record of an event, discussion, or observation by one or more participants. Any written information, whether formally or informally generated, can be considered documentary evidence if it is pertinent to a legal action or a regulatory proceeding. Included here are correspondence, memos, telephone messages, and handwritten notes, as well as the more formal documentation embodied in contracts and license agreements.

Very often, witnesses have substantially different recollections about the same events. This is usually the result of frail human memory or honest misrecall. However, eager witnesses may attempt to testify about personal memory when in fact they did not actually observe or participate in the events. Sometimes, witnesses may even be untruthful.

When recollections vary, the trier of fact must determine whom to believe. This is the crucial issue of *credibility*. Many times, witnesses whose memory is imprecise can still be very credible, *if their memory is refreshed by reviewing documents that they prepared closer to the time of the original events.*

In a copyright infringement action, the court must determine several key elements that are best proved—or disproved—by a written chronicle of events. These factors include:

- When was a copyright first obtained? Is there an effective copyright notice?
- Was the copyright properly registered, and if so when?
- Was permission to use the material sought from the copyright holder? Are there letters, phone records, or other evidence of attempts to contact the copyright holder?
- Was permission granted or denied? If permission was denied, is there a written statement to that effect? Was it properly mailed or transmitted?
- If permission was granted, were there limiting terms and conditions (e.g., number of copies, length of time, scope of content to be copied, verifying records to be maintained)?
- Was there a license agreement? What were the negotiated terms? Did the subsequent use exceed the license agreement?

These and other questions will focus the court's attention on the basis for the parties' positions in an infringement action. The case may turn on the presence or absence of clear, concise, and relevant documents. Documentation is particularly important in negotiating a license agreement, since the exchange of correspondence and the ultimate agreement should reflect the scope and limitations established for use of the copyrighted materials as well as the license fees involved. In the event of an infringement or violation of the license agreement, the documentation will serve as the best source for the court to determine the intent of the parties, and whether any violation was inadvertent or willful.

The importance of maintaining effective documentation and record retention procedures is discussed fully in Chapter 20.

References

1. H.R. Report No. 1476, 94th Cong. 2d Sess., pp. 63–64 (1976); reprinted in 1976 U.S.C.C.A.N. 5659, 5677.

2. *Playboy Enterprises, Inc. v. Frena,* 839 F.Supp. 1552 (M.D.Fla. 1993).

19
Respecting the Rights of Others and Protecting Your Own

Federal copyright law is premised on the principle that creativity, knowledge, dissemination, and artistic products should be encouraged as a matter of public policy. If unrestricted copying is permitted, authors will not write, musicians and artists will not create, knowledge will be impeded, and undesirable economic results will follow. Thus, the focus of the law is on the public benefits derived from creative and educational/informational labor. Compensation to the copyright owner is a secondary public policy.

Prior to 1976 there was a dual system of copyright, with federal law protecting published works and state common law protecting unpublished materials. Now, the Copyright Act preempts all common law protections. (Federal preemption of state laws is discussed in Chapter 1, pp. 30–31.) All works fixed in a tangible medium of expression—books, unpublished manuscripts, memoranda, notes, letters, diaries, booklets, training materials, music, art, poetry, audiovisual images, sound recordings, and even electronic media—are protected exclusively under the Copyright Act from the moment of creation. Actual "publication" is not required.

Automatic copyright protection is extended for the life of the author plus 50 years. An alternate term of 75 years from the date of publication or 100 years from creation (whichever is less) is given to anonymous and pseudonymous works and works made for hire.

Photocopied and Reproducible Publications: Know the Limits!

Before reproducing, distributing, or using any copyrighted material in training, consulting projects, or speeches, you should first obtain specific authorization from the person or organization holding the rights to the material. Copyrighted material includes the following categories:

- Literary works
- Musical works, including any accompanying words
- Dramatic works, including any accompanying music
- Pantomimes and choreographic works
- Pictorial, graphic, and sculptural works
- Videos, motion pictures, and other audiovisual works
- Sound recordings
- Multimedia presentations that combine graphic, video, and musical works

A work must be original to be copyrightable. The copyright applies to the form of expression rather than to the subject matter of the publication. Ideas are not protectable—no matter how creative or original—but only the sequence of words used to express the ideas. Likewise facts are not protectable—no matter how creatively researched—but only the words used in tangible form to explain the facts. The facts themselves are in the public domain, freely available to everyone.

The five exclusive rights of copyright holders are addressed in Chapter 18, pp. 364–371. In the context of work that may be photocopied or otherwise duplicated, the first three rights (reproduction, adaptation, and distribution) are at issue.

Reproduction Rights

Rights.   To reproduce a work is to fix it in a tangible and relatively permanent form in a material object. Reproduction is to be distinguished from the broader concept of copying.

Limits. There are five limitations on the copyright holder's exclusive right to reproduce, several of which affect training.

- Librarians and their staffs may make photocopies of books and journals under the authority of Section 108 of the act, without obtaining permission or paying a fee.

- Reproduction rights for sound recordings are limited to rerecording; making a sound-alike recording is permitted under the authority of Section 114 of the act.

- Ephemeral recordings, which are supposed to exist only temporarily, may be made without permission under the authority of Section 112 of the act.

- Reproductions of computer software for backup or archival copies, made by owners or licensees of the computer programs, are permitted under Section 117 of the act, based on the recognition that this is an essential aspect of full use of the program.

- The reproduction is a "fair use" of the material pursuant to Section 113 of the act. Fair use extends to quotes or reproductions of portions of copyrighted works for news commentaries, news reports, criticism, or other fair use.

Under the fair use doctrine, you may make limited use of a prior author's work without seeking permission. Fair use privileges are explained in the U.S. Copyright Act, Section 107, as follows:

> The fair use of a copyrighted work. . . . for purposes such as criticism, comment, news reporting, teaching . . . scholarship or research, is not an infringement of copyright. In determining whether the use made of a work in any particular case is a fair use the factors to be considered . . . include:
>
> (1) the purpose and character of the use, including whether such use is of a commercial nature or is for nonprofit educational purposes;
> (2) the nature of the copyrighted work;
> (3) the amount and substantiality of the portion used in relation to the copyrighted work as a whole; and
> (4) the effect of the use upon the potential market for, or value of, the copyrighted work.

On the first issue—the purpose and character of the use—commercialism is a key factor. Government employers, educational institutions, and nonprofit associations are granted fair use privileges more often than speakers or consultants who prepare training materials as part of a business for profit.

On balance, commercialism is less important when a work has undergone a transformation sufficient to infuse the subsequent publication with new, fresh meaning or perspective. The notion of transformation furthers the goal of copyright laws to promote human knowledge. The U.S. Supreme Court concluded that "such works...lie at the heart of the fair use doctrine's guarantee of a breathing space within the confines of copyright."[1] The Supreme Court also established that when the new work "adds something new, with a further purpose or different character, altering the first with new expression, meaning, or message," the work is a transformation that falls within the fair use exception to a copyright violation.[2]

When the intended use is for commercial purposes, the theory of most courts is that the author can afford to pay for permission to use another person's protected expression. Payment is customarily accomplished through a license agreement.

Classroom instruction has also been found to be a fair use, since teaching furthers the knowledge-enriching goals of the copyright laws. News media reporting services and nonprofit educational institutions are the most common beneficiaries.

You violate the law when you photocopy copyrighted materials, even for personal use. Individual copying of a single article from a magazine or periodical for personal use (which is not part of a business activity) has in most instances been deemed a fair use. Making multiple copies of any document, or copying entire books or other works, is not a fair use.

You cannot lawfully make multiple copies at your own photocopy machine, and you will probably find that commercial services will refuse to do so without a signed letter from the copyright holder granting you express permission. A group of major publishers obtained a $510,000 judgment against one duplicating business for copying excerpts from books without permission, compiling them into "course packets," and then selling them to college students.[3]

When you are researching your training materials, can you photocopy technical materials for your own use, even when the underlying purpose is your job (a commercial purpose)? Most courts have said yes, when it is too difficult or time-consuming to obtain permission from the copyright holder, and you are not incorporating protected expression from these materials into your own work product.

A word of caution. Many organizations publish informative newsletters on up-to-date issues affecting training, human resources management, and technical information relevant to your work and your training. Entire departments may benefit from reading the information, yet your organization may have only one subscription. It is technically a violation of copyright laws to copy the newsletter for multiple readers internal to your organization, particularly since the very reason for copying is to avoid the extra costs of additional subscriptions. Human resources departments do it; training departments do it; even law firms do it. But it clearly violates the law.

One method you can use to provide access to all interested individuals is a "routing slip," attached to the front cover with the initials of everyone who may benefit from reading the contents. The last person is generally responsible for returning the original to a central location. Another approach is posting the newsletter on a widely accessible bulletin board. You can provide an opportunity for interested parties to sign for it, as they would a library book. One option that is *not* appropriate was recently tried by an enterprising staffer: quickly typing or scanning the contents of the newsletter onto the company e-mail system, and then sending it to coworkers. Ingenious, yes. Lawful, no. Both the e-mail transmission and any subsequent printed copies violate the copyright law, and are not a fair use.

When obtaining permission, always do the following:

1. Put your request in writing. Figure 19-1 includes two sample request letters for this purpose. Figure 19-2 provides a sample response.

2. Include a complete copy of the work or excerpts with your letter. File this material with the permission letter to capture complete evidence on what rights were requested, and granted.

3. Be as specific about your intended use as possible. If you will need both reproduction and public performance rights, so specify in the letter. If you will copy multiple times, or for multiple courses, advise the owner of the intended scope in your letter.

4. Keep complete and accurate records of each time you use the material pursuant to permission.

5. Place on every copy a notice that the material is reprinted with the express permission of the copyright holder.

Adaptation Rights

Rights. Adaptation is the preparation of derivative works to exploit markets other than the one in which the work was first published. The adaptation right is infringed when a third party makes an unauthorized derivative work by recasting, reforming, adapting, translating, or dramatizing the work.

Limits. Adaptation is authorized when a phonorecord license is exercised.

Figure 19-1 Sample Letters Requesting Permission to Use Copyright-Protected Materials.

April 10, 1997

Ms. Careful Litigant, President
XYZ Corporation
1000 Indemnity Lane
Courtville, USA

Re: Request to Reproduce Materials

Dear Ms. Litigant:

The Training Conference of the Century will be held in Hawaii on September 1–3, 1997. We request permission to reproduce for our opening session 600 copies of your 53-page handout entitled *How to Keep Your Company Out of Court*, dated April 1, 1996, presented at our last conference. We will, of course, provide the appropriate legend regarding your permission.

Thank you for your consideration.

Very truly yours,

John Doe
Trainers United Against Lawsuits

October 31, 1997

Mr. Tom Trainer
10 Main Street
Anytown, USA

Dear Mr. Trainer:

I request permission to include the following material in this and all subsequent editions of my new course, *How to Train Within the Law*, and in conjunction with the promotion of my workshops:

(Continued)

Author: Tom Trainer
Title of Book: The Pitfalls of the Legal System
Title of Chapter: Dealing With Lawyers: Your Opponent's and
                        Your Own
Copyright Date: January 1988
From Page: 185, line 1, beginning with the words "Lawyers
                        are trained to be . . ."
To Page: 197, line 10, ending with the words, "so it's best
                        to avoid them."

Unless you specify otherwise, credit acknowledgment will conform
to the standard order of author, title, copyright, publisher, place, and
date of publication. Please indicate agreement by signing and
returning this letter to my attention. In signing, you warrant that you
are the sole owner of the rights granted and that your material does
not infringe upon the copyright or other rights of anyone. If you do
not control these rights, I would appreciate your letting me know to
whom I should apply.

I will look forward to receiving your response.

Sincerely,

Florence Facilitator

When you copy and tab workshop materials into notebooks, you are
affecting reproduction rights. In other contexts, particularly with
technical materials, the materials may be summarized or translated.
This is an adaptation of the original. You cannot adapt without the
express consent of the copyright owner, unless your particular context
falls within the narrow confines of the fair use exception.

Distribution Rights

When you make multiple copies of a protected work, you may infringe
a copyright, whether or not you ever distribute the copies to anyone
else. Even a single copy displayed during a workshop, or posted in a
conspicuous place during training, is improper.

April 25, 1997

John Doe, Chairman
Training Conference of the Century
Trainers United Against Lawsuits
123 Main Street
Anytown, USA

Re: Permission to Photocopy Handout Materials

Dear Mr. Doe:

Copyright holder, XYZ Corporation, grants permission to reproduce the handout materials entitled *How to Keep Your Company Out of Court*, dated April 1, 1996, for the second annual Training Conference of the Century, in an amount up to 600 copies. Permission is granted solely for distribution to attendees at the conference.

Please provide the undersigned with a copy of the document you distribute and best wishes for another successful conference.

Very truly yours,

Careful Litigant
President, XYZ Corporation

Figure 19-2 Sample Written Authorization to Use Copyright-Protected Materials.

But most presenters who photocopy entire articles, passages, or training instruments—including checklists, diagrams, job aids, games, or interactive tools—do so in order to use them with groups of people. They make multiple copies (each copy is a separate infringement!) and distribute them to workshop participants. The distribution is yet another infringement—this time of the copyright owner's exclusive right to distribution.

Rights. The copyright holder has the right to control the first public distribution of the work and to transfer physical copies or sound recordings of the work.

Limits.   There are two basic limitations to the owner's exclusive right to distribute a copyrighted work:

- The first-sale doctrine limits the copyright owner's control over copies of the work to their first sale or transfer ["the owner of a particular copy or phonorecord of a work lawfully made, or any person authorized by such owner, is entitled without authority of the copyright owner to sell or otherwise dispose of the possession of *that copy* or *phonorecord*" Section 106(3)]. This limitation prevents the owner from restraining the free transfer of owned goods, such as books.

- Libraries have the right to lend books without permission of the copyright owner (of course, the borrowers infringe copyright by copying portions of the books).

Legal and Illegal Uses of Music, Videos, and Graphics: Know What to Use, How to Get Permission, and When to Avoid "Republication"

If you use music, videos, and multimedia in your presentations, you should be aware that these works are subject to copyright protection, and unauthorized use of protected materials infringes the performance and display rights of the owner.

Public Performance Rights

Rights.   Performance rights extend to literary, musical, dramatic, and choreographic works, pantomimes, and audiovisual works. Performance includes the right to play, dance, recite, act, or portray, either directly or through a device such as a tape recording. According to the Copyright Act, public performance takes place in a public setting, before a public group, where a "substantial number of persons outside of a normal circle of family and friends is gathered." The act expressly includes devices or processes for performance where the audience may receive the work in the same place or separate places and at the same time or separate times (thus, it includes videotape, videoconference, and the like).

Limits.   There are five major exceptions to the owner's exclusive performance rights:

- Under the "worthy performances" exception of Section 110(4) of the Copyright Act, nonprofit performances given by *live performers only* are exempted. These performances cannot be for a commercial purpose, either direct or indirect. No fees or compensation may be made to the performers (except salary), and no admission may be charged beyond meeting direct expenses.

- Educational performances of copyrighted works may be given by instructors or pupils in a face-to-face live teaching situation, so long as the performance takes place in a *nonprofit educational institution.*

- Instructional television and radio broadcasts are governed by Section 110(2) of the act, and are limited to nondramatic literary and musical works through performances transmitted to classrooms or other places normally devoted to instruction. The performance must be directly related to the systematic teaching activities.

- Religious services and fraternal organizations are permitted to perform nondramatic literary and musical works during a social function. These performances cannot be open to the public, and the profits must be charitable donations.

- Television and radio transmissions to the disabled are governed by Section 110(8) of the act. Transmission of performances of a nondramatic literary work designed for the sensory-impaired, so long as there is no direct or indirect commercial advantage, is permitted through a government body or noncommercial educational broadcast station.

Sound recordings are subject to copyright laws regardless of the nature of the sounds recorded. Common examples include sound recordings of copyrighted or public domain musical works, of spoken words—such as dramas or speeches—of sounds of nature, and of special effects. Sound recordings are "works that result from the fixation of a series of musical, spoken, or other sounds…regardless of the nature of the physical medium, such as disks or tapes, in which they are embodied."[4]

Copyright protection generally extends to two elements in a sound recording: the contribution of the performers and the contribution of the producer and/or recorder—whoever is responsible for capturing, editing, and processing the sounds to make the final recording. U.S. Copyright Office Circular 56, "Copyright for Sound Recordings 1" (1991) provides that no copyright may be claimed for sounds that are "fixed by mechanical means without any originality of any kind." The required originality must come from the performer or the producer who together create the final creative product.

Many times the producer records, processes, compiles, and edits the recording for a fee, thereby creating a "work-for-hire." In these circumstances, the employer retains the copyright. Many speakers hire professional organizations to help develop and record audiotapes of their speeches. In the absence of a work-for-hire arrangement or other agreement, the recorder may claim some copyright ownership. Thus, to protect their own rights, speakers who perform on sound recordings should have a clear understanding with these service providers regarding the latter's limitations of rights pursuant to the work-for-hire arrangement.

Conversely, speakers who intend to use clips, excerpts, or other portions of a sound recording (even of their own presentations)—where the rights of the recorder are not clearly subject to a work-for-hire arrangement with the speaker or the conference sponsor—may need to obtain written permission to use the recording again or to incorporate it into other new products. Speakers should also remember that live musician-performers at their presentations may have common law copyright protection for their portion of the overall performance, unless they are providing a work-for-hire.

Chapter 13, pp. 273–279, contains further information for speakers on the use of music during live and multimedia presentations.

Public Display Rights

In addition to music and video, presenters often use graphics—including cartoons, graphic images on slides, transparencies, and computer-generated images—to enhance their presentations. The owners of these works have the same rights to reproduction, distribution, and public display.

Rights.   The copyright owner has the exclusive right to show a copy of the work, either directly or indirectly or by means of film, slide, CD-ROM, computer-generated image, or any other device or process. The definition of "public" is the same as for performance rights.

Limits.   There are two limitations to the owner's exclusive right that are helpful to presenters:

- Under Section 109(c) of the Copyright Act, an owner of a *lawfully made copy* may display *that single copy,* either directly or by the projection of no more than one image at a time, to viewers present at the place where the copy is located. Fortunately for trainers, speakers, and other presenters, fees may be charged for admission to the display.

- As with public performance, exceptions are extended to face-to-face teaching and instructional broadcasts (provided the noncommercial aspects are present).

How to Give Credit Where Credit Is Due

Once you receive express permission to use a copyrighted work, always include the complete citation to the copyrighted work and add the following statement to every copy: "Reprinted with the express written permission of the copyright holder, 1998. All rights reserved." If the copyright holder placed any limitations on the use, state them in your notice on every copy.

If you have a license to use music or sound recordings, the licensor may request that you specifically state in your written materials that the music is furnished pursuant to a license agreement or, in the absence of written materials, that you announce the permission from the platform. Include the name of the copyright holders, the dates the sound recording was made, and a statement that it is used with permission. Such permission is often requested when you anticipate large audiences, because copyright holders are reluctant to give audience members the false impression that the music is in the public domain.

Presenters should definitely make sure that anyone recording their presentation be made aware of the limitations on further uses of the recording. For example, distribution of a videotape of a speech, in which a sound recording is used pursuant to a limited license for that live presentation, will violate the rights of all copyright owners to the sound recording. The best way to avoid this problem is to include rights to videotape and distribute the presentation as part of the license agreement for the underlying sound recording. If you don't, you jeopardize your own copyright to the videotape.

How to Use Quotes Effectively and Still Comply With the Law

One of the most common myths about copyright law is that by attributing the work or placing quotation marks around a long passage, you can avoid a copyright infringement claim. In essence, trainers and speakers are often under the mistaken belief that they can quote any amount of material, as long as they give the author credit in a footnote. This is flatly untrue.

Providing credit for a quotation will *not* make the use a "fair use" if you quote an entire chapter or lengthy passages from an entire work. Likewise, if you quote large portions with only a footnote at the end to signify the source of the material, you are not protected by fair use principles.

The more material you quote, the more likely it is that your work becomes a substitute for the original. This is not a fair use, because it competes directly with the copyright holder's exclusive rights to reproduce, perform, adapt, display, or republish the work, and may affect the author financially.

Thus, even if you give the author credit, you may not come within the framework of the fair use privilege. Absent express permission of the copyright holder, you are subject to a claim of copyright infringement. However, through attribution and direct quotations, you may be able to establish that your infringement was not "willful," and thus limit the damages obtainable in an infringement suit.

The second aspect of fair use—the nature of the prior work—also provides some benefits to trainers, particularly in technical and safety programs. Factual and technical publications have copyright protection, particularly when there are limited ways to express the material in a technical compliance training program. Novels, literary works, and other fictional or dramatic publications and musical works have a significantly greater range of expression.

To avoid charges of plagiarism, authors of scholarly works must always give proper credit to the sources of their ideas and facts, as well as to any quoted words they use. Figure 19-3 provides samples of effective citation and quotation formats.

Your Rights When Providing Work-for-Hire

Designers of written materials and audiovisuals frequently ask whether they can copyright their own work. The answer depends upon whether the work is done as a work-for-hire. Prior to the 1976 Copyright Act, federal law made the employer the "author" and initial copyright holder. Definition of when the work was made "for hire" was left to the courts. Gradually, the presumption developed in the case law that anyone who paid another person to create a copyrightable work was the owner of the rights. Thus, the rights of the original "author" or creator of the work were significantly limited.

The 1976 act altered this automatic presumption, extending broader rights to the creator of copyrightable work product. The act specifies that

The complete citation should include the following:

- For books—the authors, complete title and subtitle, publisher, specification of the copyright holder, date of publication, and inclusive pages used with permission of the copyright holder.

  Patricia Eyres, *The Legal Handbook for Trainers, Speakers, and Consultants* (McGraw-Hill, 1998), pp. 22–35 and 55–90. Reprinted with the express written permission of McGraw-Hill. All rights reserved.

- For articles appearing in trade or professional journals—the authors, complete title of the article, full name of the journal, volume, number, date of publication, and inclusive pages used with permission.

  John Smith, "The Trainer's Legal Defense Fund: Keep Those Donations Coming," *Limiting Liability Journal*, Vol. 10, No. 12 (November 1997), pp. 30–35. Reprinted with the express written permission of *Limiting Liability Journal*. All rights reserved.

- For newsletters or other primary source materials—the authors, article title, name of newsletter, publisher, volume, number, date of publication, and pages (if appropriate).

  Jane Jones, "Photocopying Fax Paux," *Copyright Infringement News*, Vol. 65, No. 13 (October 22, 1997). Published by WatchDog Press, reprinted with permission of the joint copyright holders, Jane Jones and WatchDog Press. All rights reserved.

- For cartoons or graphics incorporated into your written materials—name of artist, date created, publication (if applicable), date published.

  Charles Schulz, "Peanuts," from *Los Angeles Times,* October 22, 1997, p. 5. Reprinted with express permission of Charles Schulz and the L.A. Times. All rights reserved.

If you are using copyrighted cartoons or graphics only on your slides or transparencies, place the copyright notice on the bottom of the slide:

Copyright © 1997, Charles Schulz. All rights reserved.

Identify in your written handout the graphics used, and specify that they were used with the permission of the copyright holder.

Figure 19-3 Citation Formats for Quoting from Copyrighted Text.

"copyright . . . vests initially in the author or authors of the work . . . The employer or other person for whom the work was prepared is considered the author for purposes of this title, and, *unless the parties have expressly agreed otherwise in a written instrument signed by them,* owns all of the rights comprised in the copyright."[5]

The act defines a work made for hire as:

> (1) a work prepared by an employee within the scope of his or her employment; or (2) a work specially ordered or commissioned for use as a contribution to a collective work . . . as a translation, as a supplementary work, as a compilation, as an instructional text, as a test, as answer material for a test, or as an atlas, if the parties expressly agree in a written instrument signed by them that the work shall be considered a work made for hire.[6]

Although the Copyright Act does not specifically define three key terms—employee, employer, and scope of employment—it has uniformly been interpreted that full-time employees charged with the responsibility of developing copyrightable works for their employer are providing "works-for-hire." Accordingly, in the absence of a specific agreement to the contrary, the legal owner of the copyright is your employer.

If, as an internal trainer, you are compensated for work created within the course and scope of your employment, and your employer elects to seek copyright protection, it owns the work. Should you leave the company and later wish to use materials you created, you must obtain written permission from an authorized representative of the copyright holder (your former employer). You cannot incorporate portions of copyrighted materials into new work product, even if the earlier work was your own. Failure to obtain permission jeopardizes your copyright on the new product and leaves you vulnerable to an infringement suit.

As an employee, you will be *presumed* to create works for hire unless you have a specific alternative agreement. However, work you create outside of your employment—by teaching an extension course at the local community college—may be copyrighted in your own name. It is still prudent to inform your employer of your intent to copyright the work you have done in the outside venture, in order to reduce potential confusion about which material was created while you worked for the company. If there is any potential for overlap between the works, discuss the issue up front to avoid potential ambiguities over ownership rights.

If you are an independent contractor and you provide extensive services for a single organization, the work-for-hire determination is different. (The definition of an independent contractor is addressed fully in Chapter 16, pp. 337–342.) If you are an independent contractor rather than an employee, you own the copyright in the absence of a written agreement to the contrary. The sample contracts in Appendix C provide applicable language.

External consultants are frequently retained specifically to develop training materials. Your agreement should specify who will own the copyright to any work product—handouts, audiovisual aids, sound recordings, or multimedia—when the project is concluded. Incorporate explicit language into your contract to identify which copyrights you will retain and which you will relinquish to the client as works for hire. Generally, the more customized the product is for the particular client, the greater the chance that the organization will want to secure ownership rights. The higher the fee, the more likely the client will retain the copyright. The contracts in Appendix C provide relevant sample clauses.

The following guidelines are important in preserving your rights in potential work-for-hire arrangements:

1. If you are a trainer employed full or part time by a single employer to develop copyrightable work, you do so pursuant to a work for hire, unless you have an alternative written agreement. If you want to retain rights in any work, negotiate an arrangement with your employer, put it in writing, and have an authorized company representative sign it. Ideally, you should have a separate agreement for each work-for-hire.

2. If you teach a course at the local community college, or make a presentation to a community group, you may wish to secure a separate copyright. Outside work raises several issues:

   - Are you making the presentation independently, or as a representative of your employer's organization? The educational institution may advertise the program as conducted by "C. B. Jones, Training Professional Extraordinaire of XYZ Corporation," making your status less clear.

   - When you take on outside work, clarify with your employer the nature of that work. If you want separate copyright protection for your outside work product, make sure your employer agrees with your characterization of work as outside the course and scope of your employment.

   - If you and your employer agree that this work is outside the scope of your employment, you are the owner of the handout or other product you create. However, if you use portions of your employer's copyrighted work—even when you have personally created it pursuant to work-for-hire—you must obtain the permission of the copyright holder.

- Be careful to keep the copyrights separate. Don't "commingle" the handout with material you create in employment. If you do, you may infringe your employer's copyright, or you may lose the rights to protect your separate work product.

3. If you are classified as an independent contractor rather than as an employee (e.g., if taxes are not withheld from your paycheck and your income is reported to the IRS on a 1099 form instead of a W-2), you are presumed to own the copyright to all work you create. Still, you need to take precautions.

- Make sure you are appropriately classified as an independent contractor. If you are misclassified, a later determination that you were actually an employee may render your copyrights ineffective—not to mention arouse the interest of the IRS.

- It is in your best interest, as well as your client's, to have a specific written agreement regarding your status and copyright owner- ship. If you specify that the material is work-for-hire, a later deter- mination of employee status will not affect the allocation of intellectual property rights (then, all you have to worry about is the IRS). See Chapter 16, pp. 337–342, and Appendix C.

4. Determine the nature of your relationship with the client at the outset. Build into the contract specific statements about who will own the copyright to material produced. Consider these issues:

- Is your work product used for a variety of clients? If so, generally you will retain the copyright. In most instances, the placement of a copyright notice and registration with the U.S. Copyright Office will be sufficient to protect your rights.

- If your client wants to own the copyright, it should so specify in a written agreement. Typically, with extensive customization and/or a significant fee, the client will seek to negotiate ownership interest in the handouts or training manuals and audiovisual materials.

- When you integrate some of your client's copyrighted materials directly into your final product, be careful to obtain express permission and state that you have reprinted with permission. Otherwise you risk losing protection for your original portions as well. Be sure to include the complete citation of the original source.

- When you incorporate portions of your own copyrighted work into a final product to be owned by the client, be sure to protect your interests by providing express written permission to your client, and then stating: "Reprinted with permission of the copyright holder, Skillful Consultant Co. All rights reserved."

Written permission will prevent a waiver of your rights. It will also serve as useful evidence of your consistent intent to enforce your copyrights in all settings, should you need to file an infringement action against a later unauthorized user.

Using Other People's Theories and Ideas

Copyright protection does not extend to ideas, theories, or creative ways to approach a training program. Thoughts, concepts, abstractions, and perceptions—no matter how creative or unique—cannot be registered to confer copyright protection. The exclusive rights are limited to the expression of the ideas in words, graphics, or sound. Intellectual property rights are limited to the sequence of words used to express the theories, or to the musical or artistic interpretation of the ideas.

For example, in conducting a training session on sexual harassment investigation procedures, a trainer may have a unique idea on how to structure a group exercise for maximum skill application. The idea itself is not subject to copyright protection and may be freely used or adapted by any observer. What *is* subject to protection under copyright laws are the written exercises and related instructions, an accompanying case study, and any visual aids used to enhance the exercise.

Likewise, trainers who use acronyms as memory aids may copyright the acronyms themselves, but not the idea of using acronyms. Naturally, trainers who develop creative techniques may wish to protect their unique approach without unfair competition by others. There are some legal protections in this context, but they are outside the arena of copyright protection.

Developing Training Manuals: A High-Risk Activity!

Training manuals involve a compilation of materials: research from primary and secondary sources, clips from news articles, copies of relevant articles, exercises, checklists, and related graphic materials. The materials may be drawn from research of technical publications, newsletters, internal documents subject to other copyrights, electronic media sources, and information in the public domain. Much of the material may be subject to copyright protection.

Training manuals are also frequently designed as step-by-step guides for using technical equipment or computer software. The equipment manufacturer usually holds a copyright on drawings, diagrams, and schematics. You *must* obtain express permission to use these graphics, in whole or in part, in your manual. You may be sued for infringement if you don't get permission.

Similarly, your employer or client may be the licensee of the software itself, which is typically limited to application on computers. Copying the input screens, templates, and help screens may not come within the framework of the license, particularly when you are developing a separate manual from the user's guide that accompanies the software. You must obtain permission to incorporate these graphic materials into your manual.

Once you have received authorization to use the material, you may obtain separate copyright protection for the new manual you create. Your creative input, organization, descriptions, and additional graphics transform the manual into a new work. Depending upon the extent of the transformation, the new product is a derivative work, a compilation, or an entirely new work. The more you add to reflect your own procedures, data input policies, and customized reports, the greater your benefit from copyright protection.

Conversely, you may jeopardize the validity of your own copyright if you don't obtain permission to use copyrighted materials incorporated into your final product. In a subsequent infringement action, you may be faced with a finding that your own violation precludes you from specific remedies against an unauthorized user of work product you intended to protect through copyright registration.

Some aspects of training manuals are not governed by copyright law. These include names, single technical words, ideas, concepts, scientific or mathematical equations, methods, formulas, technical facts, and theorems. In addition, most federal government publications are freely usable in the public domain. In software training manuals, blank forms, standard input screens, blank calendars, and other items too standard to be deemed "original" work are not governed by the Copyright Act.

In preparing training manuals, follow uniform procedures to give yourself maximum protection from a claim of copyright infringement. The following guidelines are a starting point.

1. Keep track of all primary and secondary sources, and develop a method for pinpointing which material came from each source. Some trainers use computer databases; others rely on index cards or even yellow pads. The method is uniquely individual. The best approach is one you can consistently follow.

2. With haphazard record keeping, you may lose citations or other direct links between the data you want to use and the source

material. It is frustrating and time-consuming to repeat research in order to find a citation for key material you want to use. It is unlawful to use such material without crediting the source and obtaining written permission of the copyright holder.

3. Develop a standard form for keeping track of copyright permissions, and use it while you research. This form will save time later, and ensure that you are keeping track of which sources require permission.

4. Use a consistent method for capturing complete citations. When using quotations, always recheck for accuracy after the material has been typed and again after final typesetting. Also carefully recheck the accuracy of page citations. See Figure 19-3 for formatting citations.

5. When using charts, graphs, pictures, diagrams, or other technical materials, you may find it easier to copy them as an appendix than to re-create the data. Specify in your permission request the method you will use to duplicate the material.

6. Be especially careful with material you receive via e-mail or through on-line research. One advantage to on-line research is that you can instantly cut and paste relevant material to a new document. If you don't keep accurate and complete records of when and where you cut or otherwise downloaded, it will become difficult to identify the sources. You will lose track of your citations and may have great difficulty locating the owners to obtain authorization to use the materials. More significantly, you may inadvertently use copyrighted material without realizing it.

The Dangers of Misappropriating Valuable Training Materials: A Case Study

Some organizations invest years of effort and millions of dollars in their training programs. Particularly in industries with specialized products and services, the misappropriation of training materials designed for technical specialists may result in devastating competitive losses. Even when the organization takes deliberate steps to obtain and enforce copyright protection, the losses from unauthorized copying of proprietary training data may be incalculable.

Under these circumstances, businesses are entitled to federal copyright protection and to a range of legal protections under state law for trade secrets and confidential data. This combination of laws is intended to protect innovative companies from misappropriation and unauthorized use and disclosure of their technological advancements or proprietary processes. When these rights are violated, remedies exist to recover and thus economically justify the investments required to develop the processes in the first place.

Many certification programs are designed to train employees to perform specialized skills. For example, software and hardware designers frequently develop formal training programs and materials to provide unique skills for servicing their computer systems. Likewise, manufacturers of unique or inventive equipment must train employees to provide the technical service—including maintenance, repair, and ongoing adjustment—that supports the customer and justifies purchase of the equipment. Such large investments in technologies and people are given broad protection from misuse by competitors and abuse by employees.

The consequences of "stealing" proprietary intellectual property—including valuable training materials—can be significant for all parties. The owner of the property risks losing substantial investments from unauthorized use by others. The employee or competitor risks substantial liabilities in a lawsuit for copyright infringement or misappropriation of trade secrets. All parties risk being consumed by years of litigation and ruinous legal fees.

The case of *Picker International Corporation v. Imaging Equipment Services, Inc.*[7] serves as a useful study for avoiding the devastating effects to both sides. Picker International was a designer, manufacturer, seller, and servicer of medical diagnostic equipment, including the tomography scanners commonly known as "CT scanners." Imaging Equipment Services was an independent servicing organization that competed with Picker to service Picker-produced CT scanners. The individual president of Imaging Equipment Services, Mr. Quinn, was named separately as a defendant in the case.

Picker alleged that Imaging and Quinn misappropriated its trade secrets and violated its copyrights through the unauthorized use of Picker proprietary information about its CT scanner, including its training materials for field service personnel. Picker sought both substantial damages and injunctive relief to stop the defendants from ongoing use of its property to compete unfairly for the business of servicing Picker CT scanners.

The results of the case could not have been more severe for the defendants. The judge wrote: "After carefully considering the evidence . . .the court finds that [the defendants] have for more than a decade engaged in a relentless and extensive campaign to misappropriate Picker's legally protected intellectual property."[8] On the basis of this finding, the court ordered the defendants to return to Picker or destroy all copyrighted materials and other confidential information they had misappropriated. The court further took the highly unusual step of appointing a former special agent of the FBI to serve as a monitor to supervise and ensure compliance with the court's order. The defendants were ordered to pay the costs of the monitor, and avoided further severe monetary damages only because they obtained protection from creditors by declaring bankruptcy.

Although Picker obtained all the relief it sought (short of damages precluded by the bankruptcy court), it still faced substantial legal fees and 10 years' worth of lost profits from improper use of its training and other materials. The facts of the case are instructive in demonstrating why such materials are subject to protection, and how to take appropriate precautions to secure that protection.

The heart of the case involved the court's determination of whether Picker took adequate measures to protect its proprietary training materials. The court concluded that it did, but not without substantial analysis useful to readers of this book.

Picker introduced its most popular CT scanner into the market after investing millions of dollars in software and documents necessary to maintain and repair the scanner. The maintenance and repair of the scanner were vitally important to purchasers, because of the delicate nature of the equipment. The court found that reliability was valued because the CT scanners were used for emergency procedures as well as on a 24-hour-a-day basis. Both routine maintenance each week and emergency diagnosis of problems were commonly needed.

In addition to technical documentation, user instructions, and periodic technical bulletins to its field service engineers, Picker developed classroom training materials that included technical information on the theory and operation of the CT scanner. The classroom materials enhanced the ability of the field engineers to provide reliable service. Evidence showed that Picker spent more than $1 million annually to develop and update its diagnostic software, service engineering technical bulletins, and classroom training materials.

Picker had a published policy requiring employees not to disclose proprietary or confidential information without the company's express authorization. Trainees and employees who serviced the scanners were required to sign confidentiality agreements. A major issue facing the court was whether Picker took reasonable steps to protect the confidentiality of its training materials. Picker trained the service engineers at a dedicated facility that was not accessible to the public or to Picker employees who had no legitimate business reason to be there. It posted a security guard at the entrance and required identification badges for entry. The training materials were kept "in a caged area, and were usually accessed only by an individual employed by Picker."

All training materials included a legend specifying that they were proprietary and confidential materials owned by Picker. In addition, at the beginning of each training class, trainees were reminded about the confidential nature of the materials, and were instructed not to share them with outsiders or to copy or take portions outside the training facility.

As part of a contract with a large hospital, Picker agreed to allow a designated representative of the client to attend training at its facility. This individual, who was falsely represented to be an employee of the hospital, was Mr. Quinn. He eventually started his own company—not surprisingly, Imaging Equipment Services, Inc.

The standard training included three levels of instruction. Quinn skipped the first level and was not present when the instructor reminded the trainees about the confidentiality of the materials they were using during training. However, evidence reflected that Quinn recognized that the training was conducted in a secure facility, that the training materials were kept in a caged area, and that they were distributed only to those in the training. Although he was not asked to sign a confidentiality agreement, he also knew he was being treated like a Picker field service engineer, and was aware of the company's confidentiality agreement.

All the materials that Quinn received during his training had considerable commercial value to him. The evidence revealed that he took extra copies from the caged area when the attendant was absent and smuggled them out of the facility. Because Picker trusted Quinn and its hospital customer, he was not asked to return the copies he was officially issued. While Quinn was being trained, there were no competitors for servicing Picker-produced CT scanners. The materials produced prior to 1993 did not contain a copyright notice. However, the software documentation included a legend that stated:

> THIS DOCUMENT CONTAINS PROPRIETARY INFORMATION. IT IS THE EXCLUSIVE CONFIDENTIAL PROPERTY OF PICKER CORPORATION. COPYING, DISCLOSURE TO OTHERS, OR OTHER USE IS PROHIBITED WITHOUT THE EXPRESS, WRITTEN AUTHORIZATION OF PICKER CORPORATION.

The following year, in anticipation of the emergence of competitive independent servicing organizations, Picker began placing copyright notices and proprietary legends on the cover of its service manuals and other documents. It also issued a memorandum reminding employees that their training and other materials were confidential. At about the same time, in return for training and continued employment, Picker required employees to execute a more specific confidentiality agreement that specified their responsibilities and mandated that they return all materials to the company upon termination of their employment. The agreement also prohibited competitive activities in servicing Picker CT scanners for one year after an employee left the company.

Finally, Picker also began conducting separate training programs for customer in-house service engineers. These classes provided only basic instruction and limited documentation. Customer representatives were not provided with the proprietary information that was given to Picker's own employees, and that Mr. Quinn had earlier obtained.

The court found that when Quinn started his business, he used materials he had received (and in some cases stolen) from Picker without permission. After Picker sued him, he agreed to a license agreement for the diagnostic software and supporting training documentation. The license was limited to one hospital. Wanting to expand the business to other sites, Quinn and Imaging sought permission from Picker, which was expressly denied. Nevertheless, Quinn copied and distributed to Imaging Equipment's employees Picker's user's guide, after removing the page with the Picker proprietary legend.

The court considered this compelling evidence that the infringement was willful. The lesson: _Never copy or use copyright-protected materials without permission, especially when permission has been denied._ To add insult to injury, Quinn placed his own legend stating "Please do not copy without prior approval of Imaging Equipment Services, Inc.," thereby passing Picker's training manual off as his own.

The court concluded that Imaging and Quinn had violated Picker's copyrights in a number of respects and had misappropriated its trade secrets. The court based its ruling in Picker's favor on several concrete pieces of evidence:

- Picker never sold its copyrighted materials.

- Picker took deliberate steps to secure the return of all materials from employees when they left the company and took other steps to obtain and enforce appropriate confidentiality agreements.

- Picker took overt steps to protect the security of its training materials from loss or misuse.

- Picker used "proprietary information" legends early in the process, and began placing copyright notices on its materials when it became aware that competitive independent servicing organizations would emerge.

- During training Picker regularly reminded employees about the confidential nature of its materials.

This combination of evidence—coupled with the flagrant unauthorized copying and distribution of copyrighted materials by the defendants—was persuasive to the court. The trial judge concluded that Picker was entitled to substantial remedies, even though its security was not absolutely impenetrable.

How to Protect Yourself and Your Employer From Copyright Violations: A Checklist

The following checklist provides a framework for developing policies and procedures to prevent inadvertent or willful copyright violations by your training staff.

1. Determine whether the material you are drawing from is copyright protected. Look for the copyright notice on the first page, or on any consecutive pages. If the notice exists, always obtain permission from the copyright holder before incorporating materials into your own work.

2. Remember that permission is required when you are using the author's creative expression, such as the sequence of words or thoughts or a unique organization of handout materials; when the material is not in the public domain and is protected by a copyright notice; and when the expression goes beyond the bounds of "fair use." For material that is to be used in a single publication, presentation, or display, a one-time nonexclusive authorization may be sufficient. For multiple uses, such as ongoing presentations or published handouts, a license agreement may be more appropriate. Follow the procedures suggested in Figure 19-1 for obtaining permission to use the material.

3. Remember that written materials are subject to a common law copyright, whether or not the author has registered the work with the U.S. Copyright Office or has included the copyright notice. If you plan to use portions of any trainer's materials, make an effort to obtain express permission. Identify those sections, passages, or constructs that you are using with permission, and include the statement "Reprinted with the express permission of the copyright holder" in your work.

4. On clearly copyrighted materials, always obtain permission to quote if you are using more than a minimal amount. Quotation marks and citations may not be enough to protect you from an

infringement action if you use significant portions of another's work.

5. While conducting your research, adopt the following procedures:

- Keep accurate records of all sources you draw from, and record the complete citation for later referral.
- When taking "bits and pieces" from a particular work, separately record the complete name of the copyright holder and contact information.
- Attempt to obtain permission as early as possible, so that you don't run afoul of a deadline and have to remove unauthorized portions of your materials at the last minute.
- When drawing from electronic sources by "cut and paste" techniques, *always* record the complete citation information and copyright holder identification. Otherwise, reconstructing your sources will be very difficult.
- Remember that photocopying protected materials, even for research purposes, may be a violation of copyright.
- Until you have completed the final product, keep all drafts, notes, or copied materials together. Once you have obtained permission to use materials, keep a copy of the written permission in your files with any older drafts.

6. If you seek permission and are denied by the copyright holder, you have two choices: offer to pay a reasonable license fee or *remove all references and passages drawn from that material.* If you use material despite an explicit refusal of permission, you risk a finding of "willful" violation.

7. Some copyright holders will be receptive to a modest donation to a charity of their choice in lieu of a fee or license. If you reach such an agreement, keep copies of the exchange of correspondence with the copyright holder and evidence that you in fact made the donation. It is courteous to send a written letter to the charity acknowledging the copyright holder as the source of the donation, with a copy to your contact.

8. Maintain clear, well-organized, and accessible files for each separate work requiring use authorization. The following items should be in the file:

- Your complete exchange of correspondence with the copyright holder.
- A complete copy of the final work product.
- Copies of all research notes or other materials used during your research and development. This includes index cards, database printouts, e-mail, faxes, and photocopies of relevant passages.

- Copies of all drafts. After you receive written authorization, you may dispose of nonrelevant drafts and extraneous materials.
- All written permissions, license agreements, or other authorization from the copyright holder.
- All copies of any license agreements for multiple uses along with documentation of the fee payment, where applicable.
- A complete tape of all music or sounds used, along with the written permission or license agreement.

9. Abide by any limitations of use requested by the copyright holder. Provide copies of the authorization letter or agreement to your printer, photocopier, or designer, with a written statement asking that service provider to abide by the same limitations.

10. Require every employee who creates audiovisual aids or other presentation materials to keep accurate records of all source materials. Provide them with appropriate forms for obtaining copyright permission.

11. Develop appropriate disciplinary policies for training department staff who do not maintain complete records and/or obtain appropriate use authorizations. Be prepared to enforce the policies consistently. In the event that your organization is sued for infringement, consistently enforced policies will serve as useful evidence that you took all reasonable steps to comply with the law. At a minimum, such policies should eliminate the potential for willful violations by your trainers.

12. Develop a compliance culture in your organization. Provide complete information to your trainers and instructional designers on the following aspects of copyright compliance:

- Limitations of the fair use doctrine
- A description of what constitutes materials in the public domain
- Your organization's internal policies and procedures to prevent copyright infringement

13. Develop strong internal policies for compliance with applicable licenses for computer software that you use in database applications, desktop publishing, word processing, multimedia, or other applications for research or presentations. At a minimum, your policies should include all of the following:

- A description of unlawful copying of software programs and the limitations of your licenses for heavily used programs
- An explanation of the limitations on use of software downloaded from on-line bulletin boards or from other organizations.

- A description of the consequences to the company and individuals for violation of copyrights, licenses, or other use restrictions on software
- Strong and consistently enforced disciplinary procedures for personnel found using unauthorized copies of software applications

14. To monitor compliance with software license agreements, develop internal audit procedures in your organization in order to ensure compliance. Make sure these procedures are enforceable and consistently enforced.

- Periodically compare purchase records for all software programs with applications on your training department network and/or individual workstations.
- Audit all hard drives on your network server and on individual workstations and laptop computers used by your employees.
- Purge all unauthorized applications and discipline the violators promptly.
- Keep clear and consistent records to establish license purchases. One approach is to use a log of authorized applications on each user's hard drive.
- Conduct periodic as well as random audits to establish compliance.

15. If you are a consulting organization, reserve the right to monitor hard disks, e-mail, and other on-line exchanges by employees throughout the company. Frequently, e-mail messages and accompanying files contain copyrighted materials. Transmission of this material is a dual problem: Employees may inadvertently waive your rights on copyrighted materials, and they may infringe on the rights of others. Develop and enforce a policy allowing your authorized representatives to inspect computer hard drives and backup disks, as necessary.

How to Protect Your Own Work Product: A Step-by-Step Guide to Getting and Enforcing Copyright Protection

Most organizations using internally prepared training materials need to protect those materials from unauthorized use by others. Your training department should develop a policy for its own copyrightable materials, which may be mass produced. Such materials include texts of training curricula and modules, study guides and manuals, videos, and audiotapes, cassettes and film strips, and multimedia presentations.

Your policy should establish that the organization owns the copyright to all materials produced by staff members within the scope of their employment. This will ensure that your employer is fairly compensated for staff time and resources used to create the work. You will also be protected if you are part of a consulting organization or a speaker who employs staff.

Since copyright protection exists from the moment the work is fixed in tangible form, you need only place a copyright notice and date on the material to obtain protection. However, in order to maintain an action for infringement, you must register the copyright with the U.S. Copyright Office.

Registration is permissive and voluntary, and can be effected at any time during the term of the copyright. Works created before January 1, 1978, must be registered and renewed during the first 28-year term to maintain copyright protection. Under the 1976 act, registration is a required step in preserving a copyright when the notice has been omitted from more than a relatively small number of publicly distributed copies of the work.

There are several advantages to formal registration of your work with the U.S. Copyright Office. Registration establishes a public record of the copyright, independent of the notice you place on the work itself. Registration also secures the right to pursue an infringement lawsuit against those who copy or use your work (in whole or in part) without your express permission, and it establishes the prima facie validity of the copyright.

Registration makes available a broader range of remedies in an infringement suit, particularly statutory damages and attorneys' fees. These costs would not otherwise be recoverable, because unauthorized users of the work would not be on "constructive notice" of the facts stated in the copyright recordation unless the work was registered. Thus, failure to register defeats many claims of willful violations.

**Procedures for Registering Your
Work Product for Copyright
Protection**

The following procedures may be utilized in registering your work for copyright protection with the U.S. Copyright Office in Washington, D.C.

1. Identify materials for which you will secure copyright protection, such as training manuals; instruments, tests, checklists or job aids; compilations or other combinations of source materials; workbooks or

instructional guides; electronically produced or other on-line materials; software programs, interactive instructional materials, CD-ROM materials, or other multimedia products; and videotapes, audiotapes, or combined recorded materials and instructional guides.

2. Place a copyright notice on the work you intend to protect, immediately upon completion.

3. Place three items in an envelope addressed to the U.S. Copyright Office:
   - A properly completed application form (photocopies are not permitted)
   - A nonrefundable fee of $10 for each item to be copyrighted
   - A deposit copy of the work to be registered

4. There are two purposes for depositing work. First, you provide a copy of the work for the collection of the Library of Congress. Second, you identify the work in conjunction with the copyright registration.

5. Deposit of the complete work is mandatory and applies to all except unpublished works, published works not containing the appropriate copyright notice, works published in foreign countries, advertising material, and individual contributions to collective works.

6. Section 407 of the Copyright Act outlines the basic procedure for registering a copyright.
   - Within three months after a work is published, the owner must deposit two copies of the best edition of the work with the Copyright Office.
   - If the work is a sound recording, the owner must deposit two complete phonorecords of the best edition, together with any printed material or other visually perceptible material published with such phonorecords. "Phonorecord" is the term used for the recording; it may be on any recording medium, including cassette tape or other type of tape, record, CD-ROM, or compact disc.
   - Failure to comply with the deposit requirements does not forfeit the copyright, but fines are imposed: initially no more than $250 plus the cost of acquiring the copies. An additional fine of $2500 may be imposed for willful refusal to comply with a demand for deposit of the work as required under the act.

7. Keep track of new methods for registering copyrights, such as CORDS, an acronym for the experimental Copyright Office Electronic Registration, Recordation, and Deposit System. The Web site address is: http://lcweb.loc.gov/copyright/cords.html.

Develop Internal Policies to Protect Your Own and Your Organization's Work Product

Every organization that designs, develops, distributes for internal use, or provides for public dissemination training materials in any tangible form—workbooks, instruments, transparencies, sound recordings, electronic or computer-based media, audiovisuals, or multimedia— should develop an internal policy for registering and protecting its copyrights.

Internal training professionals, including content specialists, curriculum designers, course materials developers, and stand-up trainers, should all be held accountable for adherence to policies for protection of copyrights on internally produced materials. Such policies have a four-fold purpose:

- To comply with procedures for copyrighting material developed by internal employees or consultants as part of their jobs

- To obtain proper authorization prior to reproducing, distributing, or using internal materials subject to copyright protection

- To follow uniform procedures allowing the limited duplication, distribution, and use of internally produced course outlines, audiovisual aids, training manuals, instruments, and job aids and company-copyrighted curriculum materials for specific purposes

- To recover, when appropriate, the costs of developing, producing, and distributing internally produced training materials and documentation

The following checklist should assist you in developing a framework for policies and procedures to protect your own work product:

1. Develop a policy that identifies the circumstances under which your organization will select work product that you will deem proprietary or otherwise protectable.

2. Utilize specific work-for-hire agreements when you retain consultants to design manuals, graphics, or other training materials. Expressly delineate the rights you are retaining and the consultant is relinquishing, and reserve your right to seek damages for copyright infringement if the consultant uses all or portions of the work product for commercial purposes. Figure 19-4 provides sample language.

3. Determine whether the consultant wishes to retain certain rights to work product developed as a work-for-hire, such as the right to provide exemplar materials when seeking future work. If this is part

---

Work Made for Hire

All work performed pursuant to this Consulting Agreement, developed or prepared for Client, is the exclusive property of Client. All right, title, and interest in and to this property shall vest in Client upon the creation and shall be deemed to be a work made for hire and made in the course of the services rendered pursuant to this Consulting Agreement. To the extent that title to any such work may not, by operation of law, vest in Client, or such work may not be considered a work made for hire, all rights, title, and interest therein are hereby irrevocably assigned by Consultant to Client. Client shall have the right to obtain and to hold in its own name any and all copyrights, registrations, or such other protection as may be appropriate to the subject matter, and any extensions and renewals thereof.

Consultant must give Client, as well as any person designated by Client, all reasonable assistance required to perfect the rights defined herein without any charge or expense beyond those amounts payable to Consultant for the services rendered under this Agreement.

Figure 19-4 Sample Contract Language Specifying a Work Made for Hire.

of your negotiated agreement, be sure to *provide a written statement authorizing the use for that limited purpose.* Authorization will protect the consultant and provide evidence of—and the consultant's knowledge of—your status as exclusive copyright holder.

4. For internal staff trainers, provide a memorandum explaining that their design and development of copyrighted materials for your organization will be pursuant to their employment. Explain the limitations on their rights to use, retain, or sell those materials during or after their employment.

5. Place a copyright notice on all written materials developed within your training department, including drafts. This is important for two reasons: It establishes the common law copyright, and it reminds your staff that the materials are intended to be proprietary. You may delete sections from one work and use it later in other work. The earlier (draft) copyright should protect your expression.

6. Date all drafts with the month, day, and year. If there is a danger that the pages will become lost, date every page and put the copyright notice on all separate sections, instruments, and adjunct materials.

7. When developing material on-line, or using e-mail to exchange materials with external consultants, put a copyright notice on all pages. Although the law is unsettled in this area, there is a strong argument that written creative expressions on e-mail are subject to copyright protection. Since the message will be date-stamped, the copyright notice will establish your proprietary intent at an early time.

8. Maintain accurate records of when you first create the final product. One useful method is to place a copy in a sealed envelope and mail it to yourself. Keep it sealed. The postmark will establish the date it was created.

9. Promptly register your final work product with the U.S. Copyright Office, and maintain clear records of the date you did so.

10. Develop a policy that you can consistently enforce regarding when you will grant permission to others to use, quote from, or adapt your copyrighted work product.

11. Keep clear, organized, and accessible files of all correspondence with people seeking your authorization to use copyrighted materials. Although it is courteous for those using your materials to send you a final copy, they are not required to do so. If you want, you may make this a condition of granting permission.

12. If possible, determine in advance your range of fees and required agreements for use of your copyrighted materials. Options include a one-time fee for a single use, a license agreement for multiple uses, a donation to a charity of your choice, or any other compensation you deem appropriate.

13. In your written permission letters or license agreements, specify precisely the materials you are authorizing for use and any limitations on that use. Attach copies or quote verbatim in the agreement itself.

14. Always specifically request that the user acknowledge in writing that the materials are "reprinted with express written permission of the copyright holder." Develop reasonable procedures for monitoring compliance with the terms of your license agreements.

15. If you are authorizing the use of material that may become dated or otherwise inappropriate, *specify the time limitations directly in your license agreement*. Limits are important, for example, with materials on legal and regulatory compliance, since the law changes from time to time. In order to ensure that the user abides by these limitations, you may wish to request either documentation that all

outdated copies have been destroyed or a liquidated-damages provision for violations.

16. Consider issuing license agreements for a limited term and then renewing them periodically. This practice is useful when it is of mutual benefit for you to provide "updates" or change the fee arrangement.

17. Follow uniform procedures for identifying materials from your training department that should be copyrighted, and for obtaining copyright ownership:

   - Have members of the training staff report potentially copyrightable materials to their supervisor or to a designated training department representative.
   - Determine whether the material should be mass produced for sale or distribution to produce income to your organization.
   - Determine whether the material will be distributed for use by people outside the organization or by employees acting outside the scope of their employment with your organization.
   - Determine whether the material would be commercially viable for sale or distribution by others outside your organization, a practice that would put your organization at a competitive disadvantage.
   - Require trainers and employees to obtain permission from the department manager or designated representative to conduct your copyrighted programs for nonemployees, including contract service providers and other agents of your organization.
   - Consider allowing single copies of copyrighted training materials to be used for informational or marketing purposes in proposals or marketing packets, or at the request of individuals or nonprofit associations other than colleges or training providers.

Proprietary Business Data and Confidentiality Agreements

Some training programs involve proprietary processes and procedures that required significant time and expense to create. These may be protected as trade secrets. A *trade secret* is a compilation of valuable technical information and procedures, generally created at great expense, and contains useful tools for technical employees in performing specialized work for your company. The unauthorized disclosure of such proprietary materials can place your company at a competitive disadvantage or devalue its products and services.

For example, certification programs for technical employees—such as computer technicians, field service engineers, and unique service providers—frequently focus on maintenance and ongoing repair of specialized equipment sold by your company. The consequences from misappropriation of such competitive and costly information may be devastating.

In addition to copyright protection, your management may wish to protect this valuable and sensitive information as a trade secret. Yet you must distribute training materials and job aids for the trainees being certified, or perhaps for selected representatives of your client or customer organization. In these circumstances, you may wish to take extra precautions to protect the confidentiality of specialized and expensive training materials.

In order for a confidentiality agreement to be enforceable, it must be reasonable in scope, meaning that it encompasses use of the material for competitive purposes against your organization and only within a reasonable geographic area. The agreement must also be reasonable in duration, meaning a limited time frame consistent with the potential harm from direct competitive uses (one to two years, maximum).

Use confidentiality agreements only when consistent with your organization's legitimate business interests in protecting the data or the unique processes and specialized procedures that are the subject of the training materials. Be sure your agreement does not unduly injure your employees' or the public interests.

Develop and publish an employee confidentiality agreement for all employees—*both* trainers and trainees—who will be part of the training program. (Consider adapting the language of the agreement in Chapter 16, Figure 16-5.) Signing the agreement should be an explicit condition of employment and training for each employee who will have access to the data or materials. The policy should require that employees not disclose proprietary or confidential information without the express prior written authorization of the company, and should mandate that employees not disclose at any time confidential information acquired during training or in the course of employment.

All materials subject to this protection should be clearly marked with both a copyright notice and a legend identifying the materials as PROPRIETARY or TRADE SECRETS or CONFIDENTIAL. The legend should specify—and verbal reminders during training should confirm—the following:

> All information contained in this [*describe with specificity the publi-*
> *cation, manual, checklist, instrument, job aid, or workbook*] is proprietary
> information and is the property of [*organization's name*]. The infor-
> mation shall not be duplicated or reproduced in any manner without

the express written permission of [*organization's name*]. The information is supplied for the sole use of [*individual trainee's name*] during training and within the course and scope of employment. Except for its intended purpose, relating to the trainee's employment with [*organization's name*], the information shall not be disclosed by [*trainee's name*].

Chapter 16, Figure 16-5, and the contracts in Appendix C provide sample confidentiality agreements.

Distribution of the materials should be tightly controlled. Print a minimum number of originals. Limit them to one set for each individual participating in the training or using the instructional materials. Distribute originals or copies only on a "need to have" basis. Prohibit employees or trainers from making copies without the express permission of management or the head of the training department.

Prohibit trainees from removing highly confidential materials from the training facility. Require employees not on the distribution list to demonstrate a direct job-related need for the materials. Require written management approval to extend access. Issue only one set of materials to each employee, trainee, and/or trainer.

Keep complete, accurate, and up-to-date records of each employee, trainee, and/or trainer who receives the issued item. A useful approach is to stamp a name on each individual set, or to provide an identifying number on each page of training materials. Require all trainees and employees—including trainers and others with "take home" access—to relinquish their individually issued materials upon completion of the training. Check each set of materials to make sure that all pages are present. For job aids used during employment, follow the same approach when the employee changes positions, no longer needs the materials for job-related activities, or separates from employment. Finally, make sure that audiovisual materials used during training sessions are similarly marked as PROPRIETARY and are accounted for at the end of each session.

Although these precautions may seem extreme—even burdensome— they are essential to ensure protection of highly proprietary materials. In fact, in litigation against an unauthorized user, the owner of proprietary trade secrets must establish that it took deliberate steps to protect the security and confidentiality of the materials. The more concrete the steps taken to protect proprietary data, the more compelling the owner's position will be to a court.

For example, in *ISC-Bunker Ramo Corporation v. Altech, Inc.*,[9] the court ruled in favor of a company whose job aids and training manuals were misappropriated by a competitor that knowingly hired its former employees, all of whom had signed confidentiality agreements. Among the most compelling evidence to the magistrate (judge) who decided the case against Altech:

> Other than from ISC's proprietary publications and software, there are no readily available sources for the information, technology, and procedures contained within ISC's service manuals, The Guide, or ISC's software. Altech admits that it does not have any service manuals for ISC's computer systems except for The Guide. As to The Guide, Altech admits that it "found" only one copy...and then made copies of that one Guide for each of Altech's field service engineers. The copy that Altech concedes it had, contained "proprietary" notices, which Altech unsuccessfully attempted to obliterate in the process of copying and redistributing it to Altech's employees. . . .
>
> One of Altech's current employees submitted an affidavit stating that he had worked at a certain bank that was a "self-maintainer" of ISC equipment, and that ISC had trained the bank employees without ever obtaining "nondisclosure" agreements from the bank or its employees. ISC then refuted these assertions by introducing nondisclosure agreements executed by the bank and its employees, including the affiant [one who swears to an affidavit].[10]

Special Considerations for Consultants and Vendors

When you elect to sell or license material, the license and confidentiality agreement should include a statement that the client or customer will abide by its terms. The license and confidentiality agreement should also provide that no rights to any intellectual property residing in the software, documents, training materials, job aids, test instruments, or other instructional or assessment materials are granted to the client and its employees except the right to use the property at the client's site. The following is an example of useful language:

> [*customer's name*] will use the same standard of care to protect [*your name*] confidential information as it uses to protect its own confidential information. [*customer's name*] shall have no right to copy, reproduce, or disclose to others in whole or in part any portion of [*describe the materials with specificity*] without [*your name*] prior written authorization.

Negotiate with your client a reasonable license fee for ongoing use of training materials. This may be a flat fee for a specific duration or a fee calculated on a per-document or per-copy basis. Develop a procedure to monitor compliance with the license agreement. The procedure should be reasonably calculated to ensure compliance without placing a burden on the customer. Select a monitoring procedure that you can effectively administer. If you place too much administrative burden on yourself, you risk failing to keep up with the process, thereby jeopardizing your proprietary rights.

Your contract documents should specify that the customer will have no right to copy, reproduce, or disclose to others in whole or in part any of the contents of your copyrighted training materials without your prior written permission.

References

1. *Campbell v. Acuff-Rose Music, Inc.*, 510 U.S. 569, 114 S.Ct. 1164 (U.S. Supreme Court 1994).

2. *Campbell v. Acuff-Rose Music, Inc.*, 510 U.S. 569, 114 S.Ct. 1164 (U.S. Supreme Court 1994).

3. *Basic Books, Inc. v. Kinko's Graphics Corp.*, 758 F.Supp. 1522 (S.D.N.Y. 1991).

4. Copyright Act, Title 17 U.S. Code, §101.

5. Copyright Act, Title 17 U.S. Code, §201(b) (emphasis added).

6. Copyright Act, Title 17 U.S. Code, §101.

7. *Picker International Corporation v. Imaging Equipment Services, Inc.*, 931 F.Supp. 18 (1995).

8. *Picker International Corporation v. Imaging Equipment Services, Inc.*, 931 F.Supp. 18 (1995).

9. *ISC-Bunker Ramo Corporation v. Altech, Inc.*, 765 F.Supp. 1310 (1990).

10. *ISC-Bunker Ramo Corporation v. Altech, Inc.*, 765 F.Supp. 1310, 1323 (1990).

PART 5

Techniques and Resources to Protect Yourself, Keep Informed, and Stay Out of Court

20

Uh-Oh! What to Do at the First Sign of Legal Trouble

Four Things You Should Never Do When Faced With a Potential Legal Problem

1. Don't ignore the problem, hoping it will go away.

Legal challenges are not like fine wine; they don't get better with age. There are several important reasons to address legal problems at the earliest possible time.

First, physical evidence may need to be preserved. The loss or destruction of physical evidence can devastate your defense or, worse, appear to be a "cover-up." Relevant documents, including those helpful to your defense, may need to be located and preserved from destruction during customary purging of records.

Second, insurance companies, particularly those issuing "claims made" policies, are contractually entitled to be placed on notice of a claim when the insured—usually the employer—is first on notice of the injury or *potential* loss. The failure to notify workers' compensation and other liability carriers may jeopardize insurance coverage. Once an agent of the employer—including the training department or an authorized facilitator—is *on notice* of a potential problem, all relevant documents must be preserved. The destruction of documents may constitute obstruction of justice—a criminal act that compounds the problem considerably, as the executives from Texaco discovered. Alteration or destruction of documents is a felony called "obstruction of justice." Former executives of Texaco Corp. have been indicted by a New York grand jury for alleged willful destruction of documents relevant to a race discrimination class action.[1] Obstruction of justice occurs when documentation is destroyed, altered, or withheld in contemplation of or after litigation is filed. *Don't turn fear into a crime.*

Most significantly, many state and federal claims have strict time frames for responding to formal lawsuits or requests for information from government agencies like OSHA and the EEOC. By waiting, you may be barred from asserting a valid defense or procedural position.

Finally, in copyright and contractual disputes, you may waive important legal rights by waiting too long to assert your rights or protect your position.

2. Do not communicate with the complaining party directly on the substance of the dispute, without obtaining advice.

Unless you are very sure you can resolve an apparent factual misunderstanding, it is prudent to obtain some advice before communicating verbally or in writing with the opposing party. The wait will give you an opportunity to "cool down," gather your thoughts, evaluate your position, consider your own documentation, and formulate an effective response. If you rush, you may say something that is later deemed an admission of fault or waive a significant available defense.

If you are an internal trainer, your organization may have in-house legal counsel. If not, check with your management and/or human resources department before taking any phone calls or responding to correspondence. A coordinated, consistent company response is a must.

If you are a speaker or consultant, you may be tempted to write off your fee or otherwise compromise your position. Resist the urge to do so until you have reviewed all the facts and the strength of your documentation. Precipitous action may cost you a fee you justly earned. In most instances, there is time to compromise on a disputed claim after you are aware of all the circumstances.

3. Do not communicate with the opposing party, its attorneys, or union personnel without representation and/or authorization.

Legal representatives have ethical rules prohibiting them from communicating directly with an opposing party who is represented by counsel. This restriction remains in effect until the dispute is resolved. If you have ongoing business (on other projects) with an adversary in litigation—a practice not unheard of in contractual or insurance disputes—be sure you alert your legal representatives when contacts may occur. Be careful to avoid any discussion of an ongoing dispute without authorization.

4. Do not—ever—back-date, fabricate, or otherwise tamper with existing documentation.

Tampering with documentation is neither smart nor legal. When such conduct comes to light—and it usually does—juries don't like it. This is the surest way to damage your credibility and hamper even an effective defense. Create and manage your documentation so you can live with it later.

If you need to go back to document something after the fact, do so, but always date the record the day it is prepared. If earlier documentation requires clarification, generate a separate memorandum dated the day it is prepared. If you become a witness, your credibility will be directly at issue; you don't need extraneous questions about the veracity of your recollection or record keeping.

Bomb-Proof Legal Protection Through Good Documentation

What Is Documentation and Why Is It Important?

Documentation is a written record of an event, discussion, or observation by one or more individuals. Most organizations rely on documentation to record their activities and those of their employees. Any written information, whether formally or informally generated, can be considered documentary evidence if it is pertinent to a legal action or a regulatory proceeding. This applies to OSHA inspections, OSHA investigations, OSHA enforcement proceedings, criminal prosecutions for violation of statute, and/or civil lawsuits for damages by an injured person.

A written record of events is the best evidence of what occurred. Many times in litigation—particularly in civil lawsuits for damages arising out of a workplace accident—the events leading up to the accident took place months *or years* before the evidence is actually presented in court. For example, in a lawsuit alleging failure to adequately train a worker whose error caused the accident, the training may have occurred long before the accident. Assuming that the worker claims there was no training, the burden shifts to the employer to establish that the training did occur. Perhaps one of the managers or trainers will remember exactly *when* this particular employee was trained, *what* content areas were included in the training, *how* the employee grasped the material, and so on.

Further, suppose the employee's primary language is not English. Will the manager or trainer remember what steps were taken to ensure that the employee understood the training, particularly the information regarding the hazards to be faced on the job? These critical issues will surely arise in an OSHA inspection or a civil lawsuit following a workplace accident. Leaving this vital information to human memory is risky. Moreover, the manager or trainer who did the training may have retired or moved to another area. In the absence of a written record of the training that took place, the employer's defense is *significantly weakened.*

To prepare for an OSHA inspection, see the discussion in Chapter 2, pp. 52–54. The effect of specific documentation as evidence in an injury action is given in Chapters 3, pp. 77–78, and 8, pp. 195–197.

An instructive Texas case shows how devastating lack of complete documentation can be. In *Truco Properties, Inc. v. Faye Charlton,*[1] a 68-year-old housekeeper employed in a nursing home operated by Truco was injured while lifting a mop bucket filled with water. The jury concluded that Truco failed to provide proper instructions and training for the job that Faye Charlton was performing and assessed damages for negligence.

The most compelling evidence supporting the jury's finding was testimony by an administrator of the nursing home regarding the injured employee's training. Her file showed a training inventory checklist noting each portion of the training received, by signature and date, but the section referring to the training on body mechanics and lifting procedures was blank. The administrator acknowledged in pretrial deposition that if Charlton had received training it would be reflected by her file. At trial, the story changed, with the same administrator testifying that the file did not necessarily reflect all the training provided to this employee.

The trainer testified that the laundry training and housekeeping training had been combined and took about two hours total time. She also testified that she had prepared a skills inventory checklist for Charlton reflecting her training in laundry skills, but no equivalent checklist for any housekeeping training.

The trainer further testified that her part of the instruction covered general instructions about the methods of lifting heavy objects, including: "I talk about lifting, the general rules. Use your thigh and leg muscles. Keep your back straight. Divide the weight between two hands....Get as close to the object as possible. Squat or bend your knees and then straighten out. Keep that object as close to your body as you can. If you need help, ask for it. Then we do some demonstrating."[3]

Finally, the laundry and housekeeping supervisor at the time of the accident testified that she knew it was dangerous for a woman to try to pick up a full industrial-size mop bucket. The administrator also confirmed her knowledge that training for employees on safety was important.

On the basis of all this evidence, the appellate court made two critical findings: (1) the jury had enough evidence to conclude that it was foreseeable that without proper training an injury could occur, and (2) there was a "clear dispute about the extent of training received by Charlton." Since the employer could not establish that effective training was provided, the adverse judgment was upheld.

How Is Documentation Used?

To Establish Compliance With a Statute. The primary purpose for maintaining documentation of training and other aspects of compliance is to present it to an inspector at the time of a regulatory visit to your place of employment. Complete, legible, concise, and easy-to-understand documentation provides the best opportunity to avoid costly enforcement proceedings.

To Avoid Criminal or Civil Proceedings. Many times, a lawsuit can be avoided by demonstrating to the potential adverse party that the employer's position will be unbeatable. In these instances, the documentation (or a portion of it) can be turned over to the adverse party in advance of any proceedings. Turning over documents is valuable if it prevents the litigation. However, legal counsel should always be consulted first, since (1) some of the documentation may be privileged and should not be produced and (2) this is usually a strategic issue that may affect any litigation filed.

To Refresh Memory. When recollections vary, the trier of fact must determine whom to believe. This is the crucial issue of *credibility*. Many times, witnesses whose memory is imprecise can still be very credible *if their memory is refreshed by reviewing documents that they prepared closer to the time of the original events*. Their memory refreshed, the witnesses can then testify to renewed or expanded personal knowledge.

To Attack Credibility.   Documentation may also be used to attack the credibility of a witness. For example, suppose an injured employee testifies that he was never trained on a hazard of his job, and as a result of that lack of training, he was injured. Suppose further that, under questioning, the employee contends he specifically remembers that he was not at work the day training took place. As the trainer, you have documentation reflecting the date, location, and substance of this employee's training. When confronted with the documentation, the employee backs down, losing credibility as a witness. Likewise, if the employee has kept documentation and you have not, your credibility—or that of your employer—is diminished, and the outcome of the proceeding is jeopardized.

Inconsistent statements in documentation, as between the testimony of a witness and the documentation he creates, can also be the source of impeachment on credibility issues. Inconsistent statements under oath are fertile grounds for the proverbial cross-examination: "Were you lying then or are you lying now?"

Use of Documentation in Court.   In most criminal or civil proceedings, written documentation is not introduced in a vacuum. Rather, oral testimony about an event will be given. Witnesses are drawn from adverse parties (e.g., an injured employee and a manager from the employer organization) and from independent persons with no stake in the litigation. The trier of fact—judge, jury, or arbitration panel—will be asked to weigh the testimony and reach a determination.

Very often, witnesses have substantially different memories about the same events, usually as a result of human memory frailties or honest misrecollection. However, eager witnesses may attempt to testify about personal memory when in fact they did not actually observe or participate in the events. Sometimes, witnesses may even be untruthful.

What Form Should Documentation Take?

There is no single correct way to construct documentation or to memorialize your activities. It is important to develop procedures that you and your organization can enforce consistently. Much will depend on your industry and the types of activities you are documenting. For example, heavily regulated industries need more detailed compliance records, while others can meet their needs with simple files. The key is to use a system that works for you consistently, so you can reconstruct past events with ease and accuracy.

Good documentation has several elements. In particular, it should be easily understandable and readable by everyone in the organization. Consistency is vital.

Document Retention Policies

The question is really not "to keep or not to keep" but rather "to create or not to create." Once a document has been created, it then falls within the parameters of the existing record retention policies of your organization. Many organizations have special training or instruction on the preparation of business records. The program could be classified as the "dos and don'ts" of preparing company records.

The general belief is that instructing employees on preparing records is best done outside the formal retention policies. The general subject matter of preparation tends to follow the lines that any document created is of necessity going to be seen by people outside the company: by vendors, government agencies, adverse parties in litigation, regulatory investigators, competitors, and the press. Instructions in record preparation counsel specifically against using terms like "top secret," "destroy or shred when done," "confidential," and "secret." The rule of thumb is to ask whether the company would be embarrassed if the record was seen by someone in the public.

Instructions in preparing records should reflect a policy that is in compliance with sound business practices. Pay attention to detail when preparing records to prevent ambiguities that might be difficult to overcome at a later date. In general, a later attempt to clear up any confusing language or impression created by the original document will be unsuccessful.

The length of time you keep records is subject to the needs of your particular organization. Regulatory documents should, at a minimum, be kept for the period of time set forth in the governing statute or regulation. Although this is a minimum requirement, retention time may be extended by company policies, for good business reasons. Once such a retention policy has been adopted, *it should be followed consistently*. Otherwise, you may find yourself explaining in court why a seemingly relevant document was destroyed in violation of your own company policy, even when the government did not require you to retain the material. The trier of fact may draw adverse inferences because the document no longer exists.

Review your personal record keeping and your training department's record retention policies to ensure that they accurately reflect your current business needs, while remaining effective to bolster a defense that you did everything required to meet your legal duties. Consult with your management or legal counsel if you have any questions about the company's overall requirements. A detailed analysis of document retention should be coordinated to guarantee that retention or nonretention meets reasonable standards and can be supported by testimony from your company's representatives, if necessary.

With the increased scrutiny of computer records in litigation, it is important for record policies to adequately address the nonretention and proper disposal of nonessential computer business records. Detailed review of all computer data systems must be made periodically to capture newly created information. A planned, cohesive record-keeping policy is essential to prevent adverse assumptions about the absence of documents.

Electronic Documents

Electronic data are fast becoming a central focus of evidence in litigation. Until a few years ago, most corporate data were maintained on large mainframe computers. Today, most organizations use personal computer workstations and local area networks. These systems, and the data stored on them, are more easily retrieved and cost-effectively analyzed in litigation.

Trial lawyers who typically represent injured parties and specialized computer consultants now have the power to process electronic data that were previously unattainable. E-mail and other electronic data evidence have become more prevalent and critical in employment litigation. Given current trends, it appears that electronic materials will become the primary type of documentation utilized by all parties to court cases. This reality makes it more important than ever to develop and consistently enforce a method for electronic data management.

Proactive training departments can take steps to develop an electronic evidence management plan for reviewing, evaluating, and retrieving electronic data to use in defending litigation as well as for managing the training function. A significant aspect of the plan is to prepare the company—and the training department—to respond to requests for documentation from regulators and opponents in litigation. You must know what you've got, where it is, and the nature of the content. When you manage electronic data in a planned manner, rather than being put on the defensive, you will present a better posture and defuse a weapon your adversary was depending upon.

Your ability to assemble relevant electronic records will assist you and your training department (or your small speaking or consulting office) in evaluating the strength and weaknesses of your position at an early stage of any dispute. Without such early review, company or client representatives may be required to respond to OSHA inspectors' questions, answer a criminal complaint, or give sworn testimony in a civil lawsuit without the benefit of reviewing the materials. If relevant materials such as e-mail messages, training records, and other memoranda exchanged within the training department are later discovered, they may be a source of embarrassment if they are inconsistent with the earlier responses. An effective electronic documentation plan will permit authorized representatives to give complete information when requested. It will also enable legal counsel to make informed judgments about the strength or weakness of your position should litigation occur.

A final advantage to electronic documentation management is the ability to address compliance problems proactively. Data backup and archiving procedures can be adjusted to make it easier to identify, evaluate, and retrieve data in connection with audits of regulatory compliance systems or training programs. Inadvertent accumulation of information with no business purpose can be minimized. Procedures can be developed to reduce inappropriate comments and discriminatory content in e-mail and other abuses of the computer systems, which in turn reduces the underlying causes of litigation and liabilities.

Three Steps for Preventing Successful Challenges to Your Documentation

1. Make sure your documentation is complete.

There is no substitute for clear, comprehensive files. If you have missing pages, illegible photocopies, or otherwise incomplete records, your documentation loses its positive impact. Remember that you may be required to produce your original files for inspection. It is best to use ink on handwritten materials, clearly label file folders, and use *complete* dates (with the month, day, and year).

2. Use objective terms to describe events and compliance.

Make the effort to ensure that your documents are correctly interpreted by a jury, even years after the underlying events have occurred. If your documents can be taken out of context by your adversary, or your records express opinions on the ultimate facts in dispute—without all the relevant facts—your position may be adversely affected. Avoid subjective or relative terms, which at best are ambiguous and at worse misconstrued, as depicted in Figure 20-1. Your documentation should have all the following elements:

OBJECTIVITY   The "five Ws" (who, what, when, where, and why)
CONSISTENCY   The same basic information *always*
RELIABILITY   Created from personal knowledge
RELEVANCY   Job-related or training-related data
VERIFICATION   Witness and document identification
CREDIBILITY   Truthful and trustworthy

3. Make sure your documentation is capable of "authentication."

To introduce documentation to a regulator or as evidence in a courtroom, you must establish that it was created as a business record, on or about the date it bears. This holds for *all* evidence: hard copies, electronic files, photographs, audiotapes and videotapes, and other tangible items. Although the parties may "stipulate" (agree) that the evidence is authentic, a difficult adversary has the option to require you to call a knowledgeable witness to authenticate, or verify, when and how the documents were created. The witness may be the photographer or videographer, or the individual *who actually generated the documents.*

Because it can be troublesome when an authenticating witness is unavailable, all trainers, speakers, and consultants should develop consistent methods for creating records maintained in the ordinary course of their business. This provides flexibility—and veracity—when you offer documents in your own defense.

A Word About Ethics

With the increasing breadth of your legal responsibilities, you may find yourself in the difficult position of having to stand up against unethical or even unlawful actions by your employer—in essence, "blow the whistle" on improper conduct. The notion of whistleblowing has been used to cover a variety of situations, such as refusing to commit or participate in an unlawful act for your employer, refusing to carry out illegal or unethical instructions, and reporting a perceived impropriety to a supervisor or through other internal channels.

In addition, you may be called upon to respond to lawful requests for information or documents by a government agency, even when instructed by an agent of your employer to withhold such information,

Avoid Subjective Labels About Trainees in Favor of Objective
Performance [*stick to the facts*]

- Aggressive
- Timid
- Uncommunicative
- Slow

Avoid Relative Terms About Events and Stick to Facts [*let the jury
decide on the basis of all the facts*]

- Excessive
- Frequent
- Untimely
- The -er words: *faster, slower, greater than*

Avoid Ultimate Conclusions in Favor of Facts [*let the experts provide
opinions*]

- Equipment was "defective"   [*use objective description*]
- Trainers were "negligent"   [*stick to what happened*]
- Consultant "breached"   [*record objective events*]
- Speaker "defamed"   [*describe actual words used*]

Figure 20-1 Effective Documentation Techniques to Ensure Objectivity and
Minimize the Potential for Turning Documentation Against You.

or to actively report improper activities to a government agency. Be
prepared to handle these situations as they arise by understanding your
role, rights, and responsibilities.

The health and safety arena presents trainers and consultants with
one of the most common grounds for whistleblowing. If your employer
or client refuses to comply with OSHA requirements, withholds information from inspectors, or otherwise refuses to maintain a safe working
environment consistent with the training you have provided, you are
faced with a dilemma: tell and risk reprisals, or keep quiet. When you
are faced with this choice, ethical standards may require actions adverse
to your employer's or client's interests.

Fortunately, you have broad legal protections for acting consistently
with the highest ethical standards. As a "whistleblower," you may bring
lawsuits for damages if you suffer retaliation. One example was *Haynes
v. Zoological Society of Cincinnati, Ohio*,[4] which involved an award of

damages and attorneys' fees to a zookeeper who suffered harassment, demotion, and constructive discharge in retaliation for making safety complaints to OSHA and the Department of Agriculture. After a fellow worker lost an arm while feeding a polar bear, the zookeeper told OSHA that hand-feeding was a common practice among the keepers and that they were not trained in bear handling. Following her complaints, she was demoted to an entry-level job, allegedly for safety reasons, and was suspended when she refused to accept the transfer without explanation.

The zookeeper then filed a private lawsuit for retaliatory demotion, and the court ordered her reinstated to her original job. Following reinstatement, she was denied access to necessary records and prevented from listening to safety tapes. She was protected from such retaliatory action both by the federal OSH Act and by Ohio whistle-blower laws.

Unlawful discrimination in the workplace is another area where you may have to make the difficult choice of opposing unlawful practices rather than participating. Once again, you can take some comfort in the strong public policy—and legal standards—that protect you from retaliation. In March 1997, an Ohio court concluded that the retaliatory termination of a personnel director of a nonprofit organization three weeks after he informed the board of directors that female employees were being sexually harassed was flatly unlawful. The personnel director had pursued the issue in meetings, even in the face of overt anger by a high-level executive. The employer claimed he was fired for encouraging former employees to submit complaints about the executive. The court disagreed, concluding that the personnel director was retaliated against for complying with his legal *and ethical* duties to address behaviors in the workplace that were both inappropriate and discriminatory.[5]

Savvy trainers, speakers, and consultants—particularly those who read this book—are sensitive to the variety of ways that documentation may affect their own position in litigation, as well as that of their employer or client. As a result, they may be tempted to "rewrite" or "clarify" prior events by altering documentation after the underlying events have occurred, usually in contemplation of or in response to litigation.

Don't do it. Ever. Put bluntly, when it becomes evident that your business records or documentation have been tampered with in any way, your credibility—and that of your client's organization—is jeopardized.

A wide variety of documents may be relevant in litigation and/or regulatory proceedings. Diversity audits, records of interviews with the client's employees, performance tests, copyrighted materials, notes and memoranda, e-mail messages, nonconfidential portions of personnel files, and a host of other materials generated during the performance of a consulting contract may all be subject to review. The standard for civil discovery of such materials is very broad—all documents that are relevant to the subject matter of the litigation or may reasonably lead to the discovery of admissible evidence. Thus, any document (even a handwritten note, telephone log, or meeting minutes) that discloses even the name of another potential witness may be subject to disclosure through discovery.

Once it becomes apparent that litigation may be filed, all potentially relevant documents may be subject to disclosure. The failure to produce the documents when lawfully requested results in significant consequences: negative publicity, unfavorable results in the case itself, monetary fines by the judge, disapproval by the jury, or adverse court orders (including default). Failure to produce relevant documents after a court order has been entered is contempt of court, with a host of additional penalties.

How to Make Your Documentation a Defensive Weapon in a Legal Proceeding

Develop and memorialize standardized documentation procedures. Once you have adopted procedures, require consistent enforcement throughout the training department, among your own staff, and with external consultants.

Keep informed about emerging statutory documentation requirements. When in doubt about the applicability of a statute to your industry, consult legal counsel. Coordinate with line management about required skill levels and then memorialize how particular training programs or activities are designed to meet those requirements.

Determine when language or cultural barriers to learning exist, and document the steps taken to overcome such obstacles. *Caveat:* Carefully develop a consistent approach and legally acceptable description of these factors to avoid giving the appearance of discriminatory attitudes or damaging reputations. When a trainee requires special language or literacy instruction, memorialize the steps you take to maximize the effectiveness of the training for that individual. Likewise, when you consider the type of reasonable accommodations you can make for a disabled trainee or test taker, document the full range of what you considered. See the detailed discussions in Chapters 2, pp. 57–59; 6, pp. 141–143; 7, pp. 167–171; and 8, pp. 192–195.

Develop measurable, job-specific learning objectives and *require* acceptable performance by each trainee. Be objective and candid about the trainee's limitations, using *factual* descriptions rather than generalized judgments whenever possible. *Caveat:* Be especially careful to confirm with line managers that an employee who has not reached an acceptable skill level will not be placed on the job without direct supervision.

Be complete and accurate, but avoid the "cover thyself" syndrome when differences arise over a trainee's job readiness. When in doubt, err by being less descriptive of such conflicts with line management.

15 Steps to Effective Documentation in a Legal Context

1. Establish objective training standards of performance for instructors and staff and memorialize why the standards are job related.

2. Establish realistic requirements for instructor qualifications in all programs, and document how the requirements are enforced.

3. Establish measurable learning objectives, tied to performance standards, and then *enforce them consistently.*

4. Train workers on job-specific safety issues, and record who attended, what was covered, and how employees performed.

5. Comply with all statutory regulations regarding content and scope of training, and specialized record-keeping requirements.

6. Develop job-specific, objective, and measurable evaluation standards, and concise records of trainees' results. Maintain confidentiality.

7. Make reasonable accommodations for trainees with language barriers or special needs and document your entire analysis.

8. Carefully evaluate testing criteria before administering tests; memorialize each step taken to accommodate language and/or cultural barriers.

9. Document the training each employee receives and follow up at regular intervals to ensure continued compliance with regulatory requirements.

10. Always provide candid, constructive criticism to trainees and employees and document that you have done so.

11. Understand the range of documents that may become "documentation" in litigation. A few examples:

- Drafts of training materials and permission letters in a copyright infringement lawsuit (see Chapters 18 and 19)
- Safety training records (existing or missing) in an injury lawsuit (see Chapters 2, 3, and 4)
- Accident reports following a training mishap (see Chapters 3, 4, and 8)
- Investigation notes about vendor safety records in adventure training (see Chapter 8, pp. 195–197)
- Performance evaluations and tests in a discrimination lawsuit (see Chapter 7, pp. 159–167)
- Flip charts and other participant notes in a diversity training discrimination claim (see Chapter 5, pp. 112–114)
- Contracts and correspondence in a contract dispute (see Chapters 13, 16, and 17)

12. Do not back-date, fabricate, destroy, or in any way alter documentation once it has been generated. Doing so is both unethical and a prescription for disaster if you are ever asked under oath to explain the evolution of particular documentation. If something needs to be clarified, create a new memorandum explaining the clarification and the basis for it, and date the new document with the current date.

13. Make sure that internal trainers can fully understand your company's record-retention policies. Follow those policies consistently. Violation of company policy may give rise to disciplinary action. Notify all appropriate company representatives of the obligation to identify and take reasonable steps to preserve potentially relevant documents.

14. Develop a record-retention policy you can consistently enforce. Don't make it too cumbersome. Establish objective indicia for which documents you keep, and which you do not. The policy should be business related, but still allow you to justify in later litigation why you did not retain a particular item. This limits the inference that you destroyed something not helpful to your position.

15. Educate trainers and staff on appropriate documentation techniques to ensure consistent enforcement of your policies.

How to Keep Up With Applicable Laws Without Becoming a Lawyer

A wealth of materials are available to assist you in keeping up with applicable laws. Most newsletters are written in plain English, with references to relevant laws or regulations for further details. Appendix A contains a state-by-state list of regulatory agencies and their telephone numbers, and Appendix B is a state-by-state guide to employment discrimination laws governing employees' EEO rights, including access to training.

How to Resolve Disputes Without Bringing in the Lawyers

Litigation is usually contentious, prohibitively expensive, frequently embarrassing, and wasteful of everyone's time and attention. *With the prime purpose of avoiding the costs of workplace litigation, some proactive employers set up three- and four-step "grievance" procedures.*

Both companies and individual employees have compelling reasons to divert workplace conflicts into internal dispute-resolution processes:

- A legitimate, user-friendly forum for airing workplace gripes and solving problems should help manage disputes, correct errors, and provide explanations.

- A prompt communication of the grievance in an "off the record" context should permit both management and employee to anticipate and possibly defuse circumstances that could develop into serious, expensive, and destructive conflicts.

- Employees and managers should be encouraged to communicate (i.e., listen to each other) in order to foster greater workplace understanding and collaboration.

Conclusion

This book is intended to provide a broad overview of the variety of legal issues you may face in your career as a professional trainer, speaker, or consultant. The objective is threefold: (1) to give you a level of awareness so you don't inadvertently get into legal trouble; (2) to provide a handy desk reference when an issue develops; and most important (3) to remove some of the "mystery" (or myths) about the legal system and *give you a comfort level that you have taken appropriate steps to protect your own interests along with those of your company and your clients.* Although accurate and up to date, this book is not a substitute for sound legal advice on specific matters. It is intended to provide focus and to alert you to the questions you may need to address with your company representatives, advisers, and legal counsel.

References

1. "On Tape Officials of Texaco Discuss Obstruction of Lawsuit," *The New York Times*, November 4, 1996.

2. *Truco Properties, Inc. v. Faye Charlton*, 749 S.W.2d 895 (1988).

3. *Truco Properties, Inc. v. Faye Charlton*, 749 S.W.2d 895 (1988).

4. *Haynes v. Zoological Society of Cincinnati, Ohio*, 567 N.E.2d 1048 (December 22, 1993).

5. *Thatcher v. Goodwill Industries*, Ohio App.Ct. No. 17817 (January 2, 1997).

APPENDIXES

Appendix A

A State-by-State Guide to Health and Safety Training and Agency Resources

The following federal statues affect the training programs, occupational safety and health plans, and right-to-know laws of individual states:

- *Occupational Safety and Health Act (OSHA).* The most comprehensive legislation is the expanded hazard communication standard, which requires employers to train all workers who may be exposed to hazardous chemicals under normal operating conditions or in foreseeable emergencies. In addition, workers who may become ill from exposure to dangerous substances in the facility—even though not in the direct performance of their job—must receive a level of hazard training that is sufficient to alleviate the risks.

- *Resource Conservation and Recovery Act (RCRA).* The act requires the EPA to establish a list of hazardous waste substances and to establish standards for generators, transporters, and disposers of such waste. RCRA provides for civil penalties of up to $25,000 per day as well as injunctive relief. Criminal penalties are also available against any person who knowingly operates without a permit or makes a false statement to the EPA.

- *Toxic Substances Control Act (TSCA).* The act requires industry testing and reporting of chemical substances where the EPA finds that certain conditions, relating to possible toxicity or widespread exposure, are met.

- *Emergency Planning and Community Right-to-Know Act (SARA).* Criminal penalties apply to *any person who knowingly and willfully fails to provide notice of hazardous substances* as required by the act. If your company must prepare or have available a material safety data sheet (MSDS) under OSHA regulations, Section 311 of Title III requires you to submit copies of the MSDS or a list of all MSDS chemicals, to the LERC (Local Emergency Response Commission), the SERC (State Emergency Response Commission), and the local fire department. Upon conviction, the fine may be $25,000 or imprisonment for two years, or both. For a second or subsequent conviction, a $50,000 fine and five years imprisonment will apply. Civil penalties may also be assessed, especially for continuing violations.

- *Superfund (CERCLA).* There are many important aspects to CERCLA. The act requires detailed record keeping by any facility that stores hazardous substances, and prompt notification to EPA of incidents involving the escape of such substances into the environment. In 1989, a federal district court in Michigan ruled that *individuals* can be held personally liable for a corporation's CERCLA liabilities. *Kelley ex rel. Michigan Natural Resources Commission v. Arco Industries Corp.*, 723 F.Supp. 1214 (W.D.Mich. 1989).

Set forth below is a summary of the details regarding state occupational safety and health plans and right-to-know laws. The following states do not have any state law covering hazardous substances in the workplace: Arkansas, Colorado, Georgia, Idaho, Kansas, Mississippi, Nebraska, Ohio, Oklahoma, South Dakota, and Wyoming.

Alabama

Law/Code:	AL Code, Secs. 22-33-1 et seq.
Implementation Date:	5/29/85
Enforcing Agency:	Department of Environmental Management 1751 Congressman W.L. Dickinson Drive Montgomery, AL 36130 205-271-7855
Covers:	Any employer in Alabama that manufactures, produces, uses, applies, or stores toxic substances. State right-to-know law applies to public sector employers; private sector employers are covered by federal OSHA.

Exceptions:	Employers with two or fewer employees; employers of professional athletes; agricultural employers; employers of domestic workers in private homes.
Required Training:	Employers must furnish employees with instructions on the nature and effect of toxic substances in the workplace. (Current employees must be given instruction within 9 months of enforcement, then annually; new employees within 30 days of starting employment, then annually.)
Other Requirements:	Employers must provide the fire department with a list of work areas where toxic substances are present; must maintain an MSDS for each toxic substance used in the workplace; must submit an annual evaluation report on the program to the governor and legislature; notice of presence of toxic substances must be posted in an obvious place.
Employee Rights:	Employees have the right to examine each MSDS for toxic substances to which they have been exposed (request must be in writing); employees may refuse to work with the toxic substance if the MSDS is not provided within 5 working days; employers may not discharge, discipline, or discriminate against employees for exercising their rights under the code.
Penalties:	None or unknown.

Alaska

Law/Code:	AK Stat., Sec. 18.60.30 (12), (13) and (14); Secs. 18.60.065, 18.60.066; 18.60.067, 18.60.068, and 18.60.105; Title 8 of the AK Admin. Code, Ch. 61.010, Sec. 15.0101.
Enforcing Agency:	Alaska Department of Labor Division of Labor Standards and Safety P.O. Box 1149 Juneau, AK 99802 907-465-4855
Covers:	Any employer with one or more employees. Applies to employers in public *and* private sectors.

Exceptions:	Employers of domestic workers in private homes; goods, food, drugs, cosmetics, or tobacco products intended for personal consumption; substances in transit in a sealed or unopened container; substances that, because of their physical state, volume, or concentration, do not pose a health hazard upon exposure.
Required Training:	Employers must conduct a safety education program before an employee begins a work assignment that may result in exposure to a toxic or hazardous substance.
Other Requirements:	Toxic and hazardous substances imported into the state must be accompanied by a federal OSHA Form 20; notice of the presence of toxic substances must be posted in an obvious place in the work area.
Employee Rights:	Employers must make a copy of the most recent OSHA Form 20 available to employees upon their request.

Arizona

Law/Code:	Ariz. Rev. Stat. Ann., Secs. 23-401 et seq.
Enforcing Agency:	Division of Occupational Safety and Health 3221 N. 16th Street, Ste. 100 Phoenix, AZ 85016 602-640-2006
Covers:	Employers in public *and* private sectors.
Required Training:	Employees must be trained on potential exposure to hazardous substances; symptoms; emergency treatment; safe use; protective equipment.

California

Law/Code:	CA Labor Code, Secs. 6300 et seq.
Enforcing Agencies:	CA Department of Industrial Relations 2151 Berkeley Way Berkeley, CA 94704 415-540-3014

Cal/OSHA Headquarters
525 Golden Gate Avenue
San Francisco, CA 94102
415-557-1946

Covers: Any employer in California whose employees may be exposed to hazardous substances; any person who sells a hazardous substance to any employer in the state; manufacturers that produce or sell hazardous substances in the state. Applies to employers in public *and* private sectors.

Exceptions: Some laboratories; pesticides; food, drug, and cosmetic products; alcoholic beverages; consumer products; hazardous waste; tobacco products; wood and wood products; articles (manufactured items); retail trade establishments.

Required Training: Employees must be given formal instruction on the employer's hazard communication program; information and training must be provided when a new employee starts work and whenever a new hazardous substance is brought into the workplace.

Other Requirements: Employers should maintain written documentation of employee training sessions; must maintain an MSDS for each toxic substance used in the workplace; must maintain a list of all toxic substances in the workplace and all relevant information about such substances; notice of the presence of toxic substances must be posted in an obvious place in the work area; containers of hazardous substances must be clearly labeled.

Employee Rights: Employees have the right to examine the MSDS for toxic substances to which they have been exposed (request must be in writing); employees cannot be discharged, disciplined, or discriminated against for exercising their rights.

Connecticut

Law/Code: CT Stat, Secs. 19a-329 through 331, 31-30c through 31-30p, and 29-307a(c).

Enforcing Agencies:	Department of Labor 200 Folly Brook Boulevard Wethersfield, CT 06109 203-566-5160
	Bureau of the State Fire Marshal 294 Colony Road Meriden, CT 06450 203-238-6623
Covers:	All public sector employers; state right-to-know law applies only to public sector employers; private sector employers are covered by federal OSHA; has a community right-to-know statute.
Required Training:	Employees must be instructed on the presence of all hazardous substances in the workplace within one month of beginning employment; employees must sign a statement acknowledging receipt of information.
Other Requirements:	Employers must maintain a list of all toxic substances in the workplace and all relevant information about such substances; community right-to-know law requires that the general public be informed about local chemical hazards.
Employee Rights:	Employees may request information from the employer and/or the labor department; Employees *can* be terminated for noncompliance with the training program.

Delaware

Law/Code:	DE Code Ann., Tit. XVI, Secs. 2401 et seq.
Enforcing Agency:	Bureau of Environmental Health Division of Public Health P.O. Box 637 802 Silver Lake Plaza Dover, DE 19903 302-736-3839
Covers:	State right-to-know law applies to public sector employers; private sector employers are covered by federal OSHA.
Exceptions:	Employers that are regulated and complying with federal OSHA; chemicals that do not release a hazardous substance under normal

conditions; products intended for personal consumption by employees in the workplace; retail food and trade establishments; workplaces where the hazardous chemical is kept sealed and is in the workplace for fewer than five days; any product regulated by the federal Food, Drug, and Cosmetic Act or Federal Alcohol Administration; certain laboratories and certain agricultural employers.

Required Training: Employers must conduct annual education and training programs and keep records of the dates of the training programs; new employees must be trained before they start work.

Other Requirements: Employers must maintain an MSDS for each toxic substance used in the workplace; must maintain a list of all toxic substances in the workplace and all relevant information about such substances; containers of hazardous substances must be clearly labeled; community right-to-know law requires that the general public be informed about local chemical hazards.

Employee Rights: Any written complaint by an employee will be investigated by the secretary of the enforcing agency; employees exposed to hazardous chemicals must be informed of the exposure; no employer may discharge, discipline, or discriminate against any employee who exercises his or her rights under the act; no employee may waive his or her rights under the act, and an employer may not request such a waiver.

District of Columbia

Law/Code: DC Code, Tit. 36, Ch. 12

Enforcing Agency: Occupational Safety and Health Board
820 1st Street NE, Ste. 440
Washington, DC 20002
202-523-1452

Covers: Applies to employers in public *and* private sectors.

Required Training: Employees must be trained on potential exposure to hazardous substances; symptoms; emergency treatment; safe use; protective equipment.

Florida

Law/Code:	West's FL Stat. Ann., Sec. 442.101 et seq. FL Admin. Code. Chapter 38F-41.
Enforcing Agency:	Department of Labor and Employment Security 2728 Centerview Drive Tallahassee, FL 32399-0663 904-488-3044
Covers:	Any employer that has two or more employees and uses, applies, stores, manufactures, or produces toxic substances. State right-to-know law applies to public sector employers; private sector employers are covered by federal OSHA.
Exceptions:	Employers with one employee; agricultural employers; employers of domestic workers in private homes.
Required Training:	Employers must furnish employees with instructions on the nature and effect of toxic substances in the workplace. (Current employees must be given instruction within 9 months of enforcement, then annually; new employees within 30 days of starting employment, then annually.)
Other Requirements:	Employers must maintain an MSDS for each toxic substance used in the workplace; must maintain a list of all toxic substances in the workplace and all relevant information about such substances.
Employee Rights:	Employees have the right to examine each MSDS for toxic substances to which they have been exposed (request must be in writing); employees may refuse to work with the toxic substance if the MSDS is not provided within five working days; employers may not discharge, discipline, or discriminate, against employees for exercising their rights under the code.

Hawaii

Law/Code:	HRS Secs. 12-203-1 et seq. and 396-4
Enforcing Agency:	Administrative and Technical Support Branch OSH Program Department of Labor and Industrial Relations 830 Punchbowl Street Honolulu, HI 96813 808-548-4155

Covers:	Applies to employers in public *and* private sectors.
Exceptions:	Employers with two or fewer employees; employers of professional athletes; agricultural employers; employers of domestic workers in private homes.
Required Training:	Employers must develop a detailed written hazard communication program that is available to all employees upon their request. *Note:* No formal classroom-type training session is required, but it is recommended.
Other Requirements:	Employers must maintain an MSDS for each toxic substance used in the workplace; must maintain a list of all toxic substances in the workplace and all relevant information about such substances.
Employee Rights:	Employees have the right to request a copy of the employer's written hazardous communication program.

Illinois

Law/Code:	56 Ill. Adm. Code 205
Enforcing Agency:	Illinois Department of Labor Toxic Substance Division 1 West Old State Capitol Plaza, Room 300 Springfield, IL 62701-1217 217-782-4102
Covers:	Employers with 20 or more part-time employees or 5 or more full-time employees. State right-to-know law applies to public sector employers; private sector employers are covered by federal OSHA; has a community right-to-know statute.
Exceptions:	Employers with fewer than 5 full-time employees or 20 part-time employees; employers of domestic workers in private homes; workplaces where the toxic substances are intended for personal consumption by employees or the toxic substances are present in concentrations of less than 1 percent.
Required Training:	Employers must hold annual training sessions.
Other Requirements:	Employers must maintain an MSDS for each toxic substance used in the workplace; must maintain a list of all toxic substances in the

workplace and all relevant information about such substances; notice of the presence of toxic substances must be posted in an obvious place in the work area; containers of hazardous substances must be clearly labeled; employers must post a sign of all employee rights; community right-to-know law requires that the general public be informed about local chemical hazards.

Employee Rights: Employees have the right to examine each MSDS for toxic substances to which they have been exposed (request must be in writing); employees may refuse to work with the toxic substance if the MSDS is not provided within five working days; employers may not discharge, discipline, or discriminate against employees for exercising their rights under the code; employers must not ask employees to waive these rights.

Indiana

Law/Code: Ind. Code, Secs. 22-8-1.1 et seq.

Enforcing Agency: Department of Labor
State Office Building
402 W. Washington Street, Room N 195
Indianapolis, IN 46204
317-232-2655

Covers: Applies to employers in public *and* private sectors.

Exceptions: Not specified.

Required Training: Employees must be trained on potential exposure to hazardous substances; symptoms; emergency treatment; safe use; protective equipment.

Iowa

Law/Code: IAC, Secs. 455D.1 et seq. IAC, Chs. 110, 120, 130, and 140.

Implementation Date: 1/1/84

Enforcing Agency: Iowa Division of Labor Service
1000 Grand Avenue
Des Moines, IA 50319
515-281-3606

Covers:	Applies to employers in public and private sectors.
Exceptions:	Employers engaged in farming; certain pesticide employers; certain research laboratories; employers dealing with certain hazardous substances that are defined as consumer products.
Required Training:	Employers must conduct a safety education program before an employee begins work and any time a new hazardous substance is introduced into the workplace; employers must also develop and implement a written hazard communication program.
Other Requirements:	Employers must maintain an MSDS for each toxic substance used in the workplace; must maintain a list of all toxic substances in the workplace and all relevant information about such substances; containers of hazardous substances must be clearly labeled; community right-to-know law requires that the general public be informed about local chemical hazards.
Employee Rights:	Employees have the right to be informed about all hazardous substances with which they work; employers may not discharge, discipline, or discriminate against employees for exercising their rights under the code.

Kentucky

Law/Code:	KY Rev. Stat. Ann., Ch. 338.
Enforcing Agency:	Division of Occupational Safety and Health Compensation Department of Workplace Standards 1047 U.S. Highway 127 South, Ste. 2 Frankfort, KY 40610 502-227-7024
Covers:	Applies to employers in public and private sectors.
Exceptions:	Not specified.
Required Training:	Employees must be trained on potential exposure to hazardous substances; symptoms; emergency treatment; safe use; protective equipment.

Louisiana

Law/Code:	R.S. 30:1150.61-79.
Enforcing Agency:	Department of Public Safety and Corrections Office of State Police Transportation and Environmental Safety Section P.O. Box 66614 Baton Rouge, LA 70896 504-925-6113
Covers:	Owners and operators engaged in business or research operations which use, manufacture, emit, or store a hazardous material at the facility. State right-to-know law applies to public sector employers; private sector employers are covered by federal OSHA.
Exceptions:	Small businesses (single establishments employing a maximum of nine employees and showing a maximum of $2 million in average gross receipts); some retail establishments; cosmetology salons and barbershops. Certain substances don't have to be reported, such as hazardous materials under military control, consumer products, or foodstuff intended for use by the general public; hazardous materials reported under the Louisiana Pesticide Law or Louisiana Structural Pest Control Law; and hazardous materials reported to the Nuclear Regulatory Commission.
Other Requirements:	Notice of the presence of toxic substances must be posted in an obvious place in the work area; community right-to-know law requires that the general public be informed about local chemical hazards.

Maine

Law/Code:	26 ME R.S.A., Secs. 1709 et seq.
Enforcing Agency:	Maine Bureau of Labor Standards Department of Labor Station 45 Hallowell Annex Augusta, ME 04333 207-289-6460

Covers:	All employers except agricultural employers. State right-to-know law applies to public sector employers; private sector employers are covered by federal OSHA.
Exceptions:	Tobacco or tobacco products; wood or wood products; food, drugs, or cosmetics intended for employee consumption at the workplace; consumer products and foodstuffs packaged for use by the general public; fire extinguishers in the workplace; common substances found in small amounts in the workplace that do not pose a significant risk of harm. *Note:* If it is determined that strict compliance with the act will not contribute to employee safety and health, the director may waive certain requirements.
Required Training:	Information and training must be provided before all employees start work and updated periodically; employers must also develop and implement a written hazard communication program; employers must maintain a list of employees by name and job title who have received training, the type of training provided, and the dates it was provided.
Other Requirements:	Employers must maintain an MSDS for each toxic substance used in the workplace; must maintain a list of all toxic substances in the workplace and all relevant information about such substances; notice of the presence of toxic substances must be posted in an obvious place in the work area; containers of hazardous substances must be clearly labeled; community right-to-know law requires that the general public be informed about local chemical hazards.
Employee Rights:	Chemical lists and MSDS records must be made available to employees, former employees, authorized representatives of employees or former employees, and physicians of employees or former employees upon request; employees must be given access to exposure tests taken to measure employee exposure in the workplace; employers may not discharge, discipline, or discriminate against employees for exercising their rights under the code.

Maryland

Law/Code:	MD Ann. Code, Art. 89, Secs. 32A to N.
Implementation Date:	5/25/86
Enforcing Agency:	Maryland Division of Labor and Industry Industrial Hygiene Division 501 St. Paul Place Baltimore, MD 21202 301-333-4219
Covers:	Any employer that uses or stores a hazardous chemical in the state; any person who imports or sells any hazardous chemical to any employer in the state; any manufacturer that produces, repackages, distributes, or sells any hazardous chemical in the state. Applies to employers in public *and* private sectors.
Exceptions:	Hazardous materials that are consumer products or foodstuff for use by the general public; some laboratories; railroads subject to the federal Railroad Safety Act of 1970.
Required Training:	Training sessions and education required prior to initial assignment of employee; training also required as new information becomes available or if an employee is subjected to increased exposure; employer must keep employee training records.
Other Requirements:	Employers must maintain an MSDS for each toxic substance used in the workplace; must maintain a list of all toxic substances in the workplace and all relevant information about such substances; notice of the presence of toxic substances must be posted in an obvious place in the work area; containers of hazardous substances must be clearly labeled; community right-to-know law requires that the general public be informed about local chemical hazards.
Employee Rights:	Employees have the right to examine each MSDS for toxic substances to which they have been exposed (request must be in writing); employees cannot be discharged, disciplined, or discriminated against for exercising their rights under the code.

Massachusetts

Law/Code:	M.G.L.A., Ch. 111F, Secs. 1 et seq.
Enforcing Agency:	Right-to-Know Office Department of Labor and Industries 100 Cambridge Street, Room 30 Boston, MA 02202 617-727-5816
Covers:	All employers that manufacture, process, use, or store hazardous substances. State right-to-know law applies to public sector employers; private sector employers are covered by federal OSHA.
Exceptions:	Employers of domestic workers in private homes; research laboratories.
Required Training:	Employers must hold annual training sessions or provide detailed written training instructions on an annual basis; new employees must receive training within the first month of employment.
Training Topics:	Names and locations of hazardous substances; first-aid treatment; proper handling of substances; employees' rights and duties.
Other Requirements:	Employers must maintain an MSDS for each toxic substance used in the workplace; must maintain a list of all toxic substances in the workplace and all relevant information about such substances; notice of the presence of toxic substances must be posted in an obvious place in the work area; containers of hazardous substances must be clearly labeled; employers must post a sign of all employee rights; community right-to-know law requires that the general public be informed about local chemical hazards.
Employee Rights:	Employees have the right to examine each MSDS for toxic substances to which they have been exposed (request must be in writing); employees may refuse to work with the toxic substance if the MSDS is not provided within five working days; employers may not discharge, discipline, or discriminate against employees for exercising their rights under the code; employers must not ask employees to waive these rights.

Michigan

Law/Code:	M.C.L.A., Secs. 408.1005, 408.1011(a)(b)(c)(d), 408.1014a through m, and 408.1031 through 1063.
Enforcing Agencies:	Michigan Department of Public Health Division of Occupational Health 3423 North Logan Street Lansing, MI 48906 517-335-8250
	Michigan Department of Labor 7150 Harris Drive Lansing, MI 48909 517-322-1809
Covers:	All employers with more than one employee. Applies to employers in public *and* private sectors.
Exceptions:	Agricultural employers; employers using chemicals regulated by the Insecticide, Fungicide, and Rodenticide Act or the Pesticide Control Act; employers using chemicals in a sealed package and in transit by a common carrier if the seal remains intact while in transit.
Required Training:	Public service announcements made by the Departments of Public Health and Labor must be distributed to employees; employees must be trained in locating MSDS records; construction employers must provide employee training.
Other Requirements:	Employers must provide protective equipment as needed; must maintain an MSDS for each toxic substance used in the workplace; containers of hazardous substances must be clearly labeled; community right-to-know law requires that the general public be informed about local chemical hazards.
Employee Rights:	Employees have the right to examine each MSDS for toxic substances to which they have been exposed (request must be in writing); employees cannot be discharged, disciplined, or discriminated against for exercising their rights; employees may not be required to operate equipment or engage in a process which the Department of Health has identified as an "imminent danger."

Minnesota

Law/Code:	MN S.A., Secs. 182.65 et seq.
Enforcing Agencies:	Minnesota Department of Labor and Industry 443 Lafayette Road St. Paul, MN 55101 612-296-2116
	Minnesota Department of Health 717 Delaware Street, SE Minneapolis, MN 55440 612-623-5333
	Department of Public Safety Minnesota Emergency Response Commission Room B-5, Capitol Building St. Paul, MN 55101 612-296-0481
Covers:	All employers, the state, and its political subdivisions.
Exceptions:	Farm employers employing fewer than 10 workers; temporary labor camps; physical agents being used by technically qualified individuals in certain laboratories, health care facilities, or pharmacies; products intended for personal consumption by employees in the workplace; consumer products packaged for distribution to and use by the general public; articles that contain hazardous substances present in a solid form that do not create a health hazard if handled by an employee; a hazardous substance found but not released under normal conditions of employment; some products used in retail food establishments and retail trade establishments; substances received by employees in a sealed package and transferred in that package with the seal intact; products for which there is no evidence that a risk to health will occur from exposure.
Required Training:	Employees must receive training prior to initial assignment during which they will work with a hazardous substance, harmful physical agent, or infectious agent; employees must also be trained annually.
Other Requirements:	Employers must establish a written accident and injury reduction program; must maintain an MSDS for each toxic substance used in the

workplace; containers of hazardous substances must be clearly labeled; employers must maintain records of employee exposure to hazardous substances and harmful physical agents; employers must conduct periodic inspections of employee exposure; community right-to-know law requires that the general public be informed about local chemical hazards.

Employee Rights: Employees have the right to request and receive access to information discussed in training programs; employees have the right to request and receive any information that is required to be on a label; employees have the right to refuse to work under conditions which they reasonably believe present an imminent danger of death or serious physical harm; employees cannot be discharged, disciplined, or discriminated against for exercising their rights; employers may not require employees to waive any rights under the law.

Penalties: Fines ranging from $7000 to $35,000, which are assessed on a daily basis until the violation is corrected.

Missouri

Law/Code: RSMO 292.600 through 292.625.

Enforcing Agency: Missouri Department of Natural Resources
Division of Management Services
P.O. Box 170
Jefferson City, MO 65102
314-751-3443

Covers: All employers that use, produce, or store toxic substances; employers of 10 or more agricultural workers; the state and its political subdivisions.

Exceptions: Agricultural employers employing fewer than 10 workers; retailers of consumer goods.

Other Requirements: Employers must provide information about any toxic or hazardous substances it uses or produces to the local fire protection services office and the Missouri Department of Natural Resources.

Montana

Law/Code:	Mon. Code Ann. Secs. 50-78-101 et seq.
Enforcing Agency:	Montana Department of Health and Environmental Services Cogswell Building Helena, MT 59620 406-444-2544
Covers:	State right-to-know law applies to public sector employers; private sector employers are covered by federal OSHA.
Exceptions:	Any consumer product intended for personal consumption or use by an employee; any retail establishment; a food, drug, or cosmetic as defined in the Montana Food, Drug, and Cosmetic Act; certain sources of ionizing radiation; the radiological properties of any source, by-product, or special nuclear material as defined in the federal Atomic Energy Act; sealed containers of hazardous chemicals during transportation or while in storage at transportation terminals.
Required Training:	Employers must hold annual training sessions and provide additional sessions whenever exposure is altered or new chemicals are introduced to the workplace.
Training Topics:	Label and MSDS interpretation; location and effects of hazardous chemicals used; safe handling, protective equipment, first aid treatment, and cleanup and disposal procedures for hazardous chemicals.
Other Requirements:	Employers must maintain an MSDS for each toxic substance used in the workplace; must maintain a list of all toxic substances in the workplace and all relevant information about such substances; containers of hazardous substances must be clearly labeled; employers must keep a record of the dates of training sessions and the names of employees attending; community right-to-know law requires that the general public be informed about local chemical hazards and that employers submit emergency and community information to the clerk and recorder of the county in which the workplace is located.

| Employee Rights: | Employees have the right to examine the chemical lists and MSDS records for toxic substances to which they have been exposed; employees may refuse to work with the toxic substance if the MSDS is not provided within five working days; employers may not discharge, discipline, or discriminate against employees for exercising their rights under the code. |

Nevada

Law/Code:	Nev. Rev. Stat., Ch. 618.
Enforcing Agency:	Division of Occupational Safety and Health Department of Industrial Relations 400 W. King Street Carson City, NV 89710 702-687-3032
Covers:	Employers with 11 or more employees. Applies to employers in public *and* private sectors.
Exceptions:	Not specified.
Required Training:	Employees must be trained on potential exposure to hazardous substances; symptoms; emergency treatment; safe use; protective equipment; precautions to take.

New Hampshire

Law/Code:	R.S.A. 277A
Enforcing Agency:	New Hampshire Department of Labor Inspection Division 19 Pillsbury Street Concord, NH 03301 601-271-3176
Covers:	State right-to-know law applies to public sector employers; private sector employers are covered by federal OSHA.
Exceptions:	Employers of domestic workers or casual laborers; liquor or beverage or other substance which is packaged for retail sale.
Required Training:	Employers must hold training sessions every time a new chemical is introduced into the workplace; new employees must be trained within one month of initial employment.

Training Topics:	Detailed information about the chemicals, hazards of exposure, and symptoms of exposure and overexposure; appropriate emergency treatment for exposure and overexposure; proper conditions for safe use of the substance; procedures for cleanup of leaks and spills of the substance; procedures in case of fire or other environmental changes that would result in increasing the substance's hazardous or toxic properties.
Other Requirements:	Employers must maintain an MSDS for each toxic substance used in the workplace; must maintain a list of all toxic substances in the workplace and all relevant information about such substances; community right-to-know law requires that the general public be informed about local chemical hazards and that employers submit information to the fire department.
Employee Rights:	Employees have the right to examine the chemical lists and MSDS records for toxic substances to which they have been exposed; employees may refuse to work with the toxic substance if the MSDS is not provided within five working days; employers may not discharge, discipline, or discriminate against employees for exercising their rights under the code.

New Jersey

Law/Code:	NJ Stat. Ann. 34:5A-1 et seq., N.J.A.C. 7:1G-1.1 eq seq., and N.J.A.C. 8:59-1 et seq.
Enforcing Agencies:	New Jersey Department of Health Right-to-Know Program CN 368 Trenton, NJ 08625 609-984-2202
	Bureau of Hazardous Substances Information New Jersey Department of Environmental Protection CN 405 Trenton, NJ 08625 609-292-6714

Covers:

All employers that keep and/or use hazardous substances in the workplace. State right-to-know law applies to public sector employers; private sector employers are covered by federal OSHA.

Required Training:

Employers must hold regular training sessions; new employees must be trained within one month of initial employment; training must be provided on paid employer time; both oral training and written instructions must be given.

Training Topics:

Detailed information about the chemicals, hazards of exposure, and symptoms of exposure and overexposure; appropriate emergency treatment for exposure and overexposure; proper conditions for safe use of the substance; procedures for cleanup of leaks and spills of the substance; procedures in case of fire or other environmental changes that would result in increasing the substance's hazardous or toxic properties.

Other Requirements:

Employers must complete the surveys developed by the Department of Environmental Protection and the Department of Health; must maintain an MSDS for each toxic substance used in the workplace; must maintain a list of all toxic substances in the workplace and all relevant information about such substances; notice of the presence of toxic substances must be posted in an obvious place in the work area; community right-to-know law requires that the general public be informed about local chemical hazards; each private employer will be assessed an annual fee of at least $50 but not more than $2 per employee to provide for implementation of the act.

Employee Rights:

Employees have the right to examine the chemical lists and MSDS records for toxic substances to which they have been exposed; employees may refuse to work with the toxic substance if the MSDS is not provided within five working days (unless it is because the government failed to send it to the employer).

New Mexico

Law/Code:	NMSA 50-9-3 and 50-9-5.1.
Enforcing Agency:	Occupational Health and Safety Bureau Environment Improvement Division P.O. Box 968 Santa Fe, NM 87504-0968 505-827-2880
Covers:	Applies to employers in public *and* private sectors.
Exceptions:	Domestic employers; "employers" of volunteer firefighters; hazardous chemicals in a sealed package or container that are subsequently sold or transferred.
Required Training:	Employers must develop and implement a written hazard communication program and make it available to all employees upon request.
Training Topics:	Labels, MSDS records, and lists of hazardous chemicals; hazards of nonroutine tasks; suggestions for appropriate protective measures.
Other Requirements:	Employers must maintain an MSDS for each toxic substance used in the workplace; must maintain a list of all toxic substances in the workplace and all relevant information about such substances; containers of hazardous substances must be clearly labeled; employers must keep a record of any employee exposure to hazardous substances.

New York

Law/Code:	Labor Law, Secs. 875 to 883; Public Health Law, Secs. 4800 to 4808.
Enforcing Agency:	Bureau of Occupational Health 2 University Place Albany, NY 12203 518-458-6392
Covers:	All employers, including the state and its subdivisions.
Exceptions:	Domestic workers; casual laborers employed at the employer's residence.

Required Training:	Training must begin prior to initial assignment and be repeated annually or whenever the potential exposure in the workplace is increased; written information on the toxic effects and circumstances under which the effects are produced must be provided.
Training Topics:	Names and locations of hazardous substances; properties of substances; effects of hazardous labels; symptoms of effects; potential for flammability, explosion, and reactivity; emergency treatment; proper conditions for safe use and exposure; leak and spill cleanup procedures.
Other Requirements:	Employers must maintain an MSDS for each toxic substance used in the workplace; must maintain a list of all toxic substances in the workplace and all relevant information about such substances; employers must keep a record of all employees (including name, address, and social security number) who handle or use hazardous substances.
Employee Rights:	Employees or their representatives may make a written request for information relating to toxic substances; employees may refuse to work with the toxic substance if the MSDS is not provided within 72 hours; employers may not discharge, discipline, or discriminate against employees for exercising their rights under the law.

North Carolina

Law/Code:	Gen. Stat., Secs. 95-173 through 218; NC Admin. Code 13; N.C.A.C. 7C01201(a)(105).
Enforcing Agencies:	North Carolina Department of Labor 214 W. Jones Street Raleigh, NC 27603
	Division of Occupational Safety and Health, 919-733-7166 Bureau of Compliance, 919-733-4880 Bureau of Consultative Services, 919-733-2360 Bureau of Education, Training, and Technical Assistance, 919-733-2486 Bureau of Management Information and Evaluation, 919-733-2385

Covers:	All employers, including the state and its political subdivisions.
Exceptions:	Hazardous substances being transported in interstate commerce into or through the state; products intended for personal consumption by employees; retail sale establishments; any food additive, color additive, drug, or cosmetic; certain laboratories; any farming operation that employs 10 or fewer employees; distilled spirits, tobacco, untreated wood products, and medicines used in direct patient care in health care facilities and laboratories.
Other Requirements:	Employers must maintain an MSDS for each toxic substance used in the workplace; must maintain a list of all toxic substances in the workplace and all relevant information about such substances; containers of hazardous substances must be clearly labeled; community right-to-know law requires that the general public be informed about local chemical hazards.
Employee Rights:	If an employee believes an unidentified substance to be a hazardous chemical and if the employer does not provide the employee with the identity of the substance within five working days of a request, the employee may refuse to work with the substance (employees may be required to work with the chemical once its identity has been provided); employers may not discharge, discipline, or discriminate against employees for exercising their rights under the law.

North Dakota

Law/Code:	ND 65-14-02 and ND 18-01-34.
Enforcing Agency:	Workers' Compensation Bureau 4007 State Street Bismarck, ND 58501 701-224-2700
Covers:	State right-to-know law applies to public sector employers; private sector employers are covered by federal OSHA.
Required Training:	Employers must implement an employee information program.

Training Topics:	Nature of the hazards; appropriate work practices; protective measures; emergency procedures.
Other Requirements:	Employers must submit a list of hazardous substances, their nature, the hazards presented by them, and the appropriate emergency response to the state fire marshal and local fire department; community right-to-know law requires that the general public be informed about local chemical hazards.
Employee Rights:	Employees and their representatives have the right to obtain information from their employers about hazardous substances with which they work.

Oregon

Law/Code:	1985 OR Laws, Ch. 683; 1985 OR Laws, Ch. 726; OAR 437 Division 155.
Enforcing Agencies:	Department of Insurance and Finance Accident Prevention Division 204 Labor and Industries Building Salem, OR 97310 503-378-3272
	Office of State Fire Marshal 3000 Market Street NE, Ste. 534 Salem, OR 97310 503-378-FIRE HazMat Section: 503-378-2885
Covers:	All employers.
Required Training:	Employees must be trained and given information prior to the initial assignment and whenever a new hazard is introduced into the workplace; employers must have a written hazardous chemical communication program.
Other Requirements:	Employers must maintain an MSDS for each toxic substance used in the workplace; must maintain a list of all toxic substances in the workplace and all relevant information about such substances; containers of hazardous substances must be clearly labeled; community right-to-know law requires that the general public be informed about local chemical hazards.

Employee Rights:	Employees have the right to request and receive information about the hazardous substances with which they work.

Pennsylvania

Law/Code:	34 PA Code, Chs. 301 to 323.
Enforcing Agency:	Department of Labor and Industry Bureau of Worker/Community Right-to-Know Program Labor and Industry Building, Room 1503 7th and Forster Streets Harrisburg, PA 17120 717-783-2071
Covers:	All employers, including the state and its political subdivisions.
Exceptions:	Manufacturers do not have to communicate information regarding hazardous substances to their own employees or to customers that are also manufacturers; when containers are labeled under certain federal laws, they are exempt from state requirements. The act does not apply to an "article" as defined under PA law; products intended for personal consumption by employees in the workplace; consumer products packaged in containers that are primarily designed for distribution to and use by the general public; food, drugs, and cosmetics; tobacco; some activities of research and development laboratories; sealed packages in the employer's possession for fewer than 20 days.
Required Training:	Employers must provide training before initial assignment, annually, whenever a new hazardous substance is introduced into the workplace, and when the employer receives new information about a hazardous substance.
Other Requirements:	Employers must maintain an MSDS for each toxic substance used in the workplace; must maintain a list of all toxic substances in the workplace and all relevant information about such substances; containers of hazardous substances must be clearly labeled; must complete Hazardous Substance Survey Forms for each workplace and update every two

	years; must keep records of employees' exposure to hazardous substances; community right-to-know law requires that the general public be informed about local chemical hazards.
Employee Rights:	Employers must furnish, upon written request of an employee or representative, hazardous substance lists, survey forms, and MSDS records; employees may refuse to work with the toxic substance if the information is not provided within five working days; employers may not discharge, discipline, or discriminate against employees for exercising their rights under the act.

Rhode Island

Law/Code:	RI Gen. Laws, Ch. 28-21-1; RI Gen. Laws, Ch. 23-24-4.
Enforcing Agency:	Department of Labor Division of Occupational Safety 220 Elmwood Avenue Providence, RI 02907 401-457-1843
Covers:	All employers that use, transport, store, or otherwise expose employees to toxic or hazardous substances. State right-to-know law applies to public sector employers; private sector employers are covered by federal OSHA.
Exceptions:	Products intended for personal consumption by employees in the workplace; consumer products packaged in containers that are primarily designed for distribution to and use by the general public; food, drugs, and cosmetics; tobacco; some activities of research and development laboratories.
Required Training:	Employers must provide training before initial assignment, annually, whenever a new hazardous substance is introduced into the workplace, and when the employer receives new information about a hazardous substance.
Training Topics:	Nature of the hazards; appropriate work practices; protective measures; emergency procedures.

Other Requirements: Employers must maintain an MSDS for each toxic substance used in the workplace; must maintain a list of all toxic substances in the workplace and all relevant information about such substances; containers of hazardous substances must be clearly labeled; must keep records of employees' exposure to hazardous substances; must provide the local fire department with a list of work areas and the toxic substances contained within them; community right-to-know law requires that the general public be informed about local chemical hazards.

Employee Rights: Employers must furnish, upon written request of an employee or representative, hazardous substance lists, survey forms, and MSDS records; employees may refuse to work with the toxic substance if the information is not provided within three working days; employers may not discharge, discipline, or discriminate against employees for exercising their rights under the act.

South Carolina

Law/Code: SC Code Ann., Sec. 41-3-10.

Enforcing Agency: Department of Labor
3600 Forest Drive
P.O. Box 11329
Columbia, SC 29211
803-731-1648

Covers: Applies to employers in public *and* private sectors.

Required Training: Employees must be trained on potential exposure to hazardous substances; symptoms; emergency treatment; safe use; protective equipment.

Tennessee

Law/Code: TN Code Ann., Secs. 50-3-2001 et seq.

Enforcing Agency: Department of Labor
OSHA Division
501 Union Building
Nashville, TN 37219-5389
615-741-7151

Covers:	Manufacturing employers and nonmanufacturing employers that use or store hazardous chemicals. Also covered is the state and its political subdivisions and volunteer fire departments. Applies to employers in public *and* private sectors.
Exceptions:	Articles formed to a specific shape during manufacture that have functions dependent on its shape and do not result in exposure to a hazardous chemical under normal use; retail trade establishments; products intended for consumption by employees in the workplace; when a hazardous chemical is received in a sealed package and sold in the package if the seal remains intact while the chemical is in the workplace and does not remain in the workplace for more than 14 days; some laboratories; items regulated by the Food and Drug Act or federal Alcohol Administration Act; agricultural employers.
Required Training:	Employees must be trained on an annual basis.
Other Requirements:	Employers should maintain written documentation of employee training sessions; must maintain an MSDS for each toxic substance used in the workplace; must maintain a list of all toxic substances in the workplace and all relevant information about such substances; containers of hazardous substances must be clearly labeled.
Employee Rights:	Employees have the right to examine each MSDS for toxic substances to which they have been exposed (request must be in writing); if the MSDS is not provided within two weeks, the employee may refuse to work with the hazardous chemical unless the employer can demonstrate that the MSDS will be forthcoming by a specified date, or that the information cannot be obtained and the employer is not at fault; employees cannot be discharged, disciplined, or discriminated against for exercising their rights.

Texas

Law/Code:	Vernon's Ann. Civ. St., Art. 5182b; 10 Tex. Reg. 4889; 11 Tex. Reg. 850; 12 Tex. Reg. 3551 to 3553.

Enforcing Agency:	Division of Occupational Safety and Health Texas Department of Health 1100 W. 49th Street Austin, Texas 78756 512-458-7410
Covers:	All employers that maintain hazardous chemicals in the workplace. State right-to-know law applies to public sector employers; private sector employers are covered by federal OSHA.
Exceptions:	Products intended for personal consumption by employees in the workplace; consumer products packaged in containers that are primarily designed for distribution to and use by the general public; food, drugs, and cosmetics; tobacco; some activities of research and development laboratories; retail food establishments; products labeled pursuant to the federal Insecticide, Fungicide, and Rodenticide Act; hazardous waste regulated pursuant to the federal Resource Conservation and Recovery Act; radioactive waste; workplaces where the hazardous chemical is received in a sealed package and is subsequently sold or transferred in that package, or, if the seal remains intact, while the chemical is in the workplace and it does not remain there more than five working days; manufacturing employers and distributors that are regulated by and complying with the OSHA hazard communication standard.
Required Training:	Employees must be trained annually.
Training Topics:	MSDS and label interpretation; the location, acute and chronic effects, and safe handling of hazardous chemicals used in the workplace; protective equipment and first-aid treatment; general safety instructions on handling, cleanup procedures, and disposal of hazardous chemicals.
Other Requirements:	Employers must maintain an MSDS for each toxic substance used in the workplace; must maintain a list of all toxic substances in the workplace and all relevant information about such substances; containers of hazardous substances must be clearly labeled; notice of the presence of toxic substances must be posted in an obvious place in the work area; must keep

records of employees' exposure to hazardous substances; must provide the local fire department with a list of work areas and the toxic substances contained within them; community right-to-know law requires that the general public be informed about local chemical hazards.

Employee Rights: Employees exposed to hazardous substances must be informed of the exposure; employees must be provided with protective equipment; employers must furnish, upon written request of an employee or representative, hazardous substance lists, survey forms, and MSDS records; employees may refuse to work with the toxic substance if the information is not provided within three working days; employers may not discharge, discipline, or discriminate against employees for exercising their rights under the act.

Utah

Law/Code: Utah Code Ann., Secs. 35-9-1 et seq.

Enforcing Agency: Industrial Commission of Utah
160 E. 300 South, 3rd Floor
Salt Lake City, UT 84114
801-530-6800

Covers: Applies to employers in public *and* private sectors.

Required Training: Employees must be trained on potential exposure to hazardous substances; symptoms; emergency treatment; safe use; protective equipment.

Other Requirements: Employers must inform employees of corrective action.

Vermont

Law/Code: 18 V.S.A., Ch. 36, Secs. 1721 et seq.

Enforcing Agency: Vermont Department of Health Laboratory
195 Colchester Avenue
Burlington, VT 05401
802-863-7335

Covers: Employers engaged in business operations
                          having certain standard industrial classifi-
                          cations as designated by the federal Office of
                          Management and Budget; the state and its
                          political subdivisions. Applies to employers in
                          public *and* private sectors.

Exceptions: Agricultural and forestry employers; tobacco or
                          tobacco products; wood or wood products;
                          food, drugs, or cosmetics intended for personal
                          consumption while in the workplace;
                          manufactured articles that do not release or
                          otherwise result in exposure to a hazardous
                          chemical under normal conditions of use;
                          wholesale and retail food; food additives, color
                          additives, and any distilled spirits, wine, or
                          malt beverages intended for nonindustrial use;
                          any consumer products defined under the
                          federal Consumer Product Safety Act; any
                          products under the federal Food, Drug, and
                          Cosmetics Act; hazardous chemicals that fall
                          below the law's minimum levels.

Other Requirements: Employers must maintain an MSDS for each
                          toxic substance used in the workplace; must
                          maintain a list of all toxic substances in the
                          workplace and all relevant information about
                          such substances; containers of hazardous sub-
                          stances must be clearly labeled; community
                          right-to-know law requires that the general pub-
                          lic be informed about local chemical hazards.

Virginia

Law/Code: VA Code Ann., Secs. 40.1-49.3 et seq.

Enforcing Agency: Department of Labor and Industries
                          Towers-Taylor Building
                          13 S. 13th Street
                          Richmond, VA 23219
                          804-786-2391

Covers: Applies to employers in public *and* private
                          sectors.

Required Training: Employees must be trained on potential
                          exposure to hazardous substances; symptoms;
                          emergency treatment; safe use; protective
                          equipment.

Other Requirements: Employers must inform employees of corrective action.

Washington

Law/Code: West's RCWA 49.70.010 to 49.70.905; Laws 1985, Ch. 409, Secs. 1 to 4.6.

Enforcing Agency: Department of Labor and Industries
Right-to-Know Program
Industrial Hygiene Section
P.O. Box 207
Olympia, WA 98504

206-753-1446

Covers: All employers of one or more employees, including the state and its political subdivisions.

Exceptions: Officers of a closely held corporation engaged in agricultural production; distributors of retail consumer products if they sell only in the retail market (no exemption if the sale is to commercial customers); transportation of hazardous chemicals or substances subject to regulations of the U.S. Department of Transportation or the Washington Utilities and Transportation Commission.

Required Training: Employees must be trained on methods and observations that may be used to detect the presence of a hazardous chemical in the work area; the physical and health hazards of the substances with which employees are working; the measures employees can take to protect themselves from the hazards; an explanation of the labeling system and the MSDS.

Other Requirements: Employers must maintain an MSDS for each toxic substance used in the workplace; must maintain a list of all toxic substances in the workplace and all relevant information about such substances; notice of the presence of toxic substances must be posted in an obvious place in the work area; containers of hazardous substances must be clearly labeled; employers will be assessed a worker right-to-know fee based on the number of worker hours reported, with an annual fee not exceeding $50,000;

community right-to-know law requires that the general public be informed about local chemical hazards; employers must notify employees immediately upon exposure.

Employee Rights: Employees may request, in writing, a workplace survey or MSDS from the employer, which must supply the information within three working days.

West Virginia

Law/Code: W. Va. Code, Ch. 21-3-128, W. Va. Code, Ch. 16-31.

Enforcing Agencies: Department of Labor
1800 Washington Street East
Building 3, Room 319
Charleston, WV 25305
304-348-7890

Department of Health
1800 Washington Street East
Charleston, WV 25305
304-348-2971

Covers: All employers that have 10 or more employees and maintain hazardous chemicals in the workplace. State right-to-know law applies to public sector employers; private sector employers are covered by federal OSHA.

Exceptions: Coal mines; coal-processing plants; agricultural or horticultural activity.

Other Requirements: Employers must maintain a list of all toxic substances in the workplace and all relevant information about such substances; notice of the presence of toxic substances must be posted in an obvious place in the work area; all employers that normally store hazardous substances in quantities greater than 55 gallons or 500 pounds must provide specified information to the director of the state department of health, the county sheriff, and the local fire chief within four months of the effective date of the law and every two years after that; community right-to-know law provides that any resident of the state may obtain information about the hazardous substances upon request.

Wisconsin

Law/Code:	WI S.A. 101.58 to 101.599.
Enforcing Agencies:	Public sector employers contact:

Wisconsin Department of Industry, Labor, and
  Human Resources
Bureau of Safety Inspections
P.O. Box 7969
Madison, WI 53707
608-266-2780

U.S. Department of Labor
Occupational Safety and Health Administration
310 W. Wisconsin Avenue, Suite 1180
Milwaukee, WI 53203
414-291-3315

Covers:	State right-to-know law applies to public sector employers; private sector employers are covered by federal OSHA.
Exceptions:	Articles containing a hazardous substance in a solid form that does not cause an acute or chronic health hazard; any product less than 2 percent of which is distributed to the general public and for which the employee's exposure during use is not significantly greater than the consumer's; any substance received by an employee in a sealed package and then sold or transferred in that package if the seal remains intact; any waste product regulated under the federal Resource Conservation and Recovery Act.
Required Training:	Employees must be trained before beginning work with hazardous substances and any time new substances are introduced into the workplace.
Training Topics:	Chemical and common names of all substances and infectious agents in the workplace; their location in the workplace; symptoms and effects of overexposure; proper conditions for safe use; potential for flammability, explosion, and reactivity; special precautions for handling, and necessary protective equipment; procedures for handling leaks or spills.
Other Requirements:	Employers must maintain a list of all toxic substances in the workplace and all relevant

information about such substances; notice of the presence of toxic substances must be posted in an obvious place in the work area.

Employee Rights: Employees have the right to request, in writing, specific information regarding toxic substances with which they work or are exposed; if the employer does not provide the information within 15 days, employees can refuse to work with the substance.

A State-by-State Guide to Discrimination Laws Providing Equal Access to Training

This appendix summarizes the state fair employment practice laws, providing information about where to find the state act, to which employers it applies, the protected classes, the areas of discrimination that are covered, and available remedies, when specified.

An asterisk (*) following *employment training opportunities* indicates that the state act specifically refers to employment training, providing that the state must not prevent individuals from participating in employment-related training programs on the basis of any of the protected classes, primarily handicap. These states include Colorado, Delaware, Kentucky, Michigan, New Jersey, New York, Ohio, and Texas.

Alabama

Act:	Alabama does not have a fair employment practice law that affects private employers; thus federal law applies. Alabama does have an act prohibiting discrimination on the basis of physical handicap.

Code Section:	Code of Alabama, Tit. 21.
Applies To:	Political subdivisions, schools, and other employment supported by public funds.
Protected Classes:	Physically handicapped individuals.
Areas of Discrimination Covered:	Adequate access to facilities, public accommodations, transportation advantages, equal housing opportunities.

Alaska

Act:	Alaska Human Rights Law
Code Section:	Alaska Statute, Secs. 18.80.010 to 18.80.300.
Applies To:	All employers, including the state.
Protected Classes:	Race, religion, color, national origin, ancestry, age, physical or mental disability, sex, marital status, changes in marital status, pregnancy, parenthood.
Enforcing Agency:	Alaska Commission for Human Rights.
Areas of Discrimination Covered:	Employment opportunities, promotion opportunities, employment compensation, housing opportunities, nonretaliation, accessibility to public accommodations, transportation, and facilities

Arizona

Act:	Arizona Civil Rights Act.
Code Section:	Ariz. Rev. Stat. Ann., Secs. 41-1461 to 41-1466.
Applies To:	All employers, including the state.
Protected Classes:	Race, color, religion, sex, age, handicap, national origin, smokers.
Enforcing Agency:	Arizona Civil Rights Division.
Areas of Discrimination Covered:	Employment opportunities, employment compensation,

employment advancement, employment privileges, transportation, housing opportunities, public accommodations, education, nonretaliation.

Arkansas

Act:	Arkansas does not have a fair employment practice law that affects private employers; thus federal law applies. Arkansas does have an act prohibiting discrimination on the basis of sex or disability.
Code Section:	Arkansas Civil Rights Act.
Applies To:	All employers, including the state.
Protected Classes:	Gender, handicap.
Enforcing Agency:	Not specified.
Areas of Discrimination Covered:	Employment opportunities, access to public accommodations, housing opportunities, transportation.

California

Act:	California Fair Employment Practices and Housing Act.
Code Section:	Cal. Govt. Code, Secs. 12900 to 12951.
Applies To:	Employment agencies, labor organizations, the state, the state's political or civil subdivisions, cities, and private employers with five or more employees.
Protected Classes:	Race, religious creed, color, national origin, ancestry, physical handicap, medical condition, marital status, sex, sexual orientation, age, pregnancy or related medical condition.
Enforcing Agency:	California Department of Fair Employment and Housing.
Areas of Discrimination:	Accommodation obligations, acceptable preemployment

inquiries, nonretaliation, prohibition on harassment, family leave.

Colorado

Act:	Colorado Antidiscrimination Act of 1957.
Code Section:	Colo. Rev. Stat., Secs. 24-34-401 to 24-34-406.
Applies To:	All employers, including the state.
Protected Classes:	Race, handicap, creed, color, sex, age, national origin, ancestry, pregnancy, marital status.
Enforcing Agency:	Colorado Civil Rights Division and Colorado Civil Rights Commission.
Areas of Discrimination Covered:	Employment hiring and discharge, employment promotions, employment opportunities, employment compensation, *employment training opportunities,** access to public accommodations, transportation, housing opportunities, education.

Connecticut

Act:	Connecticut Fair Employment Practices Act.
Code Section:	Conn. Gen. Stat., Secs. 46a-51 to 46a-57.
Applies To:	All employers, including the state.
Protected Classes:	Race, color, religion, age, sex, pregnancy, sexual orientation, marital status, national origin, ancestry, present or past history of mental disorder, mental retardation, learning disability, physical disability, previous arrest or conviction records, smokers.
Enforcing Agency:	Connecticut Commission on Human Rights and Opportunities.
Areas of Discrimination Covered:	Employment hiring, employment discharge, employment compensa-

tion, nonretaliation, access to public accommodations, transportation, housing opportunities, education.

Delaware

Act:	Delaware Fair Employment Practices Act.
Code Section:	Del. Code Ann., Tit. 19, Secs. 710 to 724.
Applies To:	All employers, including the state.
Protected Classes:	Race, marital status, color, age, religion, sex, national origin.
Enforcing Agency:	Department of Labor.
Areas of Discrimination Covered:	Employment hiring, employment discharge, employment promotion, employment opportunities, *employment training opportunities,** access to public accommodations, transportation, housing opportunities, nonretaliation.

District of Columbia

Act:	District of Columbia Human Rights Act.
Code Section:	DC Code, Secs. 1-2501 to 1-2557.
Applies To:	All employers, including the state.
Protected Classes:	Race, color, religion, national origin, sex, age, marital status, personal appearance, sexual orientation, pregnancy, family responsibilities, handicap, matriculation, political affiliation.
Enforcing Agency:	District of Columbia Commission on Human Rights, District of Columbia Office on Human Rights.
Areas of Discrimination Covered:	Employment opportunities, employment hiring, employment discharge, employment compensation, access to public accommodations, transportation, housing opportunities, education.

Florida

Act:	Florida Human Rights Act.
Code Section:	Fla. Stat. Ann., Secs. 760.01 to 760.37.
Applies To:	All employers, including the state.
Protected Classes:	Race, color, religion, sex, national origin, age, handicap, marital status.
Areas of Discrimination Covered:	Employment opportunities, employment hiring, employment discharge, employment compensation, club memberships, access to public accommodations, transportation, housing opportunities, education.

Georgia

Act:	Georgia Fair Employment Practices Act, Georgia Equal Employment for Persons With Disabilities Code.
Code Section:	GA Code Ann., Secs. 34, 45-19-20 to 45-19-45.
Applies To:	All employers, including the state.
Protected Classes:	Race, color, religion, national origin, sex, handicap, age.
Areas of Discrimination Covered:	Employment opportunities, employment hiring, employment discharge, employment compensation, access to public accommodations, transportation, housing opportunities.

Hawaii

Act:	Hawaii Fair Employment Law.
Code Section:	Haw. Rev. Stat., Secs. 378-1 to 378-38.
Applies To:	All employers, including the state.
Protected Classes:	Race, sex, age, religion, color, ancestry, handicap, marital status,

arrest and court record, sexual orientation, pregnancy.

Enforcing Agency:	Hawaii Civil Rights Commission.
Areas of Discrimination Covered:	Employment opportunities, employment hiring, employment discharge, employment compensation, access to public accommodations, transportation, housing opportunities.

Idaho

Act:	Idaho Fair Employment Practices Act.
Code Section:	Idaho Code, Secs. 67-5901 to 67-5912.
Applies To:	All employers, including the state.
Protected Classes:	Race, color, sex, national origin, handicap, age.
Enforcing Agency:	Idaho Commission on Human Rights.
Areas of Discrimination Covered:	Employment opportunities, employment hiring, employment discharge, employment compensation, access to public accommodations, transportation, housing opportunities.

Illinois

Act:	Illinois Human Rights Act.
Code Section:	Ill. Rev. Stat., Ch. 68, Secs. 1-101 to 1-103.
Applies To:	All employers, including the state.
Protected Classes:	Race, color, religion, national origin, ancestry, citizenship, age, sex, pregnancy, marital status, physical or mental handicap, arrest record, unfavorable discharge from military service.
Enforcing Agency:	Illinois Department of Human Rights, Illinois Human Rights Commission.

Areas of Discrimination Covered:	Employment opportunities, employment hiring, employment discharge, employment compensation, access to public accommodations, transportation, housing opportunities.

Indiana

Act:	Indiana Civil Rights Law.
Code Section:	Ind. Code Ann., Secs. 22-9-1-1 to 22-9-1-13.
Applies To:	All employers, including the state.
Protected Classes:	Race, religion, color, sex, handicap, national origin, ancestry.
Enforcing Agency:	Indiana Civil Rights Commission.
Areas of Discrimination Covered:	Employment, access to public accommodations, transportation, housing opportunities.

Iowa

Act:	Iowa Civil Rights Act.
Code Section:	Iowa Code Ann., Secs. 601A.1 to 601A.19.
Applies To:	All employers, including the state.
Protected Classes:	Age, race, creed, color, sex, pregnancy, national origin, religion, disability.
Enforcing Agency:	Iowa Civil Rights Commission.
Areas of Discrimination Covered:	Employment opportunities, employment hiring, employment discharge, employment compensation, access to public accommodations, transportation, housing opportunities, education.

Kansas

Act:	Kansas Act Against Discrimination.
Code Section:	Kan. Stat. Ann., Secs. 44-1001 to 44-1044.
Applies To:	All employers, including the state.

Protected Classes:	Race, religion, color, sex, disability, national origin, ancestry.
Enforcing Agency:	Kansas Commission on Civil Rights.
Areas of Discrimination Covered:	Employment opportunities, employment hiring, employment discharge, employment compensation, access to public accommodations, transportation, housing opportunities.

Kentucky

Act:	Kentucky Civil Rights Act, Kentucky Equal Employment Opportunity Act of 1978.
Code Section:	KY Rev. Stat. Ann., Secs. 344.010 to 344.990, 45.550c to 45.640, 207.130 to 207.240.
Applies To:	All employers, including the state.
Protected Classes:	Race, color, religion, national origin, sex, pregnancy, age, disability, smokers, handicap.
Enforcing Agency:	Commission on Human Rights, Department of Workplace Standards.
Areas of Discrimination Covered:	Employment opportunities, employment hiring, employment discharge, employment compensation, nonretaliation, *employment training opportunities,** access to public accommodations, transportation, housing opportunities.

Louisiana

Act:	Louisiana Fair Employment Practices Law, Louisiana Civil Rights Act for Handicapped Persons.
Code Section:	LA Rev. Stat. Ann., Secs. 23-1006, 46-2251 to 46-2256(c).

Applies To:	All employers, including the state.
Protected Classes:	Race, color, religion, sex, pregnancy, national origin, handicap.
Areas of Discrimination Covered:	Employment opportunities, employment hiring, employment discharge, employment compensation, access to public accommodations, transportation, housing opportunities, education.

Maine

Act:	Maine Human Rights Act, Maine Code of Fair Practices and Affirmative Action.
Code Section:	ME Rev. Stat. Ann., Tit. 5, Secs. 4551 to 4553(10)F.
Applies To:	All employers, including the state.
Protected Classes:	Race, color, sex, pregnancy, handicap, religion, ancestry, national origin, age.
Enforcing Agency:	Maine Human Rights Commission.
Areas of Discrimination Covered:	Employment opportunities, employment hiring, employment discharge, employment compensation, access to public accommodations, transportation, housing opportunities, education.

Maryland

Act:	Maryland Fair Employment Practices Act.
Code Section:	MD. Ann. Code, Art. 49B, Secs. 1 to 30.
Applies To:	All employers, including the state.
Protected Classes:	Race, color, religion, sex, pregnancy, age, national origin, marital status, handicap.

Enforcing Agency:	Maryland Human Relations Committee.
Areas of Discrimination Covered:	Employment, access to public accommodations, transportation, housing opportunities.

Massachusetts

Act:	Massachusetts Fair Employment Practices Act.
Code Section:	Mass. Gen. Laws Ann., Ch. 151B, Secs. 1 to 10.
Applies To:	Employers of six or more employees.
Protected Classes:	Race, color, religion, national origin, ancestry, age, sex, pregnancy, sexual orientation, handicap.
Enforcing Agency:	Massachusetts Commission Against Discrimination.
Areas of Discrimination Covered:	Employment opportunities, employment hiring, employment discharge, employment compensation, nonretaliation, access to public accommodations, transportation, housing opportunities, education.

Michigan

Act:	Elliott-Larsen Civil Rights Act, Michigan Handicappers' Civil Rights Act.
Code Section:	Mich. Comp. Laws Ann., Secs. 37.2101 to 37.2304 and 37.1101.
Applies To:	All employers, including the state.
Protected Classes:	Religion, race, color, national origin, age, sex, pregnancy, height, weight, marital status, arrest record, handicap.
Enforcing Agency:	Michigan Department of Civil Rights.

Areas of Discrimination Covered:	Employment opportunities, employment hiring, employment discharge, employment compensation, *employment training opportunities,** access to public accommodations, transportation, housing opportunities, education.

Minnesota

Act:	Minnesota Human Rights Act.
Code Section:	Minn. Stat. Ann., Sec. 363.01.
Applies To:	All employers, including the state.
Protected Classes:	Race, color, creed, religion, national origin, sex, pregnancy, marital status with regard to public assistance, disability, age, membership or activity in a local commission.
Enforcing Agency:	Minnesota Department of Human Rights.
Areas of Discrimination Covered:	Employment opportunities, employment hiring, employment discharge, employment compensation, access to public accommodations, transportation, housing opportunities, education.

Mississippi

Act:	Mississippi does not have a fair employment practice law that affects private employers; thus federal law applies. Mississippi does have an act prohibiting discrimination on the basis of political affiliation, race, national origin, sex, religious creed, age, handicap, or smoking.
Code Section:	Miss. Code Ann., Secs. 25-9-103 and 71-7-33.
Applies To:	The state.

Protected Classes: Political affiliation, race, national
                                          origin, sex, religious creed, age,
                                          handicap, or smokers.

Enforcing Agency: Not specified.

Areas of Discrimination Covered: Employment, access to public
                                          accommodations, transportation.

Missouri

Act: Missouri Human Rights Act.

Code Section: MO Rev. Stat., Secs. 213.010 to
                                          213.130.

Applies To: All employers, including the state.

Protected Classes: Race, color, religion, national
                                          origin, sex, ancestry, age,
                                          handicap.

Enforcing Agency: Missouri Commission on Human
                                          Rights.

Areas of Discrimination Covered: Employment opportunities,
                                          employment hiring, employment
                                          discharge, employment compensa-
                                          tion, access to public accommoda-
                                          tions, transportation, housing
                                          opportunities.

Montana

Act: Montana Human Rights Act.

Code Section: Mont. Code Ann., Secs. 49-1-101 to
                                          49-4-312.

Applies To: All employers, including the state.

Protected Classes: Race, creed, religion, color,
                                          national origin, ancestry, age,
                                          physical or mental handicap,
                                          marital status, sex, pregnancy,
                                          political beliefs.

Enforcing Agency: Montana Commission for Human
                                          Rights.

Areas of Discrimination Covered: Employment opportunities,
                                          employment hiring, employment
                                          discharge, employment compensa-
                                          tion, access to public accommoda-
                                          tions, transportation, housing
                                          opportunities, education.

Nebraska

Act:	Nebraska Fair Employment Practices Act.
Code Section:	Neb. Rev. Stat., Secs. 48-1101 to 48-1126, 48-1001 to 48-1010.
Applies To:	All employers, including the state.
Protected Classes:	Race, color, religion, sex, pregnancy, disability, marital status, national origin, age.
Areas of Discrimination Covered:	Employment, access to public accommodations, transportation, housing opportunities.

Nevada

Act:	Nevada Fair Employment Practices Act.
Code Section:	Nev. Rev. Stat., Secs. 613.310 to 613.430.
Applies To:	All employers, including the state, except those at or near Indian reservations.
Protected Classes:	Race, color, religion, sex, pregnancy, age, handicap, national origin, lawful use of a product.
Enforcing Agency:	Nevada Equal Rights Commission.
Areas of Discrimination Covered:	Employment opportunities, employment hiring, employment discharge, employment compensation, access to public accommodations, transportation, housing opportunities.

New Hampshire

Act:	New Hampshire Law Against Discrimination.
Code Section:	NH Rev. Stat. Ann., Secs. 354-A:1 to 354-A:14.
Applies To:	All employers, including the state.
Protected Classes:	Age, sex, race, color, marital status, disability, religious creed, national origin, smokers.

Enforcing Agency:	New Hampshire Commission for Human Rights.
Areas of Discrimination Covered:	Employment, access to public accommodations, transportation, housing opportunities.

New Jersey

Act:	New Jersey Law Against Discrimination.
Code Section:	NJ Stat. Ann., Secs. 10:5-1 to 10:5-38, 10:5-12, 10:5-4:1.
Applies To:	All employers, including the state.
Protected Classes:	Race, creed, color, national origin, nationality, ancestry, age, marital status, sex, handicap, sexual orientation, atypical hereditary cellular blood trait, service in the armed forces.
Enforcing Agency:	New Jersey Division on Civil Rights.
Areas of Discrimination Covered:	Employment opportunities, employment hiring, employment discharge, employment compensation, *employment training opportunities,** access to public accommodations, transportation, housing opportunities, nonretaliation, education.

New Mexico

Act:	New Mexico Human Rights Act.
Code Section:	NM Stat. Ann., Secs. 28-1-1 to 28-16-13.
Applies To:	All employers, including the state.
Protected Classes:	Race, age, religion, color, national origin, ancestry, sex, pregnancy, handicap.
Enforcing Agency:	New Mexico Human Rights Commission.
Areas of Discrimination Covered:	Employment, access to public accommodations, transportation, housing opportunities.

New York

Act:	New York Human Rights Law, New York City Human Rights Law.
Code Section:	NY Exec. Law, Sec. 296.
Applies To:	All employers, including the state.
Protected Classes:	Age, race, creed, color, national origin, ancestry, sex, pregnancy, disability, marital status, arrest or conviction records, sexual harassment.
Enforcing Agency:	New York State Division on Human Rights.
Areas of Discrimination Covered:	Employment opportunities, employment hiring, employment discharge, employment compensation, *employment training opportunities,** nonretaliation, access to public accommodations, transportation, housing opportunities, education.

North Carolina

Act:	North Carolina Equal Employment Practices Act.
Code Section:	NC Gen. Stat., Secs. 143-422.1 to 143-422.3, 168A-1 to 168A-12, 95-28.1.
Applies To:	All employers, including the state.
Protected Classes:	Race, religion, color, national origin, age, sex, pregnancy, handicap, sickle cell trait.
Enforcing Agency:	North Carolina Human Relations Council.
Areas of Discrimination Covered:	The North Carolina act does not prohibit employment discrimination. It merely declares that the state's policy favors nondiscrimination.

North Dakota

Act:	North Dakota Human Rights Act.

Code Section:	ND Cent. Code, Secs. 14-02.4-01 to 14-02.4-21.
Applies To:	All employers, including the state.
Protected Classes:	Race, color, religion, sex, pregnancy, national origin, age, handicap or status with respect to marriage or public assistance.
Enforcing Agency:	North Dakota Department of Labor.
Areas of Discrimination Covered:	Employment, access to public accommodations, transportation.

Ohio

Act:	Ohio Fair Employment Practices Law.
Code Section:	Ohio Rev. Code Ann., Secs. 4112.01 to 4112.99.
Applies To:	All employers, including the state.
Protected Classes:	Race, color, religion, sex, pregnancy, national origin, handicap, age, ancestry.
Enforcing Agency:	Ohio Civil Rights Commission.
Areas of Discrimination Covered:	Employment opportunities, employment hiring, employment discharge, employment compensation, access to public accommodations, transportation, housing opportunities, nonretaliation, *employment training opportunities,** education.

Oklahoma

Act:	Oklahoma Civil Rights Act.
Code Section:	Okla. Stat. Ann., Tit. 25, Secs. 1101 to 1802.
Applies To:	All employers, including the state.
Protected Classes:	Sex, race, color, religion, national origin, age, disability, smokers.
Enforcing Agency:	Oklahoma Human Rights Commission.
Areas of Discrimination Covered:	Employment, access to public accommodations, transportation, housing opportunities.

Oregon

Act:	Oregon Fair Employment Practices Act.
Code Section:	OR Rev. Stat., Secs. 659.010 to 659.990.
Applies To:	All employers, including the state.
Protected Classes:	Race, religion, color, sex, pregnancy, national origin, marital status, age, expunged juvenile record, physical or mental handicap.
Enforcing Agency:	Oregon Bureau of Labor, Civil Rights Division.
Areas of Discrimination Covered:	Employment, access to public accommodations, transportation, housing opportunities, education.

Pennsylvania

Act:	Pennsylvania Human Relations Act.
Code Section:	PA Stat. Ann., Tit. 43, Secs. 951 to 963.
Applies To:	All employers, including the state.
Protected Classes:	Race, color, religious creed, ancestry, age, sex, pregnancy, national origin, non-job-related handicap or disability, high school equivalency certification, opposition to abortion or sterilization.
Enforcing Agency:	Pennsylvania Human Relations Commission.
Areas of Discrimination Covered:	Employment opportunities, employment hiring, employment discharge, employment compensation, access to public accommodations, transportation, housing opportunities, education, nonretaliation.

Puerto Rico

Act:	Fair Employment Practices Act of Puerto Rico.

Code Section:	PR Laws Ann., Tit. 29, Secs. 146 to 154.
Applies To:	All employers, including the state.
Protected Classes:	Age, race, color, sex, social or national origin, social position.
Enforcing Agency:	The Commonwealth's Department of Labor and Human Resources.
Areas of Discrimination Covered:	Employment, accessibility, education.

Rhode Island

Act:	Rhode Island Fair Employment Practice Act.
Code Section:	RI Gen. Laws, Secs. 28-5-1 to 28-5-39, 42-87-1 to 42-87-4(b).
Applies To:	All employers, including the state.
Protected Classes:	Race, color, religion, sex, pregnancy, handicap, age, country of ancestral origin, smokers.
Enforcing Agency:	Rhode Island Commission for Human Rights.
Areas of Discrimination Covered:	Employment, access to public accommodations, transportation, housing opportunities, education.

South Carolina

Act:	South Carolina Human Affairs Law, South Carolina Bill of Rights for Handicapped Persons.
Code Section:	SC Code Ann., Secs. 1-13-10 to 1-13-110, 43-33-510 to 43-33-580
Applies To:	All employers, including the state.
Protected Classes:	Race, religion, color, sex, pregnancy, age, national origin, handicap.
Enforcing Agency:	South Carolina Human Affairs Commission.
Areas of Discrimination Covered:	Employment opportunities, employment hiring, employment discharge, employment compensation, access to public accommodations, transportation, housing opportunities.

South Dakota

Act:	South Dakota Human Relations Act.
Code Section:	SD Codified Laws Ann., Secs. 20-13-1 to 20-13-55.
Applies To:	All employers, including the state.
Protected Classes:	Race, color, creed, religion, sex, ancestry, disability, national origin, smokers.
Enforcing Agency:	South Dakota Commission on Human Relations.
Areas of Discrimination Covered:	Employment, access to public accommodations, transportation, housing opportunities, education.

Tennessee

Act:	Tennessee Antidiscrimination Act.
Code Section:	Tenn. Code Ann., Secs. 4-21-101 to 4-21-607, 8-50-103.
Applies To:	All employers, including the state.
Protected Classes:	Race, creed, color, religion, sex, age, national origin, ancestry, handicap.
Enforcing Agency:	Tennessee Human Rights Commission.
Areas of Discrimination Covered:	Employment, access to public accommodations, transportation, housing opportunities, education.

Texas

Act:	Texas Commission on Human Rights Act.
Code Section:	Tex. Rev. Civ. Stat. Ann., Arts. 5221k and 5547-300, Sec. 1.
Applies To:	All employers, including the state.
Protected Classes:	Race, color, disability, religion, sex, pregnancy, national origin, age, mental retardation.
Enforcing Agency:	Texas Commission on Human Rights.
Areas of Discrimination Covered:	Employment opportunities,

employment hiring, employment
discharge, employment compensation, *employment training opportunities,** nonretaliation, access to public
accommodations, transportation,
housing opportunities.

Utah

Act:	Utah Antidiscrimination Act.
Code Section:	Utah Code Ann., Secs. 34-35-1 to 34-35-8(12).
Applies To:	All employers, including the state.
Protected Classes:	Race, color, sex, pregnancy, childbirth, pregnancy-related conditions, age, religion, national origin, handicap.
Enforcing Agency:	Utah Antidiscrimination Division.
Areas of Discrimination Covered:	Employment, access to public accommodations, transportation, housing opportunities.

Vermont

Act:	Vermont Fair Employment Practices Act.
Code Section:	VT Stat. Ann., Tit. 21, Secs. 495 to 520(d).
Applies To:	All employers, including the state.
Protected Classes:	Race, color, religion, national origin, sex, sexual orientation, ancestry, place of birth, age, AIDS, or handicap.
Enforcing Agency:	Not specified.
Areas of Discrimination Covered:	Employment, employment compensation, access to public accommodations, transportation, housing opportunities, education.

Virgin Islands

Act:	Virgin Islands Civil Rights Act.
Code Section:	VI Code Ann., Tit. 10, Secs. 1 to 10.

Applies To:	All employers, including the state.
Protected Classes:	Age, race, creed, religion, color, national origin, ancestry, place of birth, sex, pregnancy, political affiliation.
Enforcing Agency:	Virgin Islands Civil Rights Commission.
Areas of Discrimination Covered:	Not specified.

Virginia

Act:	Virginia Human Rights Act.
Code Section:	VA Code Ann., Secs. 2.1-714 to 2.1-729.
Applies To:	All employers, including the state.
Protected Classes:	Race, color, religion, national origin, sex, age, marital status, disability, smokers.
Enforcing Agency:	Virginia Council on Human Rights.
Areas of Discrimination Covered:	Employment opportunities, employment hiring, employment discharge, employment compensation, access to public accommodations, transportation, housing opportunities, education.

Washington

Act:	Washington Law Against Discrimination.
Code Section:	Wash. Rev. Code, Secs. 49.60.010 to 49.64.040.
Applies To:	All employers, including the state.
Protected Classes:	Race, creed, color, national origin, ancestry, sex, pregnancy, marital status, age, handicap, arrest and conviction record, HIV status.
Enforcing Agency:	Washington State Human Rights Commission.
Areas of Discrimination Covered:	Employment opportunities, employment hiring, employment discharge, employment compensa-

tion, access to public accommodations, transportation, housing opportunities.

West Virginia

Act:	West Virginia Human Rights Act.
Code Section:	W.Va. Code, Secs. 5-11-1 to 5-11-19.
Applies To:	All employers, including the state.
Protected Classes:	Race, religion, color, national origin, ancestry, sex. pregnancy, age, blindness, handicap.
Enforcing Agency:	West Virginia Human Rights Commission.
Areas of Discrimination Covered:	Employment, access to public accommodations, housing opportunities.

Wisconsin

Act:	Wisconsin Fair Employment Act.
Code Section:	Wis. Stat. Ann., Secs. 111.31 to 111.395.
Applies To:	All employers, including the state.
Protected Classes:	Age, race, color, handicap, sex, pregnancy, marital status, creed, national origin, arrest or conviction record, ancestry, sexual orientation, membership in the military, off-duty use of tobacco.
Enforcing Agency:	Wisconsin Department of Industry, Labor, and Human Relations.
Areas of Discrimination Covered:	Employment opportunities, employment hiring, employment discharge, employment compensation, access to public accommodations, housing opportunities.

Wyoming

Act:	Wyoming Fair Employment Practices Act.
Code Section:	Wyo. Stat., Secs. 27-9-101 to 27-9-108.

Applies To:	All employers, including the state.
Protected Classes:	Age, sex, race, creed, color, national origin, ancestry, disability, off-duty use of tobacco products.
Enforcing Agency:	Wyoming Fair Employment Commission.
Areas of Discrimination Covered:	Employment, access to public accommodations, housing opportunities.

Sample Contracts for Trainers, Consultants, and Speakers

Consulting Agreement

This is a sample of a basic contract, covering key terms.

These provisions define the scope of work and the time frame involved.

I. Definitions and General Clauses

1. This agreement is between Consummate Consultant, Inc. ("Consultant") and Smoking Gun Legal Systems, Inc. ("Smoking Gun") (the "Parties").

2. This agreement is for the development of a comprehensive database software and automated litigation support ("ALS") seminar, including promotion, facilities management, marketing, and the solicitation of sponsors/vendors ("Marketing"); and the presentation and materials of ALS ("Presentation").

3. ALS is a seminar presented as a public conference, or to private client organizations, for the purpose of teaching document management through the use of automated litigation support databases to legal assistants, and other legal professionals who may attend from time to time.

Any variation of ALS is considered a part of this agreement.

4. All presentations will take place in 1998, within Los Angeles, San Francisco, Dallas, Houston, Tampa, Miami, and Atlanta.

II. Ownership

This preserves consultant's ownership of copyright and grants to client limited photocopy rights for use in this program *only*. The rights are granted in exchange for the overall fee agreement.

5. Consultant owns the concept, presentation, course materials, title, and any future modifications and forms of ALS, and Smoking Gun will not create or market a seminar that encompasses the content or format of Consultant without the consent of Consultant. Consultant will own the copyright on all written course materials, visual aids, and multimedia materials, and will provide written permission to Smoking Gun for duplication of such material for all ALS presentations given pursuant to this agreement.

6. Consultant will receive copies of the registration lists, including names, addresses and telephone numbers at the start of each ALS session, and copies of the evaluation forms within one month of the conclusion of the ALS sessions.

This preserves client's rights to confidential and proprietary materials generated by the consultant.

7. Consultant will not release copies of the registration lists to any person or organization without the express permission of Smoking Gun.

8. Ownership of ALS and permission to release the registration lists are binding past the nullification of this agreement.

Definition of exclusivity, which limits consultant's rights to engage in competitive activities. A negotiation point on the fee.

9. Consultant will not present ALS for any third-party vendors or seminar companies during the term of this agreement. There may be times when Consultant is asked to speak on the subject of ALS and she agrees to inform Smoking Gun of such events, at which time the parties will agree on whether or not Consultant's participation conflicts with the presentations of Smoking Gun.

Reciprocal exclusivity on the subject of the consultancy.

10. Smoking Gun will not engage speakers other than Consultant for the presentation of ALS seminars without the express permission of Consultant during the term of the agreement.

IV. Scheduling/Cancellation

Contract expressly addresses anticipated delays or foreseeable contingencies.

11. Smoking Gun reserves the right to cancel or reschedule any scheduled ALS should there be insufficient funds to market and present same, or because of acts of God.

12. Consultant agrees to present all scheduled sessions of ALS even if there are insufficient proceeds for compensation, in an effort to break even on expenses and preserve the integrity of the presentation.

V. Responsibilities of the Parties

Detailed breakdown of reciprocal responsibilities (and mutual accountability).

13. Consultant is responsible for:
   a. Oral presentation of the seminars
   b. Preparing, revising, or modifying the course materials
   c. Obtaining and shipping the course materials and/or book
   d. Assisting with the retention of sponsors

14. Smoking Gun is responsible for:
   a. Promotion and marketing
   b. Facilities management
   c. Retention and maintenance of sponsors
   d. Administrative, accounting, and office functions
   e. On-site registration of participants, or in the alternative, providing personnel for registration
   f. Evaluating the participants

15. Consent of the parties is required for:
    a. Marketing strategy
    b. Facilities selection
    c. Media relations and advertising
    d. Sponsor selection and retention
    e. Financial decisions
    f. Scheduling of presentations
    g. Creating and revising the brochure
    h. Evaluation strategy

VI. Income and Expenses

Thorough breakdown of financial arrangement.

16. Smoking Gun will handle the accounting for the income and expenses generated from the seminar and will pay all bills from the proceeds of registration and sponsors, or from funds provided by Smoking Gun.

17. Expenses will include, but not be limited to, typesetting, printing and mailing; office supplies; telephone and fax; secretarial and computer support; travel expenses including hotel, transportation, and meals; and conference expenses including room rental, banquet, course materials, finance and bank charges, and other miscellaneous charges that are directly related to the production of ALS.

18. Smoking Gun will receive 60 percent and Consultant will receive 40 percent of the net profits from the seminar.

Addresses potential contingencies in advance, rather than risking dispute or ad hoc decisions later.

19. Should the expenses exceed the profit for a seminar session, Consultant will contribute to her portion of the debt 40 percent from the proceeds of ALS in the very next season, or future seminars, whichever comes first. In the event Consultant and Smoking Gun decide not to go forward with additional seminars, and a debt exists, Consultant will pay her share of the debt to Smoking Gun.

20. Payment, and accounting of income and expenses, and reimbursement for all out-of-pocket expenses for Smoking Gun will be made to Consultant within one month of the completion of the last seminar of each season.

Dated: _____

SMOKING GUN LEGAL SYSTEMS, INC.

_____

Louis Litigator
Director

Dated: _____

CONSUMMATE CONSULTANT, INC.

_____

Florence Facilitator

Member Education and Training Contract

Recitals

Entire contract is a sample
of more detailed recitals
and terms.

This Member Education and Training
Contract ("Contract") is entered into by
Litigation Prevention Association
("Association"), a professional association,
and by Connie Consultant ("Consultant"),
for the purpose of providing education
and/or training services to the Association.

Association is authorized by the state to
contract for employee education and
training services;

Association desires to contract for
education and/or training services for its
members; and

Consultant desires to provide education
and/or training services to Association
members.

In consideration of the mutual
agreements contained herein and other
good and valuable consideration, the
receipt and sufficiency of which are hereby
acknowledged, Association and Consultant
agree as follows:

I. Consultant's Obligations

Defines scope of work.

1.1 **Services.**

 a. Consultant must provide the
    following education and/or training
    services to Association: two-hour
    keynote address and two 90-minute
    breakout sessions entitled "Handling
    High-Level Harassment."

 b. Consultant must provide services in
    accordance with the following
    specifications: At the annual
    Litigation Prevention Conference to
    be held January 5–9, 1998, in Maui,
    Hawaii. Consultant must notify and
    coordinate with Association a
    schedule for providing services
    under this Contract. Consultant's
    schedule must be mutually agreed
    upon by Consultant and Association.

1.2 **Invoice.** Consultant must submit to Association an invoice describing the services provided and the cost of such services.

Consultant specifically agrees to confidentiality over materials used to customize presentations.

1.3 **Confidentiality.** Consultant must maintain the confidentiality of information received during the performance of this Contract, including information which discloses confidential personal information or identifies any person served by Association in accordance with applicable federal and state laws and Association rules.

1.4 **Reports and Records.** Consultant must complete and file in a timely manner the following reports, records, or documentation, in a format specified by Association: _____

_____ .

Consultant relinquishes all copyright ownership in exchange for the fee.

1.5 **Work Made for Hire.** All work performed pursuant to this Contract, developed or prepared for Association, is the exclusive property of the Association. All right, title, and interest in and to said property shall vest in the Association upon the creation and shall be deemed to be a work made for hire and made in the course of the services rendered pursuant to this Contract. To the extent that title to any such work may not, by operation of law, vest in the Association, or such work may not be considered a work made for hire, all rights, title, and interest therein are hereby irrevocably assigned to the Association. The Association shall have the right to obtain and to hold in its own name any and all copyrights, registrations, or such other protection as may be appropriate to the subject matter, and any extensions and renewals thereof.

Consultant must give Association, as well as any person designated by the Association, all assistance required to perfect the rights defined herein without any charge or expense beyond those amounts payable to Consultant for the services rendered under this Contract.

Consultant will be liable to client if she uses copyrighted materials without authorization.

1.6 **Copyright Infringement.** Consultant warrants and represents that no property protected by copyright will be reproduced or used in performance of this Contract unless Consultant has previously obtained written permission from the copyright holder(s), or has otherwise demonstrated authorization to the satisfaction of the Association.

These legal compliance "warranties" protect clients that have EEO and affirmative action responsibilities. Consultant is agreeing to abide by all EEO laws in content (necessary even without contract).

1.7 **Compliance.** Consultant must provide services in compliance with the following:

  a. All applicable local, state and federal laws, rules, and regulations now in effect or that become effective during the term of this Contract including, but not limited to, the:

   1) Civil Rights Act of 1964

   2) Rehabilitation Act of 1973, §504

   3) Americans With Disabilities Act of 1990

   4) Age Discrimination in Employment Act of 1967

   and all amendments to each, and all requirements imposed by the regulations issued pursuant to these acts. These named statutes provide in part that no persons in the United States shall, on the grounds of race, color, national origin, sex, age, disability, political beliefs, or religion, be excluded from participation in, or denial of, any aid, care, service, or other benefits provided by federal and/or state funding, or otherwise be subjected to discrimination.

1.8 **W-9 Form.** Consultant must provide the Association with IRS Form W-9, Payer's Request for Taxpayer Identification Number and Certification, upon execution of this Contract.

II. Association's Obligations

Addresses client's
obligations.

2.1 **Payment.** Association must pay
Consultant for services provided pursuant
to this Contract as follows: Payment of a flat
rate of $ _____ , together with actual cost of
round-trip coach airline fare, upon
completion of services and receipt of
invoice, according to the invoice referenced
in Section 1.2. Consultant's hotel accommodations will be billed directly to the
Conference. In no event will the total
amount expended under this Contract
exceed $ _____ .

2.2 **Use of Property.** Association will allow
Consultant the use of audiovisual
equipment.

III. Independent Contractor

Affirms parties' intent to
treat consultant as inde-
pendent contractor.

It is the intent of Association and
Consultant that Consultant is an
independent contractor and not an
employee of Association for any purpose.
Consultant and Association understand and
agree that (a) Association will not withhold
or pay on behalf of Consultant any sums for
income tax, unemployment insurance,
social security, or any other withholding
pursuant to any law or requirement of any
government body, or make available to
Consultant any of the benefits, including
workers' compensation insurance coverage,
afforded to employees of Association; (b) all
such withholdings, payments, and benefits,
if any, are the sole responsibility of
Consultant, and Consultant will indemnify
and hold harmless Association from any
damages or liabilities, including attorneys'
fees and legal expenses, incurred by
Association with respect to such payments,
withholdings, and benefits.

IV. Indemnification

Sample indemnity and hold-harmless agreement by consultant to client. Client will be able to sue on this contract if consultant causes harm to any person while performing work (negligence or discrimination).

Consultant must indemnify and hold harmless Association, its board, employees, and agents from all suits, actions, claims, costs, or liability of any character, type, or description, including attorneys' fees and legal expenses, brought, made for, or on account of any death, injury, or damage received or sustained by any person or property arising out of or occasioned by the acts or omissions, including the negligence, of Consultant or Consultant's agents or employees in the execution or performance of this Contract.

Consultant further must indemnify and hold harmless Association, its board, employees, and agents from all claims, costs, and expenses, including court costs and legal fees, demands, actions, and liability of every kind and character whatsoever with respect to copyrights and the reproduction and use of works protected by copyright.

V. Miscellaneous

5.1 **Term.** This Contract will be effective on January 5, 1998, and will terminate on January 7, 1998, unless otherwise terminated. This Contract is subject to appropriated funds. In the event funds are not appropriated, this Contract will be terminated immediately.

5.2 **Amendments.** This Contract may be amended only by written agreement between Consultant and Association.

Detailed statements regarding potential grounds for termination. Demonstrates proactive addressing of issues in advance of disputes.

5.3 **Termination.**

1. *Termination for Cause.* In addition to other provisions herein allowing termination, this Contract may be terminated for the following:

   a. By either party if the other party fails to perform or comply with any covenant, term, or condition of this Contract.

b. By Association if Consultant submits falsified documents or fraudulent billings or makes false representations or certifications relating to this Contract.

c. This Contract may be terminated immediately by Association when the life, health, welfare, or safety of individuals served is endangered or could be endangered either directly or through Consultant's willful or negligent discharge of its duties under this Contract.

2. *Termination Without Cause.* This Contract may be terminated by either party upon 30 days' written notice to the other party of its intent to terminate this Contract.

3. *Termination by Mutual Agreement.* The Association and Consultant may mutually agree to termination of this Contract at any time.

Clause provides that any dispute will be submitted to ADR.

4. *Dispute Resolution.* In the event a dispute arises between the parties involving the provision or interpretation of any term or condition of this Contract, and both parties desire to attempt to resolve the dispute prior to termination or expiration of the Contract, or withholding of payments, then the parties may refer the issue to a resolution panel composed of at least three persons selected jointly. The parties agree to split the costs and fees associated with the ADR process.

5.4 **Responsibilities Prior to Termination.** Following written notification of intent to terminate and until the agreed-upon date of termination, Consultant will continue to have the responsibility to provide services under this Contract and Association will continue to have the responsibility to pay for the services in the manner specified in this Contract.

5.5 **Effect of Termination.** Upon termination of this Contract, Consultant and Association will be discharged from any further obligations created under the terms of this Contract, except for the equitable settlement of the respective accrued interests or obligations incurred prior to termination. Termination does not, however, constitute a waiver of any remedies for breach of this Contract. In addition, the obligation of Consultant to retain records and maintain the confidentiality of information will survive this Contract.

5.6 **Entire Agreement.** This Contract constitutes the entire agreement of the parties and supersedes any prior understandings or oral or written agreements between Association and Consultant on the matters contained herein.

5.7 **Consultant's Ability.** The person or persons signing and executing this Contract on behalf of the Consultant, or representing themselves as signing and executing the Contract on behalf of the Consultant, guarantee that they have been fully authorized by the Consultant to execute the Contract on behalf of the Consultant and to validly and legally bind the Consultant to all the terms and provisions contained in the Contract.

The parties have executed this Contract on the dates set forth below their signatures.

CONSULTANT

_____

Connie Consultant

Date: _____

ASSOCIATION
Litigation Prevention Association

By_____

Title: _____

Date: _____

Speaker-Client Agreement

THIS AGREEMENT is made and entered into this _____ day of November, 1997, by and between

LEGAL SPEAKERS UNITED
Sammy Speaker
300 E. Primary Blvd., #200
Urbantown, CA 90802
Federal Tax ID No. 11-1111111

hereinafter referred to as the "Speaker" and the

COMMUNITY SERVICES DISTRICT
123 Main Street
Rural City, CA 99000

hereinafter referred to as the "District."

Recitals

1. WHEREAS, the District is authorized by Section 12345 of the Anystate Local Code to contract for the procurement of goods and services as authorized by law; and

Defines independent contractor arrangement for speaker.

2. WHEREAS, the District is authorized by the State Government Code to contract with independent contractors for the provision of financial, economic, accounting, training, engineering, legal, and administrative services; and

Addresses the speaker's representations regarding expertise.

3. WHEREAS, the Speaker, Legal Speakers United, through Sammy Speaker, is specially trained, experienced, and competent to perform services pursuant to this Agreement—specifically, design and presentation of customized keynotes and workshops on Sexual Harassment Prevention for managers and full-time and part-time staff of the District.

NOW, THEREFORE, the parties agree as follows:

1. The period of this Agreement shall be from November 1, 1997, to March 30, 1998, inclusive.

2. The Speaker shall perform the following services in compliance with specifications and standards provided in accordance with a schedule to be determined.

Defines scope of work in detail.

3. **Scope/content of workshops:** To provide a series of presentations to managers, supervisors, classified employees, and staff districtwide, to be conducted at the Rural City Community Education Complex. The training shall include federal and state civil rights laws, general responsibility, liability issues, "quid pro quo vs. hostile environment" claims, the reasonable woman/reasonable person standard, and other standards of proof, as well as employer strategies and defenses. Content shall be in accordance with the Proposal submitted September 14, 1997, attached hereto as Exhibit A.

Managers and supervisors shall attend a three-hour presentation. Each managerial group shall be limited to 45 participants. Office employees and staff shall attend a two-hour speech, which shall be limited to a maximum 55 participants. Customized course materials shall be supplied for each participant. Legal Speakers United and Sammy Speaker own and will retain the copyright on the program materials. Permission to reproduce the program materials is limited to the District and its affiliates and members.

Sign-in rosters shall be maintained for each session, for District documentation of attendance. Each location shall supply a screen with an overhead projector, an easel, and flip chart, and a table for use by the Speaker.

Clauses preserve the speaker's copyright ownership and grant permission for copying under carefully defined circumstances.

4. **Videotaping of workshops:**

   a. Each location may videotape one managerial presentation and one staff speech for use as make-up sessions for participants unable to attend those originally scheduled. Use of such videos shall be at no additional cost, and shall be usable for up to one year from the date of the program.

b. Permission to copy and use the program materials for use with the video presentation is granted solely and exclusively to the District (and its authorized affiliates and members) for presentation at programs to be conducted during calendar years 1997 and 1998. The license fee for each use is $ _____ , to be reported in quarterly accountings by client.

Limitations on authorized future use by client.

c. Legal Speakers United reserves the right to update the materials as required to conform to changes in the law and will provide new camera-ready copy. Legal Speakers United also reserves the right to terminate permission to use the video if changes in the law so require. Notice will be given in writing to the District if this is necessary.

d. It is understood and agreed that the program materials will be used and distributed solely in conjunction with workshops presented via the videotape of Sammy Speaker and will not be sold to or utilized by any other instructor or used in any curriculum presented by or under the direction of the District.

Addresses issue of videographer's status as work-for-hire to preclude copyright ownership claim.

5. **Fees:** Client will use District staff as videographers, pursuant to a work-for-hire agreement.

Manager/supervisor presentation: Two 3-hour programs for managers and supervisors will be given, one at each location with a maximum attendance of 45 participants. The cost of each presentation is $ _____ for 30 participants and $ _____ for each additional participant up to 45, for a total of $ _____ each.

Detailed fee agreement and license for each handout and use of video.

Staff speech: Six 2-hour speeches will be presented for staff (full- and part-time). Each speech shall be $ _____ for 40 participants and $ _____ for each additional participant up to 55, for a total of $ _____ each.

Video facilitator workshop: One 3-hour session will be conducted for up to 10 proposed facilitators who will be trained to present the video and lead/facilitate follow-up discussion based on the video. Content shall include facilitation for both the manager/supervisor and the staff workshops. This workshop will include a *separate* customized Facilitator's Guide and related materials. The cost of this workshop is $ _____ for up to 10 participants.

6. Based on the foregoing number of workshops and attendees, the total amount encumbered pursuant to this Agreement is:

Manager/Supervisor presentation $ _____
Staff speech   _____
Video facilitator workshop   _____
            TOTAL $ _____

7. Fees shall be billed monthly for all presentations and speeches scheduled and presented during each month. Invoices shall be submitted by Legal Speakers United, and payment shall be made by the District's Accounts Payable Department within 30 days following the date of each invoice.

8. The Speaker shall assume all expenses incurred in connection with performance except as otherwise provided in this Agreement.

Reaffirms independent contractor status and client's limitation of damages.

9. While performing services hereunder, the Speaker is an independent contractor and not an officer, agent, or employee of the District.

10. The District shall not be liable to the Speaker for personal injury or property damage sustained in the performance of this contract.

Indemnity and hold-harmless clause.

11. The Speaker shall indemnify, hold harmless, and defend the District, its Board of Trustees, officers, employees, and agents from and against all claims, liability, loss, cost, and obligations on account of, or arising from, the acts or negligent omissions

of Speaker or persons acting on behalf of Speaker, however caused, in the performance of the services specified herein.

Warranties and represen-tations by speaker fulfill client's affirmative action requirements.

12. The Speaker hereby certifies that in performing work or providing services for the District, there shall be no discrimination in its hiring or employment practices because of age, sex, race, color, ancestry, national origin, religious creed, physical disability, medical condition, marital status, or sexual preference, except as provided for in federal and state law. The Speaker shall comply with applicable federal and state antidiscrimination laws, including but not limited to the California Fair Employment and Housing Act, beginning with Section 12900 of the California Government Code.

13. Neither party shall assign this Agreement or any part thereof without the written consent of the other party.

WITNESS the parties hereto the day and year first above written.

SPEAKER

LEGAL SPEAKERS UNITED
Federal Tax ID No. 11-1111111

By: _____
     Sammy Speaker

DISTRICT

COMMUNITY SERVICES DISTRICT

By: _____
     Signature

Name: _____

Title: _____

Memorandum of Understanding

Speaker Bureau Agreement

This document will serve as a Memorandum of Understanding by and between Super-Duper Speakers Bureau ("Bureau") and Suzie Speaker ("Speaker"). Both parties agree that when and for each separate speaking and/or training engagement contracted by Bureau on behalf of Speaker, an agreement shall be produced by Bureau. This specific agreement shall insert (1) the name of the client contracting the speaking engagement, (2) the fees agreed to, and (3) dates of payment of these fees along with any other pertinent information. It will not, however, change in any substantial manner, the terms agreed to below.

Bureau will to the best of its knowledge and ability represent Speaker fairly, accurately, and completely. It will not be liable for any misrepresentation that may unknowingly occur between Speaker and any business or association that Bureau has contacted on its behalf. Nor will it be liable for any misconduct that may occur during the completion by Speaker of a speaking and/or training engagement contract developed by Bureau.

1. Speaker gives permission to Bureau to actively solicit assignments for Speaker in any professional way it deems appropriate. This agreement in no way restricts Speaker from marketing herself in any other manner she deems appropriate to her business except as indicated below. In addition, this agreement does not restrict Bureau from marketing any other speaking/training businesses.

2. If Bureau is the procuring cause for Speaker being hired to deliver speaking, training, speaking/training programs, speaking/training materials, speaking/training literature, seminars, keynote speeches, coaching, retreat facilitation, or any other related or like services,

   (*PROCURING CAUSE shall be defined as that cause, event, or action which facilitates, brings about, or creates an opportunity for Speaker to deliver speaking/training expertise in some form to a paying customer.*)

   Bureau shall be entitled to and shall receive _____ percent of the total gross fee paid to Speaker by such client (including any parent companies, subsidiaries, and/or branches) contracting the services. This _____ percent commission shall be paid to Bureau in the same installments as Speaker receives payment and for the entire period of the contract regardless of its length. Payment of commissions shall be made to Bureau within 10 days of receipt of payments by Speaker.

   (*GROSS FEE shall be defined as all fees for speaking/training/materials and the like less travel expenses where (1) travel is billed separately and directly reimbursed or (2) receipts for travel expenses are provided.*)

3. Bureau shall receive _____ percent of any additional speaking/ training and like assignments contracted by Speaker in any new agreement with the same client or any of its parents/subsidiaries/branches. Speaker is responsible for maintaining accurate and complete records of these assignments and must notify Bureau in writing at the time of booking.

4. Bureau shall receive _____ percent of any spin-off business for any engagement Speaker receives as a result of a referral or recommendation from a client of Bureau's, or by a client that was contracted for Speaker by Bureau. Spin-off business includes fees for speaking engagements and product sales. Speaker is responsible for making all reasonable efforts to ascertain the source of such business as a spin-off from an engagement booked for Speaker by Bureau, keeping accurate records of such spin-off business, and reporting same to Bureau at the time the spin-off business is booked.

   If such spin-off business is the direct result of Speaker's relationship with the original client and the referral is made directly to Speaker, then Bureau shall receive _____ percent of this business or _____ percent of the customary commissions discussed in this agreement.

5. It is the understanding of Bureau that payment of a state sales tax is not required for fees earned on its brokerage services. If there should be any sales taxes due on products or items of training sold by Speaker to any client for whom it performs speaking/training services or the like, the tax shall be the sole responsibility of Speaker and not the responsibility of Bureau.

6. In the event there is any dispute between Speaker and Bureau regarding the amount, time of, or payment of fees payable to Bureau by Speaker or any other matter, both parties hereby agree to take such dispute to impartial arbitration for resolution after reasonable attempts have been made by the parties to settle the matter themselves.

7. This agreement shall be binding on and inure to the benefit of the heirs, executors, and administrators of Bureau and the successors and assigns of Speaker.

Signed on _____ 19XX, by:

_____
Super-Duper Speakers Bureau

_____
Suzie Speaker

Letter Agreement for Consulting and Training

June 9, 1997

John Doe
The Cutting Edge Company
100 West Main Street
Anytown, CA 90000-1000

Dear Mr. Doe:

Thank you for the opportunity to provide consulting services and to present the Comprehensive Training Program for Executives, Managers, and Line Supervisors addressed in our previous proposal. This Letter Agreement between The Cutting Edge Company ("Cutting Edge") and Legal Trainers United ("Trainers") shall serve as our Agreement for the design, presentation, and follow-up evaluation of the programs.

Scope of Work

Training

This Agreement is to provide a series of workshops for Cutting Edge executives, managers, and line supervisors entitled *Staying Out of Court.* The workshops will encompass executive awareness briefings and skill-building programs for all levels of management. The latter will include detailed substantive information of relevant legal, regulatory, and union contract requirements governing California employers and development of specific management and supervisory skills.

All programs and materials shall be customized for particular Cutting Edge work environments. The customization process will take place throughout the entire project, as new policies are adopted, procedures are modified, and/or relevant issues arise. We will continually prioritize the subjects we cover to address the most pressing needs of your organization.

Follow-Up Evaluation/Consultation

We will conduct a follow-up evaluation and audit of management practices to ensure effective performance management procedures, diversity awareness, and skill transfer. The audit will encompass the interviews and audit of written performance appraisals, as specified in the Detailed Scope of Work. The audit will conclude in six months, with our Final Report and Recommendations.

The Detailed Scope of Work and Fee Schedule that we have agreed upon is attached hereto as Exhibit A.

Workshop Schedule

The series will commence on July 10, 1997, with the four-hour Executive Briefing. The workshop will begin at 9:00 a.m.

We have not yet established a firm workshop schedule for the managers and supervisors. Managers/supervisor workshops will begin in July 1997, and will be conducted monthly through March 1998, as set forth at pages 4–5 of the Scope of Work. The schedule, when adopted, will be appended to this Agreement as Exhibit B.

Fee Schedule

The total cost for the comprehensive series of workshops, encompassing four separate modules, is $ _____ , payable as follows:

1. A deposit of $ _____ is payable on or about June 15, 1997, concurrent with execution of this Agreement and commitment of 1997 and 1998 dates. This deposit shall be credited to the final billing at the conclusion of all workshops.

2. The one-time course development fee of $ _____ shall be payable on July 15, 1998. As outlined in the Scope of Work, this is for design of customized curriculum for the executives' and managers' programs. The customization includes review and analysis of all Cutting Edge handbooks, collective bargaining agreements, personnel policies, grievance procedures, and other pertinent documentation.

3. Fees shall be billed monthly for all workshops scheduled and presented during each month. Invoices shall be submitted by Legal Trainers United, Inc., and payment shall be payable net 20 days.

The total cost for the six-month follow-up audit, including submission of a Final Report and Recommendations, shall be $ _____ , billable monthly in six equal payments.

Consultant shall assume all expenses incurred in connection with performance of this Agreement—specifically, printing, binding, and delivery of training materials and audiovisual aids. Cutting Edge shall provide the training facility.

Copyright Ownership of Course Materials

The principal trainer, Jane Doe, will own the concept, presentation, and course materials (with the exception of Cutting Edge policies and contract documents which are appended thereto or used as examples during the workshops) and shall retain the copyright on all written materials and visual aids. Where necessary, Trainers will provide written permission to Cutting Edge for duplication of such material for distribution to board members, officers, or managers of Cutting Edge and its affiliates.

Independent Contractor Status

While performing services under this agreement, Legal Trainers United and Jane Doe will be acting as independent contractors and not officers, agents, or employees of The Cutting Edge Company. We will comply with all federal and state laws and regulations regarding business licensing, and payment of social security and income taxes, and shall procure and maintain workers' compensation insurance and all related benefits.

Please execute one copy of this Agreement and return it in the enclosed envelope. The second copy is for your records. We have also enclosed for your records an invoice reflecting the deposit payable herewith.

Thank you for the opportunity to be of service to The Cutting Edge Company. If you have any questions or comments, please feel free to contact me.

DATED: June 9, 1997

LEGAL TRAINERS UNITED

By: Jane Doe
Title: Principal Facilitator

DATED: June ___ , 1997
THE CUTTING EDGE COMPANY

By: _____

Title: _____

Index

About the Author

Patricia S. Eyres, Esq., is a full-time professional speaker and trainer who spent 18 years as a litigator. She is president of Litigation Management and Training Services, Inc., a legal consulting and training business based in Long Beach, California. She consults with numerous business owners and government agencies on timely legal issues affecting the workplace. Ms. Eyres also advises employers on avoiding liabilities for the design and delivery of training programs, health and safety regulatory compliance issues, and the legal aspects of violence prevention and workplace security. The author of numerous articles on legal issues relevant to training and the workplace, she conducts a variety of training programs to alert management and human resource professionals to legal liabilities arising in the workplace. She also contributed the chapter "Training and the Law" to the latest edition of *The ASTD Training and Development Handbook.*